World War II

STATS AND FACTS

World War II

STATS AND FACTS

PETER DARMAN

FALL RIVER PRESS

© 2009 The Brown Reference Group Ltd

This 2009 edition published by the Fall River Press, by arrangement
with The Brown Reference Group Ltd

Editor: Dennis Cove
Designers: Kim Browne, Josephine Spencer, Lisa Robb
Production Director: Alastair Gourlay
Index: Indexing Specialists Ltd
Additional text: Robin Smith

Picture credits

Front cover: Library of Congress
All other images: Robert Hunt Library

Fall River Press
122 Fifth Avenue
New York, NY 10011

ISBN-13: 978-1-4351-1730-3

Printed and bound in China

1 3 5 7 9 10 8 6 4 2

Front cover image: The Congressional Medal Of Honor

Contents

Contents

ARMIES

German 1939 Infantry Division

A German infantry division had a paper strength of 17,000 men, although most divisions were well below this figure following losses on campaign. For example, by the end of December 1941, on the Eastern Front, the average infantry company (official strength 120 troops) was down to 60 men.

A typical infantry division consisted of a headquarters, three regiments, an artillery regiment, a reconnaissance battalion, an antitank battalion, an engineer battalion (engineers were actually pioneers trained in the use of explosives and mines rather than construction or bridging), a signals battalion, and support units. The one major advantage German infantry divisions had throughout the war was their large numbers of machine guns, which gave infantry squads massive firepower.

The German infantry divisions mostly relied on horse-drawn vehicles for their transportation. Except for the reorganization of the infantry platoon from three to four squads after the Polish Campaign in 1939, and the temporary increase in the number of horses in the divisions employed in Russia from 1941 to 1943, the German three-regiment, nine-battalion division remained unchanged until the fall of 1943.

Typical organization of a 1939 infantry division was as follows:
- Division Staff Company
- Mapping Platoon *(motorized)*
- Three Infantry Regiments: *each regiment made up of 3,250 troops; each regiment with three battalions; each battalion with three rifle companies*
- Machine Gun Company
- Infantry Gun Company
- Reconnaissance Battalion
- Mounted Squadron
- Bicycle Squadron
- Heavy Squadron
- Antitank Platoon *(motorized)*
- Infantry Gun Platoon
- Armored Reconnaissance Troop
- Artillery Regiment: *2,500 troops, with three Light Artillery Battalions and one Heavy Artillery Battalion*

Each artillery battery carried 480 rounds of ammunition (4 limbers of 12 rounds each and 8 ammunition carts of 54 rounds each), that is, 240 rounds for each piece. The ammunition consisted of high-explosive shell with percussion and double-action fuze, and smoke shell.

- Observation Battalion *(motorized)*
- Panzerjäger Battalion: *550 troops, with three Panzerjäger Companies (motorized)*
- Heavy Machine Gun Company *(motorized)*
- Pioneer Battalion: *843 troops, with two Pioneer Companies*
- Signals Battalion: *474 troops*
- Replacement Battalion
- Plus bakery, butcher, medical, and veterinary support *(2,300 troops in total)*

Divisional firepower
- Light machine guns: *527*
- Heavy machine guns: *116*
- 20mm antiaircraft/antitank guns: *11*

Mortars
- 50mm: *84*
- 81mm: *58*

Infantry guns
- 75mm: *20*
- 150mm: *6*

Artillery
- 105mm howitzers: *36*
- 105mm guns: *4*
- 150mm howitzers: *8*
- Flamethrowers: *20*

Divisional transport
The German infantry division had approximately 5,300 horses, 1,100 horse-drawn vehicles, 950 motor vehicles, and 430 motorcycles. The only fully motorized unit in the infantry division was the antitank battalion. Most of the divisional supply trains were horse drawn, motor vehicles being used chiefly to transport fuel and for the workshop company. A far greater degree of motorization existed among German headquarters troops, the supply units of which were mostly motorized. Motorization of headquarters troops was to a large degree a necessity, since these units included such types of outfits as heavy artillery, for which horses would have been a practical impossibility. These motorized headquarters units were assigned to armies, corps, and divisions as originally required.

German Infantry Division, Type 44

 In October 1943, the Germans reorganized radically their infantry divisions in reducing the infantry regiments from three to two battalions, and the other divisional components were revised accordingly. In the remaining six infantry battalions, the number of squads per rifle platoon was reduced from four to three, but without having much effect on the firepower of the division, since the caliber of the mortars and antitank guns had been increased, and the number of machine guns was kept unchanged. This type of infantry division was soon designated the Infantry Division, Type 44 (*Infanteriedivision Kriegestat 44*). This redesignation took place in May 1944, hence the name of the unit. The strength of the squad was reduced from 10 to 9, the number of light machine guns per rifle company from 16 to 13, and the strength of the logistical back-up services on all levels was reduced sharply.

Typical organization of a 1944 infantry division was as follows:
- Divisional Headquarters: *227 troops*
- Fusilier Battalion: *708 troops*
- Signals Battalion: *379 troops*
- Infantry Regiment x 3: *2,008 troops each*
- Artillery Regiment: *2,451 troops*
- Antitank Battalion: *484 troops*
- Engineer Battalion: *620 troops*
- Divisional Services: *1,459 troops*

Total strength: 12,352

Note: The reconnaissance battalion was replaced by a divisional fusilier battalion, with an organization identical with that of the usual infantry battalion. With the change from offensive to defensive warfare after 1943, and the shortage of manpower, this mobile reserve took the place of the reconnaissance unit.

Divisional firepower
- Light machine guns: *566*
- Heavy machine guns: *90*
- 20mm antiaircraft guns: *12*
- 75mm antitank guns: *21*
- 75mm self-propelled antitank guns: *14*

Mortars
- 81mm: *48*
- 120mm: *28*

Infantry guns
- 75mm: *18*
- 150mm: *6*

Artillery
- 105mm howitzers: *36*
- 150mm howitzers: *12*
- Flamethrowers: *20*

Divisional transport
- Motor vehicles: *2,081*
- Motorcycles: *168*
- Horses: *4,656*

Infantry Division, two-regiment type
Independent of the various stages of organization of the three-regiment infantry divisions, the Germans formed, from the spring of 1941, a number of two-regiment, six-battalion infantry divisions with weaker components and over-all reduced strength and firepower.

Typical organization of a two-regiment infantry division was as follows:
- Divisional Headquarters: *150 troops*
- Fusilier Company: *120 troops*
- Signals Battalion: *402 troops*
- Infantry Regiment x 2: *2,645 troops each*
- Artillery Regiment: *1,755 troops*
- Antitank Battalion: *350 troops*
- Engineer Battalion: *397 troops*
- Divisional Services: *1,395 troops*

Total strength: 9,859

Divisional firepower
- Light machine guns: *497*
- Heavy machine guns: *52*
- 20mm antiaircraft/antitank guns: *12*
- 75mm antitank guns: *20*
- 88mm antitank guns: *12*

Mortars
- 81mm: *42*
- 120mm: *24*

Infantry guns
- 75mm: *12*
- 150mm: *4*

Artillery
- 105mm howitzers: *24*
- Flamethrowers: *16*

German Mountain Division

 Small units of mountain troops were formed in World War I, when the continuous trench lines extended from the Swiss mountains to the English Channel. They were specialists in mountain warfare, with light equipment and packhorses to carry heavy weapons and ammunition where vehicles could not reach.

Nazi Germany formed its first Gebirgsjäger division, or mountain division, in 1938 from the Bavarian Gebirgs brigade. In the same year it gained two more mountain divisions when it invaded Austria and absorbed its army. Late in 1941, the Germans formed another batch of four mountain divisions.

A Gebirgs division was essentially a standard infantry division, with only two infantry regiments instead of three (see page 8). Each of the seven mountain divisions had a slightly different organization, but they were the same in many respects. Each battalion had three rifle companies, a heavy company, and a number of support platoons in the battalion headquarters company.

The mountain infantry battalion was more heavily manned and more heavily armed than the battalion in the regular German infantry division. It consisted of five companies: three rifle companies. a machine-gun company, and a heavy weapons company, which gave it about 150 men more than the regular infantry battalion. It was armed with the same number of heavy machine guns, antitank rifles, and mortars as the standard infantry battalion, but it had five more light machine guns and its firepower was augmented by four 28/20mm antitank guns, four 120mm mortars, and two 75mm mountain infantry howitzers.

Typical organization of a mountain division was as follows:
- Headquarters (*195 troops*)
- Two Gebirgsjäger Regiments (*each with 3,064 troops; each with three battalions*)
- Gebirgs Artillery Regiment (*2,230 troops, in two battalions*)
- Gebirgs Reconnaissance Battalion (*650 troops*)
- Gebirgs Panzerabwehr Battalion (*500 troops*)
- Gebirgs Pioneer Battalion (*900 troops*)
- Gebirgs Signals Battalion (*453 troops*)
- Divisional services (*2,000 troops*)

Total strength: 13,056

Divisional firepower
- Light machine guns: *485*
- Heavy machine guns: *84*
- 20mm self-propelled antiaircraft guns: *12*

Antitank weapons
- Hand-held antitank weapons: *72*
- 37mm antitank guns: *3*
- 75mm antitank guns: *24*

Mortars
- 81mm: *48*
- 120mm: *24*

Artillery
- 75mm mountain infantry howitzers: *14*
- 75mm mountain howitzers (below): *24*
- 105mm mountain howitzers: *12*
- 150mm mountain howitzers: *4*
- 150mm howitzers: *12*
- Flamethrowers: *20*

German Volksgrenadier Division

 Hitler coined the name Volksgrenadier division in the late summer of 1944. It appealed to his sense of drama and his need for "struggle." The Volk, or "German People," had mythical connotations for the Führer, who saw World War II as a racial struggle between the German master race and Jewish and Slav "sub-humans," or *Untermenschen*.

In reality, however, the Volksgrenadier divisions were little more than underequipped and undermanned line infantry divisions, repackaged with a new politically correct title. There were 13 "new" Volksgrenadier divisions, but dozens more were reformed from the remnants of line units.

The manpower strength of a Volksgrenadier division was nearly a third less than a 1939-era infantry division, with only 10,000 men compared to 17,000 men in the old type of unit. The frontline strength was badly hit, with the new divisions only having six infantry battalions, as opposed to nine infantry battalions in the earlier type of division. Improvements in firepower were made, however, with the new divisions on paper boasting more than 500 machine guns (though only on paper; the reality was often different—see below).

Volksgrenadier divisions were of very mixed quality. Those based on old formations were generally of better quality than those formed from scratch. The first big test of the new divisions was during the Ardennes Offensive in December 1944. Many of them were specifically reinforced for the offensive with assault gun battalions, and other specialist units. They were at the center of the action along the front and most acquitted themselves fairly well.

The 18th Volksgrenadier Division played a pivotal role in the destruction of the U.S. 106th Infantry Division in the opening days of the Battle of the Bulge in December 1944. Using classic infiltration tactics, the Volksgrenadiers were able to push through American lines, spreading panic and confusion among the inexperienced G.I.s. In total, some 8,000 American troops surrendered to the division in what was perhaps the most serious U.S. military defeat on mainland Europe in World War II.

For the remainder of World War II, the Volksgrenadier divisions did not taste victory again. The majority were posted to the East to hold the line in Poland, Czechoslovakia, and Hungary, where they were destroyed by the Soviet Red Army.

Typical organization of a Volksgrenadier division was as follows:

- Divisional Headquarters: *227 troops*
- Fusilier Company: *200 troops*
- Signals Battalion: *305 troops*
- Infantry Regiment x 3: *1,854 troops in each*
- Artillery Regiment: *1,744 troops*
- Antitank Battalion: *460 troops*
- Engineer Battalion: *442 troops*
- Supply Regiment: *1,075 troops*

Divisional firepower
- Light machine guns: *369*
- Heavy machine guns: *54*
- Hand-held antitank weapons: *216*
- 37mm self-propelled antiaircraft guns: *9*
- 75mm antitank guns: *9*

Mortars
- 81mm: *42*
- 120mm: *24*

Infantry guns
- 75mm: *38*

Artillery
- 75mm: *18*
- 105mm: *24*
- 150mm howitzers: *12*
- Flamethrowers: *12*

Divisional transport
- Motor vehicles: *1,562*
- Motorcycles: *119*
- Horses: *3,002*
- Bicycles: *1,522*

German Motorized Division

On the battlefield, the motorized infantry divisions (shown below) were created in order to keep up with fast-moving panzer divisions, and thus were completely equipped with motor vehicles. The first four motorized infantry divisions (2d, 13th, 20th, and 29th) were directly upgraded from infantry divisions during 1937 to 1939. They therefore kept most of the features of their parent units. Each motorized infantry division had three motorized infantry regiments, one motorized artillery regiment, and supporting units. Panzergrenadier divisions (see page opposite) of the later-war period were the successors of the motorized infantry divisions that had followed in the wake of the German panzer divisions during the Blitzkrieg years.

Contrary to popular legend, panzergrenadier divisions were not equipped with hundreds of armored SdKfz 251 troop-carrying halftracks. These were almost exclusively concentrated in either army panzer divisions or Waffen-SS panzergrenadier, later panzer, divisions. The fighting power of the panzergrenadier division was found in its two grenadier regiments. These each had three infantry battalions, supported by their own integral mortar, light gun, antiaircraft, and assault pioneer companies.

Organization of a typical 1939 motorized infantry division was as follows:
- Division headquarters (*motorized*)
- Motorized Infantry Regiment *x 3, each regiment made up of three Motorized Battalions*
- Motorized Battalion *x 3, each battalion made up of: 3 x rifle companies, 1 x heavy company, 1 x motorized antitank company, 1 x infantry support gun company, 1 x motorcycle platoon, 1 x light infantry supply column*
- Motorized Artillery Regiment, *made up four Motorized Artillery Battalions, each battalion made up of three batteries*
- Motorized Signals Platoon

Antitank Battalion
- Motorized Signals Platoon
- Motorized Antitank Company x 2
- Heavy Machine Gun Company

Reconnaissance Battalion
- Motorcycle Company
- Armored Car Company

Motorized Engineer Battalion
- Motorized Engineer Company x 3
- Motorized Bridging Company
- Motorized Engineer Supply Column

Motorized Signals Battalion
- Motorized Telephone Company
- Motorized Radio Company
- Motorized Signals Supply Column

- Motorized Supply Troop
- Divisional Services

Total strength: 17,000

Divisional firepower
- Light machine guns: *332*
- Heavy machine guns: *128*

Antitank guns
- 20mm antiaircraft/antitank guns: *22*
- 37mm antitank guns: *24*

Mortars
- 50mm: *84*
- 81mm: *54*

Infantry guns
- 75mm: *72*

Artillery
- 105mm guns: *36*
- 150mm guns: *12*

German Panzergrenadier Division

The 1943-1944 panzergrenadier divisions were essentially motorized infantry formations, but reinforced by the allocation of either a panzer or an assault gun battalion. Lucky divisions might also boast an armored reconnaissance battalion, equipped with armored cars or halftracks, along with a self-propelled antitank battalion. By 1944, tank losses meant that the panzergrenadiers lost their panzer battalions, and had to rely on Sturmgeschütz (StuG) III or IV assault guns for armored support.

All troops in a panzergrenadier division were provided with motorized transport to give the division either strategic or operational-level mobility. The division's infantry did not use their trucks to drive them into battle. The truck's main purpose was to get the panzergrenadiers to just behind the front, then they would go into action in much the same way as conventional infantry: on foot.

The one major exception to this situation was the famous *Grossdeutschland* Division which, although being designated a panzergrenadier division from June 1943 onward, usually fielded three times as many tanks as the average army panzer division. At one point, it even boasted four panzer battalions, including both Tiger I and Panther tanks. Its infantry regiments were superbly equipped as well, with one of its infantry battalions being mounted in halftracks. The majority of the specialist support units, such as reconnaissance, artillery, antitank, and antiaircraft units, were equipped with armored vehicles. Unlike other units, the *Grossdeutschland* Division was also provided with a regular stream of reinforcements to ensure it remained up to strength.

In the final months of the war, heavy losses on all fronts forced the German military authorities to no longer differentiate between panzer and panzergrenadier divisions. Henceforth, both types of units would be scaled for the same numbers of men and equipment, although by this point in the war such matters were largely academic.

Typical organization of a panzergrenadier division was as follows:
- Divisional Headquarters: *141 troops*
- Armored Reconnaissance battalion: *942 troops*
- Signals Battalion: *456 troops*
- Tank Battalion: *567 troops*
- Motorized Infantry Regiment: *3,043 troops*
- Motorized Infantry Regiment: *3,043 troops*
- Armored Artillery Regiment: *1,649 troops*
- Antiaircraft Battalion: *764 troops*
- Antitank Battalion: *513 troops*
- Engineer Battalion: *873 troops*
- Divisional Services: *1,885 troops*

Total strength: 13,876

Divisional firepower
- Light machine guns: *1,019*
- Heavy machine guns: *82*

Antiaircraft guns
- 20mm antiaircraft guns: *63*
- 88mm antiaircraft guns: *8*

Antitank guns
- 20mm antitank guns: *38*
- 75mm antitank guns: *78*
- 75mm self-propelled guns: *44*

Mortars
- 81mm: *52*
- 120mm: *24*

Infantry guns
- 150mm infantry howitzers: *12*

Artillery
- 105mm howitzers: *12*
- 105mm self-propelled howitzers: *12*
- 150mm howitzers: *12*
- 150mm self-propelled howitzers: *12*
- Flamethrowers: *26*

Tanks
- Panzer IVs: *48*

(Note that some panzergrenadier divisions had almost double this tank strength. For example, in July 1943 the Grossdeutschland Division had 45 Panzer IVs, 46 Panthers, 13 Tigers, and 35 StuG assault guns.)

- Motor vehicles: *2,637*
- Motorcycles: *469*

Early Panzer Division

The 1st Panzer Division was formed on October 15, 1935, in Weimar from the 3rd Cavalry Division. Its organization is typical of the panzer divisions of the early war years (see below).

The German panzer division was the mailed fist of the German Army, the key to the Blitzkrieg style of warfare. The panzer division was equipped to encircle and destroy the enemy by achieving local superiority in armor, firepower, and surprise. Its speed and mobility allowed it rapidly to penetrate into the enemy's rear areas once a breakthrough had been achieved.

Originally, each panzer division possessed two panzer regiments, comprising 400 tanks in total. This was unwieldy, and the division lacked motorized infantry to support the tanks. Thus, in late 1940, the panzer division was reorganized. The authorized organization now comprised: a divisional headquarters (with its own armored support company); an armored reconnaissance battalion; a tank regiment (originally three battalions, later reduced to two, comprising one of 96 Panzer IVs and one of 96 Panzer V Panthers, often with an additional company of Tiger tanks or assault guns—the Tigers were later organized into their own independent battalions); two panzergrenadier regiments; an antitank battalion (later equipped with 75mm long-barreled assault guns, while some divisions also had some self-propelled or towed 88mm guns); an antiaircraft battalion (two heavy batteries, each with 4-6 towed 88mm guns, plus a battery of 12 x 20mm guns); an artillery regiment (three battalions, one with 18 Wespe and Hummel self-propelled guns, plus one with 12 x 105mm gun-howitzers and another with 12 x 150mm gun-howitzers); an armored signals battalion; an armored engineer battalion; and divisional services.

The average manpower strength of a panzer division was around 15,000, but this could vary according to battle losses and the speed of replacements. Tank strength per panzer division varied wildly, especially toward the end of the war. From 1943, for example, it was rare for a panzer division to have more than 100 operational tanks at any one time. The panzer divisions retained a high combat efficiency throughout the war, despite falling tank inventories. This was because each division usually had a core of veteran tankers (often including an "ace") able to maintain a high level of combat proficiency and combat "kills". In addition, tank crews were not necessarily killed when their vehicles were knocked out.

Organization on September 1, 1939
- 1 Schützen Brigade Stab (*I/,II/Schützen Regiment 1 and Kradschützen Battalion 1*)
- 1 Panzer Brigade Stab (*I/,II/Panzer Regiment 1 and I/,II/Panzer Regiment 2*) (at right)
- *I/,II/Artillerie Regiment 73* (*motorized*)
- Aufklärungs Abteilung 4 (*motorized*)
- Panzerabwehr Abteilung 37 (*motorized*)
- Pionier Abteilung 37 (*motorized*)
- Nachrichten Abteilung 37 (*motorized*)
- Nachschubtruppen 81 (*motorized*)

Organization on June 22, 1941
- 1 Schützen Brigade Stab
- *I/,II/Schützen Regiment 1*
- *I/,II/Schützen Regiment 113*
- Motorcycle Abteilung 1
- *I/,II/Panzer Regiment 1*
- *I/,II/,III/Artillerie Regiment 73* (*motorized*)
- Aufklärung Abteilung 4 (*motorized*)
- Panzerjäger Abteilung 37 (*motorized*)
- Pionier Abteilung 37 (*motorized*)

KEY
Abteilung battalion
Aufklärungs reconnaissance
Nachrichten signals
Nachschubtruppen supply troops branch
Panzerabwehr antitank
Panzerjäger tank hunter
Pionier engineer
Schützen motorized

Later Panzer Division

The winter battles in the Ukraine on the Eastern Front during late 1943 and into 1944 bled the elite of the panzer divisions white. Instead of receiving large reinforcements in the spring of 1944, most of Germany's tank production was switched westward to equip divisions preparing to fight off the impending Allied invasion of France.

By mid-1944, the German Army's panzer divisions on the Eastern Front were a shadow of their former glory. On paper, they were powerful formations with two battalions of tanks, usually one of 88 Panzer IVs and one of 88 Panthers (below, right), but battle losses and delays in delivering replacement vehicles meant that divisions on the Eastern Front were lucky if they mustered on average more than 50 working tanks, of both types.

The panzer division was also supposed to boast four panzergrenadier battalions, one of which was to be equipped with armored halftracks (below, left). In reality, these "battalions" were often little more than over-sized companies, while the armored panzergrenadier battalion was lucky to muster more than a dozen halftracks.

A desperate situation was made even more critical by the destruction of Army Group Center in June and July 1944. With no respite available on either the Western or Eastern Fronts, it was no longer possible to pull worn-out panzer divisions out of the line for reequipping and refitting. More drastic measures were needed.

In July 1994, the first of 10 new so-called "panzer brigades" were formed to fill the gaps in the German battle line. These were basically strong regimental *Kampfgruppen* (battle groups) made up of a panzer battalion, with around 40 Panthers and a weak panzergrenadier battalion mounted in armored halftracks. The experiment was short-lived, and by the late fall they had been used to beef-up depleted panzer divisions.

By the spring of 1945, the panzer divisions on the Eastern Front were on their last legs. A new order of panzer divisional organization was issued in March 1945 reducing panzer divisions to a single battalion of tanks, but this was largely an academic exercise. Most could only muster a couple of dozen tanks, backed up by an equal number of assault guns or armored self-propelled antitank guns.

Tank Strength of Panzer Divisions

Time Period:	Number of Tanks:
1939–1940	*324*
1941–1942	*150–200*
1943	*170*
1944	*120–140*

Note: These are ideal numbers that usually did not reflect the strength of frontline units.

Sixth Panzer Army

This order of battle is typical of army-sized Waffen-SS formations in the final two years of the war. The army was commanded by SS-Oberstgruppenführer Josef "Sepp" Dietrich, former head of the *Leibstandarte* Division ("LSSAH"). To fill out his new army, Dietrich was given the two premier Waffen-SS corps headquarters, I SS and II SS Panzer Corps. I SS Panzer Corps boasted the *Leibstandarte* and *Hitlerjugend* Divisions, under the command of SS-Gruppenführer Hermann Priess, who had previously commanded the infamous Waffen-SS *Totenkopf* Panzer Division in Russia and was considered a sound tactician, if ruthless, even judging by Waffen-SS standards.

Ardennes, December 1944

I SS Panzer Corps *Leibstandarte Adolf Hitler*
- *(SS-Gruppenführer Hermann Priess)*
- SS-Arko I (artillery command*)*
- SS-Corps Nachrichten Abteilung 101/501

1st SS Panzer Division *Leibstandarte Adolf Hitler*
- *(SS-Oberführer Wilhelm Mohnke)*
- Total strength: 22,000 men
- SS-Panzer Nachrichten Abteilung "LSSAH" 1

Kampfgruppe *Peiper*
- *(SS-Obersturmbannführer Jochen Peiper)*
- SS-Panzer Regiment "LSSAH" 1: *38 x Panther, 34 x Panzer IV*
- SS-Panzer Abteilung 501: *30 x Tiger II (shown on page opposite)*
- SS-Panzer Artillerie Regiment "LSSAH" 1: *II Abteilung*
- SS-Panzergrenadier Regiment "LSSAH"2: *III Abteilung Abteilung (APC)*

Kampfgruppe *Hansen*
- *(SS-Standartenführer Max Hansen)*
- SS-Panzergrenadier Regiment "LSSAH" 1: *6 x 150mm IG, 12 x 20mm*
- SS-Panzerjäger Abteilung "LSSAH" 1: *21 x PzJgr IV, 11 x Pak 40*
- SS-Panzer Artillerie Regiment "LSSAH" 1: *I Abteilung*

Kampfgruppe *Sandig*
- *(SS-Standartenführer Rudolf Sandig)*
- SS-Panzergrenadier Regiment "LSSAH" 2: *6 x 150mm IG, 12 x 20mm*
- SS-Flak Abteilung "LSSAH" 1: *18 x 88mm, 18 x 37mm*
- SS-Werfer Abteilung "LSSAH" 1: *18 x 150mm, 6 x 210mm*
- SS-Panzer Pionier Abteilung "LSSAH" 1
- SS-Panzer-Artillerie-Regiment "LSSAH" 1, III Abteilung

Kampfgruppe *Knittel*
- *(SS-Sturmbannführer Gustav Knittel)*
- SS-Panzer Aufklärungs Abteilung "LSSAH" 1

12th SS Panzer Division *Hitlerjugend*
- *(SS-Standartenführer Hugo Kraas)*
- Total strength: 22,000 men
- SS-Panzer Nachrichten Abteilung: 12

Kampfgruppe *Kuhlmann*
- *(SS-Obersturmbannführer Herbert Kuhlmann)*
- SS-Panzer Regiment 12: *14 x Panther, 37 x Panzer IV*
- 506 Panzerjäger Abteilung (Army): *28 x Jagdpanzer IV, 14 x Jagdpanther*
- SS-Panzer Artillerie Regiment 12: I Abteilung
- SS-Panzergrenadier Regiment 26: III Abteilung

Kampfgruppe *Muller*
- *(SS-Sturmbannführer Siegfried Muller)*
- SS-Panzergrenadier Regiment 25
- SS-Panzerjäger Abteilung 12: *22 x Jagdpanzer IV*
- SS-Panzer Artillerie Regiment 12: II Abteilung

Sixth Panzer Army

Kampfgruppe *Krause*
- (*SS-Obersturmbannführer Bernard Krause*)
- SS-Panzergrenadier Regiment 26
- SS-Flak Abteilung 12
- SS-Werfer Abteilung 12
- SS-Panzer Pionier Abteilung 12
- SS-Panzer Artillerie Regiment 12: *III Abteilung*

Kampfgruppe *Bremer*
- (*SS-Sturmbannführer Gerhardt Bremer*)
- SS-Panzer Aufklärungs Abteilung 12

II SS Panzer Korps Headquarters
- (*SS-Obergruppenführer Willi Bittrich*)
- SS-Arko II (artillery command)
- SS-Corps Nachrichten Abteilung: 400

2nd SS Panzer Division *Das Reich*
- Total strength: 18,000 men
- (*SS-Brigadeführer Heinz Lammerding*)
- SS-Panzergrenadier Regiment 3 *Deutschland*
- SS-Panzergrenadier Regiment *Der Führer*
- SS-Infantry Regiment *Langemarck*
- SS-Panzer Regiment 2: *58 x Panther, 28 x Panzer IV, 28 x StuG III*
- SS-Panzerjäger Abteilung 2: 20 x Jagdpanzer IV
- SS-Panzer Artillerie Regiment 2
- SS-Flak Abteilung 2
- SS-Panzer Nachrichten Abteilung 2
- SS-Panzer Aufklärungs Abteilung 2
- SS-Panzer Pionier Abteilung 2

Kampfgruppe *Krag*
(*SS-Sturmbannführer Ernst-August Krag*)
- SS-Panzer Aufklärungs Abteilung: 2

9th SS Panzer Division *Hohenstaufen*
- Total strength: 16,000 men
- (*SS-Oberführer Sylvester Stadler*)
- SS-Panzergrenadier Regiment 19
- SS-Panzergrenadier Regiment 20
- SS-Panzer Regiment 9
- I Abteilung: *35 x Panther*
- II Abteilung: *28 x StuG III, 39 x Panzer IV*
- SS-Panzerjäger Abteilung 9: *21 x Jagdpanzer IV*
- SS-Panzer Artillerie Regiment 9
- SS-Flak Abteilung 9
- SS-Panzer Nachrichten Abteilung 9
- SS-Panzer Aufklärungs Abteilung 9
- SS-Panzer Pionier Abteilung 9
- 519 schwer Panzerjäger Abteilung (Army): *21 x Jagdpanther/StuG III*

KEY
Abteilung battalion
APC armored personnel carrier
Artillerie artillery
Aufklärungs reconnaissance
Ersatz replacement
Flak antiaircraft
IG infantry gun
Nachrichten signals
Nebelwerfer rocket artillery
Pak antitank
Panzerjäger tank hunter
Pionier engineer
schwer heavy

Waffen-SS Panzer Division

There were more than 40 Waffen-SS divisions by the end of World War II (see pages 33–34). The best were the panzer divisions that, during the course of the war, had a decisive impact on numerous occasions on the Eastern Front. Following the grim winter of 1941–1942 in the East, during which the German assault on Moscow had petered out and the Red Army had launched a massive counterattack all along the line, the SS divisions in Russia (*Leibstandarte, Das Reich, Wiking, Totenkopf,* and *Polizei*) had obeyed their Führer's order to stand fast and not yield an inch of ground. They had suffered terribly in doing so, but their steadfastness was a turning point in the history of the Waffen-SS.

Hitler was delighted with the performance of his SS legions during that fateful winter, pointing to their tenacity in the face of adversity as an indication of what soldiers could achieve if they were imbued with "National Socialist will." In contrast, he was particularly scathing about the performance of many army units and their commanders, who always seemed to want to withdraw to save themselves. Henceforth, Hitler would look to his Waffen-SS divisions to deliver results on the Eastern Front. But, to achieve what he wanted, they needed to be rebuilt and expanded.

The Führer, ever the fantasist, began to dream of SS corps and even SS armies, formations that would deliver victory over the Bolsheviks. The *Leibstandarte, Das Reich, Wiking,* and *Totenkopf* were already motorized when they entered Russia in June 1941, but they would now be recreated as panzergrenadier divisions. In the summer and fall of 1942, the *Leibstandarte, Das Reich,* and *Totenkopf* Divisions were withdrawn from the Eastern Front and moved to France for reorganizing as Waffen-SS panzergrenadier divisions. The *Wiking* Division remained in the southern sector of the Eastern Front and was reinforced steadily with so-called "foreign volunteers" from occupied countries, but it was never as powerful as the three original SS panzergrenadier divisions.

The Waffen-SS panzergrenadier divisions were so lavishly equipped with tanks and armored vehicles that, in reality, they were far more powerful than army line panzer divisions. The strike power of the Waffen-SS divisions lay in their panzer regiments, which boasted two battalions of tanks. In 1942, a tank battalion had three companies—one of heavy Panzer IVs and two with lighter Panzer IIIs, each having a complement of 22 tanks. The *Leibstandarte*'s companies, however, all had Panzer IVs in frontline roles, with Panzer IIIs reduced to command tasks. For added punch, each

Waffen-SS panzer regiment also had a company of the heavy Tiger I tanks attached in 1942. This gave them massive antitank firepower.

To give an idea of the tank inventories of the Waffen-SS panzer divisions, in February 1943 the *Leibstandarte* had the following panzers in its order of battle: 12 Panzer IIs, 10 Panzer IIIs, 52 Panzer IVs, 9 Tiger Is, and 9 command tanks. Five months later, just before the Battle of Kursk, the division could field 4 Panzer IIs, 13 Panzer IIIs, 67 Panzer IVs, 13 Tiger Is and 9 command tanks.

At the heart of the Waffen-SS divisions were their two panzergrenadier regiments (although due to shortages only one was equipped with armored halftracks; the other used trucks to transport its troops—not even the Waffen-SS was spared Germany's armaments shortages). These units were able to trace their lineage back to the original SS regiment, and they made great play of their Nazi heritage. They generally had honorific titles as well as numerical designations. For example, *Das Reich* had the *Deutschland* and *Der Führer* Regiments, *Totenkopf* had the *Thule* (later *Totenkopf*) and *Theodor Eicke* Regiments, and *Wiking* had the *Germania, Nordland,* and *Westland* Regiments. The *Leibstandarte* was, however, unique in that all its sub-units included numerical designations and the title *Leibstandarte SS Adolf Hitler,* abbreviated to LSSAH.

By 1944, the elite Waffen-SS divisions were fully fledged panzer divisions, with an authorized order of battle as follows: one panzer regiment (two battalions); two panzergrenadier regiments; an artillery regiment (one battalion of 12 x 150mm howitzers, one battalion of 8 towed 150mm howitzers and 3 field guns, and one battalion of 8 self-propelled 105mm howitzers and 4 self-propelled 150mm howitzers); an armored reconnaissance battalion; an assault gun battalion (around 40 StuG III assault guns); an antitank battalion (28 x 75mm assault guns or tank destroyers and 12 towed antitank guns); an antiaircraft battalion (12 x 88mm guns and 9 x 37mm guns); an engineer battalion; an armored signals brigade; and divisional services. Authorized divisional strength was around 19,500 troops in total.

SS Chief Heinrich Himmler tried to ensure that his panzer divisions were always up to strength. Thus, in June 1944, despite high losses the previous year on the Eastern Front, the *Leibstandarte* had 103 Panzer IVs, 72 Panthers, and 45 StuG IIIs, and *Das Reich* had 50 Panzer IVs, 26 Panthers, and 41 StuG IIIs.

Typical Waffen-SS Panzer Division

 Total strength: 13–15,000 men

Divisional HQ Company (2 x Panzer V), band, and field police (450 men)

SS-PANZER REGIMENT
- HQ Company: *320 men*

I Abteilung *(500-600 men)*
- HQ Company: 2–8 Panzer V, 3 x 20mm Flakvierling and 12 x LMG
- 1, 2, 3, & 4 Companies *(each 14-17 Panzer V and/or Panzer IV)*

II Abteilung *(500 men)*
- HQ Company, as above but all Panzer IV
- 5 & 6 Companies *(each 14 x Panzer IV)*
- 7 & 8 Companies *(each 10-14 x 75mm Jagdpanzer IV/70)*

I SS-PANZERGRENADIER REGIMENT *(2,000 men)*
- HQ Company, SdKfz 250 & 251 halftracks: *160 men*

I Abteilung (all SdKfz 251 halftracks) *(850 men)*
- HQ Company
- 1, 2, & 3 Companies *(each 2 x 75mm Pak 40, 7 x 20mm Flak 38, 2 x 80mm GrW 34 mortar, 4 x HMG & 29 x LMG)*
- 4 Company *(6 x 75mm Pak 40, 4 x 120mm sGrW 42 mortar, 2 x HMG & 4 x LMG)*

II Abteilung (all truck-mounted) *(850 men)*
- HQ Company
- 5, 6, & 7 Companies *(each 2 x 80mm GrW 34 mortar, 4 x HMG)*
- 8 Company *(6 x 20mm Flak 38, 4 x sGrW 42 & 2 x HMG) (NB: No 9-14 Companies)*
- 15 Company *(6 x Hummel, siG 33 or Wespe)*
- Engineer Company *(24 x Flamethrower, 1 x 20mm Flak 38, 2 x 80mm GrW 34, 2 x HMG)*

II SS-PANZERGRENADIER REGIMENT
- As above, except both abteilungen as II/I and Engineer Company only 16 x Flammenwerfer and 12 x LMG

SS-PANZER ARTILLERY REGIMENT
- HQ Company *(2 x LMG) (90 men)*

I Abteilung *(550 men)*
- HQ Company *(1 x Wespe, 3 x 20mm Flak 38)*
- 1 & 2 Batteries *(each 6 x Wespe)*
- 3 Battery *(6 x Hummel)*

II Abteilung *(450 men)*
- HQ Company *(as above)*
- 4 & 5 Batteries *(each 6 x towed 105mm leFH 18)*

III Abteilung *(500 men)*
- HQ Company *(as above)*
- 6 & 7 Batteries *(each 4 x towed 150mm sFH 18)*
- 8 Battery *(4 x 170mm K18)*

SS-PANZER RECONNAISSANCE ABTEILUNG *(500 men)*
- HQ Company
- Scout Company *(26 x SdKfz 221 & 16 x SdKfz 231)*
- Light Company *(SdKfz 251s) (2 x 75mm PaK 40, 2 x 80mm GrW 34 & 44 x LMG)*
- 3 Company *(2 x 75mm Pak 40, 7 x 20mm Flak 38, 2 x 80mm GrW 34, 4 x HMG & 29 x LMG)*
- 4 Company *(6 x 75mm PaK 40, 6 x 80mm GrW 34, 18 x LMG)*
- Maintenance Company *(5 x LMG)*

SS-PANZERJÄGER ABTEILUNG *(500 men)*
- HQ Company *(3 x 75mm Jagdpanzer 1V/70)*
- 1 & 2 Companies *(each 10 x 75mm Jagdpanzer IV/70)*
- 3 Company *(12 x towed 75mm Pak 40)*
- Maintenance Company *(3 x LMG)*

SS-PANZER FLAK ABTEILUNG *(750 men)*
- HQ Company *(2 x LMG)*
- 1 & 2 Companies *(each 6 x towed 88mm Flak 18 or 36 & 3 x 20mm Flak 38)*
- 3 Company *(9 x 37mm Flak 36 or 37)*
- 4 Company *(4–12 x 20mm Flakvierling on halftracks)*

SS-PANZER ENGINEER ABTEILUNG *(850 men)*
- HQ Company *(4 x LMG & 4 x flamethrower)*
- 1 Company *(motorized) (4 x HMG, 36 x LMG & 4 x 80mm GrW 34)*
- 2 Company *(SdKfz 251s) (2 x HMG, 43 x LMG, 2 x 8cm GrW 34, 6-8 x flamethrower)*

SS-PANZER SIGNALS ABTEILUNG *(500 men)*
- HQ Company
- 3 companies

SS-PANZER ROCKET ARTILLERY ABTEILUNG *(500 men)*
- HQ Company *(1 x LMG)*
- 1, 2, & 3 Batteries *(each 6 x 150mm WGr 41)*
- Maintenance Company *(1 x LMG)*

SS-MAINTENANCE ABTEILUNG (motorized)
- HQ Company
- 1, 2, 3, 4, & 5 Transport Companies

Waffen-SS Panzer Divisions in Normandy, 1944

By the fall of 1943, new Waffen-SS units were being formed in training depots in Belgium, although the *Leibstandarte* Division itself would not join them until the following spring, when it was to be released from defensive duties on the Eastern Front.

But Hitler wanted more Waffen-SS panzer divisions. II SS Panzer Corps was pulled out of Russia after the failed Kursk Offensive and moved to France to begin raising another two Waffen-SS divisions, the *Hohenstaufen* and *Frundsberg*. In the fall of 1943, a new designation system was introduced, with the panzergrenadier divisions officially being renamed panzer divisions. For example, the premier Waffen-SS unit became the 1st SS Panzer Division *Leibstandarte-SS Adolf Hitler* ("LSSAH").

Although it was not affiliated to the two Waffen-SS panzer corps, the 17th SS Panzergrenadier Division *Götz von Berlichingen* was also formed at this point, and it would later go on to play a prominent part in the battles on the Western Front during the following year.

The new Waffen-SS panzer units were initially slow to take shape, with new recruits and equipment arriving in dribs and drabs. As winter approached and it became clear that the British and Americans would soon launch their invasion of France, the pace of training and equipping took on greater urgency. Soon new tanks, armored halftracks, and other weapons were flowing to the Waffen-SS in France.

The *Hitlerjugend* Division received the highest priority for men and equipment. Its cadre of *Leibstandarte* instructors were soon whipping the young 17- and 18-year-olds of the division into shape. Lack of time meant the division concentrated on battlefield skills, not parade drills. Tactical exercises with live ammunition were the norm. Panzer crews were sent to tank factories in Germany to help build the vehicles they would soon drive into battle.

The *Hitlerjugend* Division was soon conducting complicated battalion, then regimental, and finally divisional exercises. By the spring of 1944, the division boasted nearly 20,000 soldiers and an almost complete inventory of vehicles and equipment, as well as a high standard of training.

The *Frundsberg* and *Hohenstaufen* Divisions were not quite as lavishly equipped and trained, but nonetheless they were to benefit from a trip to the Eastern Front in April 1944 to help the First Panzer Army break out of a Soviet encirclement. They saw limited action and allowed Hausser's successor, Willi Bittrich, to see his units in battle and to sideline a number of incompetent unit commanders. The troops themselves fought well and showed much potential. They stayed in the Ukraine on temporary "loan" to the Eastern Front until early June, when they were recalled to France to fight in Normandy. On their return, they would put up an impressive performance, on a par with the other Waffen-SS units. Bittrich's headquarters team was also first rate, and would later inflict the only strategic defeat on the Allies during the entire northwest European campaign. This famous defeat was one which would take place at Nijmegen and Arnhem in September 1944.

Languishing in the south of France, the 17th SS Panzergrenadier Division was right at the bottom of the list for receiving new equipment. Its inventory was to number only a single assault gun battalion of StuG IIIs by the time the Allied landings occurred in Normandy in June.

Shattered by their experiences on the Eastern Front, the *Leibstandarte* and *Das Reich* Divisions were pulled back to France in the spring of 1944. Here they would be rebuilt in order that they could act as the spearhead for Hitler's counter-invasion strategy. The half-starved and lice-infested remnants of the two divisions were in no shape to do much beyond clean and repair their paltry stocks of weapons and vehicles.

Then the Waffen-SS replacement and supply system started to kick in. New soldiers and equipment were suddenly beginning to arrive in large quantities from Germany. Time was short, however, and the quality of the new recruits left a lot to be desired. Most of them were drafted youngsters, or former Luftwaffe (air force) and Kriegsmarine (navy) personnel. They were not of the same ilk as the volunteers who had made their way into the ranks of the elite Waffen-SS divisions earlier in the war. The cadre of *Leibstandarte* and *Das Reich* veterans had to begin almost from scratch. They found themselves teaching these new Waffen-SS men basic soldiering skills while, at the same time, having to indoctrinate them into the special philosophy of their "divisional family."-

By the late spring of 1944, the five Waffen-SS panzer divisions and one panzergrenadier division earmarked to repulse the impending Allied invasion of France boasted some of the most powerful weapons in the German arsenal. The most common tank was the Panzer V Panther. With its sloped armor, wide tracks, and powerful, long 75mm cannon, it could outshoot, and out-armor almost every Allied tank.

Waffen-SS Panzer Strength in Normandy, 1944

 June 6 to August 13, 1944

	June 1	July 1	July 18	July 25	August 5	August 13
PANTHER TANKS						
Leibstandarte Division	38	25	46	34	46	7
Das Reich Division	25	26	unknown	41	1	3
Hohenstaufen Division	30	19	25	23	11	15
Hitlerjugend Division	48	24	21	37	9	7
PANZER IV TANKS						
Leibstandarte Division	42	30	61	45	57	14
Das Reich Division	44	50	unknown	37	4	5
Hohenstaufen Division	41	10	20	21	8	11
Frundsberg Division	34	20	12	14	10	11
Hitlerjugend Division	91	32	16	21	37	17
STUG III ASSAULT GUNS						
Leibstandarte Division	44	31	35	32	27	8
Das Reich Division	33	36	unknown	25	6	8
Hohenstaufen Division	38	22	15	14	8	14
Frundsberg Division	32	25	6	11	7	5
17th SS Division	42	18	unknown	10	unknown	unknown
TIGER I TANKS						
101st SS Battalion	37	11	6	13	20	8
102d SS Battalion	28	14	19	30	20	7
PANZERJÄGER IV						
Hitlerjugend Division	–	–	–	–	10	5
17th SS Division	–	–	–	–	31	unknown

German Forces in the Kharkov Sector, August 1943

 The German defeat at Kursk in July 1943 greatly weakened those German divisions and corps that had taken part in the battle. III Panzer Corps under Lieutenant General Hermann Breith, for example, was ordered to take charge of the operation to defeat the Soviet attack at Kharkov in August 1943. He was to have the *Totenkopf*, *Das Reich*, and *Wiking* Divisions for the mission, as well as the 3rd Panzer Division. However, at this time all the Waffen-SS divisions were still en route by train from the Izyum and Mius Fronts. In the meantime, the 3rd Panzer Division would have to hold the ring as best it could, and prevent Soviet tanks driving into Kharkov and capturing the de-training points of the Waffen-SS divisions.

Although it could only put 35 tanks in the field, the 3rd Panzer Division was a seasoned formation and it put up a good fight, staging a spirited rearguard action on August 5 against a push by the Soviet XVIII Tank Corps of the Fifth Guards Tank Army. The division repulsed this attack, and became a firm anchor on the right flank of III Panzer Corps.

Farther to the west, there were no German forces to stop the First Tank Army seizing the key rail junction at Bogodukhov on August 6. Over the next two days, the lead elements of the *Das Reich* Division started to arrive south of Kharkov, and they were fed piecemeal into the battle to try to shore up the front to the west of the city. Luftwaffe aerial reconnaissance was providing Breith with valuable photographs that showed thousands of Russian tanks moving southward to the west of Kharkov. The Germans had never had to deal with an enemy offensive on this scale before.

By August 8, *Das Reich* was deployed in strength, with four Tigers and 20 assault guns in action. Even though its panzer regiment was still to arrive, the division was able to inflict heavy losses on the Soviet III Mechanized Corps and XXXI Tank Corps, which were spearheading the First Tank Army's advance. VI Tank Corps, however, was still advancing southward unopposed.

It was now the turn of the *Totenkopf* Division to enter the battle, and try to close down the Soviet breakthrough. During the night of August 8/9, the division deployed across VI Tank Corps' axis of advance, ready to stop it in its tracks. In reserve was a company from SS Panzer Regiment 3 with 12 tanks. The remainder of the regiment's 14 Panzer IIIs and 27 Panzer IVs were still en route. By this time the SS divisions were a shadow of their former selves.

III Panzer Corps (west of Kharkov)
- 3rd Panzer Division
- SS *Wiking* Division
- SS *Das Reich* Division
- SS *Totenkopf* Division (*at right, top*)
- 34th Infantry Division
- 223rd Infantry Division

IX Corps (defense of Kharkov)
- 3rd Panzer Division
- 6th Panzer Division
- SS *Das Reich* Division (*relocated*) (*at right, bottom*)
- 106th Infantry Division
- 168th Infantry Division
- 198th Infantry Division
- 320th Infantry Division
- 248th Infantry Division

German Order of Battle, Cherkassy Pocket, February 1944

Six months after the Battle of Kursk (July 1943), Army Group South had been pushed back 187 miles (300 km) by the advancing Red Army across the Ukraine. The retreating Germans hoped to use the Dnieper River as a defensive barrier to halt the Soviet pursuit, but this plan was doomed when the first Soviet spearheads crossed at Bukrin on September 22, 1943. Army Group South's depleted formations were unable to establish an effective defense before the Soviets forced other crossings of the Dnieper, with General Ivan S. Konev's 2d Ukrainian Front breaking out of the Mishurin Rog bridgehead in October, while General Mikhail F. Vatutin's 1st Ukrainian Front recaptured Kiev on November 6. Although Army Group South's commander, Field Marshal Manstein, was able to mass his remaining armor in early November and launch a series of partly successful counterattacks west of Kiev and near Kirovograd that slowed both Soviet drives, the German position in the Ukraine was increasingly desperate.

After the Soviet offensives culminated in early January 1944, Army Group South was left with a salient formed around Korsun that split the 1st and 2d Ukrainian Fronts. Hitler was determined to hold the Korsun Pocket—despite Manstein's objections—since it was the only significant area where German troops still held part of the Dnieper line. However, only two weak German infantry corps held the salient: General Wilhelm Stemmermann's XI Corps and Generalleutnant Theo Lieb's XXXXII Corps, with five weak infantry divisions and the SS *Wiking* Panzer Division. The Soviet Stavka (High Command) realized the vulnerability of the Korsun salient and intended to create another Stalingrad by cutting off the salient at its base. Despite the fact that their forces were still badly depleted from the fighting around Kiev and Kirovograd, Vatutin and Konev were able to mount powerful pincer attacks with tank armies that penetrated the exposed flanks of the Korsun Salient on January 24–25, and their spearheads linked up near Zvenigorodka on January 28, 1944. About 65,000 tired and ill-equipped German troops were cut off in the Korsun Pocket.

The initial German reaction to the breakthrough was slow due to Manstein's absence at a meeting with Hitler in East Prussia, but, on his return, he began organizing a relief effort. He was determined to rescue the encircled forces in the Korsun Pocket, and he was able to assemble two weak panzer corps for the operation. General Nikolaus von Vormann's XXXVII Panzer Corps began attacking northward into Konev's flank on February 1, inflicting some damage, but the effort was too weak to succeed. General Hermann Breith's III Panzer Corps was stronger, but this formation had to move 94 miles (150 km) before it could begin its assault northward on February 4. Marshal Georgi Zhukov, charged by the Stavka with coordinating efforts to block the German relief operations, shifted his own armor reserves to counter Breith's attack. In a series of tough tank battles, III Panzer Corps' advance toward the pocket was gradually exhausted by mud, lack of supplies, and casualties. A final effort on February 11–13 succeeded in seizing the town of Lysyanka on the Gniloy Tikich stream, but was still more than 6.25 miles (10 km) short of the pocket. Manstein's first relief effort to reach the pocket had failed.

Inside the pocket, the trapped German troops were being ground down in a merciless battle of attrition that favored the attackers. After much confusion about command and control, General Stemmermann was finally placed in command of both corps on February 7. However, by that point it was obvious that Group *Stemmermann* could no longer merely wait for rescue, but would have to free itself. On February 12–13, Stemmermann used his few remaining combat-capable troops in the SS *Wiking* Division and the 72d Infantry Division to seize the towns of Shanderovka, Novo Buda, and Komarovka, which lay on the route to III Panzer Corps. Despite fierce Soviet counterattacks to retake the towns, Group *Stemmermann* held on to its gains and gradually shifted its remaining 45,000 troops for a breakout, abandoning Korsun itself on February 13, 1944. The breakout from the Korsun Pocket began at 11:00 hours on February 16.

Approximately 13,000 German troops were lost during the breakout on February 16–18, with about 8,500 killed and 4,500 captured. Very little equipment was brought out of the Cherkassy Pocket, and for all intents Group *Stemmermann* was wrecked as a fighting force. Of the five infantry divisions that escaped the pocket, all were reduced to disarmed fragments; the loss of virtually all their horses and vehicles would be impossible to replace. The SS *Wiking* Division was in slightly better shape, with 8,278 survivors, and the unit's recovery was assisted by the fact that three of its battalions that had been reequipping in Germany returned shortly. The *Wiking* Division was soon back in action in Poland, and it was the only unit that escaped from the Cherkassy Pocket that played any significant role in subsequent operations. Although Soviet losses in tanks and men were heavy, these were quickly made good.

German Order of Battle, Cherkassy Pocket, February 1944

The Rescue Force
III Panzer Corps
- SS *Leibstandarte* Division
- 1st Panzer Division
- 6th Panzer Division
- 16th Panzer Division
- 17th Panzer Division
- Heavy Panzer Regiment *Bake*
- 249th Assault Gun Brigade
- 54th Rocket Regiment

Operating in support of Rescue Force
XLVII Panzer Corps
- 3rd Panzer Division
- 11th Panzer Division
- 13th Panzer Division
- 14th Panzer Division
- 106th Infantry Division
- 282d Infantry Division
- 320th Infantry Division
- 911st Assault Gun Brigade

In the Pocket
XLII Corps
- 88th Infantry Division
- 417th Infantry Regiment
- Kampfgruppe B (*elements of the 112th, 332d, and 255th Infantry Divisions*) (*below*)
- 805th Assault Gun Brigade

XI Corps
- SS *Wiking* Division
- SS *Walloon* Assault Brigade
- 57th Infantry Division
- 72d Infantry Division
- 389th Infantry Division
- 202d Assault Gun Brigade
- GHQ Light Artillery Battalion

Waffen-SS Order of Battle, Arnhem, September 1944

In the first week of September 1944, Willi Bittrich's II SS Panzer Corps was ordered to move to a reorganizing and refitting area north of the Dutch town of Arnhem. The unit had been in action continuously for just over two months, and was now desperately in need of a quiet period to get itself ready for battle again.

Plans were already in train to bring Bittrich's two divisions, the *Hohenstaufen* and *Frundsberg*, back up to strength, and Arnhem seemed like a good place to begin this time-consuming task. There they would be safe from Allied attack. Lightly wounded personnel were sent to hospitals in Germany in order to recover, and those in need of training were sent on courses in specialist depots.

Remaining in the Dutch barracks which had been taken over by the Waffen-SS corps were probably no more than 6,000 men, who were equipped with whatever tanks, artillery, and vehicles they had managed to bring with them out of the summer defeat in France. It was doubtful if the whole of the corps would be able to put more than 30 tanks or assault guns into the field. Walther Harzer's *Hohenstaufen* was then ordered to move to Germany to be rebuilt

there. Before it left, it was to hand over its remaining operational vehicles and heavy weapons to Heinz Harmel's *Frundsberg*, which was to remain in Holland. At the same time as this reorganization process was under way, contingency orders were issued stating that the two units were to be prepared to dispatch "alarm" Kampfgruppen (battle groups) to crisis zones. Not believing intelligence reports that the Allied advance had run out of steam, Harzer decided to keep hold of many of his precious remaining tanks and heavy weapons until the very last minute, in case he had to send his men into battle.

The conventional organization of both divisions had all but collapsed. Instead, the remaining troops were grouped into a number of ad hoc Kampfgruppen. Harmel gutted his panzergrenadier heavy weapons companies to form the division's only antitank gun company. Likewise, all the armored halftracks in the division were grouped in the reconnaissance battalion to provide him with a powerful strike force. The artillery regiment's self-propelled gun drivers and crews were all transferred to the panzer regiment, and all the infantry were combined into three very weak panzergrenadier battalions.

II SS Panzer Corps Headquarters
(SS-Obergruppenführer Willi Bittrich)
- SS-Arko II (*artillery command*)
- SS-Corps Nachrichten Abteilung: *400*

9th SS Panzer Division Hohenstaufen
- (*SS-Obersturmbannführer Walther Harzer*)
- SS-Panzer Nachrichten Abteilung 9, (*plus Military Police, intelligence, escort troops, repair troops, medical staff; 280 men total*)
- SS-Panzergrenadier Regiment 19: *no heavy weapons or APCs*
- SS-Panzergrenadier Regiment 20: *no heavy weapons or APCs*
-

Kampfgruppe Spindler
- (*SS-Obersturmbannführer Ludwig Spindler*)
- SS-Panzer Artillerie Regiment 9: *120 men, no guns*
- SS-Panzer Regiment 9: *no tanks, 200–300 men*
- SS-Panzerjäger Abteilung 9: *no heavy weapons, 2 x Pzjg IV, 2 x Pak 40, 2 x APC (120 men)*

Kampfgruppe von Allworden
- (*SS-Hauptsturmführer Klaus von Allworden*)

Kampfgruppe Moeller
- (*SS-Hauptsturmführer Hans Moeller*)
- SS-Panzer Pionier Abteilung 9: *90 men*

Kampfgruppe Gropp
- (*SS-Untersturmführer Gropp*)
- SS-Flak Abteilung 9: *87 men, 1 x 88mm, 4 x 20mm*
- SS Depot and Reserve Abteilung 16: *440 men (SS-Hauptsturmführer Sepp Kraft)*
- Total: *2,500 men*

10th SS Panzer Division Frundsberg
- (*SS-Brigadeführer Heinz Harmel*)
- SS-Panzer Nachrichten Abteilung 10
- SS-Panzergrenadier Regiment 21: *1.5 battalions*
- SS-Panzergrenadier Regiment 22: *1 battalion plus 8 x Pak 40, 4 x SP 75mm AT*
- SS-Panzer Artillerie Regiment 10: *40 guns*
- SS-Flak Abteilung 10
- SS Training and Replacement Regiment 5
- Kampfgruppe Brinkmann
- SS-Panzer Aufklärungs Abteilung 10

Waffen-SS Order of Battle, Arnhem, September 1944

NIJMEGEN DEFENSE

Kampfgruppe *Graebner* *(at right, top and center)*
- *(SS-Hauptsturmführer Viktor Graebner)*
- SS-Panzer Aufklärungs Abteilung 9: *30 armored vehicles, 400 men*
- SS-Panzer Regiment 10: *16 x Pz IV tanks*
- SS-Panzer Pionier Abteilung 10
- *(SS-Hauptsturmführer Albert Brandt)*

Kampfgruppe *Reinhold*
- tank crews as infantry
  (SS-Hauptsturmführer Leo Hermann Reinhold)
- 22d Panzergrenadier Regiment, plus 3rd Company, 21st Regiment

Kampfgruppe *Euling* *(at right, bottom)*
- 100 men plus 4 x PzJg IV
  (SS-Hauptsturmführer Karl Heinz Euling)

Detached to Kampfgruppe *Walther*
- Kampfgruppe *Heinke*
- SS-Panzerjäger Abteilung 10: *15 x PzJgr IV*
- SS Kampfgruppe *Seger*
- Artillery battery: *6 x 105mm field guns, plus infantry battalion from 9th SS Panzer Division*
- SS Kampfgruppe *Richter*
- *(SS-Hauptsturmführer Richter)*

I SS Panzer Corps' Order of Battle, 1943

 At the end of March 1943, Hitler informed the *Leibstandarte* Division's commander, SS-Obergruppenführer Josef "Sepp" Dietrich, that his unit would be the core of a new corps, to be known as I SS Panzer Corps *Leibstandarte Adolf Hitler*. Scores of staff officers from Dietrich's division would form the new corps staff, while hundreds of officers and noncommissioned officers were to be drafted to form a training cadre to establish the new Hitler Youth SS panzergrenadier division. A number of artillery, assault gun, and antitank battalions were also transferred from the *Leibstandarte* to the new division, to provide the core of its specialist regiments.

As trainloads of *Leibstandarte* veterans headed westward, those who remained behind were ordered to prepare their units for action in a few weeks' time. Thousands of replacement soldiers were now arriving on a daily basis. These were mostly a mix of raw conscripts and drafted Luftwaffe ground personnel. Gone were the days when the Waffen-SS could pick and choose who served in its ranks. When Dietrich greeted the first batch of ex-Luftwaffe men in Kharkov, he asked for volunteers for the panzergrenadiers. There were few takers—most of the new Waffen-SS men wanted to serve in maintenance and repair teams. In future the replacements were not to be given a choice regarding which units they would serve in. Most of these recruits were directed to the *Leibstandarte* Division, because of the heavy casualties it had suffered during the previous two months.

A constant stream of trains arrived at Kharkov with new tanks, artillery, vehicles, and other equipment. Waffen-SS repair teams worked overtime to restore the scores of tanks damaged in action back to fighting condition. No one trusted them to be returned in time for the coming offensive if they were shipped back to workshops in Germany.

The panzer regiments of the Waffen-SS divisions were extensively reorganized to absorb their new equipment. The *Leibstandarte* and *Das Reich* Divisions were both ordered to send the first battalion of their panzer regiments back to Germany, for training in the use of the new Panther tank. This process would not be complete by the time Operation Citadel began, contrary to the many accounts of the Battle of Kursk which have stated that the Waffen-SS divisions fielded hundreds of the new tanks during the offensive. In fact, the Panther would not make its appearance on the Eastern Front in Waffen-SS service until the middle of August 1943.

The Waffen-SS was also not equipped with hundreds of Tiger I tanks at Kursk: only three companies of the heavy tanks saw service with II SS Panzer Corps during July 1943. Each division did have a battalion of Sturmgeschütz (StuG) III assault guns and a strong contingent of Marder III self-propelled antitank guns.

By the time Operation Citadel got under way, the *Leibstandarte*'s panzer regiment boasted one battalion, with 67 Panzer IV and 13 Panzer III tanks, along with 13 Tiger Is. The *Das Reich* Division was less well equipped, with only 33 Panzer IVs, 62 Panzer IIIs, and 14 Tiger Is. To boost its fighting power, the division pressed 25 captured T-34s into service. The *Totenkopf* Division still had two battalions in its panzer regiment, but 63 of its tanks were Panzer IIIs. It also had 44 heavier Panzer IVs and 15 Tiger Is.

The *Wiking* Division's panzer unit had been upgraded to regimental status. However, it had yet to grow beyond battalion strength. In July 1943, it could only muster 23 Panzer III and 17 Panzer IV tanks. It had no Tigers, and was kept in reserve throughout the Kursk Offensive.

To further increase the firepower of II SS Panzer Corps, the army provided two heavy artillery and two rocket launcher regiments, as well as a special command headquarters to coordinate fire missions of all artillery units in the corps. This meant that huge amounts of firepower could be brought down on individual targets in a very short space of time.

To prepare his command for battle, Hausser ordered a series of training exercises to be held. Noncommissioned officers drilled the new recruits to turn them into combat soldiers. Tank driving and gunnery courses were run on the new vehicles and weapons being delivered to the Waffen-SS. Senior commanders were given top-secret briefings on the Operation Citadel plan, and were shown scores of Luftwaffe aerial photographs of the Soviet defenses in their respective sectors.

Company and battalion field exercises were held on the steppe around Kharkov to familiarize the troops with equipment and to practice the tactics to be used during the coming battle. Finally, divisional and corps "command post" exercises were put on to acquaint the Waffen-SS commanders and staff officers with the plan. They based their planning on intelligence that said four Russian infantry divisions were holding the enemy's first defensive line in II SS Panzer Corps' sector. Two more held the second line, and behind them were two tank corps with at least 360 tanks. After defeating these forces, counterattacks were to be expected from several more enemy tank corps. Although many Waffen-SS men were superbly confident regarding their own equipment and abilities, some of the older veterans knew the coming battle would be like no other that they had previously faced.

I SS Panzer Corps' Order of Battle, 1943

Panzer Corps Headquarters (later II SS Panzer Korps)
- SS-Panzer Abteilung 102/schw (*heavy*)
- SS-Panzer Abteilung 502
- (*Tiger tanks from 1944*)
- Arko II. SS Panzer Corps/SS-Arko 102 (*artillery command*)
- SS-Artillerie Abteilung 102
- 1. u. 2. SS-Gr. Werfer. Kompanie 102 (*rocket*)
- SS-Flak Kompanie 102
- SS-Werfer Abteilung. Generalkommando II.SS Panzer Corps/ SS-Werfer Abteilung 102 (*rockets*)
- Corps Nachr. Abteilung 400 (*motorized*) (*signals*)

Leibstandarte Division
- SS-Musik Corps "LSSAH"
- SS-Panzergrenadier Regiment 1 "LSSAH"
- SS-Panzergrenadier Regiment 2 "LSSAH"
- SS-Panzer Regiment "LSSAH" 1
- SS-Panzerjäger Abteilung "LSSAH" 1 (*antitank*)
- SS-Sturmgeschütz Abteilung "LSSAH" 1
- SS-Panzer Artillerie Regiment "LSSAH" 1
- SS-Flak Abteilung "LSSAH" 1
- SS-Werfer Abteilung "LSSAH" 1 (*rocket*)
- SS-Panzer Nachrichten Abteilung "LSSAH" 1 (*radio*)
- SS-Panzer Aufklärungs Abteilung "LSSAH" 1 (*reconnaissance*)
- SS-Panzer Pionier Abteilung "LSSAH" 1 (*combat engineer*)
- SS-Wach Abteilung (*motorized*) "LSSAH" (*often detached in Berlin for security work*)

Das Reich Division
- SS-Panzergrenadier Regiment 3 *Deutschland*
- SS-Panzergrenadier Regiment *Der Führer*
- SS-Infantry Regiment *Langemarck*
- SS-Panzer Regiment 2
- SS-Panzerjäger Abteilung 2 (*antitank*)
- SS-Sturmgeschütz Abteilung 2
- SS-Panzer Artillerie Regiment 2
- SS-Flak Abteilung 2
- SS-Werfer Abteilung 2 (*rocket*)
- SS-Panzer Nachrichten Abteilung 2 (*radio*)
- SS-Panzer Aufklärungs Abteilung 2 (*reconnaissance*)
- SS-Panzer Pionier Battalion 2 (*combat engineer*)

Totenkopf Division
- SS-Panzergrenadier Regiment 5 *Thule* (*later titled Totenkopf*)
- SS-Panzergrenadier Regiment 6 *Theodor Eicke*
- SS-Panzer Regiment 3
- SS-Panzerjäger Abteilung 3 (*antitank*)
- SS-Sturmgeschütz Abteilung 3
- SS-Panzer Artillerie Regiment 3
- SS-Flak Abteilung 3
- SS-Werfer Abteilung 3 (*rocket*)
- SS-Panzer Nachrichten Abteilung 3 (*radio*)
- SS-Panzer Aufklärungs Abteilung 3 (*reconnaissance*)
- SS-Panzer Pionier Battalion 3 (*combat engineer*)

Wiking Division
- SS-Panzergrenadier Regiment 9 *Germania*
- SS-Panzergrenadier Regiment 10 *Westland*
- SS-Panzergrenadier Regiment *Nordland* (*left the division on March 22, 1943*)
- Estnisches SS-Freiwilligen Panzergrenadier Battalion *Narwa* (*part of the division in the summer of 1943 and withdrawn in July 1944*)
- SS-Sturmbrigade *Wallonien* (*temporarily attached in 1943–1944*)
- SS-Panzer Regiment 5
- SS-Panzerjäger Abteilung 5 (*antitank*)
- SS-Sturmgeschütz Abteilung 5
- SS-Panzer Artillerie Regiment 5
- SS-Flak Abteilung 5
- SS-Werfer Abteilung 5 (*rocket*)
- SS-Panzer Nachrichten Abteilung 5 (*radio*)
- SS-Panzer Aufklärungs Abteilung 5 (*reconnaissance*)
- SS-Panzer Pionier Battalion 5 (*combat engineer*)
- 1./SS-Panzergrenadier Regiment 23 *Norge* *
- 1./SS-Panzergrenadier Regiment 24 *Danmark* *
- SS-Panzer Abteilung Wiking (*1942–1943*)

* These units were attached to the division in 1944–1945

Key
Abteilung: battalion
Aufklärungs: reconnaissance
Flak: antiaircraft
Generalkommando: General Headquarters
Kompanie: company
Nachrichten: signals
Panzerjäger: antitank
Pionier: engineer
Sturm: assault
Wach: guard
Werfer: rocket artillery

Parachute Division Order of Battle

At the beginning of 1939, there was a complete reorganization of Germany's airborne detachments. The loose framework that had hitherto sufficed needed to be replaced by a more formal establishment if the 7th Flieger Division was to become a division in the full sense of that term. The establishment of a standard German infantry division was three rifle regiments, each of three battalions. The 7th Flieger Division had, at the beginning of 1939, only one parachute rifle regiment with one battalion. Though divisional strength included Heidrich's Parachute Infantry Battalion and Sydow's Airlanding Battalion of the General Göring Regiment, these had not been formally established as part of the parachute regiment. When that amalgamation was carried out, Heidrich's unit became the 2d Parachute Battalion and Sydow's unit the 3rd Parachute Battalion of the 1st Parachute Regiment respectively. A headquarters was established, and Bräuer assumed command of the 1st Parachute Regiment. He was succeeded in the post of commander of the 1st Battalion by Major von Grazy. With the formal establishment of the first of the division's three regiments at last completed, in June 1939 work commenced on forming the 2d Parachute Regiment. By the end of July, two battalions had been raised for this unit. The order of battle below is for a 1944 parachute division.

The maximum strength of the division was 15,976 men. It was composed of three parachute regiments, an antitank battalion, headquarters and supporting units.

Parachute regiment (3,206 men)
Composed of:
Three battalions, plus
One antitank company (186 men),
with three towed 75mm antitank guns
One mortar company (163 men) with
9–12 x 120mm mortars

Parachute battalion (853 men)
Composed of:
Three rifle companies (170 men each)
One machine gun company (205 men)
with eight heavy machine guns
Four 81mm mortars
Two 75mm light recoilless guns

Artillery regiment (1,571 men)
Composed of:
One battalion of three batteries, with
12 x 75mm mountain guns
One battalion of three batteries, with
12 x 105mm recoilless guns

Mortar battalion (594 men)
Composed of:
Three mortar companies,
each equipped with 12 x 120mm mortars

Antitank battalion (484 men)
Composed of:
One company with
12 towed 75mm antitank guns
One company with
14 x 75mm self-propelled guns
One antiaircraft company with
12 x 20mm self-propelled antiaircraft guns

Pioneer battalion (620 men)
Composed of:
Three pioneer companies
One machine gun company

Antiaircraft battalion (824 men)
Composed of:
Two heavy antiaircraft batteries (each
one equipped with 6 x 88mm guns)
One light antiaircraft company with
18 towed 20mm antiaircraft guns

Signals battalion (379 men)
Composed of:
One radio company
One telephone company
One light signals company

Medical battalion (800 men)
Composed of:
Two medical companies
One field hospital
One light medical company

Reconnaissance company (200 men)

Waffen-SS Order of Battle, Normandy, June 1944

On June 6, 1944, the *Hitlerjugend* and Panzer Lehr Divisions were ordered to move against the British beaches as the Allies poured ashore on D-Day. They were under the command of "Sepp" Dietrich's I SS Panzer Corps.

The *Leibstandarte* Division remained in Belgium to counter the threat of an Allied landing in the Pas de Calais, the region which so dogged Hitler. In the meantime, the *Das Reich* and the 17th SS Panzergrenadier Divisions began moving northward from southwest France. Despite their determination, it would be at least a week before they managed to reach the invasion front. It would also be six days until Hitler finally agreed to release II SS Panzer Corps from the Eastern Front in order that it could return to Normandy. Far from being able to hammer the Allies with a decisive, knock-out blow, the Germans ended up committing their reserves piecemeal in a desperate bid to shore up a crumbling front.

While Dietrich was easily able to establish contact with his old comrade, Fritz Witt, he nevertheless had great problems in trying to link up with the 21st Panzer Division or the remnants of the infantry divisions resisting the British north of the large Norman city of Caen.

Dietrich and other staff officers from the Waffen-SS criss-crossed the German front in order to try to pull together some sort of cohesion. All during the night they worked out various formulae for counterattack plan after counterattack plan. But all of their plans were rapidly overtaken by events. The commander of the 21st

Panzer Division could not be found at his command post, and this was to further frustrate plans to mount a joint attack with the *Hitlerjugend* Division.

Of even more concern was the fact that the arrival of the *Hitlerjugend* Division was still stalled because of the chaotic conditions on the roads. The Panzer Lehr Division was even further behind, and would not arrive at the front for days. In the meantime, thousands more Allied troops and tanks were rapidly pouring ashore.

As a result of the expansion of the Waffen-SS panzer corps in the summer of 1943, it was decided to remove the divisional Tiger companies and form two corps-level heavy tank battalions. These were nominally to have three Tiger I companies, each with 14 tanks each. The continued commitment of the *Leibstandarte*, *Das Reich*, and *Totenkopf* on the Eastern Front through the winter of 1943, and into the spring of 1944, meant the two new battalions were not ready for action until just before the invasion of France. The 101st SS Heavy Panzer Battalion itself was assigned to support I SS Panzer Corps, and the 102d SS Heavy Panzer Battalion worked for the sister corps. They were to provide each of the Waffen-SS corps with a hard-hitting strike force, or a reserve counter-punch.

The 101st SS Battalion had been ordered to Normandy immediately after the Allied invasion, but persistent Allied air raids delayed the advance of its 37 operational tanks. It arrived in I SS Panzer Corps' sector west of Caen on June 12, just as the Panzer Lehr Division was taking up position alongside the *Hitlerjugend* Division.

PANZER GROUP WEST
(then Fifth Panzer Army from August 6, 1944)
(Date in brackets is when unit reached the Normandy Front)

I SS Panzer Corps *Leibstandarte Adolf Hitler* **(June 7)**
- *(SS-Obergruppenführer Josef "Sepp" Dietrich)*
- schwer SS-Panzer Abteilung 101: *37 x Tiger I*
- SS-Arko I *(artillery command)*
- SS-Artillerie Abteilung 101: *4 x 210mm, 6 x 170mm*
- SS-Corps Nachrichten Abteilung: *101/501*

1st SS Panzer Division *Leibstandarte Adolf Hitler* **(June 25 to July 6)**
- *(SS-Brigadeführer Teddy Wisch)*
Total strength: 19,618 men

- SS-Panzergrenadier Regiment 1 "LSSAH":
  I & II Abteilungen only, 36 APC
- SS-Panzergrenadier Regiment 2 "LSSAH"

- SS-Panzer Regiment "LSSAH": *103 x Panzer IV, 72 x Panther*
- SS-Sturmgeschütz Abteilung "LSSAH" 1: *45 x StuG III*
- SS-Panzer Artillerie Regiment "LSSAH" 1:
  *I & II Abteilungen: 8 x 105mm, 6 x 150mm,
  4 x 100mm, 8 x Wespe, 5 x Hummel*
- SS-Flak Abteilung "LSSAH" 1: *12 x 88mm,
  9 x 37mm*
- SS-Werfer Abteilung "LSSAH" 1: one battery,
  5 x Nebelwerfer
- SS-Panzer Nachrichten Abteilung "LSSAH" 1
- SS-Panzer Aufklärungs Abteilung "LSSAH" 1
- SS-Panzer Pionier Abteilung "LSSAH" 1

Waffen-SS Order of Battle, Normandy, June 1944

12th SS Panzer Division *Hitlerjugend* (June 7)
- *(SS-Oberführer Fritz Witt until June 14, 1944, then SS-Standartenführer Kurt Meyer)*

Total strength: 17,000 men, 306 armored personnel carriers

- SS-Panzergrenadier Regiment 25
- III Abteilung: *12 x Pak 40, 12 x 75mm IG, 6 x 150mm IG, 2 x 20mm flak*
- SS-Panzergrenadier Regiment 26: *12 x Pak 40, 22 x 75mm IG, 6 x 150mm IG, 2 x 20mm Flak*
- SS-Panzer Regiment 12: *66 x Panther, 98 x Panzer IV*
- SS-Panzerjäger Abteilung 12: *one company with 10 x Pzjgr IV*
- SS-Panzer Artillerie Regiment 12: *12 x Wespe, 6 x Hummel, 18 x 105mm, 4 x 150mm, 4 x 100mm*
- SS-Flak Abteilung 12: *12 x 88mm, 9 x 37mm*
- SS-Werfer Abteilung 12: one battery *(arrived June 12, balance in July)*
- SS-Panzer Nachrichten Abteilung 12
- SS-Panzer Aufklärungs Abteilung 12
- SS-Panzer Pionier Abteilung 12
- SS-Panzer Ersatz Abteilung 12 *(in Arnhem with 2,000 men)*

II SS Panzer Corps Headquarters (June 28)
- *(SS-Obergruppenführer Paul Hausser, then Willi Bittrich from June 28, 1944)*
- schwer SS-Panzer Abteilung 102: *28 x Tiger I*
- SS-Arko II *(artillery command)*
- SS-Corps Nachrichten Abteilung 400

9th SS Panzer Division *Hohenstaufen* (June 28)
- *(SS-Gruppenführer Willi Bittrich until June 28, 1944, SS-Standartenführer Thomas Müller until July 14, 1944, then SS-Standartenführer Sylvester Stadler)*

Total strength: 15,898 men, 345 trucks

- SS-Panzergrenadier Regiment 19: *9 x Pak 40, 12 x 75mm IG, 6 x 150mm IG, 11 x 20mm Flak*
- SS-Panzergrenadier Regiment 20: *9 x Pak 40, 14 x 75mm IG, 6 x 150mm IG, 12 x 20mm flak*
- SS-Panzer Regiment 9
- I Abteilung: *79 x Panther*
- II Abteilung: *48 x Panzer IV and 40 x StuG III*
- SS-Panzerjäger Abteilung 9: *one company with 12 x Pak 40*
- SS-Panzer Artillerie Regiment 9: *12 x Wespe, 2 x Hummel, 12 x 105m, 12 x 150mm, 4 x 100mm*
- SS-Flak Abteilung 9: *12 x 88mm, 9 x 37mm*
- SS-Panzer Nachrichten Abteilung 9
- SS-Panzer Aufklärungs Abteilung 9
- SS-Panzer Pionier Abteilung 9

10th SS Panzer Division *Frundsberg* (June 28)
- *(SS-Oberführer Heinz Harmel)*

Total strength: 15,800 men

- SS-Panzergrenadier Regiment 21
- SS-Panzergrenadier Regiment 22
- SS-Panzer Regiment 10: *II Abteilung only with 39 x Panzer IV, 38 x StuG III*
- SS-Panzer Artillerie Regiment 10: *11 x Wespe, 6 x Hummel, 12 x 105mm, 12 x 150mm, 4 x 100mm*
- SS-Flak Abteilung 10: *12 x 88mm, 9 x 37mm*
- SS-Panzer Nachrichten Abteilung 10
- SS-Panzer Aufklärungs Abteilung 10
- SS-Panzer Pionier Abteilung 10
- SS Ersatz Battalion 9: *1,000 men*

SEVENTH ARMY
2nd SS Panzer Division *Das Reich*
(July 1)
(SS-Brigadeführer Heinz Lammerding)

Total strength: 11,175 men, 227 armored personnel carriers, 768 trucks

- SS-Panzergrenadier Regiment 3 *Deutschland* (*I & III Abteilung only*)
- SS-Panzergrenadier Regiment *Der Führer* (*I & III Abteilung only*)
- SS-Panzer Regiment 2: *50 x Panzer IV, 26 x Panther*
- SS-Sturmgeschütz Abteilung 2: *41 x StuG III*
- SS-Panzer Artillerie Regiment 2: *12 x 105mm, 4 x 100mm, 4 x 15mm, 6 x Wespe, 5 x Hummel*
- SS-Flak Abteilung 2: *12 x 88mm, 9 x 37mm*
- SS-Panzer Nachrichten Abteilung 2
- SS-Panzer Aufklärungs Abteilung 2: *4 companies*
- SS-Panzer Pionier Abteilung 2: *three companies only*

Attached
- SS-Werfer Abteilung 102: *18 x Nebelwerfer*
- II/Artillery Regiment 275: *4 x 105mm, 4 x 100mm*
- II/Artillery Regiment 191: *9 x 75mm, 2 x 150mm*
- Panzerjäger Abteilung 1041: *15 x 88mm*

Waffen-SS Order of Battle, Normandy, June 1944

17th SS Panzergrenadier Division *Götz von Berlichingen*
(June 10)
(SS-Standartenführer Otto Baum)

Total strength: 17,321 men

- SS-Panzergrenadier Regiment 37
- SS-Panzergrenadier Regiment 38
- SS-Panzerjäger Abteilung 1: *12 x Marder,*
  22 x Pak 40 (arrived later in the month)
- SS-Panzer Abteilung 17: *42 x StuG III (below)*
- SS-Panzer Artillerie Regiment 17: *25 x 105mm, 12 x 150mm,*
  4 x 100mm
- SS-Flak Abteilung *17: 8 x 88mm (at right),*
  9 x 37mm (arrived later in the month)
- SS-Panzer Nachrichten Abteilung 17
- SS-Panzer Aufklärungs Abteilung 17
- SS-Panzer Pionier Abteilung 17 (*arrived later in the month*)

Waffen-SS Divisions

Originally, the Waffen-SS developed its unique ethos. Recruits were screened for ethnic purity. They had to be able to trace their "blood line" back through several generations in order to prove they had no Jewish relatives. Any physical imperfections, such as tooth fillings or poor eyesight, also counted against the much sought-after membership of the Waffen-SS. The prominent public role of the first Waffen-SS unit, the SS *Leibstandarte Adolf Hitler*, guarding their Führer and public buildings in Berlin, quickly led to them being dubbed the "Asphalt Soldiers" by the army, fit only for parades. By the end of the war, the Waffen-SS had grown into a separate army, though by this time many of its divisions were of poor quality.

FINAL TITLE	FORMED AS DIVISION	RECRUITMENT ZONE	MAIN COMBAT ZONES
1. SS Panzer Division *Leibstandarte Adolf Hitler*	1942	Germany	Poland, Belgium, Balkans, Russia, France, Hungary
2. SS Panzer Division *Das Reich*	1939	Germany	Poland, France, Balkans, Russia, France, Hungary
3. SS Panzer Division *Totenkopf*	1939	Germany	Poland, France, Russia, Hungary
4. SS Panzergrenadier Division *Polizei*	1939	Germany	France, Russia
5. SS Panzer Division *Wiking*	1940	Western Europe, Scandinavia	Russia, Hungary
6. SS Gebirgs Division *Nord*	1940	Germany	Norway
7. SS Freiwilligen Gebirgs Division *Prinz Eugen*	1942	Southeastern Europe	Yugoslavia, Hungary
8. SS Cavalry Division *Florian Geyer*	1942	Germany	Yugoslavia, Hungary
9. SS Panzer Division *Hohenstaufen*	1943	Germany	Russia, Western Europe, Hungary
10. SS Panzer Division *Frundsberg*	1943	Germany	Russia, Western Europe, Hungary
11. SS Freiwilligen Panzergrenadier Division *Nordland*	1943	Western Europe, Scandinavia	Russia, Poland
12. SS Panzer Division *Hitlerjugend*	1943	Germany	France, Hungary
13. Waffen Gebirgs Division der SS *Handschar* (kroatische Nr 1)	1943	Yugoslavia (Muslims)	Yugoslavia
14. Waffen Grenadier Division der SS *Galicia* (ukrainische Nr 1)	1943	Ukraine	Ukraine
15. Waffen Grenadier Division der SS (lettische Nr 1)	1943	Latvia	Russia, Poland, Germany
16. SS Panzergrenadier Division *Reichsführer-SS*	1943	Germany	Italy, Yugoslavia
17. SS Panzergrenadier Division *Götz von Berlichingen*	1943	Germany	France
18. SS Freiwilligen Panzergrenadier Division *Horst Wessel*	1944	Hungary	Poland, Czechoslovakia

Waffen-SS Divisions

FINAL TITLE	FORMED AS DIVISION	RECRUITMENT ZONE	MAIN COMBAT ZONES
19. Waffen Grenadier Division der SS (lettische Nr 2)	1944	Latvia	Russia
20. Waffen Grenadier Division der SS (estnische Nr 1)	1944	Estonia	Russia, Germany, Czechoslovakia
21. Waffen Gebirgs Division der SS *Skanderberg* (albanische Nr 1)	1944	Albania	Albania
22. SS Freiwilligen Cavalry Division *Maria Theresia*	1944	Hungary	Hungary
23. SS-Freiwilligen Panzergrenadier Division *Nederland* (niederlandische Nr 1)	1944	Netherlands	Hungary
23. Waffen Gebirgs Division der SS *Kama* (kroatische Nr 2)	1944	Croatia	Yugoslavia
24. Waffen Gebirgs Division der SS *Karstjäger*	1944	Italy	Italy
25. Waffen Grenadier Divison der SS *Hunyadi* (ungarnische Nr 1)	1944	Hungary	Hungary
26. Waffen Grenadier Division der SS *Gombos* (ungarnische Nr 2)	1945	Hungary	Hungary
27. SS Freiwilligen Grenadier Division *Langemarck*	1945	Flemish regions of Belgium	Russia, Poland, Germany
28. SS Freiwilligen Panzergrenadier Division *Wallonien*	1945	French regions of Belgium	Russia, Poland, Germany
29. Waffen Grenadier Division der SS RONA (russische Nr. 1)	1945	Russia	Czechoslovakia
29. Waffen Grenadier Division der SS (italienische Nr 1)	1945	Italy	Italy
30. Waffen Grenadier Division der SS (russische Nr 2)	1945	Russia	France, Czechoslovakia
31. SS Freiwilligen Grenadier Division *Bohmen-Mahren*	1945	Czechoslovakia	Czechoslovakia
32. SS Freiwilligen Grenadier Division *30 Januar*	1945	Germany	Germany
33. Waffen Grenadier Division der SS (ungarnische Nr 4)	1945	Hungary	Hungary
33. Waffen Grenadier Division der SS *Charlemagne* (französische Nr 1)	1945	France	Russia, Germany
34. SS Freiwilligen Grenadier Division *Landstorm Nederland*	1945	Netherlands	Russia
35. SS und Polizei Grenadier Division	1945	Germany	Czechoslovakia
36. Waffen Grenadier Division der SS	1945	Germany/ Eastern Europe	Russia, Poland, Germany
37. SS Freiwilligen Cavalry Division *Lutzow*	1945	Hungary	Hungary
38. SS Grenadier Division *Nibelungen*	1945	Germany	Germany

Army Group South, Average Tank Strength, February 1943

XXXX Panzer Corps
- 3rd Panzer Division: *35 tanks*
- 7th Panzer Division: *19 tanks*
- 11th Panzer Division: *52 tanks*
- SS *Wiking* Division: *10 tanks*

XXXXVIII Panzer Corps
- 17th Panzer Division: *6 tanks*
- 6th Panzer Division: *17 tanks*

SS Panzer Corps
- SS *Leibstandarte* Division: *37 tanks (including 3 Tiger Is)*
- SS *Das Reich* Division: *66 tanks (including 7 Tigers Is, below)*
- SS *Totenkopf* Division: *95 tanks (including 9 Tiger Is)*

Army Detachment *Kempf*
- *Grossdeutschland* Motorized Division: *103 tanks (including 4 Tiger Is)*

Army Group North, Operation Barbarossa, June 22, 1941

Hitler issued Directive No. 21, confirming plans for the attack on the USSR, codenamed Operation Barbarossa, on December 18, 1940. It stated: "In the theater of operations, which is divided by the Pripet Marshes into a Southern and a Northern sector, the main weight of attack will be delivered in the Northern area. Two Army Groups will be employed here.

"The more southerly of these two Army Groups (in the center of the whole front) will have the task of advancing with powerful armored and motorized formations from the area about and north of Warsaw, and routing the enemy forces in White Russia [Belorussia]. This will make it possible for strong mobile forces to advance northward and, in conjunction with the Northern Army Group operating out of East Prussia in the general direction of Leningrad, to destroy the enemy forces operating in the Baltic area. Only after the fulfilment of this first essential task, which must include the occupation of Leningrad and Kronstadt, will the attack be continued with the intention of occupying Moscow, an important center of communications and of the armaments industry.

"It will be the duty of the main body of the Finnish Army, in conjunction with the advance of the German North flank, to hold down the strongest possible Russian forces by an attack to the West, or on both sides of Lake Ladoga, and to occupy Hanko. It will be the duty of the navy during the attack on Soviet Russia to protect our own coasts and to prevent the breakout of enemy naval units from the Baltic. As the Russian Baltic fleet will, with the capture of Leningrad, lose its last base and will then be in a hopeless position, major naval action will be avoided until this occurs.

"After the elimination of the Russian fleet, the duty of the navy will be to protect the entire maritime traffic in the Baltic and the transport of supplies by sea to the Northern flank (clearing of minefields)."

The attack on the Soviet Union was to be conducted by three massive army groups. More than three million German and allied troops began the invasion of the USSR, accompanied by 3,330 tanks, 600,000 motor vehicles, and 750,000 horses. The Luftwaffe deployed 2,770 aircraft, or approximately 65 percent of its frontline strength.

German and Axis
German Army in Norway
- Mountain Corps Norway (*2d and 3rd Mountain Divisions*); XXXVI Corps (*169th Infantry Division, SS Group* Nord)

Finnish Army
- 14th Division
- Finnish III Army Corps (3rd and 6th Divisions)
- Karelian Army: Group Oinonen (*three brigades*); VI Corps (*5th, 11th Divisions*); VII Corps (*1st, 7th, 19th Divisions*); II Corps (*2d, 10th, 15th, 18th Divisions*); IV Corps (*4th, 8th, 12th, 17th Divisions*)

Army Group North (at right)
- Eighteenth Army: XXVI Corps (*61st, 217th, 291st Infantry Divisions*); XXXVIII Corps (*58th Infantry Division*); I Corps (*1st, 11th, 12th Infantry Divisions*)
- Fourth Panzer Group: XXXXI Panzer Corps (*1st, 6th Panzer Divisions, 269th Infantry Division, 36th Motorized Division*); LVI Panzer Corps (*290th Infantry Division, 8th Panzer Division, 3rd Motorized Division*); SS Totenkopf Division
- Sixteenth Army: X Corps (*30th, 126th Infantry Divisions*); XXVIII Corps (*122d, 123rd Infantry Divisions*); II Corps (*12th, 32d, 121st, 253rd Infantry Divisions*)
- Army Group Reserve: 251st, 254th, 206th Infantry Divisions
- OKH Reserve (*in Army Group North*):
- L Corps (*86th Infantry Division, SS* Polizei *Division*)
- Rear area security: 207th, 281st, 285th Security Divisions

Army Group Center, Operation Barbarossa, June 22, 1941

 Directive No. 21 stated: "The bulk of the Russian Army stationed in western Russia will be destroyed by daring operations led by deeply penetrating armored spearheads. Russian forces still capable of giving battle will be prevented from withdrawing into the depths of Russia.

"It will be the duty of the Luftwaffe to paralyze and eliminate the effectiveness of the Russian Air Force as far as possible. It will also support the main operations of the Army, i.e., those of the central Army Group and of the vital flank of the Southern Army Group. Russian railways will either be destroyed or, in accordance with operational requirements, captured at their most important points (river crossings) by the bold employment of parachute and airborne troops.

"In order that we may concentrate all our strength against the enemy air force and for the immediate support of land operations, the Russian armaments industry will not be attacked during the main operations. Such attacks will be made only after the conclusion of mobile warfare, and they will be concentrated first on the Urals area."

In June 1941, the German Army was at its peak, its ranks filled with veterans of the Polish and French campaigns. At the start of Barbarossa nearly all of its 120 line infantry divisions were at their full offensive power. German divisions usually recruited from a single geographic area, thus many soldiers began military service having already known each other for years. Each division had a training battalion in Germany to train replacements. Noncommissioned officers (NCOs) were rotated from the front to the training battalion. Thus the trainees were taught the latest battle tactics by combat soldiers.

Junior and middle-grade officers (lieutenants to colonels) were excellent, being well trained and expertly evaluated for specific command posts. Officers were selected on the basis of their suitability for command, and promotion was on merit.

- Third Panzer Group: VI Corps (*6th, 26th Infantry Divisions*); *XXXIX Panzer Corps (14th, 20th Motorized Divisions, 7th, 20th Panzer Divisions); V Corps (5th, 35th Infantry Divisions); LVII Panzer Corps (18th Motorized Division, 12th, 19th Panzer Divisions)*
- Ninth Army: VIII Corps (*8th, 28th, 161st Infantry Divisions*); *XX Corps (162d, 256th Infantry Divisions); XXXXII Corps (87th, 102d, 129th Infantry Divisions)*
- Fourth Army: VII Corps (*7th, 23rd, 258th, 268th Infantry Divisions*)
- XIII Corps (*17th, 78th Infantry Divisions); IX Corps (137th, 263rd, 292d Infantry Divisions); XXXXIII Corps (131st, 134th, 252d Infantry Divisions)*
- Second Panzer Group (*at right): XXXXVI Panzer Corps (Grossdeutschland Infantry Regiment, SS Das Reich Motorized Division, 10th Panzer Division); XXXXVII Panzer Corps (29th Motorized Division, 167th Infantry Division, 17th, 18th Panzer Divisions); XII Corps (31st, 34th, 45th Infantry Divisions); XXIV Panzer Corps (10th Motorized Division, 3rd, 4th Panzer Divisions, 267th Infantry Division); Reserve 255th Infantry Division*
- Army Group Reserve: LIII Corps (*293rd Infantry Division*)
- OKH Reserve (*in Army Group Center): XXXV Corps (15th, 52d, 112th, 197th Infantry Divisions); XXXXII Corps (106th, 110th Infantry Divisions, 900th Motorized Brigade)*
- Rear area security: 221st, 286th, 403rd Security Divisions

Army Group South, Operation Barbarossa, June 22, 1941

The mission of Army Group South, as directed by Hitler, was: "The Army Group operating South of the Pripet Marshes will also seek, in a concentric operation with strong forces on either flank, to destroy all Russian forces west of the Dnieper in the Ukraine. The main attack will be carried out from the Lublin area in the general direction of Kiev, while forces in Romania will carry out a wide enclosing movement across the lower Prut. It will be the task of the Romanian Army to hold down Russian forces in the intervening area. When the battles north and south of the Pripet Marshes are ended, the pursuit of the enemy will have the following aims:

"In the South, the early capture of the Donets Basin, important for war industry; in the North, a quick advance to Moscow. The capture of this city would represent a decisive political and economic success and would also bring about the capture of the most important railway junctions."

The Luftwaffe element of Barbarossa comprised the 1st Air Fleet (379 aircraft), which supported Army Group North; 2d Air Fleet (1,223 aircraft), which would support Army Group Center; and 4th Air Fleet (630 aircraft), which would support Army Group South. Crucially,

German doctrine demanded close cooperation between the Luftwaffe and the army. To this end, staff officers were regularly exchanged between the two services, resulting in an excellent working relationship between ground and air forces.

Behind the army groups came the Einsatzgruppen (Special Action Groups), which were formed by the SS prior to Operation Barbarossa, being attached to Amt (Office) IV of the RSHA (Reichssicherheitshauptamt—Reich Central Security Office). Their task was to follow immediately behind the German armies as they advanced into the USSR, and round up Jews, gypsies, political commissars, and anyone else who was perceived by the Nazis as being a real or potential threat to the "New Order" being established in the East. All persons thus taken were to be executed immediately. As they advanced into the USSR, the Einsatzgruppen were able to enlist the help of thousands of the indigenous population in their gruesome undertaking. Thus, Lithuanians, Latvians, Estonians, Ukrainians, and even Poles assisted the Einsatzgruppen as willing executioners. The Einsatzgruppen were responsible for the deaths of 730,000 Jews during their killing spree in the USSR between 1941 and 1944.

- First Panzer Group: XIV Panzer Corps (*SS Wiking Motorized Division, 9th, 16th Panzer Divisions*); III Panzer Corps (*14th Panzer Division, 44th, 298th Infantry Divisions*); XXIX Corps (*111th, 299th Infantry Divisions*); XXXXVIII Panzer Corps (*11th Panzer Division, 57th, 75th Infantry Divisions*); reserve (*16th, 25th SS Leibstandarte Motorized Divisions, 13th Panzer Division*)
- Sixth Army: XVII Corps: (*56th, 62d Infantry Divisions*); XXXXIV Corps (*9th, 297th Infantry Divisions*); LV Corps (*168th Infantry Division*)
- Seventeenth Army (*at right*): IV Corps (*24th, 71st, 262d, 295th, 296th Infantry Divisions*); XXXXIX Mountain Corps (*1st Mountain Division, 68th, 257th Infantry Divisions*); LII Corps (*101st Jäger Division*); reserve (*97th, 100th Jäger Divisions*)
- Eleventh Army: Romanian Mountain Corps (*1st, 2d, 4th Mountain Brigades, 8th Cavalry Brigade, 7th Infantry Division*); XI Corps (*76th, 239th Infantry Divisions, 6th, 8th Romanian Infantry Divisions, 6th Romanian Cavalry Brigade*); XXX Corps (*5th Romanian Cavalry Brigade, 14th Romanian Infantry Division, 198th Infantry Division*); LIV Corps (*50th, 170th Infantry Divisions*); reserve (*Romanian cavalry HQ, 22d Infantry Division*)
- Army Group Reserve: 99th *Jäger Division*
- OKH Reserve (*in Army Group South*): XXXIV Corps HQ; 4th Mountain Division, 113th, 125th, 132d Infantry Divisions; LI Corps (*79th, 95th Infantry Divisions*)
- Rear area security: 213th, 444th, 454th Security Divisions

OKH reserve
- XXXX Panzer Corps: *60th Motorized Division; 46th, 73rd, 93rd, 94th, 96th, 98th, 183rd, 260th, 294th Infantry Divisions; 2d, 5th Panzer Divisions; 707th, 713th Security Divisions; Romanian Third and Fourth Armies (four corps, nine divisions, two brigades)*

Typical Luftwaffe Air Fleet, Battle of Britain, 1940

 Luftflotte (Air Fleet) Headquarters

The headquarters for Luftflotte III was in Paris and was commanded by Field Marshal Hugo Sperrle. The fleet consisted of 9 jagdgruppen (fighter groups), 15 kampfgruppen (bomber groups), 7 Stukagruppen (dive-bomber groups), 4 zerstörergruppen (heavy-fighter or destroyer groups), 1 schlachtgruppe (battle group), and a variety of long-range patrol, weather, and reconnaissance units. It was split into command administrative units as follows:

- VIII Fliegerkorps: With headquarters at Deauville under the command of General Richtofen, the korps consisted of three Stuka wings, some fighter-bomber, zerstörer, and support units.

- V Fliegerkorps: With headquarters at Villacoublay under the command of General Ritter von Greim, the korps consisted of three bomber wings and two reconnaissance units.

- IV Fliegerkorps: With headquarters at Dinard under the command of Major General Pflugbeil, the korps consisted of two bomber wings, an independent kampfgruppe, a Stuka wing staff flight, and a reconnaissance unit.

- Jafu 3: The Jagdfliegerführer had headquarters at Wissant under the command of Colonel von Massow, and consisted of nine day-fighter Groups in three wings and one zerstörer wing.

Fighter units and stations

Beaumont le Roger
- Stab JG 2: *Me 109E*
- I./JG 2: *Me 109E*
- II./JG 2: *Me 109E*

Brest
- III./JG 53: *Me 109E*
Also operating from Brest as part of Luftflotte II were:
- Stab KG 40: *Ju 88A*
- I./KG 40: *Fw 200C*

Cherbourg
- Stab JG 27: *Me 109E*
- Stab JG 53: *Me 109E*

Crepon
- II./JG 27: *Me 109E*

Dinan
- II./JG 53: *Me 109E*

Le Havre
- III./JG 2: *Me 109E*

Plumetot
- I./JG 27: *Me 109E*

Rennes
- I./JG 53: *Me 109E*

Bomber units and stations

Bretigny
- Stab StG 3: *Ju 87B, He 111H*

Caen
- Kampfgruppe 806: *Ju 88A*

Chartres
- II./KG 55: *He 111H, He 111P*

Chateaudun
- III(K)./LG 1: *Ju 88A*

Raum Cherbourg
- 4(F)./14: *Do 17M, Do 17P, Me 110D*

Dreux
- I./KG 55: *He 111H, He 111P*

Etampes
- III./KG 51: *Ju 88A*

Evreux
- Stab KG 54: *Ju 88A*
- I./KG 54: *Ju 88A*

Melun
- I./KG 51: *Ju 88A*

Luftflotte III, Battle of Britain, 1940

Orleans (Bricy)
- Stab LG 1: *Ju 88A*
- I(*K*)./LG 1: *Ju 88A*
- II(*K*)./LG 1: *Ju 88A*

Orly
- Stab KG 51: *Ju 88A*
- II./KG 51: *Ju 88A*

St Andre
- II./KG 54: *Ju 88A*

Tours
- Stab KG 27: *He 111P*
- I./KG 27: *He 111P*
- II./KG 27: *He 111H, He 111P*
- III./KG 27: *He 111P*

Villacoublay
- Stab KG 55: *He 111P*
- III./KG 55: *He 111P*
- 4(F)/121: *Do 17P, Ju 88A*

Dive-bomber units and stations

Angers
- Stab StG 1: *Ju 87B*
- I./StG 1: *Ju 87R*
- III./StG 1: *Ju 87B*

Caen
- Stab StG 77: *Ju 87B*
- I./StG 77: *Ju 87B*
- II./StG 77: *Ju 87B*
- III./StG 77: *Ju 87B*

Lannion
- II./StG 2: *Ju 87R*

St Malo
- Stab StG 2: *Ju 87B*
- I./StG 2: *Ju 87B*

Zerstörer units and stations

Caen
- V(Z)/LG 1: *Me 110C, Me 110D*
- I./ZG 2: *Me 110D*

Toussus le Noble
- Stab ZG 2: *Me 110C*

KEY
Fliegerdivision (FD) Air Division
Fliegerkorps (FK) Air Corps, contains several Fliegerdivisionen
Geschwader Wing the largest Luftwaffe flying unit
Gruppe (Gr) Group, basic Luftwaffe command unit
Jabo abbreviation of Jagdbomber, fighter-bomber
Jabostaffel Fighter-Bomber Squadron
Jäger Fighter
Jagddivision (JD) Fighter Division
Jagdführer (Jafu) Area fighter commander, usually covered several JGs
Jagdgeschwader (JG) Fighter Wing, containing three or four Gruppen
Jagdgruppe (JGr) Fighter Group; containing three or four Staffeln
Jagdkorps (JK) Fighter Corps
Jagdstaffel Fighter Squadron
Jagdwaffe Fighter arm of the Luftwaffe
Kampfgeschwader (KG) Bomber Wing
Kampfgruppe(KGr) Bomber Group
Kampfgruppe-Jäger (KGj) Bomber Group converted to fighter operations
Luftflotte (Lfl) Air Fleet
Schlachtgeschwader (SG) Ground-Attack Wing (below)
Schnelleskampfgeschwader (SKG) Fast Bomber Wing
Stab Staff
Staffel Squadron (pl. Staffeln).
Stukageschwader (StG) Dive-Bomber Wing
Zerstörer "Destroyer", term used for twin-engined fighters
Zerstörergeschwader (ZG) Destroyer Wing

U-Boats

 At the outbreak of the war, Germany had 57 U-boats, most of them not capable of operations in the Atlantic. It was planned to build about 250 in the naval construction program called the "Z-Plan," but since this plan was never realized, Germany entered the war with a much lower number of submarines than the Allied nations. During the war, over 1,100 U-boats were built, and this force was often seen as the biggest threat to Britain during the whole of the conflict.

Those submarines operated in all oceans of the world, including the North Sea, the Atlantic, the American seaboard (Operation Donnerschlag), the Arctic, and even the Indian Ocean and the Pacific. Until mid-1943,

German U-boats were superior to their Allied hunters, but, with the introduction of detection technology such as radar and Huff-Duff, and a continuous air cover for Allied convoys, the hunter became the hunted. Even the introduction of new, revolutionary submarines such as the Type XXI could not alter this.

Despite their success in the early years of the war, the U-boats ultimately paid a heavy price. About 80 percent of all U-boats were destroyed, 28,000 out of 40,000 U-boat personnel were killed during the war, and 8,000 were captured.

U-boats in wolfpacks

Note: Some 265 U-boats operated as a part of a wolfpack (or group) during the war. After each boat number, the number of wolfpacks the boat belonged to is shown. For example, U-221 (11) means that U-221 operated in 11 wolfpacks.

U-25 (1), *U-28* (2), *U-29* (2), *U-30* (1), *U-32* (2), *U-38* (2), *U-43* (6), *U-46* (4), *U-47* (5), *U-48* (4), *U-51* (1), *U-52* (1), *U-65* (2), *U-66* (2), *U-67* (2), *U-68* (1), *U-69* (2), *U-71* (6), *U-84* (9), *U-86* (5), *U-87* (2), *U-89* (5), *U-90* (1), *U-91* (5), *U-92* (6), *U-94* (1), *U-96* (3), *U-98* (1), *U-99* (2), *U-100* (3), *U-101* (4), *U-103* (5), *U-106* (2), *U-107* (6), *U-108* (3), *U-109* (1), *U-116* (1), *U-123* (4), *U-124* (1), *U-125* (2), *U-130* (2), *U-132* (2), *U-134* (5), *U-135* (6), *U-136* (1), *U-155* (1), *U-156* (1), *U-159* (2), *U-164* (1), *U-167* (3), *U-168* (4), *U-169* (1), *U-172* (3), *U-174* (1), *U-176* (1), *U-183* (1), *U-185* (1), *U-186* (7), *U-187* (2), *U-188* (2), *U-190* (3), *U-191* (3), *U-192* (2), *U-193* (1), *U-201* (3), *U-202* (2), *U-203* (5), *U-209* (2), *U-210* (1), *U-211* (6), *U-213* (1), *U-214* (3), *U-216* (4), *U-217* (2), *U-218* (2), *U-221* (11), *U-223* (7), *U-224* (1), *U-225* (1), *U-226* (5), *U-228* (5), *U-229* (4), *U-230* (3), *U-231* (3), *U-232* (3), *U-238* (1), *U-254* (4), *U-256* (1), *U-257* (6), *U-258* (6), *U-259* (1), *U-260* (9), *U-262* (3), *U-264* (3), *U-266* (4), *U-267* (4), *U-268* (3), *U-270* (4), *U-274* (1), *U-301* (2), *U-303* (2), *U-305* (3), *U-306* (2), *U-332* (5), *U-333* (6), *U-336* (7), *U-338* (2), *U-341* (1), *U-353* (2), *U-356* (4), *U-358* (6), *U-359* (3), *U-373* (5), *U-376* (1), *U-377* (6), *U-378* (3), *U-379* (1), *U-380* (2), *U-381* (4), *U-382* (4), *U-383* (7), *U-384* (3), *U-386* (2), *U-402* (6), *U-403* (3), *U-404* (7), *U-405* (2), *U-406* (8), *U-407* (2), *U-409* (5), *U-410* (4), *U-411* (1), *U-413* (6), *U-414* (2), *U-415* (2), *U-422* (1), *U-432* (5), *U-435* (6), *U-436* (3), *U-437* (5), *U-438* (7), *U-439* (6), *U-440* (5), *U-441* (6), *U-442* (4), *U-443* (2), *U-444* (3), *U-445* (3), *U-447* (3), *U-448* (6), *U-454* (6), *U-455* (3), *U-456* (2), *U-458* (1), *U-465* (3), *U-466* (4), *U-468* (4), *U-469* (1), *U-504* (5), *U-509* (1), *U-510* (1), *U-511* (2), *U-513* (2), *U-514* (3), *U-515* (3), *U-519* (2), *U-520* (1), *U-521* (2), *U-522* (2), *U-523* (2), *U-524* (3), *U-525* (5), *U-526* (4), *U-527* (4), *U-528* (1), *U-529* (1), *U-530* (4), *U-531* (2), *U-532* (2), *U-533* (2), *U-552* (6), *U-553* (3), *U-558* (4), *U-563* (5), *U-564* (4), *U-566* (6), *U-569* (8), *U-571* (4), *U-572* (7), *U-575* (6), *U-578* (1), *U-582* (2), *U-584* (11), *U-590* (6), *U-591* (5), *U-592* (2), *U-593* (1), *U-594* (5), *U-595* (2), *U-596* (2), *U-597* (5), *U-598* (3), *U-600* (5), *U-602* (2), *U-603* (4), *U-604* (6), *U-605* (2), *U-606* (3), *U-607* (7), *U-608* (8), *U-609* (5), *U-610* (7), *U-611* (2), *U-613* (5), *U-614* (3), *U-615* (6), *U-616* (2), *U-617* (2), *U-618* (7), *U-619* (1), *U-620* (1), *U-621* (7), *U-623* (3), *U-624* (5), *U-628* (5), *U-630* (4), *U-631* (5), *U-632* (4), *U-633* (1), *U-634* (4), *U-635* (1), *U-638* (2), *U-641* (8), *U-642* (7), *U-645* (1), *U-648* (2), *U-650* (3), *U-653* (7), *U-658* (1), *U-659* (7), *U-660* (2), *U-662* (7), *U-663* (2), *U-664* (4), *U-665* (3), *U-666* (5), *U-704* (6), *U-705* (1), *U-706* (9), *U-707* (6), *U-709* (5), *U-731* (1), *U-732* (2), *U-752* (5), *U-753* (8), *U-755* (2), *U-756* (1), *U-757* (2), *U-758* (5), *U-759* (1), *U-951* (3), *U-952* (1), *U-953* (3), *U-954* (2), *U-963* (1)

Germany's Surface Fleet

 The "Z-Plan" was Germany's fleet-building program started shortly before World War II. In the mid-1930s, a major discussion about a new fleet program started in Germany. There were two major opinions about what kind of program should be chosen. One plan focused on a large submarine fleet and a relatively small surface fleet for coastal protection. This plan was preferred by the U-boat faction in the Kriegsmarine high command. The other alternative was a mixed fleet of various surface ships and a much smaller U-boat fleet, similar to the German Imperial Navy in World War I or the British Royal Navy. In the end, this plan was chosen.

According to the Z-Plan, the German Kriegsmarine should have grown to about 800 units, consisting of 13 battleships and battlecruisers (such as the *Scharnhorst*, shown below), 4 aircraft carriers, 15 Panzerschiffe, 23 cruisers, and 22 so-called "Spähkreuzer," which were basically large destroyers. In addition, many smaller vessels would also have been built. It was an ambitious program, and these ships should have been built

between 1939 and 1946. During the same period, the personnel of the Kriegsmarine would have increased to 201,000 men. Over 33 billion Reichsmarks should have been earmarked for building the new units.

However, the Z-Plan never achieved reality. It was questionable whether German industry would have had the resources for such a construction program, even if the war had not started in September 1939. The Z-Plan started on January 29, 1939, when two H-Class battleships were laid down. However, in September 1939 Germany attacked Poland and work on all Z-Plan projects was stopped. During the next few months, all incomplete ships in the Z-Plan program were scrapped and the material was directed toward building additional U-boats.

Typical German battle fleet

German naval forces at the Battle of the Barents Sea, December 31, 1942

Admiral Kübler, Commander, Northern Sector
Vice Admiral Kummetz, Commander Task Force

- *Lützow* – Pocket Battleship

- *Hipper* – Heavy Cruiser

- *Friedrich Eckholdt* – Destroyer

- *Richard Beitzen* - Destroyer

- *Z-29* – Destroyer

- *Z-30* – Destroyer

- *Z-31* – Destroyer

Italian Second Army, Invasion of Yugoslavia, April 1941

SECOND ARMY
Commander: General Des A. Vittorio Ambrosio
V CORPS (*General R. Balocco*)
- 15th Infantry Division "Bergamo" (*General P. Belletti*)
- 57th Infantry Division "Lombardia" (*General V. Zatti*)
- GAF (Frontier Guards) Sectors XXV, XXVI and XXVII (*General A. Torriano*)
- (*Reinforced with 3 CCNN battalions, 3 field artillery battalions and the 10th GAF Group*)
- V Machine Gun (MG) Battalion (*packed*)
- CV Machine Gun Battalion (*motorized*)
- V Guastatori Battalion
- V Corps Artillery Group
- III Engineer Battalion

Detached from Army Command
- VII MG Battalion
- CVII MG Battalion
- 10th Army Artillery Aroup
- XXII AA Artillery Battalion

VI CORPS (*General R. Dalmazzo*)
- 12th Infantry Division "Sassari" (*General F. Monticelli*)
- 20th Infantry Division "Friuli" (*General V. Ferroni*)
- 26th (*Mountain*) Infantry Division "Assietta" (*General E. Girlando*)
- VI Machine Gun Battalion (*packed*)
- CVI Machine Gun Battalion (*motorized*)
- VI Corps Artillery Support

Detached from Army Command
- 13 Army Artillery Battalions
- 1 AA Artillery Battalion

XI CORPS (*General M. Robotti*)
- 3rd (*Mountain*) Infantry Division "Ravenna" (*General E. Nebbia*)
- 13th Infantry Division "Re" (*General B. Fiorenzoli*)
- 14th Infantry Division "Isonzo" (*General F. Romero*)
- 3rd Valley Alpine Group (*Colonel A. Bruzzone*)
- GAF Sectors XVII, XXI, XXII, and XXIII (*General C. Viale*)
- (*Reinforced with 6 CCNN battalions, 1 machine gun battalion, 15 artillery battalions*)
- XI MG Battalion (*packed*)
- CXI MG Battalion (*motorized*)
- XI Corps Artillery Group
- VII Engineer Battalion

Detached from Army Command
- First Army Artillery Group
- Third Army Artillery Group

AUTO TRANSPORTABLE CORPS (*General F. Zingales*)
- 133rd Armored Division "Littorio" (*General G. Bitossi*)
- 9th Autotransportabile Division "Pasubio" (*General V. Giovannelli*)
- 52d Autotransportabile Division "Torino" (*General L. Manzi*)
- XXX Corps Artillery Group
- IV Engineer Battalion
- VII Signal Battalion

CELERE CORPS (*General F. Ferrari Orsi*)
- 1st Celere Division "Eugenio di Savoia" (*General C. Lomaglio*)
- 2d Celere Division "Emanuele Filiberto Testa di Ferro" (*General C. Ceriana Manieri*)
- 3rd Celere Division "principe Amedeo Duca d'Aosta" (*General M. Marazzani*)
- * all with an additional regiment
- Army Support 3rd Engineer Group
- II Chemical Battalion
- 15 Territorial Battalions, 2 Static Battalions

ZARA FRONT/ZARA GARRISON
- Commander (*General E. Giglioli*)
- 3 Machine Gun Battalions
- "Zara" Bersaglieri Battalion
- CIII GAF Group
- III DICAT Group
- XXX Engineer Battalion

ALBANIAN FRONT (DEPLOYED AGAINST YUGOSLAVIA)
UPPER COMMAND ARMED FORCES ALBANIA
- Commander (*General U. Cavallero*)
- XIV CORPS (*General G. Vecchi*)
- 38th (*Mountain*) Infantry Division "Puglie" (*General A. d'Aponte*)
- 4th Alpine Division "Cuneense" (*General E. Battisti*)
- 6th "Aosta Lancers" Calvary Regiment
- IV, CVI, CXIV, GAF Battalions
- 2 Carabinieri Battalions
- 1 Finance Guard Battalion
- Forestal Militia Group

XVII (ARMORED) CORPS (*General G. Pafundi*)
- 131st Armored Division "Centauro" (*General G. Pizzolato*)
- 18th Infantry Division "Messina" (*General F. Zani*)
- 32d (*Mountain*) Infantry Division "Marche" (*General R. Pentimalli*)
- Blackshirt Groups "Diamanti" and "Skanderbeg"
- 72d Infantry Regiment
- 19th "Guide Light Cavalry" Regiment
- 23rd Blackshirt Legion
- XXII Motorcycle Bersaglieri Battalion
- XI Carabinieri Battalion
- 1 Finance Guard Battalion, 3 GAF Battalions
- 21st Motorized Field Artillery Regiment

LIBRAZID SECTOR (*General G. Nasci*)
- 24th Infantry Division "Pinerolo" (*General G. de Stefanis*)
- 41st Infantry Division "Firenze" (*General P. Negri*)
- 53rd (*Mountain*) Infantry Division "Arezzo" (*General E. Ferone*)
- Blackshirt Group "Biscaccianti"
- 4th Bersaglieri Regiment
- 7th "Milano Lancers" Cavalry Regiment
- Finance Guard Tactical Group (*3 battalions*)
- 8th Corps Artillery Group

Italian Infantry Divisions

The binary infantry division organization was adopted on the eve of World War II. It was, by doctrine, supposed to be capable only of frontal attack. Manuever was the prerogative of army corps only. The divisions were to function as attack columns to create and exploit any tactical opportunity. Control both of the movement of individual divisions and of the medium-caliber guns was retained by corps headquarters. This flaw became apparent in France in 1940. Italian units dashed forward into the killing zone of French artillery and were stopped, with heavy casualties. The high command misinterpreted the failure and blamed inadequate artillery support rather than an operational concept that assigned to poorly trained infantry the task of deep penetrations. In reality, this doctrine meant that Italian numerical superiority on the battlefield only produced higher numbers of dead, wounded, or captured.

Typical organization of an Italian Libyan division in 1940 was as follows:
- Two Infantry Regiments, *each with three battalions*
- Antitank Company
- Artillery Regiment
- Engineer Battalion

Total strength: 7,400

Divisional firepower
- *No machine guns specified*

Antitank weapons
- 47mm antitank guns: *8*

Artillery
- 65mm howitzers: *24*
- 75mm guns: *12*
- 100mm howitzers: *12*

Typical organization of a 1940 Italian truck-borne division was as follows:
- Two Infantry Regiments
- Artillery Regiment
- Machine Gun Battalion
- Tankette Battalion
- Engineer Battalion

Total strength: 11,000

Divisional firepower
- Light machine guns: *262*
- Heavy machine guns: *232*

Antitank weapons
- 47mm antitank guns: *8*

Artillery
- 65mm guns: *8*
- 75mm guns: *24*
- 100mm howitzers: *12*
- 20mm antiaircraft guns: *16*

Transport
- Trucks and assorted vehicles: *683*
- Bicycles: *100*

Typical organization of a 1942 Italian North Africa division was as follows:
- Two Infantry Regiments, *each with two battalions*
- Support Battalion
- Antitank Company
- Mortar Company
- Machine Gun Company
- Antiaircraft Company
- Light Tank Battalion
- Support Battalion
- Engineer Battalion

Total strength: 6,800

Divisional firepower
- Light tanks: *46*

Italian Motorized and Armored Divisions

 The Italian armored division was originally envisaged to be a mobile reserve, to be used in the exploitation of a breakthrough and to counter enemy penetrations. It could also engage in reconnaissance with mobile units, or in a wide envelopment of an enemy flank, infiltration through gaps, or in an assault against hastily prepared defensive positions. Italian tank tactics and training were poor until the armored divisions came under German command in North Africa from 1941, where German training and tactical doctrines were introduced. Since it was weak in divisional infantry, the armored division was organized and trained primarily to operate in conjunction with infantry and motorized divisions and not on its own, unlike the German panzer division. Independent tank units of the Italian Army were designed to serve primarily as shock elements on the battlefield and to support the infantry arm.

Typical organization of a 1940 Italian mobile division was as follows:
- Two Cavalry Regiments, *each with four cavalry squadrons*
- Machine Gun Squadron
- Bersaglieri Regiment, *with two battalions*
- Support Battalion
- Motorcycle Company
- Artillery Regiment
- Support Battalion
- Engineer Battalion

Total strength: 7,750

Divisional Firepower
- Light machine guns: *165*
- Heavy machine guns: *78*

Antitank weapons
- 47mm antitank guns: *8*

Mortars
- 81mm: *57*

Artillery
- 20mm antiaircraft guns: *8*
- Assorted artillery pieces: *24*

Armor
- Tanks: *61*

Transport
- Assorted motor vehicles: *641*
- Motorcycles: *431*
- Bicycles: *2,565*
- Horses: *2,012*

Typical example of a 1942 Italian motorized division was as follows:
- Two Motorized Infantry Regiments, *each with two battalions and a support battalion*
- Bersaglieri Regiment, *with two battalions, plus a support battalion and a motorcycle company*

- Artillery Regiment
- Support Battalion
- Engineer Battalion

Total strength: 9,200

Divisional firepower
- Light machine guns: *200*
- Heavy machine guns: *110*

Antitank weapons
- 47mm antitank guns: *48*

Artillery
- 20mm antiaircraft guns: *40*
- Other artillery pieces: *36*

Transport
- Assorted motor vehicles: *850*

Typical example of a 1942 Italian armored division was as follows:
- Two Tank Regiments, *each with three battalions*
- Bersaglieri Regiment, *each with two Bersaglieri Battalions*
- Mechanized Artillery Regiment
- Two Support Battalions
- Engineer Company

Total strength: 6,500

Divisional firepower
- Tanks: *55*
- 20mm antiaircraft guns: *12*

Antitank weapons
- 47mm antitank guns: *4*

Artillery
- 105mm howitzers: *18*
- 75mm guns: *24*
- 90mm guns: *8*

Italian Alpine and Parachute Divisions

The Alpine division was an elite unit made up of men native to Italy's mountainous regions. Standards of physical fitness and training were high. The regiments had their own detachments of artillery, engineers, and auxiliary services permanently attached. This made the regiment self-supporting and capable of independent action for long periods. Decentralization did not stop at regiments. Alpine battalions and companies were often detached from their parent units and regrouped with artillery units. This was made easier by the existence of independent transport.

Despite the fact that the Italians had experimented with paratroopers at the end of World War I, the Italian high command was skeptical about their usefulness. German airborne successes in 1940–1941, though, brought about a rethink and Italy began to create its own airborne divisions.

Typical organization of an Italian Alpine division in 1940 was as follows:
- Two Alpine Regiments, *each with three battalions (below)*
- Artillery Regiment
- Engineer Battalion
- Chemical Warfare Company
- Antitank Platoon

Total strength: 13,000

Divisional firepower
- Light machine guns: *162*
- Heavy machine guns: *66*

Mortars
- 45mm mortars: *54*
- 81mm mortars: *24*

Artillery
- 75mm pack howitzers: *24*
- Flamethrowers: *27*

Transport
- Motor vehicles: *50*
- Motorcycles: *22*
- Bicycles: *53*
- Horses and mules: *5,400*

Typical organization of a 1942 Italian parachute division was as follows:
- Two Parachute Regiments, *each with three battalions*
- Artillery Regiment, *each with three artillery groups*
- Motorcycle Company
- Mortar Company
- Engineer Company

Divisional firepower
- Light machine guns: *54*

Mortars
- 80mm mortars

Italian Air Force, June 1940

Italy entered World War II on June 10, 1940, when Mussolini declared war on France. The German Blitzkrieg in Western Europe was almost complete. The Italian Air Force was only lightly involved in the campaign, undertaking reconnaissance flights over southern France and carrying out a number of attacks against French airfields. The French surrendered on June 24. Several squadrons of the Italian Air Force based in Belgium then took part in a total of 150 bombing raids against England during the Battle of Britain, beginning in October 1940. The first major operational effort of the Italian Air Force took place in the Balkans, against Greece and Yugoslavia, between October 1940 and April 1941. The air force's role was primarily one of close ground support. Later, the Italian Air Force took part in the war in North Africa against the British, and in the bombing campaign against the British-held island of Malta.

1ST AIR REGION *(MILANO)*
4TH BOMBER DIVISION "DRAGO" *(Dragon) (Novara)*

43rd Bomber Wing
- 98th Bomber Squadron *(BR20: Cameri)*
- 99th Bomber Squadron *(BR20: Cameri)*

7th Bomber Wing
- 4th Bomber Squadron *(BR20: Lonate Pozzolo)*
- 25th Bomber Squadron *(BR20: Lonate Pozzolo)*

13th Bomber Wing
- 11th Bomber Squadron *(BR20: Piacenza)*
- 43rd Bomber Squadron *(BR20: Piacenza)*

2d Fighter Division "BOREA"
(Boreas, poetic name of the North Wind)
(Torino-Caselle)

3rd Fighter Wing
- 18th Fighter Squadron *(CR42: Novi Ligure)*
- 23rd Fighter Squadron *(CR42: Novi Ligure)*

53rd Fighter Wing
- 150th Fighter Squadron *(CR42: Torino-Caselle)*
- 151st Fighter Squadron *(CR42: Torino-Caselle)*

6TH BOMBER DIVISION "FALCO" *(Hawk) (Padova)*
- 9th *(independent) Fighter Squadron (CR42: Gorizia)*

16th Bomber Wing
- 50th Bomber Squadron *(Cant Z1007bis: Vicenza)*
- 50th Bomber Squadron *(Cant Z1007bis: Vicenza)*

18th Bomber Wing:
- 31st Bomber Squadron *(BR20: Aviano)*
- 37th Bomber Squadron *(BR20: Aviano)*

47th Bomber Wing:
- 106th Bomber Squadron *(Cant Z1007bis: Ghedi)*
- 107th Bomber Squadron *(Cant Z1007bis: Ghedi)*

1ST AIR REGION *(ROMA)*

5TH BOMBER DIVISION "EOLO" *(Aeolus, Latin God of the winds) (Viterbo)*

46th Bomber Wing
- 104th Bomber Squadron *(SM79: Pisa)*
- 105th Bomber Squadron *(SM79: Pisa)*

9th Bomber Wing:
- 26th Bomber Squadron *(SM79: Viterbo)*
- 29th Bomber Squadron *(SM79: Viterbo)*
- 8th Fighter Brigade "ASTORE" *(Goshawk) (Roma-Ciampino)*
- 7th Independent Fighter Squadron *(Ba88: Campiglia)*

51st Fighter Wing:
- 20th Fighter Squadron *(G50: Roma-Ciampino)*
- 21st Fighter Squadron *(G50: Roma-Ciampino)*

52d Fighter Wing:
- 22d Fighter Squadron *(G50: Pontedera)*
- 24th Fighter Squadron *(G50: Pontedera)*

SARDINIA AIR COMMAND *(CAGLIARI)*
- 10th Bomber Brigade "MARTE" *(Mars, God of war) (Cagliari)*
- 3rd Independent Fighter Squadron *(CR32: Monserrato)*
- 19th Independent Ground Attack Squadron *(Ba88: Alghero)*
- 124th Recon Flight *(Ro37: Cagliari-Elmas)*

8th Bomber Wing:
- 27th Bomber Squadron *(SM79: Villacidro)*
- 28th Bomber Squadron *(SM79: Villacidro)*

31st Bomber Wing:
- 93rd Bomber Squadron *(Cant Z506bis: Cagliari-Elmas)*
- 94th Bomber Squadron *(Cant Z506bis: Cagliari-Elmas)*

32d Bomber Wing:
- 88th Bomber Squadron *(SM79: Decimomannu)*
- 89th Bomber Squadron *(SM79: Decimomannu)*

Italian Air Force, June 1940

LIBYA AIR COMMAND—WEST *(TRIPOLI)*
- 1st Sahara Recon Squadron (*Ca309: Mellaha*)
- 26th Independent Recon Squadron (*Ca309: Hon*)
- 122d Recon Flight (*Ro37bis: Mellaha*)
- 136th Recon Flight (*Ro37bis: Tripoli*)

15th Bomber Wing:
- 46th Bomber Squadron (*SM79: Tarhuna*)
- 47th Bomber Squadron (*SM79: Tarhuna*)

33rd Bomber Wing:
- 35th Bomber Squadron (*SM79: Bir Bhera*)
- 37th Bomber Squadron (*SM79: Bir Bhera*)

50th Ground Attack Wing:
- 12th Ground Attack Squadron (*Ba65: Sorman*)
- 16th Ground Attack Squadron (*Ca310bis: Sorman*)

2d Fighter Wing:
- 13th Fighter Squadron (*CR42: Castel Benito*)
- 1st Recon Squadron (*Ca309: Mellaha*)

ITALIAN EAST AFRICA AIR COMMAND—NORTH *(ASSAB)*
- 25th Bomber Squadron (*Ca133: Bahar Dar*)
- 26th Bomber Squadron (*Ca133: Gondar*)
- 27th Bomber Squadron (*Ca133: Assab*)
- 28th Bomber Squadron (*SM81: Zula*)
- 118th Bomber Flight (*Ca133: Assab*)
- Recon Flight "North" (*Ca133: Agordat*)
- 409th Fighter Flight (*CR42: Massaua*)
- 413th Fighter Flight (*CR42: Assab*)

SPECIAL AIR SERVICES COMMAND
(Militarized airlines, long-range aircraft)
- 147th Squadron (*SM75*)
- 148th Squadron (*SM73*)
- 149th Squadron (*SM82*)
- 604th Flight (*SM75*)
- 608th Flight (*SM82*)
- 610th Flight (*SM75*)
- 615th Flight (*SM83*)
- 616th Flight (*SM74*)
- 604th Flight (*SM75*)

Italian East Africa Detachment *(SM73/Ca148c/ Ca133T/Fokker F)*

AIR FORCE COMMAND FOR THE ARMY
- Under Army GHQ control
- 27th Recon Flight (*Ro37bis: Casabianca*)
- 42d Recon Flight (*Ro37bis: Bari*)
- 121st Recon Flight (*Ro37bis: Airasca*)
- 131st Recon Flight (*Ro37bis: Napoli-Capodichino*)

UNDER ARMY GROUP WEST CONTROL
- 31st Recon Flight (*Ro37: Venaria Reale*)
- 33rd Recon Flight (*Ro37bis: Bresso*)

- 34th Recon Flight (*Ca311: Cervere*)
- 39th Recon Flight (*Ro37: Venaria Reale*)
- 40th Recon Flight (*Ro37: Venaria Reale*)
- 114th Recon Flight (*Ro37: Tornino-Mirafiori*)
- 118th Recon Flight (*Ro37bis: Levaldigi*)
- 119th Recon Flight (*Ca311: Bologna*)
- 123rd Recon Flight (*Ro37bis: Levaldigi*)
- 129th Recon Flight (*Ro37bis/Ca311: Mondovi'*)
- 132d Recon Flight (*Ro37bis: Levaldigi*)

UNDER ARMY GROUP EAST CONTROL
- 24th Recon Flight (*Ro37: Verona-Boscomantico*)
- 25th Recon Flight (*Ro37: Jesi*)
- 28th Recon Flight (*Ro37: Lucca-Tassignano*)
- 29th Recon Flight (*Ro37: Arezzo*)
- 32d Recon Flight (*Ro37bis: Udine-Campoformido*)
- 34th Recon Flight (*Ro37: Parma*)
- 35th Recon Flight (*Ro37: Verona-Boscomantico*)
- 36th Recon Flight (*Ro37: Padova*)
- 38th Recon Flight (*Ro37bis: Gorizia-Merna*)
- 87th Recon Flight (*Ro37: Padova*)
- 113th Recon Flight (*Ro37bis: Bologna-Borgo Panigale*)
- 115th Recon Flight (*Ro37: Verona-Boscomantico*)
- 116th Recon Flight (*Ro37bis: Gorizia-Merna*)
- 125th Recon Flight (*Ro37bis: Udine-Campoformido*)
- 128th Recon Flight (*Ro37: Parma*)

2D AIR REGION *(PALERMO)*
3rd Bomber Division "CENTAURO" *(Centaur) (Catania)*

11th Bomber Wing:
- 33rd Bomber Squadron (*SM79: Comiso*)
- 34th Bomber Squadron (*SM79: Comiso*)

41st Bomber Wing
- 59th Bomber Squadron (*SM79: Gela*)
- 60th Bomber Squadron (*SM79: Gela*)

24th Bomber Wing:
- 52d Bomber Squadron (*SM79: Catania*)
- 53rd Bomber Squadron (*SM79: Catania*)
- 11th Bomber Brigade "NIBBIO" (*Kite*) *(Castelvetrano)*
- 96th Independent Bomber Squadron (*SM-95c: Reggio Calabria*)

30th Bomber Wing
- 87th Bomber Squadron (*SM79: Sciacca*)
- 90th Bomber Squadron (*SM79: Sciacca*)

36th Bomber Wing
- 108th Bomber Squadron (*SM79: Castelvetrano*)
- 109th Bomber Squadron (*SM79: Castelvetrano*)

FIGHTER DIVISION "AQUILA" *(Eagle) (Palermo)*
- 6th Independent Fighter Squadron (*MC200: Comiso*)
- 30th Recon Flight (*Ro37bis: Palermo*)

Italian Air Force, June 1940

1st Fighter Wing
- 17th Fighter Squadron (*CR42: Palermo*)
- 157th Fighter Squadron (*CR42: Palermo*)

TERRITORIAL AIR ZONE *(BARI)*
- 116th Independent Bomber Squadron (*BR20: Grottaglie*)
- 2d Independent Fighter Squadron (*CR32: Grottaglie*)

35th Bomber Wing:
- 86th Bomber Squadron (*Cant Z501: Brindisi*)
- 96th Bomber Squadron (*Cant Z506bis: Brindisi*)
- 37th Bomber Wing: 54th Bomber Squadron (*SM81: Lecce*)
- 29th Bomber Squadron (*SM81: Lecce*)

ALBANIA AIR COMMAND *(TIRANA)*
- 38th Independent Bomber Squadron (*SM81: Tirana*)
- 160th Independent Fighter Squadron (*CR32: Tirana*)
- 120th Recon Flight (*Ro37bis: Tirana*)

AEGEAN AIR COMMAND *(RHODES)*
- 161st Independent Fighter Squadron (*Ro44: Leros*)
- 163rd Independent Fighter Squadron (*CR32: Maritza*)

39th Bomber Wing:
- 56th Bomber Squadron (*SM81: Gadurra*)
- 92d Bomber Squadron (*SM81: Maritza*)

LIBYA AIR COMMAND - EAST *(BENGHAZI)*
- 2d Sahara Recon Squadron (*Ca309: El Adem*)
- 127th Recon Flight (*Ro37bis: El Adem*)
- 137th Recon Flight (*Ro37bis: El Adem*)
- 13th Bomber Division "PEGASO" (*Benghazi*)

14th Bomber Wing:
- 44th Bomber Squadron (*SM81: El Adem*)
- 45th Bomber Squadron (*SM81: El Adem*)

10th Bomber Wing:
- 30th Bomber Squadron (*SM79: Benina*)
- 32nd Bomber Squadron (*SM79: Benina*)
- 14th Fighter Brigade "REX" (*King, in Latin*) (*Tobruk*)
- 8th Fighter Squadron (*CR32: Tobruk*)
- 10th Fighter Squadron (*CR42: Tobruk*)

ITALIAN EAST AFRICA AIR COMMAND—CENTRAL
(ADDIS ABABA)
- 4th Bomber Squadron (*SM81: Scenele*)
- 29th Bomber Squadron (*SM81: Assab*)
- 44th Bomber Squadron (*SM79: Ghiniele*)
- 49th Bomber Squadron (*Ca133: Gimma*)
- 41st Recon Flight (*Ca133: Addis Abeba*)
- 110th Recon Flight (*Ro37: Dire Daua*)
- 410th Fighter Flight (*CR32: Dire Daua*)
- 411th Fighter Flight (*CR32: Dire Daua*)

ITALIAN EAST AFRICA AIR COMMAND—SOUTH
(MOGADISHU)
- 31st Bomber Squadron (*Ca133: Neghelli*)
- Recon Flight "South" (*Ca133: Mogadiscio*)

AIR FORCE COMMAND FOR THE NAVY UNDER UPPER ADRIATIC SEA DEPARTMENT CONTROL
- 4th Recon Section (*Cant Z-501: Pola*)

UNDER IONIAN & LOWER ADRIATIC SEA DEPARTMENT CONTROL
- 142d Recon Flight (*Cant Z501: Taranto*)
- 145th Recon Flight (*Cant Z501: Brindisi*)
- 171st Recon Flight (*Cant Z501: Brindisi*)
- 3rd Recon Section (*Cant Z501: Taranto*)

UNDER UPPER TYRRENHIAN SEA DEPARTMENT CONTROL
- 141st Recon Flight (*Cant Z501: La Spezia-Cadimare*)
- 187th Recon Flight (*Cant Z501: La Spezia -Cadimare*)
- 1st Recon Section (*Cant Z501: La Spezia-Cadimare*)

UNDER LOWER TYRRENHIAN SEA DEPARTMENT CONTROL
- 182d Recon Flight (*Cant Z501: Nisida*)

UNDER SARDINIA NAVAL COMMAND CONTROL
- 146th Recon Flight (*Cant Z501: Cagliari-Elmas*)
- 148th Recon Flight (*Cant Z501: Vigna*)
- 183rd Recon Flight (*Cant Z501: Cagliari-Elmas*)
- 188th Recon Flight (*Cant Z501: Cagliari-Elmas*)
- 199th Recon Flight (*Cant Z506: Santa Giusta*)
- 5th Recon Section (*Cant Z501: Olbia*)

UNDER SICILY NAVY COMMAND CONTROL
- 144th Recon Flight (*Cant Z501: Stagnone*)
- 170th Recon Flight (*Cant Z506bis: Augusta*)
- 184th Recon Flight (*Cant Z501: Augusta*)
- 186th Recon Flight (*Cant Z501: Augusta*)
- 189th Recon Flight (*Cant Z501: Siracusa*)

UNDER ALBANIA NAVAL COMMAND CONTROL
- 288th Recon Flight (*Cant Z506bis: Brindisi*)

UNDER LIBYAN NAVAL COMMAND CONTROL
- 143rd Recon Flight (*Cant Z501: Menelao*)

UNDER AEGEAN SEA NAVAL COMMAND CONTROL
- 147th Recon Flight (*Cant Z501: Leros*)
- 185th Recon Flight (*Cant Z501: Leros*)

The Italian Navy, Order of Battle, June 1940

 When it entered World War II, the Italian Navy was one of the most formidable naval fighting forces in the world. It posed a great threat to British interests in the Mediterranean.

Unfortunately, the lack of aircraft carriers plus a lack of aggression displayed by senior Italian naval officers would have a devastating effect on the navy's ability to combat the Royal Navy between 1940 and 1943.

1ST FLEET *(Vice Admiral Campioni)*
Auxiliary Units:
- Seaplane Tender *GIUSEPPE MIRAGLIA*
- Water Tanker *ISONZO*
- Water Tanker *PO*
- Water Tanker *GARDA*
- Tug *ATLANTE*
- Tug *LIPARI*

5th Battleship Division *(Rear Admiral Brivonesi)*
- BB *GIULIO CESARE*
- BB *CONTE DI CAVOUR*

7th Destroyer Squadron
- DD *FRECCIA*
- DD *DARDO*
- DD *SAETTA*
- DD *STRALE*

8th Destroyer Squadron
- DD *FOLGORE*
- DD *FULMINE*
- DD *BALENO*
- DD *LAMPO*

9th Battleship Division *(Rear Admiral Bergamini)*
- BB *LITTORIO*
- BB *VITTORIO VENETO*

14th Destroyer Squadron
- DD *UGOLINO VIVALDI*
- DD *ANTONIO DA NOLI*
- DD *LEONE PANCALDO*

15th Destroyer Squadron
- DD *ANTONIO PIGAFETTA*
- DD *NICOLO' ZENO*
- DD *ALVISE DA MOSTO*
- DD *GIOVANNI DA VERRAZZANO*
- DD *LANZEROTTO MALOCELLO*

1st Cruiser Division *(Rear Admiral Matteucci)*
- CA *ZARA*
- CA *GORIZIA*
- CA *FIUME*

9th Destroyer Squadron
- DD *VITTORIO ALFIERI*
- DD *ALFREDO ORIANI*
- DD *GIOSUE' CARDUCCI*
- DD *VINCENZO GIOBERTI*

4th Cruiser Division *(Rear Admiral Marenco)*
- CL *ALBERICO DA BARBIANO*
- CL *LUIGI CADORNA*
- CL *ALBERTO DA GIUSSANO*
- CL *ARMANDO DIAZ*
- DD *LANCIERE*

8th Cruiser Division *(Rear Admiral Legnani)*
- CL *LUIGI DI SAVOIA DUCA DEGLI ABRUZZI*
- CL *GIUSEPPE GARIBALDI*

16th Destroyer Squadron
- DD *NICOLOSO DA RECCO*
- DD *ANTONIOTTO USODIMARE*
- DD *TARIGO*
- DD *EMANUELE PESSAGNO*

2D FLEET *(Vice Admiral Paladini)*
- CA *POLA*

12th Destroyer Squadron
- DD *CARABINIERE*
- DD *CORAZZIERE*
- DD *ASCARI*

3rd Cruiser Division *(Rear Admiral Cattaneo)*
- CA *TRENTO*
- CA *BOLZANO*
- CA *TRIESTE*

11th Destroyer Squadron
- DD *ARTIGLIERE*
- DD *CAMICIA NERA*
- DD *AVIERE*
- DD *GENIERE*

7th Cruiser Division *(Rear Admiral Sansonetti)*
- CL *EUGENIO DI SAVOIA*
- CL *EMANUELE FILIBERTO DUCA D'AOSTA*

- CL *MUZIO ATTENDOLO*
- CL *RAIMONDO MONTECUCCOLI*

13th Destroyer Squadron
- DD *GRANATIERE*
- DD *FUCILIERE*
- DD *BERSAGLIERE*
- DD *ALPINO*

2d Cruiser Division *(Rear Admiral Casardi)*
- CL *GIOVANNI DALLE BANDE NERE*
- CL *BARTOLOMEO COLLEONI*

10th Destroyer Squadron
- DD *MAESTRALE*
- DD *LIBECCIO*
- DD *GRECALE*
- DD *SCIROCCO*

SUBMARINE FLEET *(Vice Damiral Falangola)*
1st Group
11th Squadron
- SS *CALVI*
- SS *FINZI*
- SS *TAZZOLI*
- SS *ETTORE FIERAMOSCA*

12th Squadron
- SS *CAPPELLINI*
- SS *FAA DI BRUNO*
- SS *LAZZARO MOCENIGO*
- SS *SEBASTIANO VENIERO*
- SS *GLAUCO*
- SS *OTARIA*

13th Squadron
- SS *BERILLIO*
- SS *ONICE*
- SS *GEMMA*

14th Squadron
- SS *IRIDE*
- SS *ARGO*
- SS *VALELLA*
- SS *GONDAR*
- SS *NEGHELLI*
- SS *ASCIANGHI*
- SS *SCIRE'*

The Italian Navy, Order of Battle, June 1940

16th Squadron
- SS *MICCA*
- SS *FOCA*

17th Squadron
- *H1*
- *H2*
- *H4*
- *H6*
- *H8*

2d Group
21st Squadron
- SS *MARCELO*
- SS *NANI*
- SS *ENRICO DANDOLO*
- SS *PROVANA*

22d Squadron
- SS *BARBARIGO*
- SS *ANGELO EMO*
- SS *FRANCESCO MOROSINI*
- SS *GUGLIELMO MARCONI*
- SS *LEONARDO DA VINCI*

3rd Group
31st Squadron
- SS *VETTOR PISANI*
- SS *COLONNA*
- SS *BAUSAN*
- SS *DES GENEYES*

33rd Squadron
- SS *FRATELLI BANDIERA*
- SS *LUCIANO MANARA*
- SS *CIRO MENOTTI*
- SS *SANTORE DI SANTAROSA*

34th Squadron
- SS *GOFFREDO MAMELI*
- SS *PIER CAPPONI*
- SS *TITO SPERI*
- SS *DA PROCIDA*

35th Squadron
- SS *DURBO*
- SS *TEMBIEN*
- SS *BEILUL*

37th Squadron
- *X2*
- *X3*

4th Group
40th Squadron
- SS *BALILLA*
- SS *AMATORE SCIESA*

- SS *ENRICO TOTI*
- SS *DOMENICO MILLELIRE*

41st Squadron
- SS *LIUZZI*
- SS *ATTILIO BAGNOLINI*
- SS *GIULIANI*
- SS *TARANTINI*

42d Squadron
- SS *BENEDETTO BRIN*

43rd Squadron
- SS *SETTIMO*
- SS *SETTEMBRINI*

44th Squadron
- SS *ANFITRITE*

45th Squadron
- SS *SALPA*
- SS *SERPENTE*

46th Squadron
- SS *DESSIE'*
- SS *DAGABUR*
- SS *UAR-SCIECK*
- SS *UEBI-SCEBELI*

47th Squadron
- SS *MALACHITE*
- SS *RUBINO*
- SS *AMBRA*

48th Squadron
- SS *ONDINA*

49th Squadron
- SS *ATROPO*
- SS *ZOEA*
- SS *FILIPPO CORRIDONI*

7th Group
71st Squadron
- SS *ALAGI*
- SS *ADUA*
- SS *AXUM*
- SS *ARADAM*

72d Squadron
- SS *DIASPRO*
- SS *CORALLO*
- SS *TURCHESE*
- SS *MEDUSA*

UPPER ADRIATIC SEA DEPARTMENT
(Vice Admiral Ferdinando di Savoia)
15th Torpedo-Boat Squadron
- TB *CONFIENZA*
- TB *SOLFERINOTB SAN MARTINO*
- TB *PALESTRO*
- TB *GIOVANNINI*

LIBYA NAVAL COMMAND *(Rear Admiral Brivonesi)*
1st Destroyer Squadron
- DD *TURBINE*
- DD *AQUILONE*
- DD *EURO*
- DD *NEMBO*

11th Torpedo Boat Squadron
- TB *CIGNO*
- TB *CASTORE*
- TB *CLIMENE*
- TB *CENTAURO*
- CA *SAN GIORGIO*

6th Submarine Group
61st Squadron
- SS *SIRENA*
- SS *ARGONAUTA*
- SS *FISALIA*
- SS *SMERALDO*
- SS *NEREIDE*

62d Squadron
- SS *DIAMANTE*
- SS *TOPAZIO*
- SS *NEREIDE*
- SS *GALATEA*
- SS *LAFOLE*

FAR EAST NAVAL COMMAND
(Commander Galletti)
- Minelayer *LEPANTO*
- Gunboat *CARLOTTO*

UPPER TYRRENHIAN SEA DEPARTMENT
(Vice Admiral Aimone di Savoia-Aosta)
10th Torpedo Boat Squadron
- TB *VEGA*
- TB *SAGITTARIO*
- TB *PERSEO*
- TB *SIRIO*
- TB *GIACINTO CARINI*
- TB *ANTONIO LA MASA*

LOWER TYRRENHIAN SEA DEPARTMENT
(Vice Admiral Pini)
1st Torpedo Boat Squadron
- TB *AIRO E*

The Italian Navy, Order of Battle, June 1940

- TB *ARIEL*
- TB *ARETUSA*
- TB *ALCIONE*
- TB *ALBATROS*

2d Torpedo Boat Squadron
- TB *PAPA*
- TB *MONTANARI*
- TB *CASCINO*
- TB *CHINOTTO*

3rd Torpedo Boat Squadron
- TB *PRESTINARI*
- TB *CANTORE*

4th Torpedo Boat Squadron
- TB *PROCIONE*
- TB *ORIONE*
- TB *ORSA*
- TB *PERSEO*

5th Torpedo Boat Squadron
- TB *SIMONE SCHIAFFINO*
- TB *DEZZA*
- TB *GIUSEPPE LA FARINA*
- TB *ABBA*

9th Torpedo Boat Squadron
- TB *CASSIOPEA*
- TB *CANOPO*
- TB *CAIROLI*
- TB *ANTONIO MOSTO*

12th Torpedo Boat Squadron
- TB *ALTAIR*
- TB *ANTARES*
- TB *ALDEBARAN*
- TB *ANDROMEDA*

13th Torpedo Boat Squadron
- TB *CIRCE*
- TB *CLIO*
- TB *CALLIOPE*
- TB *CALIPSO*

14th Torpedo Boat Squadron
- TB *PARTENOPE*
- TB *POLLUCE*
- TB *PLEIADI*
- TB *PALLADE*

IONIAN AND LOWER ADRIATIC DEPARTMENT *(Vice Admiral Pasetti)*
- CL *BARI*
- CL *TARANTO*

2d Destroyer Squadron
- DD *ESPERO*
- DD *BOREA*
- DD *ZEFFIRO*
- DD *OSTRO*

6th Destroyer Squadron
- DD *ROSOLINO PILO*
- DD *FRANCESCO STOCCO*
- DD *GIUSEPPE MISSORI*
- DD *SIRTORI*
- DD *AUGUSTO RIBOTY*

7th Torpedo Boat Squadron
- TB *ANGELO BASSINI*
- TB *COSENZ*
- TB *GIACOMO MEDICI*
- TB *NICOLA FABRIZI*

AEGEAN SEA NAVAL COMMAND
(Rear Admiral Biancheri)
4th Destroyer Squadron
- DD *FRANCESCO CRISPI*
- DD *QUINTINO SELLA*

8th Torpedo Boat Squadron
- TB *LUPO*
- TB *LINCE*
- TB *LIRA*
- TB *LIBRA*

5th Submarine Group
51st Squadron
- SS *NARVALO*
- SS *SQUALO*
- SS *TRICHECO*
- SS *DELFINO*

52d Squadron
- SS *JALEA*
- SS *IANTINA*
- SS *AMETISTA*
- SS *ZAFFIRO*

ITALIAN EAST AFRICA NAVAL COMMAND *(Rear Admiral Balsamo)*
3rd Destroyer Squadron
- DD *FRANCESCO NULLO*
- DD *NAZARIO SAURO*
- DD *CESARE BATTISTI*
- DD *DANIELE MANIN*

5th Destroyer Squadron
- DD *PANTERA*
- DD *TIGRE*
- DD *LEONE*

8th Submarine Group
81st Squadron
- SS *GUGLIELMOTTI*
- SS GALILEO FERRARIS
- SS *GALILEO GALILEI*
- SS *LUIGI GALVANI*

82nd Squadron
- SS *PERLA*
- SS *MACALLE'*
- SS *ARCHIMEDE*
- SS *EVANGELISTA TORRICELLI*

Auxiliary Units
- Gunboat *PORTO CORSINI*
- Gunboat *BIGLIERI*
- Minelayer *OSTIA*
- Oil Tanker *NIOBE*
- Water Tanker *SILE*
- Water Tanker SEBETO
- Water Tanker *BACCHIGLIONE*
- Royal Yacht *AURORA*
- Royal Yacht *SAVOIA*
- Royal Yacht ILLIRIA
- Radio-controlled target ship *SAN MARCO*
- Hydrographic Ship *AMMIRAGLIO MAGNAGHI*
- Hydrographic Ship *CARIDDI*
- Transport Ship *ENRICHETTA*
- Transport Ship *TRIPOLI*
- Transport Ship *VALLELUNGA*
- Transport Ship *PANIGAGLIA*
- Transport Ship *ASMARA*
- Hospital Ship *AQUILEIA*
- Cable-layer *CITTA' DI MILANO*
- Cable-layer *GIASONE*
- Oil Tanker *TARVISIO*
- Oil Tanker *BRENNERO*
- Oil Tanker *URANO*
- Oil Tanker *BRONTE*
- Oil Tanker *NETTUNO*
- Oil Tanker *GIOVE*
- Oil Tanker *MARTE*
- Oil Tanker *STIGE*
- Tug *TESEO*
- Tug *TITANO*
- Tug *CICLOPE*
- Tug *MARETTIMO*
- Tug *LUNI*
- Tug *EGADI*
- Tug *NEREO*
- Tug *MARSIGLI*
- Tug *MONTECRISTO*

Japanese Thirty-Second Army, March 1945

The Japanese constitution stated that the Emperor was Commander-in-Chief of the army and navy. He determined their organization, he declared war, made peace, and concluded treaties. He was advised by two military councils: the Board of Marshals and Admirals, and the Supreme Military Council. In wartime, or in cases of grave emergency, an Imperial Headquarters was established, under the supervision of the Emperor, to assist in the exercise of supreme military command. It consisted of the Chiefs of the Army and Navy General Staffs, the Ministers of War and of Navy, and a staff of specially selected officers. Subordinate to the Emperor and Imperial Headquarters, the direction of the army was in the hands of four principal agencies: The General Staff (Sambo Hombu); the Ministry of War; the Inspectorate General of Military Training; and the Inspectorate General of Aviation. The Thirty-Second Army (below) defended Okinawa in 1945.

Thirty-Second Army, Order of Battle, March 1945

- Headquarters (1,070 troops)
- Ordnance Depot (1,498 troops)
- Ordnance Duty Unit (150 troops)
- Field Freight Depot (1,167 troops)
- 36th Signal Regiment (1,912 troops)
- Okinawa Army Hospital (204 troops)
- 27th Field Water Purification Unit (224 troops)
- Well Digging Unit (34 troops)
- Defense Construction Unit (108 troops)
- 7th Fortress Construction Duty (322 troops)
- 2d Field Construction Duty Company (366 troops)

24th Infantry Division
- Headquarters (267 troops)
- 22d Infantry Regiment (2,796 troops)
- 32d Infantry Regiment (2,870 troops)
- 89th Infantry Regiment (2,809 troops)
- 42d Field Artillery Regiment (2,321 troops)
- 24th Reconnaissance Regiment (346 troops)
- 24th Engineer Regiment (777 troops)
- 24th Transport Regiment (1,158 troops)
- Signal Unit (275 troops)
- Decontamination Training Unit (77 troops)
- Ordnance Repair Unit (57 troops)
- Veterinary Hospital (11 troops)
- Water Supply and Purification Unit (241 troops)
- 1st Field Hospital (174 troops)
- 2d Field Hospital (181 troops)

62d Infantry Division
- Headquarters (65 troops)
- 63rd Brigade Headquarters (129 troops)
- 11th Independent Infantry Battalion (1,091 troops)
- 12th Independent Infantry Battalion (1,085 troops)
- 13th Independent Infantry Battalion (1,058 troops)
- 14th Independent Infantry Battalion (1,085 troops)
- 273d Independent Infantry Battalion (683 troops)
- 64th Brigade Headquarters (121 troops)
- 15th Independent Infantry Battalion (1,076 troops)
- 21st Independent Infantry Battalion (1,080 troops)
- 22d Independent Infantry Battalion (1,071 troops)

- 23rd Independent Infantry Battalion (1,089 troops)
- 272d Independent Infantry Battalion (683 troops)
- Engineer Unit (255 troops)
- Signal Unit (359 troops)
- Transport Unit (300 troops)
- Field Hospital (371 troops)
- Veterinary Hospital (22 troops)

44th Independent Mixed Brigade
- Headquarters (63 troops)
- 2d Infantry Unit (2,046 troops)
- 15th Independent Mixed Regiment (1,885 troops)
- Artillery Unit (330 troops)
- Engineer Unit (161 troops)

5th Artillery Command
- Headquarters (147 troops)
- 1st Medium Artillery Regiment (856 troops)
- 23rd Medium Artillery Regiment (1,143 troops)
- 7th Heavy Artillery Regiment (526 troops)
- 100th Independent Heavy Artillery Battalion (565 troops)
- 1st Independent Artillery Mortar Regiment (613 troops)
- 1st Light Mortar Battalion (633 troops)
- 2d Light Mortar Battalion (615 troops)

21st Antiaircraft Artillery Command
- Headquarters (71 troops)
- 27th Independent Antiaircraft Artillery Battalion (505 troops)
- 70th Field Antiaircraft Artillery Battalion (513 troops)
- 80th Field Antiaircraft Artillery Battalion (517 troops)
- 81st Field Antiaircraft Artillery Battalion (514 troops)
- 103rd Independent Machine Cannon Battalion (336 troops)
- 104th Independent Machine Cannon Battalion (338 troops)
- 105th Independent Machine Cannon Battalion (337 troops)

Machine Gun Units
- 3rd Independent Machine Gun Battalion (340 troops)
- 4th Independent Machine Gun Battalion (344 troops)
- 14th Independent Machine Gun Battalion (334 troops)
- 17th Independent Machine Gun Battalion (331 troops)

Japanese Thirty-Second Army, March 1945

Antitank Units
- 3rd Independent Antitank Battalion *(363 troops)*
- 7th Independent Antitank Battalion *(353 troops)*
- 22d Independent Antitank Battalion *(402 troops)*
- 32d Independent Antitank Company *(144 troops)*

11th Shipping Group
- Headquarters *(100 troops)*
- 7th Shipping Engineer Branch Depot *(600 troops)*
- 23rd Shipping Engineer Regiment *(850 troops)*
- 26th Shipping Engineer Regiment *(550 troops)*
- 5th Sea Raiding Base Headquarters *(42 troops)*
- 1st Sea Raiding Squadron *(104 troops)*
- 2d Sea Raiding Squadron *(104 troops)*
- 3rd Sea Raiding Squadron *(104 troops)*
- 26th Sea Raiding Squadron *(104 troops)*
- 27th Sea Raiding Squadron *(104 troops)*
- 28th Sea Raiding Squadron *(104 troops)*
- 29th Sea Raiding Squadron *(104 troops)*
- 1st Sea Raiding Base Battalion *(886 troops)*
- 2d Sea Raiding Base Battalion *(874 troops)*
- 3rd Sea Raiding Base Battalion *(877 troops)*
- 26th Sea Raiding Base Battalion *(908 troops)*
- 27th Sea Raiding Base Battalion *(897 troops)*
- 28th Sea Raiding Base Battalion *(900 troops)*
- 29th Sea Raiding Base Battalion *(900 troops)*

49th Line of Communication Sector
- Headquarters *(202 troops)*
- 72d Land Duty Company *(508 troops)*
- 83rd Land Duty Company *(496 troops)*
- 103rd Sea Duty Company *(711 troops)*
- 104th Sea Duty Company *(724 troops)*
- 215th Independent Motor Transport Company *(181 troops)*
- 259th Independent Motor Transport Company *(182 troops)*

Engineer Units
- 66th Independent Engineer Battalion *(865 troops)*
- 14th Field Well Drilling Company *(110 troops)*
- 20th Field Well Drilling Company *(110 troops)*

19th Air Sector Command
- Headquarters *(41 troops)*
- 29th Field Airfield Construction Battalion *(750 troops)*
- 44th Airfield Battalion *(377 troops)*
- 50th Airfield Battalion *(360 troops)*
- 56th Airfield Battalion *(380 troops)*
- 3rd Independent Maintenance Unit *(120 troops)*
- Makoto 1st Maintenance Company *(90 troops)*
- 118th Independent Maintenance Unit *(100 troops)*
- 6th Fortress Construction Duty Company *(330 troops)*
- Detachment, 20th Air Regiment *(27 troops)*
- 10th Field Meteorological Unit *(80 troops)*
- 26th Air-Ground Radio Unit *(117 troops)*
- 46th Independent Air Company *(132 troops)*
- 1st Branch Depot, 5th Field Air Repair Depot *(130 troops)*
- 21st Air Signal Unit *(310 troops)*

- Okinawa Branch, Army Air Route Department *(359 troops)*
- 223d Specially Established Garrison Company *(200 troops)*
- 224th Specially Established Garrison Company *(200 troops)*
- 225th Specially Established Garrison Company *(200 troops)*
- 27th Tank Regiment *(750 troops)*

Army Unit Total 66,636

Navy Units
- Okinawa Base Force (*Headquarters, Coast Defense, and Antiaircraft Personnel*) (3,400 troops)
- 27th Motor Torpedo Boat Squadron *(200 troops)*
- 33rd Midget Submarine Unit *(130 troops)*
- 37th Torpedo Maintenance Unit *(140 troops)*
- Torpedo Working Unit *(130 troops)*
- 81mm Mortar Battery *(150 troops)*
- Oroku Transmitting Station *(30 troops)*
- Naha Branch, Sasebo Naval Stores Department *(136 troops)*
- Naha Branch, Sasebo Transportation Department *(136 troops)*
- Naha Navy Yard, Sasebo Naval Base *(53 troops)*
- Oroku Detachment, 951st Air Group *(600 troops)*
- Nansei Shoto Air Group *(2,000 troops)*
- 226th Construction Unit *(1,420 troops)*
- 3210th Construction Unit *(300 troops)*
- Navy Unit Total *(8,825 troops)*

Okinawa
- 502d Special Guard Engineer Unit *(900 troops)*
- 503rd Special Guard Engineer Unit *(700 troops)*
- 504th Special Guard Engineer Unit *(700 troops)*
- Blood-and-Iron-for-the-Emperor Duty Unit *(750 troops)*
- Boeitai Assigned to the Army *(16,600 troops)*
- Boeitai Assigned to the Navy *(1,100 troops)*
- Students *(600 troops)*
- Regular Conscripts Not Included Under Army Units *(2,000 troops)*
- Okinawan Total *(23,350 troops)*

Grand Total *(Rounded Out)*
- Army Units: *67,000*
- Navy Units: *9,000*
- Okinawans: *24,000*
- Japanese Strength on Okinawa: *100,000*

Japanese Infantry Division

 A division was commanded by a lieutenant general, with a colonel of the General Staff as Chief of Staff. The staff was in two sections—the General Staff section and the administrative section. To the staff were attached five departmental sections and an ordnance, a signal, and a veterinary detachment. In all, there were about 300 officers and enlisted men. The General Staff section was composed of about 75 officers and enlisted men. The Chief of Staff supervised and coordinated the work of the General and Administrative Staffs. He acted as the link between the division commander and the unit commanders, heads of departments, and the civil authorities.

Each infantry division normally contained either one cavalry or one reconnaissance regiment or unit. Within both the standard and the strengthened divisions, the regimental cavalry was organized basically along the same lines.

Typical organization of a Japanese standard army division in 1941 was as follows:
- Cavalry Regiment, *with three Rifle Companies*
- Machine Gun Company
- Reconnaissance Regiment, *with a Mounted Company, a Motor Company, and an Armored Car Company*
- Infantry Group (at right), *comprising three Infantry Regiments, each with three Battalions*
- HQ Company
- Artillery Regiment, *with three Artillery Battalions*
- Engineer Regiment
- Transport Regiment

Total strength: 20,000

Divisional firepower
- Light machine guns: *382*
- Heavy machine guns: *112*
- Grenade launchers: *340*

Antitank guns
- 47mm antitank guns: *37*
- 20mm antitank rifles: *18*

Infantry guns
- 75mm: *12*

Artillery
- 75mm field guns: *36*
- 70mm guns: *18*

Armor
- Armored cars: *7*

Transport
- Carts: *250*
- Trucks: *50*

Japanese Brigades and Tank Regiments

 Until 1929, Japan did not produce any tanks of its own. As was common with many weapons systems, Japanese ideas were borrowed from the West, particularly from the British and French. The first Japanese tanks were versions of early Renault, Vickers, and Carden-Lloyd models. Later, Japan turned to Russia for new developments.

Prior to 1941, the Japanese had every opportunity to study the experience of Allied tanks under combat conditions. During 1935–1937, the Japanese concentrated on tankettes, light tanks, and medium tanks, perfecting one model in each class. Their tanks fell into four main types, divided according to weight. These were: Tankette (Chokei Sensha); light tanks (Kei Sensha); medium tanks (Chu Sensha); and heavy tanks (Ju Sensha). During World War II, Japanese tanks were inferior to their U.S. counterparts, especially the M4 Sherman medium tank.

Typical organization of a 1941 Japanese special garrison division was as follows:
- Infantry Brigade, *with three Independent Battalions*
- Engineer Unit
- Signals Unit
- Transport Unit

Total strength: 13,000

Divisional Firepower
- Light machine guns: *110*
- Heavy machine guns: *32*
- Grenade launchers: *112*

Mortars
- 16 light mortars

Infantry guns
- 70mm: *8*

Transport
- 2,700 horses

Typical organization of a 1941 Japanese independent brigade was as follows:
- Five Infantry Battalions
- Artillery Unit
- Engineer Unit
- Signals Unit

Total strength: 5,600

Brigade firepower
- Light machine guns: *36*
- Heavy machine guns: *4*

Antitank weapons
- 20mm antitank rifles: *4*

Mortars
- 150mm mortars: *4*

Artillery
- 105mm howitzers: *8*

Typical organization of a 1941 Japanese tank regiment was as follows:
- Three Tank Companies, *each with four platoons*
- Company Headquarters
- Combat Train

Total strength: 850

Regimental firepower
- Medium, light tanks, or tankettes. The combat train carried 15 replacements.

Japanese Landing Forces

 Until several years after World War I, Japan had no separate permanent naval landing organization corresponding to the U.S. Marine Corps. Instead, naval landing parties were organized temporarily from fleet personnel for a particular mission and were returned to their ships at its conclusion. This practice was made possible by the fact that every naval recruit was given training in land warfare concurrently with training in seamanship. The results of such training,

together with any special skills such as machine gunner and truck driver, were noted on the seaman's service record to serve as a basis for his inclusion in a landing party. Normally, the fleet commander designated certain ships to furnish personnel for the landing party. This practice, however, depleted their crews and lowered their efficiency for naval action. Therefore, in the late 1920s, Japan began to experiment with more permanent units known as Special Naval Landing Forces (Rikusentai).

Typical organization of a 1941 Japanese Special Naval Landing Force was as follows:
- Two Rifle Companies, *each with four Rifle Platoons (at right)*
- Heavy Machine Gun Platoon
- Heavy Weapons Company, *with a Regimental Gun platoon and a Howitzer Platoon*

Total strength: 10,060

Landing force firepower
- Light machine guns: *55*
- Heavy machine guns: *12*
- Grenade launchers: *33*

Infantry guns
- 75mm: *2*

Artillery
- 70mm howitzers: *4*

Typical organization of a 1943 Japanese Special Landing Force was as follows:
- Two Rifle Companies
- Three Coastal Defense Companies
- Antitank Platoon
- Mortar Platoon

Total strength: 1,800

Landing force firepower
- Light machine guns: *12*
- Heavy machine guns: *24*
- 40mm antiaircraft guns: *2*
- 13mm antiaircraft machine guns: *10*

Infantry guns
- 80mm: *16*
- 120mm: *8*

Artillery
- 75mm antiaircraft guns: *4*

Japanese Fleet, Battle at Midway, June 1942

 At Midway, the U.S. Navy inflicted a smashing defeat on the Japanese Navy. Although the performance of the three American carrier air groups would later be considered uneven, their pilots and crew had won the day through courage, determination, and heroic sacrifice. The Japanese lost the four large carriers that had attacked Pearl Harbor in December, while the Americans only lost one carrier. In addition, the Japanese lost over 100 trained pilots, who could not be replaced. The balance of sea power in the Pacific shifted; Japan was now on the defensive. Soon after the Battle of Midway, the United States and its allies would take the offensive in the Pacific Ocean.

COMBINED FLEET
- Admiral Isoroku Yamamoto, in *Yamato*
- Chief of Staff, Rear Admiral Matome Ugaki
- Main Body, Admiral Yamamoto

Battleship Division 1, Admiral Yamamoto
- BB *Yamato* (flagship)
- BB *Nagato*
- BB *Mutsu*

Carrier Group, Captain Kaoru Umetani
- CVL *Hosho*
- Air Unit (8 bombers)
- DD *Yukaze*

Special Force, Captain Kaku Harada
- *Chiyoda* (seaplane carrier)
- *Nisshin* (seaplane carrier)

SCREEN, Rear Admiral Shintaro Hashimoto
- CL *Sendai* (flagship, *Jintsu*)

Destroyer Division 11, Captain Kiichiro Shoji
- DD *Fubuki*
- DD *Shirayuki*
- DD *Hatsuyuki*
- DD *Murakumo*

Destroyer Division 19, Captain Ranji Oe
- DD *Isonami*
- DD *Uranami*
- DD *Shikinami*
- DD *Ayanami*

1st Supply Unit, Captain Shigeyasu Nishioka
- *Naruto* (Oiler)
- *Toei Maru* (Oiler)

GUARD (Aleutians Screening) FORCE, Vice Admiral Shiro Takasu in *Hyuga*
- Chief of Staff, Rear Admiral Kengo Kobayashi

Battleship Division 2
- BB *Hyuga*
- BB *Ise*
- BB *Fuso*
- BB *Yamashiro*

Cruiser Division 9, Rear Admiral Fukuji Kishi
- CL *Kitakami*
- CL *Oi*

Destroyer Division 20, Captain Yuji Yamada
- DD *Asagiri*
- DD *Yugiri*
- DD *Shirakumo*
- DD *Amagiri*

Destroyer Division 24, Captain Yasuji Hirai
- DD *Umikaze*
- DD *Yamakaze*
- DD *Kawakaze*
- DD *Suzukaze*

Destroyer Division 27, Captain Matake Yoshimura
- DD *Ariake*
- DD *Yugure*
- DD *Shigure*
- DD *Shiratsuyu*

2nd Supply Unit, Captain Matsuo Eguchi
- *San Clemente Maru* (oiler)
- *Toa Maru* (oiler)

FIRST CARRIER STRIKING FORCE (1st Air Fleet), Vice Admiral Chuichi Nagumo

Carrier Group, Vice Admiral Nagumo

Carrier Division 1
- CV *Akagi* (flagship, shown opposite), 21 Zero fighters, 21 dive-bombers, 21 torpedo-bombers (Sunk)
- CV *Kaga*, 21 Zero fighters, 21 dive-bombers, 30 torpedo-bombers (Sunk)

Carrier Division 2, Rear Admiral Tamon Yamaguchi
- CV *Hiryu* (flagship), 21 Zero fighters, 21 dive-bombers, 21 torpedo-bombers (Sunk)
- CV *Soryu* (Hiryu) 21 Zero fighters, 21 dive-bombers, 21 torpedo-bombers (Sunk)

SUPPORT GROUP, Rear Admiral Hiroaki Abe
Cruiser Division 8
- CA *Tone* (flagship)
- CA *Chikuma*

Battleship Division 3
- BB *Haruna*
- BB *Kirishima*

SCREEN, Rear Admiral Susumu Kimura
- CL *Nagara* (flagship)
- Destroyer Division 4: 4 DDs
- Destroyer Division 10: 3 DDs
- Destroyer Division 17: 4 DDs
- Supply Group: 5 oilers, 1 DD

MIDWAY INVASION FORCE, (2d Fleet), Vice Admiral Nobutake Kondo

INVASION FORCE MAIN BODY
Cruiser Division 4 (less 2nd section)
- CA *Atago* (flagship)
- CA *Chokai*

Japanese Fleet, Battle at Midway, June 1942

Cruiser Division 5 (less 2d section)
- CA *Myoko*
- CA *Haguro*

Battleship Division 3 (less 2d section) –
- BB *Kongo*
- BB *Hiei*

SCREEN, Rear Admiral Shoji Nishimura
- CL *Yura* (flagship)
- Destroyer Division 2: *4 DDs*
- Destroyer Division 9: *3 DDs*
- Carrier Group *Zuiho* (CVL), 12 Zero fighters, 12 torpedo-bombers; 1 DD
- Supply Group: 4 oilers, 1 repair ship

Close Support Group, Vice Admiral Takeo Kurita
Cruiser Division 7
- CA *Kumano* (flagship)
- CA *Suzuya*
- CA *Mikuma* (Sunk)
- CA *Mogami*

Destroyer Division 8
- 2 DDs
- 1 oiler

TRANSPORT GROUP, Rear Admiral Raizo Tanaka
- 12 transports carrying troops
- 3 patrol boats carrying troops
- 1 oiler

ESCORT, Rear Admiral Tanaka
- CL *Jintsu* (flagship)
- Destroyer Division 15: *2 DDs*
- Destroyer Division 16: *4 DDs*
- Destroyer Division 18: *4 DDs*

SEAPLANE TENDER GROUP, Rear Admiral Riutaro Fujita
Seaplane Tender Division 11
- *Chitose* (CVS), 16 fighter seaplanes, 4 scout planes
- *Kamikawa Maru* (AV), 8 fighter seaplanes, 4 scout planes
- 1 DD
- 1 patrol boat carrying troops

Minesweeper Group
- 4 minesweepers
- 3 submarine chasers
- 1 supply ship
- 2 cargo ships

NORTHERN (ALEUTIANS) FORCE (5th Fleet), Vice Admiral Moshiro Hosogaya
Northern Force Main Body
- CA *Nachi* (flagship)
- Screen: *2 DDs*

Supply Group
- 2 oilers, 3 cargo ships

SECOND CARRIER STRIKING FORCE, Rear Admiral Kakuji Kakuta
Carrier Group
- CVL *Ryujo* (flagship), 16 Zero fighters, 21 torpedo-bombers
- CV *Junyo*, 24 Zero fighters, 21 torpedo-bombers

Support Group
- CA *Maya*
- CA *Takao*

Screen
- 3 DDs
- 1 oiler

ATTU INVASION FORCE, Rear Admiral Sentaro Omori
- CL *Abukuma* (flagship)

Destroyer Division 21
- 4 DDs
- 1 minelayer
- 1 transport carrying troops

KISKA INVASION FORCE, Captain Takeji Ono
Cruiser Division 21
- CL *Kiso*
- CL *Tama*
- AMC *Asaka Maru* (auxiliary cruiser)

SCREEN (Destroyer Division 6)
- 3 DDs
- 2 transports carrying troops

Minesweeper Division 13
- 3 minesweepers

SUBMARINE DETACHMENT, Rear Admiral Shigeaki Yamazaki
- *I-9* (flagship)
- Submarine Division 2: *3 submarines*
- Submarine Division 4: *2 submarines*

ADVANCE (SUBMARINE) FORCE (6th Fleet), Vice Admiral Teruhisa Komatsu
- CL *Katori* (flagship)
- *Rio de Janeiro Maru* (flagship)
- Submarine Division 19: *4 submarines*
- Submarine Division 30: *3 submarines*
- Submarine Division 13: *3 submarines*

SHORE-BASED AIR PATROL (11th Air Fleet), Vice Admiral Nishizo Tsukahara
- Midway Expeditionary Force: *36 Zero fighters (aboard Nagumo's carriers), 10 land-based bombers at Wake; 6 flying boats at Jaluit*
24th Air Flotilla, Rear Admiral Minoru Maeda at Kwajalein
- Chitose Air Group: *36 Zero fighters, 36 torpedo-bombers at Kwajalein*
- 1st Air Group: *36 Zero fighters, 36 torpedo-bombers at Aur and Wotje*
- 14th Air Group: *18 flying boats at Jaluit and Wotje*

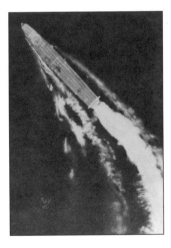

Hungarian Divisions

 According to the agreement between the Hungarian General Staff and the German High Command, Hungarian divisions assumed rear area security on the Eastern Front. The territory they had to secure against partisan activity was 60–70 miles (96–112 km) wide and 250–300 miles (400–480 km) deep, at a distance of 60–70 miles (96–112 km) behind the front. The forces assigned to this duty in 1943 were so-called "light" divisions. Each comprised two infantry regiments, one artillery regiment, one signal corps company, one engineering company, and logistic units with a stronger medical corps unit. With outdated weapons, they also suffered from manpower shortages. The vast territory assigned to them compelled each division to operate as an independent unit. Divided into smaller garrisons at crucial points, they built fortified bases, sometimes only a platoon, sometimes battalion strength. Under such conditions the central command of the "Hungarian Occupational Group" in

Kiev could not provide effective leadership. Still, the Hungarian troops fulfilled their duties and stood fast against partisan attacks.

The underequipped, undermanned light divisions faced an enemy which was unexpectedly strong. The Hungarian divisions searched out, attacked, and annihilated the most dangerous and strongest partisan bases. These bases were well fortified, supplied by air, and settled in thick, unapproachable forests or marshes.

The most "modern" and best-equipped unit of the Hungarian Army was the Gyorshadtest ("fast-moving army corps"). It was only partly mechanized. Each of the two motorized brigades of this mechanized corps had a reconnaissance battalion with small and medium tanks; two motorized infantry battalions, two bicycle battalions, one medium-caliber howitzer division, and one antiaircraft battery. Supporting engineering, communication, and supply troops enabled the brigades to perform as independent tactical units.

Typical organization of an Hungarian light infantry division was as follows:
- Infantry Brigade, *with two Infantry Regiments, each with three Battalions and a Weapons Company*
- Artillery Regiment
- Cavalry Troop
- Antiaircraft Company
- Signals Company
- Reconnaissance Battalion (from 1942)

Total strength: 11,000

Divisional Firepower
- Antitank weapons
- 37mm antitank guns: *80*

Artillery
- Artillery pieces: *24*

Typical organization of an Hungarian mobile corps in 1941 was as follows:
- Two Motorized Brigades, *each with three Motorized Regiments*
- Motorized Artillery Group
- Two Cycle Battalions
- Reconnaissance Battalion
- Two Cavalry Brigades, *each with two Cavalry Regiments*
- Cavalry Motorized Artillery Group

Total strength: 24,000

Typical organization of an Hungarian armored division in 1943 was as follows:
- Reconnaissance Battalion
- Armored Regiment
- Motorized Infantry Regiment
- Artillery Regiment
- Antitank Battalion
- Engineer Battalion

Typical organization of an Hungarian security division in 1941 was as follows:
- Two Infantry Regiments
- Artillery Battery
- Cavalry Squadron

Romanian Infantry Division

The infantry division was organized after the German model: three infantry regiments; one partially motorized reconnaissance group; one antitank company (6 x 47mm Schneider model 1936); a pioneer battalion; and two artillery regiments. It had a total of 17,500 men.

During 1941, several reserve divisions were formed: the 25th, 27th, 30th, 31st, 32d, and 35th. Only the 35th Reserve Infantry Division actually took part in the battles for Bessarabia. They had the same organization as the normal divisions, but were formed from the recently mobilized regiments: 41st-81st, 111th, and 112th, which were equipped with older weapons. There was also the 1st Fortification Division.

The infantry regiments (1st-40th, 82d-96th) and the "Vanatori" (hunters) regiments (1st-10th), from which the active divisions were organized, had the same structure. The name was only a 19th century tradition. Each regiment consisted of three battalions (each battalion of three companies, each company of three platoons, each platoon of three sections), a heavy weapons company (an 81.4mm Brandt mortar platoon, a 37mm Bofors antitank gun platoon, and a 47mm Schneider antitank gun platoon; each one with 6 artillery pieces), and a reconnaissance company. At battalion level, there was also a heavy weapons company (a machine gun platoon and one mortar platoon).

In 1941, Romanian infantry divisions fought well enough against a demoralized and retreating Red Army, but, when on the defensive, their lack of heavy, modern weapons, especially effective antitank guns, resulted in them suffering heavy losses.

On September 4, 1939, 18 new mixed artillery regiments were formed for the 9 infantry divisions newly created, as well as 19 independent heavy artillery battalions. Subsequently, the 12th and the 34th Heavy Artillery Battalions were combined into the 10th Horse-drawn Heavy Artillery Regiment. During the course of World War II, six heavy artillery battalions of fortification were also created.

Motorization of the Romanian artillery was initiated in 1937, when, at the fall maneuvers, the field guns were towed by Fiat tractors and the 150mm howitzers were towed by Skoda tractors. The first motorized heavy artillery batteries were formed in 1938, and in two years (1938-1940) almost the entire heavy artillery (eight regiments and six battalions) was motorized.

Typical organization of a 1941 Romanian infantry division was as follows:

- Reconnaissance Company
- Three Infantry Regiments, *each with three battalions (at right)*
- Artillery Regiment, *with two Artillery Battalions*
- Antitank Company
- Pioneer Battalion

Total strength: 17,500

Romanian Mountain Divisions

 The *vanatori de munte* (mountain hunters) units were created in November 1916 and represented the elite troops of the Romanian infantry. On June 22, 1941, the Mountain Corps consisted of four brigades (1st–4th) made up of 12 groups (1st–12th), each with two battalions. There were 24 battalions (1st–24th), out of which the first 16 were active units, very well trained and armed, and the rest (17th–24th) were formed after the general mobilization and were of lower quality. Thus, the 4th Mountain Brigade (created in 1939) was never able to match the other brigades.

A mountain brigade had the following structure: six battalions, one mountain artillery group (one or two battalions of 75mm or 76.2mm mountain guns and one battalion of 100mm mountain howitzers), and one mountain pioneer battalion. At the beginning of World War II, the Mountain Corps was made up of the 1st, 2d, and 4th Mountain Brigades. The 3rd Mountain Brigade was stationed on the frontier with Hungary. At the end of the 1941 campaign on the Eastern Front, the 2d Mountain Brigade was brought back to Romania and the 1st and 4th Mountain Brigades remained in the Crimea. During the winter, an Expeditionary Skier Group was formed from some troops of the 3rd Mountain Brigade. The 5th and 6th Mountain Battalions became the 25th and 26th Skier Battalions. The Group also had a communications platoon, a pioneer platoon, an antiaircraft gun platoon (4 x 20mm), an antitank gun company (6 x 47mm), and a 75mm mountain howitzer battalion. For transportation, the Group had 60 donkeys, 60 sleds, and 6 trucks. In January 1942, the Skier Group was sent to the Crimea and subordinated to the 1st Mountain Brigade, but soon it was put under the direct command of the Eleventh German Army and used in the area around Izyum.

Typical organization of a 1944 Romanian mountain division was as follows:

- Reconnaissance Company
- Two Infantry Regiments, *each with three battalions*
- Three Artillery Battalions and an Artillery Battery
- Antitank Company
- Pioneer Company

Total strength: 15,900

Romanian Cavalry Division

 At the beginning of the war, there were 26 cavalry regiments in the Romanian Army: 12 rosiori regiments; 13 calarasi regiments; and the Horse Guard Regiment. These names were a 19th century tradition. The rosiori were the regular cavalry, the elite of the Romanian Army. The calarasi were the territorial cavalry. After World War I, the differences between them disappeared and only the names remained.

The 12 rosiori regiments (1st–12th) and 6 calarasi regiments (2d, 3rd, 5th, 9th, 11th, and 13th) formed 6 cavalry brigades (1st, 5th–9th). The other seven calarasi regiments were divided among the large units and formed their reconnaissance groups. Each corps had a cavalry battalion and each division a cavalry squadron attached to it.

In 1941, the process of motorization started. The aim was to have one motorized regiment out of three per brigade. The lack of vehicles meant that only three brigades were partially motorized before the war began. These were the 5th, 6th, and 8th Cavalry Brigades, which formed the Cavalry Corps that was subordinated to the Third Army during the 1941 campaign. A motorized brigade was made up from one motorized cavalry regiment, two cavalry regiments, one horse artillery regiment (two battalions of two 75mm howitzer batteries each), one motorized 81.4mm mortar squadron, one motorized antitank and antiaircraft gun squadron, one motorized machine gun squadron, one motorized pioneer squadron, one motorized communications squadron, and one mechanized reconnaissance squadron (two light tank platoons of three tanks each, one motorized cavalry platoon, one motorcycle platoon). Such a brigade had 204 light machine guns, 24 heavy machine guns, 20 x13.2mm antiaircraft machine guns, 7 x 60mm Stokes mortars, 12 x 81.4mm Brandt model 1927/31 mortars, 20 x 37mm antitank guns, 16 x 75mm field guns, and 6 R-1 tanks. A second category was made up from the 1st, 7th, and 9th Cavalry Brigades.

Typical organization of a 1942 Romanian cavalry division was as follows
- Reconnaissance Squadron
- Three Mounted Cavalry Regiments (at right)
- Artillery Regiment
- Antitank Company
- Pioneer Company

Total strength: 6,500

Divisional Firepower

Antitank weapons
- 37mm antitank guns: *9*

Artillery
- 75mm field guns: *16*

French Army Divisions

In 1940, a French infantry division was made up of three infantry regiments (each one having a headquarters company, a weapons company, and three battalions), one cavalry unit tasked with reconnaissance, one antitank company (12 x 25mm antitank guns), one light field artillery regiment with three groups of 12 x 75mm guns each (plus an antitank and antiaircraft company to protect the field guns from enemy tanks and aircraft), one heavy field artillery regiment (two groups of 12 x 105mm howitzers and 12 x 150mm field guns), two engineer companies, two signals companies, two transport companies, one ammunition company, one medical group, and divisional services.

On paper, an infantry division, the backbone of the French Army, was a formidable fighting machine. But in reality things were far from satisfactory. For one thing, some Type B reserve infantry divisions, such as those in the Sedan sector in 1940, had only one mixed artillery regiment with four groups of 12 x 75mm guns and one group of 12 x 155mm howitzers. With regard to the infantrymen themselves there were glaring problems. For example, each 12-man infantry squad had a mixture of rifles and machine guns. Unfortunately, the rifles fired 7.5mm ammunition, whereas the machine guns fired 8mm rounds. This meant the squad had to carry two calibers of ammunition. In addition, French artillery was also sadly deficient. German General Heinz Guderian had this to say of French gunners in 1940: "Their shooting was not adaptable enough, and their speed in putting down strong concentrations of fire fell far short of the standard required in a war of movement. What was more, they had not developed forward observation techniques to anything like the same extent as we had, nor were their specialists in this field of the same quality as our own observation battalions."

The most effective French units were those of the Foreign Legion. For example, during the fighting around Narvik in 1940, the Foreign Legion's 1st battalion (I/13e DBLE) spearheaded assault landings at Bjerkvik and near Narvik in May 1940 that succeeded in overcoming tough German defenses in both cases. The I/13 DBLE had been formed from various African garrisons just two months before the Narvik campaign, but included a hard-core of desert veterans, as well as Spaniards with recent experience in the Spanish Civil War. Sadly for the French, such units were in short supply at the start of World War II.

Typical organization of a French infantry division was as follows:
- Three Infantry Regiments, *each with three Battalions*
- HQ Company
- Weapons Company
- Two Artillery Regiments
- Reconnaissance Group
- HQ Squadron
- Motorcycle Squadron
- Weapons Squadron
- Horse Squadron
- Telephone Radio Company
- Two Engineer Companies
- Antitank Company

Total strength: 17,500

Divisional firepower
- Light machine guns: *360*
- Heavy machine guns: *360*

Antitank weapons
- 25mm antitank guns: *34*
- 47mm antitank guns: *6*

Mortars
- Light mortars: *27*
- Heavy mortars: *24*

Artillery
- 75mm field guns: *36*
- 105mm howitzers: *12*
- 155mm field guns: *12*

Typical organization of a French armored division was as follows:
- Brigade de Combat, *with two Demi-Brigades and two Tank Battalions*
- Chasseur Battalion
- Weapons Company
- Three Rifle Companies
- Engineer Company

Total strength: 6,510

Divisional firepower
- Char B tanks: *68*
- Hotchkiss tanks: *90*

French Army Divisions

Antitank weapons
- 25mm antitank guns: *12*
- 37mm antitank guns: *84*
- 47mm antitank guns: *71*

Artillery
- 105mm howitzers: *25*

Transport
- Assorted vehicles: *1,100*
- Motorcycles: *400*

Typical organization of a French light mechanized division was as follows:
- Brigade de Combat, *with two Demi-Brigades, each with four Tank Squadrons*
- Artillery Regiment (below right)
- Reconnaissance Brigade
- Reconnaissance Regiment, *with two Motorcycle Squadrons and two Armored Car Squadrons*
- Dismounted Dragoon Regiment, *with three Battalions, each with two Rifle Squadrons*
- Engineer Battalion
- Armored Car Squadron
- Weapons Squadron
- Rifle Squadron

Total strength: 10,400

Divisional firepower
- Somua tanks: *80*
- Hotchkiss tanks: *80*
- Renault tanks: *60*
- Armored cars 40

Antitank weapons
- 37mm antitank guns: *80*
- 47mm antitank guns: *90*

Artillery
- 75mm filed guns: *24*
- 105mm howitzers 12

Transport
- Assorted motor vehicles 1,800
- Motorcycles 1,500

Typical organization of a French light cavalry division was as follows:
- Cavalry Brigade
- Two Cavalry Regiments
- Mechanized Brigade
- Three Motorcycle Squadrons
- Armored Car Squadron
- Tank Squadron
- Mechanized Infantry Regiment

- Light Tank Squadron
- Two Weapons Squadrons
- Two Mechanized Infantry Squadrons

Divisional firepower
- Hotchkiss tanks: *12*
- Renault tanks: *20*
- Armored cars :*12*

Antitank weapons
- 47mm antitank guns: *8*

Artillery
- 75mm field guns: *12*
- 105mm howitzers: *12*

U.S. Infantry Division

 The United States mobilized 67 infantry divisions in World War II. They were the 1st–9th, 10th Mountain, 24th–38th, 40th–45th, 63rd, 65th, 66th, 69th–71st, 75th–81st, 83rd–91st, 92d, and 93rd Colored, 94th–100th, 102nd–104th, 106th, and American Infantry Divisions, 11th, 13th, 17th, 82nd, and 101st Airborne Divisions, and the 1st Cavalry Division, which was dismounted and utilized as infantry. Forty-two of the infantry divisions and four of the airborne divisions served in Europe and the Mediterranean, the remainder served in the Pacific.

The infantry regiment was organized with three battalions, 12 lettered companies (A–M, skipping J), an Infantry Cannon Company (first equipped with two halftrack-mounted 105mm howitzers and six halftrack-mounted 75mm howitzers or guns, and later with a towed, short-barreled 105mm howitzer), an Antitank (AT) Company (initially with 12 x 37mm and later 9 x 57mm AT guns), and a Service Company. The fourth company in each battalion (D, H, M) were heavy weapons companies with sustained-fire heavy machine guns and mortars. The regiment and each battalion also had a Headquarters Company. The regimental Headquarters Company included an Intelligence and Reconnaissance Platoon. The battalion Headquarters Company included an Ammunition and Pioneer (A&P, responsible for light engineering duties and for transporting ammunition forward to the line companies) Platoon and an AT Platoon (initially with 4 x 37mm AT guns and later with 3 x 57mm AT guns).

Typical organization of a 1943 United States infantry division was as follows:
- Reconnaissance Troop
- Three Infantry Regiments, *each with three Infantry Battalions, an Antitank Company, and a Cannon Company*
- Three Light Artillery Battalions
- Medium Artillery Battalion
- Engineer Battalion
- Signals Company

Total strength: 14,253

Divisional firepower
- Medium machine guns: *157*
- Heavy machine guns: *236*

Antitank weapons
- 57mm antitank guns: *57*

Mortars
- 60mm mortars: *90 (opposite, top)*
- 81mm mortars: *54*

Infantry guns
- Bazookas: *607*

Artillery
- 105mm howitzers: *54 (opposite, bottom)*

Transport
- All types of vehicles: *2,012*
- Halftracks: *5*

5th INFANTRY DIVISION (fall 1944)
"Red Diamond Division" (Major General S. Leroy Irwin)

Organic units
- 2d Infantry Regiment
- 10th Infantry Regiment
- 11th Infantry Regiment
- 5th Reconnaissance Troop (Mechanized)
- 7th Engineer Combat Battalion
- 5th Medical Battalion
- 5th Division Artillery
- 19th Field Artillery Battalion (105mm Howitzer)
- 46th Field Artillery Battalion (105mm Howitzer)
- 50th Field Artillery Battalion (105mm Howitzer)
- 21st Field Artillery Battalion (155mm Howitzer)
- Special Troops
- 705th Ordnance Light Maintenance Company
- 5th Quartermaster Company
- 5th Signal Company
- Military Police Platoon
- Headquarters Company
- Band

Attachments
- 449th Antiaircraft Artillery Battalion
- Battery D, 116th AAA Gun Battalion (Mobile)
- 735th Tank Battalion
- 3rd, 38th Cavalry Reconnaissance Squadrons
- 81st Chemical Mortar Battalion, 84th Chemical SG Company
- 150th Combat Engineer Battalion, 994th Engineer Treadway Bridging Company
- 537th, 509th Engineer Light Pontoon Companies, 160th Combat Engineer Battalion
- 989th Engineer Treadway Bridging Company
- 187th, 204th, 282d, 241st, 284th, 434th Field Artillery Battalions

U.S. Infantry Division

- 7th FA Observation Battalion
- 5th Ranger Infantry Battalion
- 3rd Battalion, 8th Infantry Regiment
- 818th, 774th Tank Destroyer Battalions

8TH INFANTRY DIVISION (fall 1944)
"Pathfinder Division"
"Arrow Division" (Major-General Donald A. Stroh)

Organic units
- 13th Infantry Regiment
- 28th Infantry Regiment
- 121st Infantry Regiment
- 8th Reconnaissance Troop (Mechanized)
- 12th Engineer Combat Battalion
- 8th Medical Battalion
- 8th Division Artillery
- 43rd Field Artillery Battalion (105mm Howitzer)
- 45th Field Artillery Battalion (105mm Howitzer)
- 56th Field Artillery Battalion (105mm Howitzer)
- 28th Field Artillery Battalion (155mm Howitzer)
- Special Troops
- 708th Ordnance Light Maintenance Company
- 8th Quartermaster Company
- 8th Signal Company
- Military Police Platoon
- Headquarters Company
- Band

Attachments
- 445th Antiaircraft Artillery Battalion (Mobile)
- 709th Tank Battalion
- 86th Chemical Mortar Battalion
- 174th, 196th, 402d Field Artillery Groups
- 2d Ranger Infantry Battalion
- 644th Tank Destroyer Battalion

35th INFANTRY DIVISION
"Sante Fe Division" (Major-General Paul W. Baade)

Organic units
- 134th Infantry Regiment
- 137th Infantry Regiment
- 320th Infantry Regiment
- 35th Reconnaissance Troop (Mechanized)
- 60th Engineer Combat Battalion
- 110th Medical Battalion
- 35th Division Artillery
- 161st Field Artillery Battalion (105mm Howitzer)
- 216th Field Artillery Battalion (105mm Howitzer)
- 219th Field Artillery Battalion (105mm Howitzer)
- 127th Field Artillery Battalion (155mm Howitzer)
- Special Troops
- 735th Ordnance Light Maintenance Company
- 35th Quartermaster Company
- 35th Signal Company
- Military Police Platoon

- Headquarters Company
- Band

Attachments
- 448th, 459th, 116th Antiaircraft Battalions (Mobile)
- 69th, 737th Tank Battalions
- Company D, 32d Armored Regiment
- 44th, 212th Armored Infantry Battalions
- Troop B, 86th Cavalry Reconnaissance Squadron
- Company C, 25th Armored Engineer Battalion
- 4th Cavalry Reconnaissance Squadron
- 106th Cavalry Group
- 81st, 82d, 86th Chemical Mortar Battalions
- 183rd, 255th, 967th, 974th Field Artillery Battalions
- 29th Division Artillery
- 182d Field Artillery Group
- 654th, 821st, 691st Tank Destroyer Battalions

U.S. Armored Divisions

 A total of 16 U.S. armored divisions were eventually organized during World War II (1st–14th, 16th, and 20th). Of these, only two, the 2d and the 3rd, retained the "heavy" organization throughout the war. All of the other divisions were reorganized as light divisions prior to leaving the U.S. (except the 1st, which converted to the light organization while in Italy during July 1944). All of the armored divisions served in the West or in Italy.

The main battle tank issued to the U.S. Army during the war was the M4 Sherman, which was available in two main versions. The basic M4 was armed with a 75mm cannon and powered by a Continental R-975 radial engine. The up-armored, up-gunned, and up-powered M4A2 boasted a long-barreled 76mm cannon and twin GM diesels, with a top speed of 30 mph (48 kmh). Specialist versions of the Sherman were available in large numbers, including a close-support version fitted with a 105mm howitzer to neutralize soft targets, such as infantry, trucks, and antitank guns. There were also engineer and recovery versions, equipped with bulldozer blades and towing arms respectively.

These tanks were specially designed for the fast-moving type of armored warfare envisaged by generals such as Patton. They were reliable and fuel-efficient, allowing them to drive between 100 miles (160 km) and 120 miles (192 km) on a full tank of fuel. The Sherman, however, was not designed for head-to-head combat with heavy German Panther and Tiger tanks. These monster tanks could easily pick off a Sherman, even the up-armored M4A2, at ranges in excess of 3,280 ft (1,000 m). At these ranges, the American tank's guns stood little chance of penetrating the armor of its German opponents. Soon U.S. tank crews had dubbed their Shermans "Ronsons," after the famous cigarette lighter, due to their habit of exploding when hit by German 75mm and 88mm shells.

Typical organization of a 1943 United States armoured division was as follows:
- Reconnaissance Battalion
- Three Tank Battalions
- Three Armored Infantry Battalions
- Three Armored Field Artillery Battalions
- Engineer Battalion
- Signals company

Total strength: 10,937

Divisional firepower
- 30mm machine guns: *465*
- 50mm machine guns: *404*

Antitank weapons
- 57mm antitank guns 27

Mortars
- 60mm mortars: *63*
- 81mm mortars: *30*

Infantry guns
- Bazookas: *607*

Artillery:
- 105mm howitzers: *54*

Armor:
- Light tanks: *77*
- Medium tanks: *186 (opposite)*

Transport
- Halftracks: *501*
- Assorted vehicles: *2,653*

4th ARMORED DIVISION (fall 1944)
(Major General John Wood)

Organic units
- Headquarters Company
- Reserve Command
- Combat Command A
- Combat Command B
- 8th Tank Battalion
- 35th Tank Battalion
- 37th Tank Battalion
- 10th Armored Infantry Battalion
- 51st Armored Infantry Battalion
- 53rd Armored Infantry Battalion
- 25th Cavalry Recon Squadron (Mechanized)
- 24th Armored Engineer Battalion
- 144th Armored Signal Company
- 4th Armored Division Artillery
- 22d Armored Field Artillery Battalion
- 66th Armored Field Artillery Battalion
- 94th Armored Field Artillery Battalion
- 4th Armored Division Trains
- 126th Ordnance Maintenance Battalion
- 4th Armored Medical Battalion
- Military Police Platoon
- Band

U.S. Armored Divisions

Attachments
- 489th Antiaircraft Artillery Battalion
- Co A 86th Chemical Mortar Battalion
- 995th Engineer Treadway Bridging Company
- 77th, 179th, 191st, 216th, 219th, 253rd, 695th, 696th FA Battalions
- 5th, 177th Field Artillery Groups
- 13th, 137th, 319th, 230th Infantry Regiments
- 1st Battalion, 318th Infantry Regiment
- 2nd Battalion, 320th Infantry Regiment

5th ARMORED DIVISION (fall 1944)
"Victory" (Major General Lundsford E. Oliver)

Organic units
- Headquarters Company
- Reserve Command
- Combat Command A
- Combat Command B
- 10th Tank Battalion
- 34th Tank Battalion
- 81st Tank Battalion
- 15th Armored Infantry Battalion
- 46th Armored Infantry Battalion
- 47th Armored Infantry Battalion
- 85th Cavalry Recon Squadron (Mechanized)
- 22d Armored Engineer Battalion
- 145th Armored Signal Company
- 5th Armored Division Artillery
- 47th Armored Field Artillery Battalion
- 71st Armored Field Artillery Battalion
- 95th Armored Field Artillery Battalion
- 5th Armored Division Trains
- 127th Ordnance Maintenance Battalion
- 75th Armored Medical Battalion
- Military Police Platoon
- Band

Attachments
- 387th Antiaircraft Artillery Battalion
- 208th, 975th, 987th Field Artillery Battalions
- 400th Armored Field Artillery Battalion
- 628th Tank Destroyer Battalion

6th ARMORED DIVISION
"Super Sixth" (Major General Robert W. Grow)

Organic units
- Headquarters Company
- Reserve Command
- Combat Command A
- Combat Command B
- 15th Tank Battalion
- 68th Tank Battalion
- 69th Tank Battalion
- 9th Armored Infantry Battalion
- 44th Armored Infantry Battalion
- 50th Armored Infantry Battalion
- 86th Cavalry Recon Squadron (Mechanized)
- 25th Armored Engineer Battalion
- 146th Armored Signal Company
- 6th Armored Division Artillery
- 128th Armored Field Artillery Battalion
- 212th Armored Field Artillery Battalion
- 231st Armored Field Artillery Battalion
- 6th Armored Division Trains
- 128th Ordnance Maintenance Battalion
- 76th Armored Medical Battalion
- Military Police Platoon
- Band

Attachments
- 777th Antiaircraft Artillery Battalion
- 965th, 969th, 45th, 28th Field Artillery Battalions
- 83rd, 174th Armored Field Artillery Battalions
- 28th, 134th Infantry Battalions

U.S. Airborne Division

 Impressed by the successful employment of airborne troops by the Germans in their invasion of the Low Countries in 1940, U.S. military branches began an all-out effort to develop their own airborne units. The Air Corps made the most unique proposal. Its staff proposed that the Air Infantry be called "Air Grenadiers" and be members of the "Marines of the Air Corps."

In April 1940, the U.S. War Department approved plans for the formation of a test platoon of Airborne Infantry to form, equip, and train under the control of the Army's Infantry Board. In June, the Commandant of the Infantry School was directed to organize a test platoon of volunteers from Fort Benning's 29th Infantry Regiment. Later that year, the 2d Infantry Division was directed to conduct the necessary tests to develop reference data and operational procedures for air-transported troops. By the summer of 1944 the U.S. Army had formed five airborne divisions and six airborne regiments. By the end of World War II, the U.S. had used airborne troops in 14 major offensives and dozens of smaller operations. Anglo-American airborne forces mounted major assaults in Sicily in July 1943, Normandy in June 1944, and across the Rhine in March 1945. Smaller airborne landings occurred in North Africa in 1942 and in the Pacific.

Typical organization of a 1942 United States airborne division was as follows:
- Parachute Infantry Regiment, *with three Parachute Infantry Battalions*
- Two Glider Infantry Regiments, *each with three Glider Infantry Battalions*
- Parachute Field Artillery Battalion
- Airborne Antiaircraft Battalion
- Airborne Engineer Battalion
- Airborne Signals Company

Total strength: 8,505

Divisional firepower
- 30mm machine guns: *187*
- 50mm machine guns: *105*
- 37mm antiaircraft guns: *24*

Mortars
- 60mm mortars: *75*
- 81mm mortars: *36*

Infantry guns
- Bazookas: *182*

Artillery
- 75mm pack howitzers: *36*
- Flamethrowers: *27*

Transport
- Trucks: *385*

U.S. 82ND AIRBORNE DIVISION
Arnhem 1944
- Divisional HQ
- Commander: *Brigadier General James Gavin*
- Chief of Staff: *Colonel Robert Wienecke*

504th Parachute Infantry Regiment
- Commander: *Lieutenant Colonel Reuben Tucker*
1st Battalion
- Commander: *Major William Harrison*
2d Battalion
- Commander: *Lieutenant Colonel Edward Wellems*
3rd Battalion
- Commander: *Major Julian Cook*

505th Parachute Infantry Regiment
- Commander: *Lieutenant Colonel Ben Vandervoort*
1st Battalion
- Commander: *Major Talton Long*
2d Battalion
- Commander: *Major Vandervoort*
3rd Battalion
- Commander: *Major James Krause*

508th Parachute Infantry Regiment
- Commander: *Lieutenant Colonel Roy Lindquist*
1st Battalion
- Commander: *Lieutenant Colonel Shields Warren*
2d Battalion
- Commander: *Major Otho Holmes*
3rd Battalion
- Commander: *Lieutenant Colonel Louis Mendez*

325th Glider Infantry Regiment
- Commander: *Colonel Charles Billingslea*
1st Battalion
- Commander: *Lieutenant Colonel Teddy Sanford*
2d Battalion
- Commander: *Major Charles Major*

2d Battalion, 401st Glider Infantry Regiment
- Commander: *Major Osmond Leahy*

DIVISIONAL ARTILLERY
- Commander: *Colonel Francis March*

376th Parachute Field Artillery Battalion
- Commander: *Lieutenant Colonel Wilbur Griffith*

456th Parachute Field Artillery Battalion
- Commander: *Lieutenant Colonel Wagner d'Allesio*

319th Glider Field Artillery Battalion
- Commander: *Lieutenant Colonel James Todd*

320th Glider Field Artillery Battalion
- Commander: *Lieutenant Colonel Paul Wright*

80th Antitank Battalion
- Commander: *Colonel Raymond Sangleton*

U.S. Airborne Division

DIVISIONAL UNITS

307th Airborne Engineer Battalion
- Commander: *Colonel Edwin Bedell*

307th Airborne Medical Company
- Commander: *Major Jerry Belden*

Divisional Signals Company

Quartermaster Company

Ordnance Company

101ST AIRBORNE DIVISION
Arnhem 1944
- Divisional HQ
- Commander: *Major General Maxwell Taylor*
- Chief of Staff: *Colonel Gerald Higgins*

501st Parachute Infantry Regiment
- Commander: *Lieutenant Colonel Howard Johnson*
1st Battalion
- Commander: *Lieutenant Colonel Harry Kinnard*
2d Battalion
- Commander: *Major Robert Ballard*
3rd Battalion
- Commander: *Major Julian Ewell*

502nd Parachute Infantry Regiment
- Commander: *Lieutenant Colonel John H. Michaelis*
1st Battalion
- Commander: *Lieutenant Colonel Patrick Cassidy*
2d Battalion
- Commander: *Lieutenant Colonel Elbridge Chapman*
3rd Battalion
- Commander: *Lieutenant Colonel Robert Cole*

506th Parachute Infantry Regiment
- Commander: *Colonel Robert F. Sink*
1st Battalion
- Commander: *Lieutenant Colonel James LaPrade*
2d Battalion
- Commander: *Lieutenant Colonel Robert Strayer*
3rd Battalion
- Commander: *Major Oliver Horton*

327th Glider Infantry Regiment
- Commander: *Colonel Joseph P. Harper*
1st Battalion
- Commander: *Lieutenant Colonel Hartford Sallee*
2d Battalion
- Commander: *Lieutenant Colonel Thomas Rouzie*

1st Battalion, 401st Glider Infantry Regiment
- Commander: *Lieutenant Colonel Roy Allen*

DIVISIONAL ARTILLERY
- Commander: *Brigadier General Anthony McAuliffe*

377th Parachute Field Artillery Battalion
- Commander: *Lieutenant Colonel Harry Elkins*

321st Glider Field Artillery Battalion
- Commander: *Lieutenant Colonel Edward Carmichael*

907th Glider Field Artillery Battalion
- Commander: *Colonel Clarence Nelson*

81st Antitank Battalion
- Commander: *Lieutenant Colonel X. Cox*

DIVISIONAL UNITS

326th Airborne Engineer Battalion
- Commander: *Lieutenant Colonel John Pappas*

326th Airborne Medical Company
- Commander: *Major William Barfield*

426th Airborne Quartermaster Company

Signals Company
- Reconnaissance Platoon
- Military Police Platoon

U.S. Amphibious Corps

 The Battle of Iwo Jima in the Pacific (February–March 1945) represented the pinnacle of U.S. amphibious operations during World War II. This particular amphibious assault was the ultimate "storm landing," the Japanese term describing the American propensity for concentrating overwhelming force at the point of attack. The huge striking force was more experienced, better armed, and more powerfully supported than any other offensive campaign in the Pacific War. Vice Admiral Raymond A. Spruance's Fifth Fleet enjoyed total domination of air and sea around the small, sulfuric island, and the 74,000 Marines in the landing force would outnumber the Japanese garrison by three to one.

U.S. order of battle at Iwo Jima

UNITED STATES MARINE CORPS

V AMPHIBIOUS CORPS
(Major General Harry Schmidt)

3RD DIVISION (Major General Graves B. Erskine)
9th Regiment, Colonel Howard N. Kenyon
- 1st Battalion
- 2d Battalion
- 3rd Battalion

21st Regiment, Colonel Hartnoll J. Withers
- 1st Battalion
- 2d Battalion
- 3rd Battalion

12th Regiment [Artillery], Lieutenant Colonel Raymond F. Crist, Jr.
- 1st Battalion
- 2d Battalion
- 3rd Battalion
- 4th Battalion
- 3rd Tank Battalion
- 3rd Engineer Battalion
- 3rd Pioneer Battalion
- 3rd Service Battalion
- 3rd Motor Transport Battalion
- 3rd Medical Battalion
- 3rd Joint Assault Signal Company (JASCO)
- Marine Observation Squadron 1
- 3rd War Dog Platoon
- JICPOA Intelligence Team

4TH DIVISION (Major General Clifton B. Cates)
23rd Regiment, Colonel Walter W. Wensinger
- 1st Battalion
- 2d Battalion
- 3rd Battalion

24th Regiment, Colonel Walter I. Jordan
- 1st Battalion
- 2d Battalion
- 3rd Battalion

25th Regiment, Colonel John R. ("Pat") Lanigan
- 1st Battalion
- 2d Battalion
- 3rd Battalion

14th Regiment [Artillery], Colonel Louis G. De Haven
- 1st Battalion
- 2d Battalion
- 3rd Battalion
- 4th Battalion
- 4th Tank Battalion
- 4th Engineer Battalion
- 4th Pioneer Battalion
- 4th Service Battalion
- 4th Motor Transport Battalion
- 4th Medical Battalion
- 5th Amphibian Tractor Battalion
- 10th Amphibian Tractor Battalion
- 1st Joint Assault Signal Company (JASCO)
- Marine Observation Squadron 4
- 7th War Dog Platoon
- 1st Provisional Rocket Detachment
- JICPOA Intelligence Team

5TH DIVISION (Major General Keller E. Rockey)
26th Regiment, Colonel Chester B. Graham
- 1st Battalion
- 2d Battalion
- 3rd Battalion

27th Regiment, Colonel Thomas A. Wornham
- 1st Battalion
- 2d Battalion
- 3rd Battalion

28th Regiment, Colonel Harry B. Liversedge
- 1st Battalion
- 2d Battalion
- 3rd Battalion

13th Regiment [Artillery], Colonel James D. Waller
- 1st Battalion
- 2d Battalion
- 3rd Battalion
- 4th Battalion
- Service Troops
- 5th Tank Battalion
- 5th Engineer Battalion
- 5th Pioneer Battalion
- 5th Service Battalion
- 5th Motor Transport Battalion
- 5th Medical Battalion
- 3rd Amphibian Tractor Battalion
- 11th Amphibian Tractor Battalion
- 5th Joint Assault Signal Company (JASCO)
- Marine Observation Squadron 5
- 6th War Dog Platoon
- 3rd Provisional Rocket Detachment
- JICPOA Intelligence Team

U.S. Amphibious Corps

**V AMPHIBIOUS CORPS
(MAJOR ATTACHED UNITS)**
- Corps Troops Commander
- 1st Provisional Field Artillery Group
- 8th Field Depot
- Air Support Control Unit
- Signal Battalion
- Medical Battalion
- Provisional Signal Corps
- 2d Separate Engineer Battalion
- 2d Armored Amphibian Battalion
- Evacuation Hospital No. 1
- 2d Bomb Disposal Company
- Company B, Amphibious Reconnaissance Battalion
- Medical Section, Civil Affairs
- JICPOA Intelligence Team
- JICPOA Enemy Material and Salvage Platoon

**U.S. NAVY FIFTH FLEET
Admiral Raymond A. Spruance**

**TASK FORCE 58
Vice Admiral Marc A. Mitscher**
Carrier aircraft of TF 58 supported the Iwo Jima operation through diversionary strikes on the enemy homeland and supplied close air support at the objective. Fire support vessels of TF 58 also provided valuable firepower at Iwo Jima for several days commencing on D-Day.

Task Group 58.1, Rear Admiral Joseph J. Clark
- Carriers: *Hornet, Wasp, Bennington, Belleau Wood*
- Battleships: *Massachusetts, Indiana*
- Cruisers: *Vincennes, Miami, San Juan*
- 15 destroyers

Task Group 58.2, Rear Admiral Ralph E. Davison
- Carriers: *Lexington, Hancock, San Jacinto*
- Battleships: *Wisconsin, Missouri*
- Cruisers: *San Francisco, Boston*
- 19 destroyers

Task Group 58.3, Rear Admiral Frederick C. Sherman
- Carriers: *Essex, Bunker Hill, Cowpens*
- Battleships: *South Dakota, New Jersey*
- Cruisers: *Alaska, Indianapolis, Pasadena, Wilkes-Barre, Astoria*
- 14 destroyers

Task Group 58.4, Rear Admiral Arthur W. Radford
- Carriers: *Yorktown, Randolph, Langley, Cabot*
- Battleships: *Washington, North Carolina*
- Cruisers: *Santa Fe, Biloxi, San Diego*
- 17 destroyers

Task Group 58.5
- Carriers: *Enterprise, Saratoga*
- Cruisers: *Baltimore, Flint*
- 12 destroyers

**LOGISTIC SUPPORT GROUP
Rear Admiral Donald B. Beary**
This group was mainly used to resupply Task Force 58 with planes, ammunition, fuel, spare parts, and general supplies. It included:
- 15 escort carriers
- 1 cruiser
- 11 destroyers
- 18 destroyer escorts
- 33 tankers
- 4 ocean tugs
- 2 ammunition ships
- 1 general supply ship

Service Squadron 10, Commodore Worrall R. Carter
This squadron of more than 250 ships had headquarters at Ulithi and provided repairs and supplies for all vessels staging through Ulithi, Eniwetok, Guam, and Saipan.

UNITED STATES ARMY ASSAULT FORCES
- 471st Amphibian Truck Company (attached to 5th Marine Division)
- 473rd Amphibian Truck Company (attached to V Amphibious Corps)
- 476th Amphibian Truck Company (attached to 4th Marine Division)
- 138th Antiaircraft Artillery Group
- Headquarters Battery, 138th AAA
- 506th AA Gun Battalion
- 483rd AAAW Battalion
- 38th Field Hospital, Reinforced
- Detachment, 568th Signal Air Warning Battalion (attached to V Amphibious Corps)
- Detachments, 726th Signal Warning Company (attached to V Amphibious Corps, 4th & 5th Marine Divisions)
- Detachment, 49th Signal Construction Battalion
- Detachment 44, 70th Army Airways Communications Systems
- Detachment, Communications Unit 434
- 442d Port Company (attached to 4th Marine Division)
- 592d Port Company (attached to 5th Marine Division)
- Garrison Forces, Major General James E. Chaney
- Detachment, Island Command Headquarters
- Detachment, 147th Infantry Regiment
- Detachment, Headquarters 7th Fighter Command
- Detachment, Headquarters 15th Fighter Group
- 47th Fighter Squadron
- 78th Fighter Squadron
- 548th Night Fighter Squadron
- 386th Air Service Group, Special
- 1st Platoon, 604th Graves Registration Company
- 223rd Radar Maintenance Unit, Type C
- Port Director Detachment
- Garrison Beach Party

U.S. Marine Corps Division

 The basic structure of the division remained fairly constant during World War II. The core fighting power was built around three infantry regiments, and organic fire support came from an artillery regiment. Armored support came from the divisional tank battalion. The division had its own headquarters, engineer, motor transport, medical, pioneer, and service battalions. As the war progressed, each campaign brought new lessons learned and these were used to adapt and improve the Marine division's organization and structure. During World War II, the divisional size often swelled to over 25,000 men for major operations, especially later in the conflict. During the war, six Marine divisions served in combat.

Typical organization of a 1944 United States Marine Corps Division was as follows:

- Tank Battalion
- Three Infantry Regiments, *each with three Infantry Battalions*
- Weapons Company
- Artillery Regiment, *with four Artillery Battalions*
- Engineer Battalion
- Pioneer Battalion

Total strength: 17,455

Divisional firepower
- 30mm machine guns: *464*
- 50mm machine guns: *161*

Antitank weapons
- 37mm antitank guns: *36*
- 75mm antitank guns: *12*

Mortars
- 60mm mortars: *117*
- 81mm mortars: *36*

Infantry guns
- Bazookas: *172*

Artillery
- 105mm howitzers: *24*
- 75mm pack howitzers: *24*

Armor
- M4 tanks: *46*

Transport
- Assorted vehicles: *1,056*

Firepower of a late war Marine Corps division
- Carbine, .30 cal., M1: *10,371*
- Flamethrower, portable, M2-2: *108*
- Flamethrower, mechanized, M 3-4-3: *18*
- Gun, 37mm, antitank: *24*
- 105mm M7 motor carriage: *12*
- M1919A4 machine gun: *356*
- M1917A1 machine gun: *162*
- M2 HB machine gun: *161*
- M1A1 .45 submachine gun (below) *49*
- Howitzer, 155mm, M1: *12*
- Howitzer, 105mm, M2A1: *36*
- 2.36 in. rocket launcher, M9A1: *153*
- 60mm mortar: *117*
- 81mm mortar: *36*
- M1911A1 .45 cal. pistol: *1,707*
- Rifle, .30 cal., M1: *6,261*
- M1918A2 BAR: *867*
- Shotgun, 12 gauge: *306*
- M4 medium tank: *46*
- M4 medium tank, flamethrower: *9*
- M32B2 tank retriever: *3*

Bomber & Fighter Groups of The Eighth Air Force

During World War II, the Eighth Air Force was a United States Army Air Forces command and control organization, which primarily carried out strategic daytime bombing operations in Western Europe from airfields in eastern England from 1942 through to the end of the war in 1945. The order of battle given below is for January 1, 1945.

FIRST AIR DIVISION (all B-17)
1st Combat Wing
- 91st BG. Sqdns: *322d, 323rd, 324th, 401st*
- 381st BG. Sqdns: *532d, 533rd, 535th, 536th*
- 398th BG. Sqdns: *600th, 601st, 602d, 603rd*

40th Combat Wing
- 92d BG. Sqdns: *325th, 326th, 327th, 407th*
- 305th BG. Sqdns: *364th, 365th, 366th, 422d*
- 306th BG. Sqdns: *367th, 368th, 369th, 423rd*

41st Combat Wing
- 303rd BG. Sqdns: *358th, 359th, 360th, 427th*
- 379th BG. Sqdns: *524th, 525th, 526th, 527th*
- 384th BG. Sqdns: *544th, 545th, 546th, 547th*

94th Combat Wing
- 351st BG. Sqdns: *508th, 509th, 510th, 511th*
- 401st BG. Sqdns: *612th, 613th, 614th, 615th*
- 457th BG. Sqdns: *748th, 749th, 750th, 751st*

FIGHTER GROUPS
67th Fighter Wing
- 20th FG. Sqdns: *55th, 77th, 79th*
- 352d FG. Sqdns: *328th, 486th, 487th*
- 356th FG. Sqdns: *359th, 360th, 361st*
- 359th FG. Sqdns: *368th, 369th, 379th*
- 364th FG. Sqdns: *383rd, 384th, 385th*
- 495th FG. Sqdns: *551st, 552d (Training)*

SECOND AIR DIVISION (all B-24)
2d Combat Wing
- 389th BG. Sqdns: *564th, 565th, 566th, 567th*
- 445th BG. Sqdns: *700th, 701st, 702d, 703rd*
- 453rd BG. Sqdns: *732d, 733rd, 734th, 735th*

14th Combat Wing
- 44th BG. Sqdns: *66th, 67th, 68th, 506th*
- 392d BG. Sqdns: *576th, 577th, 578th, 579th*
- 491st BG. Sqdns: *852d, 853rd, 854th, 855th*
- 492d BG. Sqdns: *856th, 857th, 858th, 859th*

28th Combat Wing
- 93rd BG. Sqdns: *328th, 329th, 330th, 409th*
- 446th BG. Sqdns: *704th, 705th, 706th, 707th*
- 448th BG. Sqdns: *712th, 713th, 714th, 715th*
- 489th BG. Sqdns: *844th, 845th, 846th, 847th*

96th Combat Wing
- 458th BG. Sqdns: *752d, 753rd, 754th, 755th*
- 466th BG. Sqdns: *784th, 785th, 786th, 787th*
- 467th BG. Sqdns: *788th, 789th, 789th, 781st*

FIGHTER GROUPS
65th Fighter Wing
- 4th FG. Sqdns: *334th, 335th, 336th*
- 56th FG. Sqdns: *61st, 62d, 63rd*
- 355th FG. Sqdns: *354th, 357th, 358th*
- 361st FG. Sqdns: *374th, 375th, 376th*
- 479th FG. Sqdns: *434th, 435th, 436th*
- 496th FG. Sqdns: *554th, 555th (Training)*

THIRD AIR DIVISION (all B-17 after August 1944)
4th Combat Wing
- 94th BG. Sqdns: *331rd, 332d, 333rd, 410th*
- 447th BG. Sqdns: *708th, 709th, 710th, 711th*
- 486th BG. Sqdns: *832d, 833rd, 834th, 835th*
- 487th BG. Sqdns: *836th, 837th, 838th, 839th*

13th Combat Wing
- 95th BG. Sqdns: *334th, 335th, 336th, 412th*
- 100th BG. Sqdns: *349th, 350th, 351st, 418th*
- 390th BG. Sqdns: *568th, 569th, 570th, 571st*

45th Combat Wing
- 96th BG. Sqdns: *337th, 338th, 339th, 413th*
- 388th BG. Sqdns: *561st, 562d, 563rd, 564th*
- 452nd BG. Sqdns: *728th, 729th, 730th, 731st*

93rd Combat Wing
- 34th BG. Sqdns: *4th, 7th, 18th, 391st*
- 385th BG. Sqdns: *548th, 549th, 550th, 551st*
- 490th BG. Sqdns: *848th, 849th, 850th, 851st*
- 493rd BG. Sqdns: *860th, 861st, 862d, 863rd*

FIGHTER GROUPS
66th Fighter Wing
- 55th FG.. Sqdns: *38th, 338th, 343rd*
- 78th FG. Sqdns: *82d, 83rd, 84th*
- 339th FG. Sqdns: *503rd, 504th, 505th*
- 353rd FG. Sqdns: *350th, 351st, 352th*
- 357th FG. Sqdns: *362d, 363rd, 364th*

SPECIAL GROUPS
- 7th PhotoRecon Group. Sqdns: *13th, 14th, 22d, 27th*
- Special Operations Group. Sqdns: *36th ("Deception Sqdn"), 406th, 788th, 850th*

ABBREVIATIONS
- AD: Air Division
- BG: Bomb Group (*H*) (*heavy*)
- CBW: Combat Wing
- FG: Fighter Group
- Sqdn: Squadron

Bomber & Fighter Groups of The Eighth Air Force

Aircraft types
Fighter groups (4th Fighter Group)
- Spitfire V September 1942 to April 1943
- P-47C March 1943 to February 1944
- P-47D June 1943 to February 1944 (*at right, top*)
- P-51B February 1944
- P-51D June 1944
- P-51K December 1944

55th Fighter Group
- P-38H September 1943 to end December 1943
- P-38J December 1943 to July 1944
- P-51D from July 1944
- P-51K December 1944

Bomb groups (25th Bomb Group)
- B-17F September 1943 to May 1944
- B-17G from November 1943 (below)
- B-24J July 1944 to November 1944
- Mosquito XVI from April 1944 with the 653BS and 654BS
- B-26G: *654BS*

U.S. Fifth Fleet, June 1944

This order of battle is for the U.S. Fifth Fleet, commanded by Admiral Raymond A. Spruance, at the Battle of the Philippine Sea in June 1944. The Fifth Fleet consisted primarily of the landing forces ("Joint Expeditionary Force") under Vice Admiral R.K. Turner, and the fast carriers and their escorts (Task Force 58) under Vice Admiral Mitscher.

The battle consisted of a struggle between the Japanese carrier forces on one side, and Mitscher's Task Force 58 (and the American submarines) on the other.

TASK FORCE 58
Vice Admiral Marc A. Mitscher in carrier *Lexington*
- 7 fleet carriers, 8 light fleet carriers, 7 battleships, 8 heavy cruisers, 12 light cruisers, 67 destroyers.
- Task Force 58 was organized into four carrier groups, plus Vice Admiral Lee's Battle Line, as detailed below.

TASK GROUP ONE (TG58.1)
Rear Admiral J.J. Clark in carrier *Hornet*
- 2 fleet carriers, 2 light fleet carriers, 2 heavy cruisers, 2 light cruisers, 14 destroyers
- CV-12 *Hornet*: Air Group 2
- CV-10 *Yorktown*: Air Group 1
- CVL-24 *Belleau Wood*: Air Group 24
- CVL-29 *Bataan*: Air Group 50
- CA *Boston*
- CA *Canberra*
- CA *Baltimore*
- CL Antiaircraft light cruiser *Oakland*
- CL Antiaircraft light cruiser *San Juan*
- DD *Izard*
- DD *Bell*
- DD *Burns*
- DD *Conner*
- DD *Charrette*
- DD *Boyd*
- DD *Bradford*
- DD *Brown*
- DD *Cowell*
- DD *Maury*
- DD *Craven*
- DD *Gridley*
- DD *Helm*
- DD *McCall*

TASK GROUP TWO (TG38.2)
Rear Admiral A.E. Montgomery in carrier *Bunker Hill*
- 2 fleet carriers, 2 light fleet carriers, 1 heavy cruiser, 4 light cruisers, 12 destroyers
- CV-17 *Bunker Hill*: Air Group 8
- CV-18 *Wasp*: Air Group 14
- CVL-26 *Monterey*: Air Group 28
- CVL-28 *Cabot*: Air Group 31
- CL *Santa Fe*
- CL *Mobile*
- CL *Biloxi*
- DD *Miller*
- DD *Owen*
- DD *Stephen Potter*
- DD *The Sullivans*
- DD *Tingey*
- DD *Hickox*
- DD *Hunt*
- DD *Lewis Hancock*
- DD *Marshall*
- DD *Macdonough*
- DD *Dewey*
- DD *Hull*

TASK GROUP THREE (TG58.3)
Rear Admiral J.W. Reeves in carrier *Enterprise*
- 2 fleet carriers, 2 light fleet carriers, 1 heavy cruiser, 4 light cruisers, 13 destroyers
- CV-6 *Enterprise*: Air Group 10
- CV-16 *Lexington*: Air Group 16
- CVL-23 *Princeton*: Air Group 27
- CVL-30 *San Jacinto*: Air Group 51
- CA *Indianapolis*
- CL *Montpelier*
- CL *Cleveland*
- CL *Birmingham*
- DD *Clarence K. Bronson*
- DD *Cotten*

- DD *Dortch*
- DD *Gatling*
- DD *Healy*
- DD *Caperton*
- DD *Cogswell*
- DD *Ingersoll*
- DD *Knapp*
- DD *Anthony*
- DD *Wadsworth*
- DD *Terry*
- DD *Braine*

TASK GROUP FOUR (TG58.4)
Rear Admiral W.K. Harrill in carrier *Essex*
- 1 fleet carrier, 2 light fleet carriers, 4 light cruisers, 14 destroyers
- CV-9 *Essex*: Air Group 15
- CVL-25 *Cowpens*: Air Group 25
- CVL-27 *Langley*: Air Group 32
- CL *Vincennes*
- CL *Miami*
- CL *Houston*
- CL Antiaircraft light cruiser *San Diego*
- DD *Lansdowne*
- DD *Lardner*
- DD *McCalla*
- DD *Case*
- DD *Lang*
- DD *Sterett*
- DD *Wilson*
- DD *Ellet*
- DD *Charles Ausburne*
- DD *Stanly*
- DD *Dyson*
- DD *Converse*
- DD *Spence*
- DD *Thatcher*

TASK GROUP 58.7, Battle Line
Vice Admiral Willis A. Lee in battleship *Washington*
- 7 battleships, 4 heavy cruisers, 14 destroyers
- BB *Washington*
- BB *North Carolina*
- BB *Iowa*
- BB *New Jersey*
- BB *South Dakota*
- BB *Alabama*
- BB *Indiana*
- CA *Wichita*
- CA *Minneapolis*
- CA *New Orleans*
- CA *San Francisco*
- DD *Mugford*
- DD *Conyngham*
- DD *Bagley*
- DD *Patterson*
- DD *Selfridge*
- DD *Halford*
- DD *Fullam*
- DD *Hudson*
- DD *Guest*
- DD *Bennett*
- DD *Yarnall*
- DD *Monssen*
- DD *Twining*
- DD *Stockham*

KEY
CV: Fleet Carrier
CVL: Light Fleet Carrier
BB: Battleship
CA: Heavy Cruiser
CL: Light Cruiser
DD: Destroyer

U.S. Navy Fast Carrier Task Force

 From the start of the Pacific War, the U.S. fleet contained what are referred to as "fast carrier task forces." But the formation known as "The Fast Carrier Task Force" came into being in late 1943, after the arrival in the central Pacific of the first ships of the Essex and Independence classes. This force was the Pacific War's equivalent of the great gun-armed battlefleets of earlier conflicts. By the time of the Battle for Leyte Gulf, it had already proved itself to be one of the most potent instruments in the history of naval warfare, obliterating Japanese air power and sweeping enemy warships and merchant shipping from the seas.

It was divided into carrier task groups. Each group contained between three and five carriers, with each group having its own strong escort—a large number of cruisers and destroyers—and often two or more battleships. From early 1944, the Fast Carrier Force was known as Task Force 58 and Task Force 38.

FAST CARRIER TASK FORCE FIREPOWER

Vice Admiral Marc A. Mitscher's Fast Carrier Task Force, operating as part of the Third Fleet, made the first attack against Okinawa on October 10, 1944.

- 9 carriers
- 5 fast battleships
- 8 escort carriers
- 4 heavy cruisers
- 7 light cruisers
- 3 antiaircraft cruisers
- 58 destroyers

In one day, the task force delivered:
- 1,356 air strikes
- 652 rockets fired
- 21 torpedoes launched
- 541 tons (550 tonnes) of bombs dropped

This resulted in the following Japanese losses:
- 23 enemy aircraft shot down
- 88 destroyed on the ground
- 20 cargo ships sunk
- 45 smaller vessels sunk
- 4 midget submarines sunk
- 1 destroyer escort sunk,
- 1 submarine tender sunk
- 1 minesweeper sunk

U.S. Navy Air Groups

 Numerical designation of air groups began in 1942, the first being Carrier Air Group Nine (CVG-9), established in March 1942. The carrier air group was sometimes referred to as CAG. However, the official designation was CVG. Existing air groups continued to be known by their carrier names until they were reformed or disbanded, only two of the early groups escaping the latter fate. On June 29, 1944, U.S. Navy Carrier Air Groups were standardized for all commands under the following designations: CVBG, large carrier air group; CVG, medium carrier air group; CVLG, light carrier air group; and CVEG, escort carrier air group. The other CVE carrier classes were assigned Composite Squadrons (VC) and listed as air groups. They remained in that category throughout the war period. The CVBG designation was for assignment to the Midway Class carriers, sometimes referred to as the large carriers.

U.S. Navy Air Group

Originally, the air wing was called an air group and had a name, not a number; the air group title was based upon the carrier it was assigned to. For instance, an air group on CV-3 USS *Saratoga* would have simply been called the "Saratoga Air Group." In 1942, air groups lost the carrier name and began to be numbered.

The number given to each air group came from the hull number of the carrier to which it was assigned, i.e. CAG-3 for the "Saratoga Air Group" on CV-3 USS *Saratoga*, CAG-14 for the "Ticonderoga Air Group" on CV-14 USS *Ticonderoga*.

Typical air group
(Example is USS *Enterprise*, June 1942, seen below)

- 36 Douglas SBD-2/3 Dauntless
- 27 Grumman F4F-4 Wildcats
- 14 Douglas TBD-1 Devastators

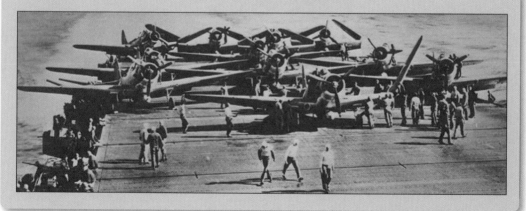

British 1939 and 1940 Infantry Divisions

 As with most armies, the British Army's organization was decided by its General Staff, in accordance with the available manpower and the army's doctrine. However, the detailed organization of units was prepared and proposed by the "owning" arm or service. Organizations were manifested in three main types of document: the War Office's Order of Battle (ORBAT) that established the number of formations and their composition in terms of the units they commanded in accordance with the General Staff's Policy Decisions; the unit War Establishment (WE) prepared by the "owning" arm or service, approved by the War Office's Establishments Committee, published by the Staff Duties branch and authorized by the Army Council; and the Unit Equipment Table (Army Form G1098), giving the entitlement of stores and equipment for the establishment and prepared by the "owning" arm or service directorate's staff quartermasters.

Changes to unit organization were often the result of General Staff policy decisions concerning the scales of equipment such as weapons, vehicles, and wirelesses, with Establishments and G1098 being subsequently amended.

British units had "peace" and "war" establishments, the former being called "reduced" prior to 1939.

War establishments were the full quota of men and equipment, while the first were reduced numbers appropriate to peacetime training. In 1939, regular and Territorial Army (TA) units in Britain, and most regular units overseas and west of India, were mobilized and brought up to war strength with reservists.

On the outbreak of World War II, the British prime minister, Neville Chamberlain, agreed to send a British Expeditionary Force to France. Under the command of General Lord John Gort, the force included four regular infantry divisions and 50 light tanks.

Following the German invasion of Poland in 1939, the British Expeditionary Force was sent to the Franco-Belgian border. By May 1940, when the German attack began, it consisted of 10 infantry divisions in three corps (I, II, and III), 1st Army Tank Brigade, and an RAF detachment of about 500 aircraft, the BEF Air Component. Also in France was a separate long-range RAF force, the Advanced Air Striking Force (AASF). Commanded by General Lord Gort, although constituting only a tenth of the defending Allied force, it sustained heavy losses during the German advance and most of the remainder (roughly 330,000 men) were evacuated from Dunkirk between May 26 and June 4, 1940, leaving much of their equipment behind.

Typical organization of a 1939 British infantry division was as follows:
- Cavalry Regiment
- Three Infantry Brigades, *with three Infantry Battalions and an Antitank Company*
- Three Field Artillery Regiments
- Antitank Regiment
- Three Royal Engineers Field Companies and a Field Park Company
- Divisional Signals Company

Total strength: 13,863

Divisional firepower
- light machine guns: *644*
- heavy machine guns: *56*

Antitank weapons
- 25mm antitank guns: *27*
- antitank rifles: *24*
- 2-pdr antitank guns: *48*

Mortars
- 2in mortars: *108*
- 3in mortars: *18*

Artillery
- 18/25-pdr guns: *72*

Armor
- Light tanks: *28*

Transport
- Carriers: *140*
- Vans and trucks: *864*
- Lorries and tractors: *844*

1st Infantry Division in France 1940
- Major General The Hon. H. R. L. G. Alexander

1st Guards Brigade (Brigadier M. B. Beckwith-Smith)
- 3rd Battalion, Grenadier Guards
- 2nd Battalion, Coldstream Guards

- 2nd Battalion The Hampshire Regiment

2nd Brigade (Brigader C. E. Hudson)
- 1st Battalion, The Loyal Regiment
- 2nd Battalion, The North Staffordshire Regiment
- 6th Battalion, The Gordon Highlanders

3rd Brigade (Brigadier T. N. F. Wilson)
- 1st Battalion, The Duke of Wellington's Regiment
- 2nd Battalion, The Sherwood Foresters
- 1st Battalion, The King's Shropshire Light Infantry

Divisional Troops
- Royal Artillery
- 2nd, 19th, 67th Field Regiments; 21st Antitank Regiment
- Royal Engineers
- 23rd, 238th, 248th Field Companies; 6th Field Park Company

British 1941 and 1944 Infantry Divisions

The ultimate staying power of the battalion remained founded on its four rifle companies, subdivided into platoons and sections. Each rifle section was commanded by a corporal, and consisted of a rifle group of six men, and a gun group with a lance-corporal, gunner, and loader. The Thompson submachine gun was now being increasingly replaced by the British-made Sten. The Sten was a cheap, nasty, and initially unreliable item, and fired more controllable 9mm ammunition than the Thompson. It was also simple to produce and was cheaper to replace than repair. The six men of the rifle group were each now armed with the bolt-action Rifle No. 4, the more easily-produced version of the previous Lee-Enfield, still firing the powerful .303-inch round. While a perfectly sound weapon, like all bolt-action rifles it was handicapped by its relative slow rate of fire.

The company was commanded by a major, with a captain as his second-in-command. The rifle platoons lost their individual trucks in the 1943 reorganization. Company transport now became three 15-cwt trucks and one Jeep, while a Universal Carrier was added, with a Bren and 2in mortar on board. By 1944, rifle platoon commanders were provided with their own Sten guns. In the absence or loss of the officer, the sergeant would become the platoon leader.

Typical organization of a 1941 British infantry division was as follows:

- Armored Reconnaissance Regiment
- Machine Gun Battalion
- Three Infantry Brigades, *each with three Infantry Battalions*
- Three Field Artillery Regiments
- Antitank Regiment
- Light Antiaircraft Regiment
- Three Royal Engineers Field Companies and a Field Park Company
- Divisional Signals Company

Total strength 17,298

Divisional firepower
- Light machine guns: *819*
- Medium machine guns: *48*
- 40mm antiaircraft guns : *48*

Antitank weapons
- 2-pdr antitank guns: *48*

Mortars
- 2in mortars: *162*
- 3in mortars: *56*

Artillery
- 25-pdr guns: *72*

Armor
- Armored cars: *6*

Transport
- Carriers: *256*
- Motorcycles: *1,064*
- Vans and trucks: *994*
- Lorries and tractors: *1,164*

Typical organization of a 1944 British infantry division was as follows:

- Reconnaissance Regiment
- Machine Gun Battalion
- Three Infantry Brigades, *each with three Infantry Battalions*
- Three Field Artillery Regiments
- Antitank Regiment
- Light Antiaircraft Regiment
- Three Royal Engineers Field Companies, a Field Park Company, and a Bridging Platoon
- Divisional Signals Company

Total strength: 18,347

Divisional firepower
- Light machine guns: *1,262*
- Medium machine guns: *48*
- 20mm antiaircraft guns: *71*
- 40mm antiaircraft guns: *54*
-

Antitank guns
- PIAT guns: *436*

Mortars
- 2in mortars: *283*
- 3in mortars: *60*

Armor
- Armored cars: *31*

Transport
- Carriers: *595*
- Trucks: *881*
- Lorries and tractors: *1,261*
- Motorcycles: *983*

British Armored Divisions

 TANKS The range of tanks that served with the division was quite large, starting with the Matilda II (Infantry Tank), the MK 6 Light Tank, and then the A9, A10, and A13 Cruiser Tanks. The most powerul gun fitted to these tanks was the 2-pdr, which had little impact on German tanks, but later on when the Valentine and Crusader made their appearance, they were eventually armed with the 6-pdr. The British-produced tanks were to be followed by the U.S.-supplied Stuart (37mm gun), Grant (37mm and 75mm guns), and Sherman (75mm gun). The latter was also modified by fitting a 17-pdr gun, to become the Sherman Firefly.

Toward the end of the war, the British Cromwell (75mm gun) and Challenger tanks (17-pdr gun), became the mainstay of the division, with a few Chaffee tanks (76mm gun) serving in the reconnaissance units. Finally, the armored division was supplied with the Comet tank after the end of World War II, but used them as part of the Berlin Victory Parade in July 1945.

ARTILLERY REGIMENTS, (INCLUDING ANTITANK, TANK DESTROYERS, AND ANTIAIRCRAFT) At the start of World War II, the majority of artillery units were equipped with the 18-pdr Field Gun, which was of World War I vintage (converted to towing by a tractor unit), or with 3.7in howitzers. The other field gun in service, which then became the standard weapon of the Royal Horse Artillery and Field Artillery units, was the versatile 25-pdr howitzer. This excellent piece of ordnance was even capable of antitank fire. During the course of the war, a number of tractor units were used, but by far the most widely used was the "Quad," plus a limber, for the field artillery, while the Morris CDSW 6x4 Tractor was used for the light antiaircraft guns.

As the war progressed and became increasingly mechanized, there was a clear need for the artillery support to become mechanized too. This was achieved initially by the "Bishop" Self-Propelled Gun (SPG), equipped with a 25-pdr, and later the "Sexton" SPG (again equipped with a 25-pdr). Also, some 105mm U.S.-manufactured "Priests" were deployed within the SP artillery regiments.

At the start of the war, the heaviest antitank weapon available was the 2-pdr antitank gun, which had little effect against some of the heavier German tanks.

However, these were in short supply, so the Bofors Model 1936 antitank gun was also used in North Africa in the early stages of the war. By 1941, this was being replaced by the better 6-pdr antitank gun, which saw service through to the end of the war. This was deployed within both the infantry battalions and antitank regiments. Normally, the antitank guns were towed by normal lorries, but to make the guns more mobile they were carried "Portee" on the back of the vehicles, ready for action. This made them easier to move, but more susceptible to enemy fire. As the war progressed, the lighter antitank guns were towed by Bren Gun and Loyd Carriers.

In May 1942, the general outline of the British armored division that would serve until the end of the war was decided upon. Armored divisions in North Africa would continue to deploy a fluid organization until the end of the campaign in that theater, but their experience had shown that an increased infantry presence was required to assist the armored units.

As a result, armored divisions moved to one armored brigade, with its own motor battalion, and one infantry brigade, displaying only detail differences from that found in the infantry division. There were still many changes to come, however, in other parts of the armored division.

Reconnaissance was initially provided by an armored car regiment, but in early 1943 an experimental mix of cruiser tanks, scouts cars, and Universal carriers was tested. This proved somewhat unsatisfactory, and in late 1943 a new Armored Reconnaissance Regiment Type "B" was introduced, operating both light tanks and cruisers. This was used in Italy, but armored divisions in Northwest Europe went to war with their armored reconnaissance regiments organized on similar lines to their usual armoured regiments.

Self-propelled artillery had first been used in North Africa, with U.S. 105mm Priests. By late 1943, the British-Canadian 25-pdr RAM was being introduced. The Priest continued in service in Italy with British armored divisions, while the RAM was used throughout the Northwest European theater of war.

Armored divisions in Italy and Northwest Europe found it necessary to further amend their organization in the light of circumstances in their particular theater. This involved combined infantry/armor battle groups.

British Armored Divisions

Typical organization of a 1940 British armored division was as follows:

- Two Armored Brigades, *each with three armored regiments*
- Support Group with Motor Battalion, Royal Horse Artillery Regiment and Light Antiaircraft/Antitank Regiment
- Royal Engineers Field Squadron and Field Park Troop
- Divisional Signals Company

Total strength: 10,750

Divisional firepower
- Light machine guns: *475*
- 40mm antiaircraft guns: *24*
- Antitank rifles: *254*

Mortars
- 2in mortars: *364*

Artillery
- 25-pdr guns: *16*

Armor
- Close support tanks: *36*
- Cruiser tanks: *304*

Transport
- Carriers: *88*
- Vans and trucks: *602*
- Lorries and tractors: *858*

British Motor Battalion, circa 1940. When the 1st Armoured Division was rushed to France in May 1940, it was deployed in a decidedly fragmented fashion. Both of its Motor Battalions, plus an Armored Regiment, and other supporting elements, were rushed to defend the port of Calais, where the composite brigade they formed was subsequently captured at the end of May 1940.

- Battalion Headquarters: *(5 officers, 26 men)*
- Headquarter Company: *(5 officers, 116 men), comprised of:*
- Company HQ: *(1 officer, 5 men)*
- Signals Platoon: *(1 officer, 27 men)*
- Administrative Platoon: *(3 officers, 86 men)*

- Four Motor Companies: *(4 officers, 158 men), each comprised of:*
- Company HQ: *(2 officers, 28 men)*
- Scout Platoon: *(1 officer, 41 men)*
- One Motor Platoon, *comprised of:*
- Platoon HQ *(1 officer, 5 men)*
- Three Motor Sections, *each comprised of 8 men*
- Two Motor Platoons, *each comprised of:*
- Platoon HQ: *(6 men)*
- Three Motor Sections, *each comprised of 8 men*

Total strength of 800 all ranks (26 officers and 774 men)

Typical organization of a February 1942 Middle East British armored division was as follows:

- Armored Car Regiment
- Armored Brigade Group, *with three Armored Regiments, Motor Battalion Royal Horse Artillery Regiment and Light Antiaircraft Battery*
- Infantry Brigade Group, *with three Motor Battalions, a Royal Horse Artillery, or Light Antiaircraft Battery*

Typical organization of a British armored division in May, 1942, was as follows:

- Armored Car Regiment
- Armored Brigade, *with three Armored Regiments, and a Motor Battalion*
- Infantry Brigade, *with three Infantry Battalions*
- Field Artillery Regiment
- Antitank Regiment
- Light Antiaircraft Regiment
- Royal Engineers Field Squadron and Field Park Troop
- Divisional Signals Company

Total strength: 13,235

Divisional firepower
- Light machine guns: *860*
- 20mm antiaircraft guns: *52*
- 40mm antiaircraft guns: *36*

Antitank weapons
- 2- or 6-pdr antitank guns: *220*

Mortars
- 2in mortars: *60*
- 3in mortars: *18*

Artillery
- 25-pdr guns: *48*

Armor
- Stuart and Grant tanks, or Crusader and Grant tanks: *200*
- Armored cars: *64*

Transport
- Carriers : *151*
- Vans and trucks: *417*
- Lorries and tractors: *1,051*

The British Motor Battalion, 1941 to 1942

- Battalion Headquarters: *(5 officers, 26 men)*
- Headquarter Company: *(5 officers, 116 men), comprised of:*
- Company HQ: *(1 officer, 5 men)*
- Signals Platoon: *(1 officer, 27 men)*
- Administrative Platoon: *(3 officers, 86 men)*

- Four Motor Companies *(6 officers, 156 men), each comprised of:*
- Company HQ *(2 officers, 28 men)*
- Scout Platoon *(1 officer, 41 men)*

- Three Motor Platoons, *each comprised of:*
- Platoon HQ: *(1 officer, 5 men)*
- Three Motor Sections, *each comprised of 8 men*

Total strength of 800 all ranks (34 officers and 766 men)

British Armored Divisions

NORTH AFRICAN VARIATIONS, 1942–1943 (RIGHT)
By early 1942, British and Commonwealth units were reorganizing themselves to meet the demands of the new type of warfare emerging in the North African campaign. This led to a notable increase in the firepower of the Motor Battalions, bringing antitank guns, medium machine guns, and 3in mortars into their organization for the first time.

The Motor Battalion (Middle East) August 1942
- Battalion Headquarters: *(10 officers, 102 men)*
- Four Motor Companies: *(6 officers, 161 men), each comprised of:*
- Company HQ: *(2 officers, 42 men)*
- Scout Platoon: *(1 officer, 37 men)*
- Machine Gun Platoon: *(1 officer, 29 men)*
- Motor Platoon: *(1 officer, 23 men)*
- Antitank Platoon: *(1 officer, 30 men)*

Total strength of 780 all ranks (34 officers and 746 men)

The Motor Battalion (Middle East) October 1942
- Battalion Headquarters: *(10 officers, 110 men)*
- Three Motor Companies: *(6 officers, 158 men), each comprised of:*
- Company HQ: *(2 officers, 46 men)*
- Scout Platoon: *(1 officer, 37 men)*
- Machine Gun Platoon: *(1 officer, 29 men)*
- Two Motor Platoons *(each with 1 officer, 23 men)*
- Antitank Company: *(7 officers, 146 men)*
- Company Headquarters: *(3 officers, 30 men)*
- Four Antitank Troops: *(each with 1 officer, 29 men)*

Total strength of 765 all ranks (35 officers and 730 men)

1944 British Armored Division

 Toward the end of the war, the 17-pdr antitank gun was available to British divisions. This could knock out a German Tiger tank at a range of 1,000 yards (914 m), though the Tiger could knock out a Sherman at twice this range. This was the gun fitted to the British Sherman Firefly and Challenger tanks, and also the Achilles/Wolverine tank destroyers. It was a good gun, but it was unfortunate for the British Army that it was not introduced earlier.

Antiaircraft defense was provided mainly by the famous 40mm Bofors Gun, but, for a while, captured 20mm Breda guns were also used, and just before the end of the war, M16 Quad 0.5in Browning halftracks were also in use.

From 1944, German mortars were becoming a significant threat and so counter-mortar batteries were formed, using sound detection equipment and radar to help locate them, ready for counter-bombardment.

Typical organization of a 1944 British armored division was as follows:

- Armored Reconnaissance Regiment
- Machine Gun Company
- Armored Brigade, *with three Armored Regiments and a Motor Battalion*
- Infantry Brigade, *with three Infantry Battalions*
- Field Artillery Regiment
- Antitank Regiment
- Light Antiaircraft Regiment
- Royal Engineers Field Squadron and Field Park Squadron
- Divisional Signals Company

Total strength: 14,964

Divisional firepower
- Light machine guns: *1,376*
- Medium machine guns: *22*
- 20mm antiaircraft guns: *18*
- 40mm antiaircraft guns: *36*

Antitank weapons
- 6-pdr antitank guns: *30*
- 17-pdr antitank guns: *48*
- PIAT guns: *302*

Mortars
- 2in mortars: *132*
- 3in mortars: *24*
- 4.2in mortars: *4*

Artillery
- 25-pdr field guns: *24*

Armor
- Light tanks: *63*
- Cruiser tanks: *246 (at right)*

Transport
- Carriers: *261*
- Trucks: *789*

- Lorries and tractors: *1,453*
- Motorcycles: *853*

British Airborne Division

Typical organization of a 1944 British airborne division was as follows:

Airborne Armored Reconnaissance Regiment
- Independent Parachute Company
- Parachute Brigade, *with three Parachute Battalions*
- Air-Landing Brigade, *with three Air-Landing Battalions*
- Air-Landing Light Artillery Regiment
- Air-Landing Antitank Regiment
- Royal Engineers Parachute Squadron, and Airborne Field Company and Field Park Company
- Divisional Signals Company

Total strength: 12,148

Divisional firepower
- Light machine guns: *966*
- Medium machine guns: *46*
- 20mm antiaircraft guns: *23*

Antitank weapons
- PIAT guns: *392*
- 6-pdr antitank guns: *84*
- 17-pdr antitank guns: *16*

Mortars
- 2in mortars: *474*
- 3in mortars: *56*

Artillery
- 75mm pack howitzers: *27*
- Flamethrowers: *38*

Armour
- Light tanks: *11*
- Cruiser tanks: *11*

Transport
- Carriers: *25*
- Bicycles: *3,269*
- Motorcycles: *1,233*
- Jeeps: *904*
- Trucks: *129*
- Lorries and tractors: *464*

1ST AIRBORNE DIVISION
Order of battle, Arnhem, September 1944

Divisional HQ and Defense Platoon
- Commander: *Major-General Roy Urquhart*
- GSO 1 (Operations): *Lieutenant Colonel Charles Mackenzie*
- GSO 2 (Air): *Major David Madden*
- GSO 2 (Intelligence): *Major Hugh Maguire*
- Commander Royal Artillery: *Lieutenant Colonel Robert Loder-Symonds*
- Commander Royal Engineers: *Lieutenant Colonel Eddie Myers*
- Commander Royal Electrical and Mechanical Engineers: *Captain A. F. Ewens*
- Commander Royal Army Service Corps: *Lieutenant Colonel Michael Packe*
- Assistant Adjutant and Quartermaster-General: *Lieutenant Colonel Henry Preston*
- Assistant Director of Medical Services: *Colonel Graeme Warrack*
- Assistant Director of Ordnance Services: *Lieutenant Colonel Gerald Mobbs*
- Assistant Provost Marshal: *Major O. P. Haig*
- Defense Platoon: *Lieutenant A. D. Butterworth*

Based at Fulbeck Hall. Flew in 7 C-47s from Barkston Heath and Saltby, and 29 Horsa gliders from Fairford, Down Ampney, and Manston.
- Went in: *142 men*
- Died: *14*
- Evacuated: *70*
- Missing: *58*

1ST PARACHUTE BRIGADE
Brigade HQ and Defense Platoon
- Commander: *Brigadier Gerald Lathbury*
- Brigade Major: *Major Tony Hibbert*

Based at Syston Old Hall. Flew in 9 C-47s from Barkston Heath, and 8 Horsa gliders from Blakehill Farm.
- Went in: *82 men*
- Died: *5*
- Evacuated: *3*
- Missing: *74*

1st Parachute Battalion
- Commander: *Lieutenant Colonel David Dobie*
Headquarters/Support Company
- Signals Platoon
- Assault Platoon
- Mortar Platoon
- Medium Machine Gun Platoon
- R Company
- No. 1 Platoon
- No. 2 Platoon
- No. 3 Platoon
- S Company
- No. 5 Platoon
- No. 6 Platoon
- No. 7 Platoon
- T Company
- No. 9 Platoon
- No. 10 Platoon
- No. 11 Platoon

Based at Grimsthorpe Castle and Bourne. Flew in 34 C-47s from Barkston Heath, vehicles in 7 Horsa gliders from Keevil and a Hamilcar from Tarrant Rushton.
- Went in: *548*
- Died: *82*
- Evacuated: *89 or 108 (reports differ)*
- Missing: *377 or 358*

2nd Parachute Battalion
- Commander: *Lieutenant Colonel John Frost*
Headquarters Company
- Signals Platoon
- Support Company
- Assault Platoon
- Mortar Platoon
- Medium Machine Gun Platoon
- A Company
- No. 1 Platoon
- No. 2 Platoon
- No. 3 Platoon
- B Company
- No. 4 Platoon
- No. 5 Platoon
- No. 6 Platoon
- C Company
- No. 7 Platoon
- No. 8 Platoon
- No. 9 Platoon

British Airborne Division

Based at Stoke Rochford and Grantham. Flew in 34 C-47s from Saltby, vehicles in 7 Horsas from Keevil, and a Hamilcar from Tarrant Rushton.
- Went in: *525 men*
- Died: *57*
- Evacuated: *16*
- Missing: *452*

3rd Parachute Battalion
- Commander: *Lieutenant Colonel J. Fitch*

Headquarters Company
- Signals Platoon
- Assault/Pioneer Platoon
- Mortar Platoon
- Medium Machine Gun Platoon
- A Company
- No. 1 Platoon
- No. 2 Platoon
- No. 3 Platoon
- B Company
- No. 4 Platoon
- No. 5 Platoon
- No. 6 Platoon
- C Company
- No. 7 Platoon
- No. 8 Platoon
- No. 9 Platoon

Based at Spalding. Flew in 34 C-47s from Saltby, vehicles in 7 Horsas from Keevil, and a Hamilcar from Tarrant Rushton.
- Went in: *588 men*
- Died: *65*
- Evacuated: *28*
- Missing: *495*

1st Airlanding Antitank Battery, RA
- Commander: *Major Bill Arnold*
- A Troop
- B Troop
- C Troop
- D Troop
- P Troop
- Z Troop

Based at Heckington and Helpringham, with P Troop at Tarrant Rushton. Flew in 30 Horsas from Manston (mostly) and Blakehill Farm, P Troop in 8 Hamilcars from Tarrant Rushton.
- Went in: *191 men*
- Died: *24*
- Evacuated: *52*
- Missing: *115*

1st Parachute Squadron, RE
- Commander: *Major Douglas Murray*
- A Troop
- B Troop
- C Troop

Based at Donington. Flew in 9 C-47s from Barkston Heath, and 4 Horsas from Keevil.
- Went in: *143 men*
- Died: *20*
- Evacuated: *13*
- Missing: *110*

16 Parachute Field Ambulance, RAMC
- Commander: *Lieutenant Colonel E. Townsend*

Based at Culverthorpe. Flew in 6 C-47s from Barkston Heath and Saltby, and 6 Horsas from Keevil.
- Went in: *135 men*
- Died: *6*
- Evacuated: *0*
- Missing: *129*

4TH PARACHUTE BRIGADE
Brigade HQ and Defense Platoon
- Commander: *Brigadier John Hackett*
- Brigade Major: *Major Charles Dawson*

Based at Knossington Grange. Flew in 8 C-47s from Spanhoe, and 1 C-47 with Advance Party from Barkston Heath, and 8 Horsas from Keevil.
- Went in: *86 men*
- Died: *12*
- Evacuated: *43*
- Missing: *31*

10th Parachute Battalion
- Commander: *Lieutenant Colonel Ken Smyth*

Headquarters Company: *Major Charles Ashworth*
- Signals Platoon
- Support Company
- Assault Platoon
- Mortar Platoon
- Medium Machine Gun Platoon
- A Company
- No. 3 Platoon
- No. 4 Platoon
- No. 5 Platoon
- B Company
- No. 10 Platoon

- No. 11 Platoon
- No. 12 Platoon
- D Company
- No. 16 Platoon
- No. 17 Platoon
- No. 18 Platoon

Based at Somerby, Thorpe Satchville, Burgh-on-the-Hill, and Twyford. Flew in 33 C-47s from Spanhoe, 1 C-47 with Advance Party from Barkston Heath, vehicles in 7 Horsas from Keevil, and a Hamilcar from Tarrant Rushton.
- Went in: *582 men*
- Died: *92*
- Evacuated: *86*
- Missing: *404*

11th Parachute Battalion
- Commander: *Lieutenant Colonel George Lea*

Headquarters Company
- Signals Platoon
- Support Company: *Captain Frank King*
- Assault Platoon
- Mortar Platoon
- Medium Machine Gun Platoon
- A Company
- No. 1 Platoon
- No. 2 Platoon
- No. 3 Platoon
- B Company
- No. 4 Platoon
- No. 5 Platoon
- No. 6 Platoon
- C Company
- No. 7 Platoon
- No. 8 Platoon
- No. 9 Platoon

Based at Melton Mowbray. Flew in 33 C-47s from Saltby, 1 C-47 with Advance Party from Barkston Heath, vehicles in 7 Horsas from Keevil, and 1 Hamilcar from Tarrant Rushton.
- Went in: *571 men*
- Died: *92*
- Evacuated: *72*
- Missing: *407*

British Airborne Division

156th Parachute Battalion
- Commander: *Lieutenant Colonel Sir Richard Des Voeux*

Headquarters Company
- Signals Platoon
- Support Company
- Antitank Platoon
- Mortar Platoon
- Medium Machine Gun Platoon
- A Company
- No. 3 Platoon
- No. 4 Platoon
- No. 5 Platoon
- B Company
- No. 6 Platoon
- No. 7 Platoon
- No. 8 Platoon
- C Company
- No. 9 Platoon
- No. 10 Platoon
- No. 11 Platoon

Based in and around Melton Mowbray. Flew in 33 C-47s from Saltby, 1 C-47 with Advance Party from Barkston Heath, vehicles in 7 Horsas from Keevil, and a Hamilcar from Tarrant Rushton.
- Went in: *621–625 men*
- Died: *98*
- Evacuated: *68*
- Missing: *455–459*

2nd (Oban) Airlanding Antitank Battery
- Commander: *Major A. Haynes*
- E Troop
- F Troop
- G Troop
- H Troop
- X Troop

Based at Harrowby. Flew in 24 Horsas from Blakehill Farm and 8 Hamilcars from Tarrant Rushton.
- Went in: *168 men*
- Died: *25*
- Evacuated: *37*
- Missing: *106*

4th Parachute Squadron, RE
- Commander: *Major Aeneas Perkins*
- No. 1 Troop
- No. 2 Troop
- No. 3 Troop

Based at Uppingham. Flew in 9 C-47s from Spanhoe, and 4 Horsas from Keevil.

- Went in: *155 men*
- Died: *19*
- Evacuated: *64*
- Missing: *72*

133 Parachute Field Ambulance, RAMC
- Commander: *Lieutenant Colonel W. Alford*

Based at Barleythorpe Hall. Flew in 6 C-47s from Spanhoe and Saltby, and 6 Horsas from Keevil.
- Went in: *129 men*
- Died: *6*
- Evacuated: *3*
- Missing: *120*

1ST AIRLANDING BRIGADE
- Brigade HQ and Defense Platoon
- Commander: *Brigadier Philip Hicks*
- Deputy Commander: *Colonel H. Barlow*
- Brigade Major: *Major C. A. H. B. Blake*

Based at Woodhall Spa. Flew in 11 Horsas from Broadwell.
- Went in: *69 men*
- Died: *7*
- Evacuated: *39*
- Missing: *23*

1st Battalion The Border Regiment
- Commander: *Lieutenant Colonel Tommy Haddon*

Headquarters Company
- Signals Platoon
- Pioneer Platoon
- Support Company
- Mortar Group
- No. 23 Mortar Platoon
- No. 24 Mortar Platoon

Antitank Group
- No. 25 Antitank Platoon
- No. 26 Antitank Platoon

Medium Machine Gun Group
- No. 27 Medium Machine Gun Platoon
- No. 28 Medium Machine Gun Platoon

A Company
- No. 7 Platoon
- No. 8 Platoon
- No. 9 Platoon
- No. 10 Platoon

B Company
- No.11 Platoon
- No.12 Platoon
- No.13 Platoon
- No. 14 Platoon

C Company
- No. 15 Platoon
- No. 16 Platoon
- No. 17 Platoon
- No. 18 Platoon

D Company
- No. 19 Platoon
- No. 20 Platoon
- No. 21 Platoon
- No. 22 Platoon

Based at Woodhall Spa, with B Company at Bardney. Flew in 56 Horsas from Broadwell and Blakehill Farm, and a Hamilcar from Tarrant Rushton.
- Went in: *788 men*
- Died: *121*
- Evacuated: *235*
- Missing: *432*

2nd Battalion South Staffs. Regiment
- Commander: *Lieutenant Colonel Derek McCardie*

Headquarters Company
- Signals Platoon
- Pioneer Platoon
- Support Company

Mortar Group
- No. 1 Mortar Platoon
- No. 2 Mortar Platoon

Medium Machine Gun Group
- No. 1 Medium Machine Gun Platoon
- No. 2 Medium Machine Gun Platoon

Antitank Group
- No. 1 Antitank Platoon
- No. 2 Antitank Platoon

A Company
- No. 7 Platoon
- No. 8 Platoon
- No. 9 Platoon
- No. 10 Platoon

B Company
- No. 11 Platoon
- No. 12 Platoon
- No. 13 Platoon
- No. 14 Platoon

C Company
- No. 15 Platoon
- No. 16 Platoon
- No. 17 Platoon
- No. 18 Platoon

D Company
- No. 19 Platoon
- No. 20 Platoon
- No. 21 Platoon
- No. 22 Platoon

British Airborne Division

Based at Woodhall Spa. Flew to Arnhem over two days in 62 Horsas from Manston and Broadwell, and a Hamilcar from Tarrant Rushton.
- Went in: *767 men*
- Died: *85*
- Evacuated: *124*
- Missing: *558*

7th (Galloway) Battalion The King's Own Scottish Borderers
- Commander: *Lieutenant Colonel Robert Payton-Reid*

Headquarters Company
- Signals Platoon
- Pioneer Platoon
- Support Company

Mortar Group
- No. 1 Mortar Platoon
- No. 2 Mortar Platoon

Medium Machine Gun Group
- No. 1 Medium Machine Gun Platoon
- No. 2 Medium Machine Gun Platoon

Antitank Group
- No. 1 Antitank Platoon
- No. 2 Antitank Platoon

A Company
- No. 1 Platoon
- No. 2 Platoon
- No. 3 Platoon
- No. 4 Platoon

B Company
- No. 5 Platoon
- No. 6 Platoon
- No. 7 Platoon
- No. 8 Platoon

C Company
- No. 9 Platoon
- No. 10 Platoon
- No. 11 Platoon
- No. 12 Platoon

D Company
- No. 13 Platoon
- No. 14 Platoon
- No. 15 Platoon
- No. 16 Platoon

Based at Woodhall Spa. Flew in 56 Horsas from Down Ampney and Blakehill Farm, and a Hamilcar from Tarrant Rushton.
- Went in: *765 men*
- Died: *112*
- Evacuated: *76*
- Missing: *577*

181 Airlanding Field Ambulance
- Commander: *Lieutenant Colonel Marrable*

Based at Stenigot House and Martin. Flew in 12 Horsas from Down Ampney.
- Went in: *137 men*
- Died: *5*
- Evacuated: *10*
- Missing: *122*

1st Airlanding Light Regiment
- Commander: *Lieutenant Colonel Thompson*

1st Airlanding Light Battery
- A Troop
- B Troop

2nd Airlanding Light Battery
- C Troop
- D Troop

3rd Airlanding Light Battery
- E Troop
- F Troop

Based at Boston. Flew in 57 Horsas from Fairford, Blakehill Farm, Down Ampney, Manston and Keevil on the First Lift; No. 2 Battery and remainder flew in 33 Horsas from Manston on the Second Lift.
- Went in: *372 men*
- Died: *36*
- Evacuated: *136*
- Missing: *200*

1 Forward (Airborne) Observation Unit
- Commander: *Major Denys Wight-Boycott*

Flew in 3 Horsas from Keevil and various small groups in C-47s and Horsas of other brigades.
- Went in: *73 men*
- Died: *7*
- Evacuated: *23*
- Missing: *43*

1st Airborne Divisional Signals
- Commander: *Lieutenant Colonel Tom Stephenson*

No. 1 Company

No. 2 Company

Based at Caythorpe. Flew in C-47s and Horsas from several airfields.
- Went in: *348 men*
- Died: *28*
- Evacuated: *149*
- Missing: *171*

1st Airborne Reconnaissance Squadron
- Commander: *Major Freddie Gough*

Headquarters Troop
- Support Troop: *Lieutenant John Christie*

A Troop
- No. 1 Section
- No. 2 Section
- No. 3 Section

C Troop
- No. 7 Section
- No. 8 Section
- No. 9 Section

D Troop
- No. 10 Section
- No. 11 Section
- No. 12 Section

Flew in 8 C-47s from Barkston Heath, and 22 Horsas from Tarrant Rushton.
- Went in: *181 men*
- Died: *30*
- Evacuated: *73*
- Missing: *78*

21st Independent Parachute Company
- Commander: *Major "Boy" Wilson*
- No. 1 Platoon
- No. 2 Platoon
- No. 3 Platoon

Flew in 12 Stirlings from Fairford, and a Horsa.
- Went in: *186 men*
- Died: *20*
- Evacuated: *120*
- Missing: *46*

9th (Airborne) Field Company, RE
- Commander: *Major John Winchester*
- No. 1 Platoon
- No. 2 Platoon
- No. 3 Platoon

Flew in 22 Horsas (two lifts from Keevil).
- Went in: *194 men*
- Died: *44*
- Evacuated: *71*
- Missing: *79*

261 (Airborne) Field Park Company
- Commander: *Lieutenant W. Skinner*

Flew in 3 Horsas and a Hamilcar.
- Went in: *13 men*
- Died: *2*
- Evacuated: *5*
- Missing: *6*

British Airborne Division

250 (Airborne) Light Composite Company
- No. 1 Para Platoon & 1st Para Jeep Section (1st Para Brigade)
- No. 2 Para Platoon & 2nd Para Jeep Section (4th Para Brigade)
- No. 3 Para Platoon & 3rd Para Jeep Section (1st Airlanding Brigade)

Based at Longhills Hall, Branston, and Lincoln. Flew in 4 C-47s from Barkston Heath and Saltby, and 34 Horsas and 3 Hamilcars from Keevil, Harwell, and Tarrant Rushton.
- Went in: *226 men*
- Died: *29*
- Evacuated: 75
- Missing: *122*

1st (Airborne) Divisional Field Park
- Commander: *Captain Bill Chidgey*

Based at Grantham. Flew in a shared C-47 from Barkston Heath, and a Horsa from Keevil.
- Went in: *19 men*
- Died: *2*
- Evacuated: *2*
- Missing: *15*

1st (Airborne) Divisional Workshops
- Advanced Workshop Detachment
- 1st Para Brigade Light Aid Detachment
- 4th Para Brigade Light Aid Detachment

Based at Sleaford. Flew in 4 Horsas from Fairford and Down Ampney, with other men flying in with various units.
- Went in: *61 men*
- Died: *6*
- Evacuated: *29*
- Missing: *26*

1st (Airborne) Divisional Provost Company, CMP
- Commander: *Captain Bill Gray*
- No. 1 Provost Sectiony
- No. 2 Provost Section
- No. 3 Provost Section
- No. 4 Provost Section

Based at Stubton Hall and Newark, with sections at Divisional and brigade HQs. Company HQ flew in a Horsa from Down Ampney, sections in C-47s and Horsas with other units.
- Went in: *69 men*
- Died: *7*
- Evacuated: *13*
- Missing: *49*

89th (Parachute) Field Security Section, Intelligence Corps
- Commander: *Captain J. Killick*

Based at Wellingore. HQ flew in shared Horsa from Fairford, with other men flying in with various units.
- Went in: *16 men*
- Died: *2*
- Evacuated: *4*
- Missing: *10*

UNITS ATTACHED TO THE DIVISION
The Glider Pilot Regiment
- Commander: *Colonel George Chatterton*

No. 1 Wing
- Commander: *Lieutenant Colonel Iain Murray*

A Squadron
- No. 1 Flight
- No. 17 Flight

B Squadron
- No. 3 Flight
- No. 4 Flight
- No. 19 Flight
- No. 20 Flight

D Squadron
- No. 5 Flight
- No. 8 Flight
- No. 13 Flight
- No. 21 Flight
- No. 22 Flight

G Squadron
- No. 9 Flight
- No. 10 Flight
- No. 23 Flight
- No. 24 Flight

No. 2 Wing
- Commander: *Lieutenant Colonel John Place*

C Squadron
- No. 6 Flight
- No. 7 Flight

E Squadron
- No. 11 Flight
- No. 12 Flight
- No. 25 Flight

F Squadron
- No. 14 Flight
- No. 15 Flight
- No. 16 Flight

No. 1 Wing HQ based at Harwell. A Squadron based at and flew from Harwell. B Squadron based at Brize Norton, but flew from Manston. D

Squadron based at and flew from Keevil. G Squadron based at and flew from Fairford.
No. 2 Wing HQ based at Broadwell. C Squadron based at and flew from Tarrant Rushton. E Squadron based at and flew from Down Ampney. F Squadron based at and flew from Broadwell and Blakehill Farm.
- Went in: *1,262 men*
- Died: *219*
- Evacuated: *532*
- Missing: *511*

Dutch Liaison Mission: No.2 Troop of No. 10 (Inter-Allied) Commando
- Commander: *Lieutenant M. J. Knottenbelt*
- Flew in with various units.
- Went in: *12*
- Died: *1*
- Evacuated: *9*
- Missing: *2*

6080 and 6341 Light Warning Units, RAF
- Flew in 4 Horsas with the Second Lift.
- Went in: *45*
- Died: *9*
- Evacuated: *4*
- Missing: *32*

U.S. Air Support Signals Team—306th Fighter Control Squadron
- Flew in 4 Wacos from Manston.
- Went in: *10*
- Died: *0*
- Evacuated/Missing: *Unknown*

GHQ Signal Liaison Regiment Detachment—"Phantom"
- Went in: *10*
- Died: *0*
- Evacuated/Missing: *Unknown*

Jedburgh Team
- Went in: *3*
- Died: *1*
- Evacuated: *1*
- Missing: *1*

Public Relations Team
- Went in: *15*
- Died: *0*
- Evacuated: *14 (Unconfirmed)*
- Missing: *1*

RAF Fighter Command, August 1940

 This is the order of battle of RAF Fighter Command on August 8, 1940.

At the time of the Battle of Britain, Fighter Command was split into four groups: 13 Group covered the North of England and Scotland; 12 Group the Midlands and Wales; 10 Group South West England; and, most importantly, 11 Group covered the South East and London. 11 Group was also nearest to the Germans in an area where the German invasion of Britain, Operation Sealion, was most likely to take place. The Royal Air Force Chief of Staff was Air Chief Marshal Sir Cyril Newall, and the Fighter Command Air Officer Commanding-in-Chief was Air Chief Marshal Sir Hugh Dowding.

HEADQUARTERS NO. 10 GROUP
- *(Box, Wilts)*
Squadron Nos.
- 92 *(Spitfires), Pembrey*
- 87 *(Hurricanes), Exeter*
- 213 *(Hurricanes), Exeter*
- 234 *(Spitfires), St. Eval*
- 247 *(Gladiator), Roborough (1 Flight only)*
- 28 *(Hurricanes), Middle Wallop*
- 608 *(Spitfires), Middle Wallop*
- 604 *(Blenheims), Middle Wallop*
- 152 *(Spitfires), Warmwell*

HEADQUARTERS NO. 11 GROUP
- *(Uxbridge)*
Squadron Nos.
- 17 *(Hurricanes), Debden*
- 85 *(Hurricanes), Martlesham*
- 56 *(Hurricanes), Rochford*
- 151 *(Hurricanes), North Weald*
- 25 *(Blenheims), Martlesham*
- 54 *(Spitfires), Hornchurch*
- 65 *(Spitfires), Hornchurch*
- 74 *(Spitfires), Hornchurch*
- 41 *(Spitfires), Hornchurch*
- 43 *(Hurricanes), Tangmere*
- 145 *(Hurricanes), Westhampnett*
- 601 *(Hurricanes), Tangmere*
- 1 *(Hurricanes), Northolt*
- 257 *(Hurricanes), Northolt*
- 615 *(Hurricanes), Kenley*
- 64 *(Spitfires), Kenley*
- 111 *(Hurricanes), Biggin Hill*
- 610 *(Spitfires), Biggin Hill*
- 501 *(Hurricanes), Gravesend*
- 600 *(Blenheims), Manston*

HEADQUARTERS NO. 12 GROUP
- *(Watnall, Noss)*
Squadron Nos.
- 73 *(Hurricanes), Church Fenton*
- 249 *(Hurricanes), Church Fenton*
- 616 *(Spitfires), Leconfield*
- 222 *(Spitfires), Kirton-in-Lindsey*
- 264 *(Defiants), Kirton-in-Lindsey ('A' Flight at Ringway)*
- 46 *(Hurricanes), Digby*
- 611 *(Spitfires), Digby*
- 29 *(Blenheims), Digby*
- 242 *(Hurricanes), Coltishall*
- 66 *(Spitfires), Coltishall*
- 229 *(Hurricanes), Wittering*
- 26 *(Spitfires), Wittering*
- 23 *(Blenheims), Colly Weston*
- 19 *(Spitfires), Duxford*

HEADQUARTERS NO. 13 GROUP
- *(Newcastle-on-Tyne)*
Squadron Nos.
- 79 *(Spitfires), Acklington*
- 607 *(Hurricanes), Usworth*
- 72 *(Spitfires), Acklington*
- 605 *(Hurricanes), Drem*
- 232 *(Hurricanes), Turnhouse*
- 253 *(Hurricanes), Turnhouse*
- 141 *(Defiants), Prestwock*
- 219 *(Blenheims), Catterick*
- 245 *(Hurricanes), Aldergrove*
- 3 *(Hurricanes), Wick*
- 504 *(Hurricanes), Castletown*
- 232 *(Hurricanes), Sumburgh (1 Flight only)*
- 603 *(Spitfires):*
- "A" Flight at Dyce
- "B" Flight at Montrose

RAF Bomber Command

 When World War II began in September 1939, Bomber Command's capability was still restricted to small numbers of slow aircraft carrying primitive navigation equipment including sextants. The British did not want to provoke the Germans by actually bombing Germany itself. So the first flights by RAF bombers over the German homeland were only to drop propaganda leaflets at night.

On May 14, 1940, the German Luftwaffe bombed the Dutch city of Rotterdam. Bomber Command, though still a relatively small and underequipped force, was immediately ordered to bomb Germany itself. Specific targets were the German Air Force, oil refineries, communications (railways, bridges, and roads), and factories involved in war production.

From August 1942, a specialized target-finding force, called the "Pathfinders," began operating. Their task was to fly ahead of the other bombers, locate the target, and mark it with large colored flares which the main force then aimed at. An experienced commander, known as the "Master Bomber," would circle the target throughout the raid, sending instructions to the incoming stream of bombers to ensure accuracy was maintained.

For three-and-a-half years Bomber Command pounded Germany night after night, sometimes sending 800 or more aircraft against a major industrial center, sometimes, if weather conditions precluded a heavy raid, sending a few fast Mosquitoes over Berlin or the Ruhr industrial area to keep the air raid sirens sounding all night and German war workers out of their beds.

These are all the RAF Bomber Command squadrons that served in World War II:

7 Squadron	63 Squadron	110 Squadron
9 Squadron	75 Squadron	114 Squadron
10 Squadron	76 Squadron	115 Squadron
12 Squadron	77 Squadron	128 Squadron
15 Squadron	78 Squadron	138 (Special) Squadron
18 Squadron	82 Squadron	139 Squadron
21 Squadron	83 Squadron	141 Squadron
35 Squadron	88 Squadron	142 Squadron
37 Squadron	90 Squadron	144 Squadron
38 Squadron	97 Squadron	148 Squadron
40 Squadron	98 Squadron	149 Squadron
44 Squadron	99 Squadron	150 Squadron
49 Squadron	100 Squadron	153 Squadron
50 Squadron	101 Squadron	156 Squadron
51 Squadron	102 Squadron	158 Squadron
52 Squadron	103 Squadron	161 (Special) Squadron
57 Squadron	104 Squadron	162 Squadron
58 Squadron	105 Squadron	163 Squadron
61 Squadron	106 Squadron	166 Squadron
	107 Squadron	169 Squadron
	108 Squadron	170 Squadron
	109 Squadron	180 Squadron

RAF Bomber Command

185 Squadron
186 Squadron
189 Squadron
192 (Special) Squadron
195 Squadron
196 Squadron
199 Squadron
207 Squadron
214 Squadron
215 Squadron
218 Squadron
223 Squadron
226 Squadron
227 Squadron

Polish and Czechoslovak Squadrons
300 (Polish) Squadron
301 (Polish) Squadron
304 (Polish) Squadron
305 (Polish) squadron
311 (Czechoslovak) Squadron

Free French Air Force Squadrons
346 Squadron
347 Squadron

Royal Canadian Air Force Squadrons
405 Squadron
408 Squadron
415 Squadron
419 Squadron
420 Squadron
424 Squadron
425 Squadron
426 Squadron

427 Squadron
428 Squadron
429 Squadron
431 Squadron
432 Squadron
433 Squadron
434 Squadron

Royal Australian Air Force Squadrons
455 Squadron
458 Squadron
460 Squadron
462 Squadron
463 Squadron
464 Squadron
466 Squadron
467 Squadron

Royal New Zealand Air Force Squadrons
487 Squadron

Royal Air Force Squadrons
514 Squadron
515 Squadron
550 Squadron
571 Squadron
576 Squadron
578 Squadron
582 Squadron
608 Squadron
617 Squadron
619 Squadron
620 Squadron
622 Squadron
623 Squadron
625 Squadron

626 Squadron
627 Squadron
630 Squadron
635 Squadron
640 Squadron
692 Squadron

Royal Navy Wings

 Royal Navy Wings were first created in October 1943, following an order that embarked squadrons were to be grouped in numbered wings, as either Fighter or Torpedo-Bomber Reconnaissance (TBR) Wings. Some 19 naval wings were formed in total, and they saw action in a number of theaters. Finally, those serving in the Pacific theater were merged into the new Carrier Air Groups in June 1945, and the remainder disbanded as their ships returned home.

In the Illustrious-class aircraft carrier, armor was carried at the flight deck level—which became the strength deck—and formed an armored box-like hangar that was an integral part of the ship's structure. However, to make this possible without increasing the displacement, it was necessary to significantly reduce the size and headroom of the hangar. The later three vessels, *Indomitable*, *Indefatigable*, and *Implacable*, had redesigned two-level hangars which enabled them to carry larger air groups than the original design. The size of the air wings was also increased by using outriggers and deck parks. The original design was for 36 aircraft, but eventually the vessels operated with a complement of up to 72 aircraft. This armor scheme was designed to withstand 1,000 pound bombs (and heavier bombs which struck at an angle). In the Home and Mediterranean theaters, it was likely that the carriers would operate within the range of shore-based aircraft. The main belt protected the machinery, petrol stowage, magazines, and aerial weapon stores. The lifts were placed outside the hangar, at either end, with access through sliding armored doors in the end bulkheads.

2nd Naval TBR Wing
- 1st 828/841 Squadrons on HMS *Implacable*, HMS *Formidable*
- 2nd 820/849 reformed as No. 2 Strike Wing

3rd Naval Fighter Wing
- 1st: *808, 886, 897 on HMS* Hunter, *HMS* Attacker, *HMS* Stalker
- 2nd: *808, 886, 897; Wing attached to 2nd Tactical Air Force*
- 3rd: *800, 808, 885, 1840; (881, 882 briefly attached), HMS* Emperor, *HMS* Khedive, *HMS* Ruler, *HMS* Speaker

4th Naval Fighter Wing
- 1st: *807/808, on HMS* Hunter, *879, 886, HMS* Attacker *809, 897, HMS* Stalker *(not realized).*
- 2nd: *807, 809 & 879 on HMS* Hunter, *HMS* Attacker, *HMS* Stalker

5th Naval Fighter Wing
- 1839/1844 on HMS Begum & HMS Indomitable

6th Naval Fighter Wing
- 1st: *1837 on HMS* Atheling *& HMS* Illustrious
- 2nd: *1841/1842 on HMS* Formidable

7th Naval Fighter Wing
- 800/804 on HMS *Emperor*; 881/896 on HMS *Pursuer*; 882/898 on HMS *Searcher*

8th Naval TBR Wing
- 827/830 on HMS *Furious*, and also HMS *Victorious*

9th Naval TBR Wing
- 820/826 on HMS *Indefatigable*

10th Naval Fighter Wing
- 1843/1845 in BPF separately on HMS *Slinger* and HMS *Arbiter*

11th Naval TBR Wing
- 822/823 at Ulunderpet, India

12th Naval TBR Wing
- 815/817 on HMS *Begum*

15th Naval Fighter Wing
- 1830, 1831, & 1833 on HMS *Illustrious*

21st Naval TBR Wing
- 810/847 on HMS *Illustrious*

24th Naval Fighter Wing
- 887/894 on HMS *Indefatigable*

30 Naval Fighter Wing
- 801/880 on HMS *Implacable*

31st Naval TBR Wing
- Proposed to consist of 832/845 for HMS *Victorious* (canceled)

45th Naval TBR Wing
- 822/823 on HMS *Atheling*

47th Naval Fighter Wing
- 1834/1836 on HMS *Victorious*

52nd Naval TBR Wing
- 1st: *815/817 on HMS* Victorious/HMS Begum
- 2nd: *829/831 HMS* Victorious

Royal Navy Carrier Air Groups, 1945

 Carrier Air Groups were first created in June 1945 to align with U.S. Navy policy in the Pacific following the end of the war in Europe, involving frontline squadrons reorganized into Carrier Air Groups (CAGs). The CAG organization continued into the postwar period, being reorganized in September 1946 so that each Air Group had one Firefly squadron and one of Seafires.

1st Carrier Air Group
- Formed June 30, 1945, for HMS *Victorious*, disbanded September 1945
- Avenger and Corsairs: *849, 1834, 1836 Squadrons*

2nd Carrier Air Group
- Formed June 30, 1945, for HMS *Formidable*, disbanded October 1945
- Avenger and Corsairs: *848, 1841, 1842*

3rd Carrier Air Group
- Formed at Nowra on August 2, 1945, disbanded on October 20, 1945
- Corsairs: *1843, 1845*

4th Carrier Air Group
- Planned to form for HMS *Illustrious*, but not realized by VJ-Day
- Corsairs: *1837, 1853*

5th Carrier Air Group
- Planned to form for Illustrious-class carrier, but not realized by VJ-Day
- Corsairs: *1832, 1838*

6th Carrier Air Group
- Planned to form for Illustrious-class carrier, but not realized by VJ-Day
- Avenger, Corsairs, Wildcats: *853, 882, 1830*

7th Carrier Air Group
- Formed for HMS *Indefatigable* at Scholfields on June 30, 1945
- Seafires, Avengers, Firefly: *820, 887, 894, 1770, 1772*

8th Carrier Air Group
- Formed for HMS *Implacable* on June 30, 1945
- Seafires, Avengers, Firefly: *801, 828, 880, 1771*

9th Carrier Air Group
- Planned to form for Implacable-class carrier, but not realized by VJ-Day
- Seafires, Avengers, Firefly: *802, 851, 899, 1773*

10th Carrier Air Group
- Planned to form for Implacable-class carrier, but not realized by VJ-Day
- Seafires, Avengers, Firefly: *856, 883, 1833, and planned 1775*

11th Carrier Air Group
- Formed for HMS *Indomitable*
- Hellcats, Avengers, Firefly: *857, 1839, 1844*, and planned but not realized *1772*

12th Carrier Air Group
- Planned to form for HMS *Indomitable*, but not realized by VJ-Day
- Hellcats, Avengers, Firefly: *845, 881, 885*, and planned but not realized *1774*

13th Carrier Air Group
- Formed for HMS *Vengeance* on June 30, 1945
- Barracudas and Corsairs: *812, 1850*

14th Carrier Air Group
- Formed for HMS *Colossus* on June 30, 1945
- Barracudas and Corsairs: *827, 1846*

15th Carrier Air Group
- Formed for HMS *Venerable* June 30, 1945
- Barracudas and Corsairs: *814, 1851*

16th Carrier Air Group
- Formed for HMS *Glory* June 30, 1945
- Barracudas and Corsairs: *837, 1831*

17th Carrier Air Group
- Planned to form for Colossus-class carrier, but not realized by VJ-Day
- Barracudas and Corsairs: *824, 1835*

18th Carrier Air Group
- Planned to form for Colossus-class carrier, but not realized by VJ-Day
- Barracudas and Corsairs: *822, 1852*

22nd Carrier Air Group
- Planned to form for Colossus-class carrier, but not realized by VJ-Day
- Barracudas and Seafire: *818, 884*

Royal Navy Mediterranean Fleet

ORDER OF BATTLE, 1940
Admiral Sir Andrew Cunningham

1st Battle Squadron (Vice Admiral Geoffrey Layton)
Battleships
- *BARHAM*
- *RAMILLIES*
- *WARSPITE*

Aircraft Carrier
- *GLORIOUS*

1st Cruiser Squadron (Vice Admiral John H. D. Cunningham)
Heavy cruisers
- *DEVONSHIRE*
- *SUSSEX*
- *SHROPSHIRE*

3rd Cruiser Squadron (Rear Admiral Henry R. Moore)
Light cruisers
- *ARETHUSA*
- *PENELOPE*

Destroyer Flotillas (Rear Admiral John C. Tovey)
- Light cruiser *GALATEA*
- Depot ship *WOOLWICH*

1st Destroyer Flotilla (Captain G. E. Creasy)
- *GALLANT*
- *GARLAND*
- *GIPSY*
- *GLOWWORM*
- *GRAFTON*
- *GRENADE*
- *GRENVILLE*
- *GREYHOUND*
- *GRIFFIN*

2nd Destroyer Flotilla (Captain Warburton-Lee)
- *HARDY*
- *HASTY*
- *HEREWARD*
- *HERO*
- *HOSTILE*
- *HAVOCK*
- *HOTSPUR*
- *HUNTER*
- *HYPERION*
-

3rd Destroyer Flotilla (Captain Talbot)
- *ICARUS*
- *ILEX*
- *IMOGEN*
- *IMPERIAL*
- *IMPULSIVE*
- *INGLEFIELD*
- *INTREPID*

- *ISIS*
- *IVANHOE*

4th Destroyer Flotilla (Captain Creswell)
- *AFRIDI*
- *COSSACK*
- *GURKHA*
- *MAORI*
- *MOHAWK*
- *NUBIAN*
- *SIKH*
- *ZULU*

1st Submarine Flotilla (Captain Ruck-Keene)
Submarines
- *CLYDE*
- *SEVERN*
- *SALMON*
- *SEALION*
- *SHARK*
- *SNAPPER*

1st Motor Torpedo Boat Flotilla
- Motor torpedo boats MTB.1, MTB.2, MTB.3, MTB.4, MTB.5, MTB.6, MTB.14, MTB.15, MTB.16, MTB.17, MTB.18, MTB.19

Malta Reserve
Destroyers
- *WOLSEY*
- *WRESTLER*
Minesweepers
- *ALBURY*
- *DUNOON*
- *DUNDALK*

Alexandria Reserve
Minesweepers
- *ELGIN*
- *FERMOY*
- *LYDD*
- *PANGBOURNE*
- *ROSS*
- *SALTASH*
- *SUTTON*

Gibraltar Reserve
Destroyers
- *ACTIVE*
- *WISHART*
- *WRYNECK*

Royal Navy Home Fleet

ORDER OF BATTLE, 1939
Admiral Sir Charles M. Forbes

2nd Battle Squadron (Rear Admiral Lancelot E. Holland)
Battleships
- *NELSON*
- *RAMILLIES*
- *RESOLUTION*
- *RODNEY*
- *ROYAL OAK*
- *ROYAL SOVEREIGN*

BATTLECRUISER SQUADRON (Rear Admiral William J. Whitworth)
- *HOOD (below)*
- *REPULSE*

Aircraft Carriers (Vice Admiral Lionel V. Wells)
- *ARK ROYAL*
- *FURIOUS*

Destroyers
- *BEAGLE*
- *BOREAS*

2nd Cruiser Squadron (Vice Admiral Sir George F. B. Edwards-Collins)
- heavy cruiser *CUMBERLAND*

Light cruisers
- *BELFAST*
- *EDINBURGH*
- *GLASGOW*
- *NEWCASTLE*
- *SHEFFIELD*
- *SOUTHAMPTON*

Destroyer Flotillas (Rear Admiral Ronald H. C. Hallifax)
- light cruiser *AURORA*

6th Destroyer Flotilla (Captain R. S. G. Nicholson)
- *ASHANTI*
- *BEDOUIN*
- *ESKIMO*
- *MASHONA*
- *MATABELE*
- *SOMALI*
- *TARTAR*
- *PUNJABI*

7th Destroyer Flotilla (Captain P. J. Mack)
- *ECHO*
- *ENCOUNTER*
- *JACKAL*
- *JAVELIN*
- *JERSEY*
- *JERVIS*
- *JUPITER*

8th Destroyer Flotilla (Captain C. S. Daniel)
- *FAME*
- *FAULKNOR*
- *FEARLESS*
- *FIREDRAKE*
- *FORESIGHT*
- *FORESTER*
- *FORTUNE*
- *FOXHOUND*
- *FURY*

SUBMARINES (Rear Admiral Bertram Chalmers Watson)

2nd Submarine Flotilla (Captain W. D. Stephens)
- destroyer *MACKAY*

Submarines
CACHALOT
NARWHAL
PORPOISE
SEAHORSE
STARFISH

Dominion Navies 1939

 In World War II, the foundation of Britain's sea power was, as in previous wars, her battle fleets in European waters. By their presence, and the implied ability so to dispose their forces as to meet threats in other parts of the world, they controlled, or at any rate influenced, the activities of hostile or possibly-hostile battle fleets elsewhere. Their existence, even on the other side of the world, afforded a measure of security to Canada, New Zealand, and Australia, under cover of which their own naval forces could look to their local defenses against seaborne raids on trade and territory. In addition, the navies of the former colonies of the British Empire lightened the Royal Navy's burden when it came to the war in the Mediterranean Sea, Pacific, and Atlantic Oceans. This was particularly important in 1940–1941 when the British Isles were under virtual U-boat siege and Axis forces were on the offensive in the Mediterranean and North Africa. Though the dominion navies were small in comparison to the Royal Navy, their crews were highly trained and motivated, and in the Pacific the fleets of Australia and New Zealand provided valuable counter forces to the Imperial Japanese Navy. Their contribution in the early years of the war was truly invaluable.

ROYAL AUSTRALIAN NAVY
Rear Admiral Wilfred N. Custance

Cruiser Squadron (Rear Admiral Custance)
• heavy cruiser *CANBERRA*
Light cruisers
• *SYDNEY*
• *HOBART*
• *PERTH*

Destroyers
• *VAMPIRE*
• *VENDETTA*
• *VOYAGER*

Escort sloops
• *SWAN*
• *YARRA*

Depot ship *PENGUIN*
Survey ship *MORESBY*
Refitting—heavy cruiser *AUSTRALIA*
In reserve
• light cruiser *ADELAIDE*
• destroyers *STUART, WATERHEN*

ROYAL CANADIAN NAVY
Chief of Staff Rear Admiral P. W. Nelles

Destroyers
• SAGUENAY
• SKEENA
• FRASER
• OTTAWA
• RESTIGOUCHEST
• LAURENT

Minesweeping trawlers
• *GASPE*
• *FUNDY*
• *ARMENTIERES*
• *COMOX*
• *NOOTKA*

NEW ZEALAND DIVISION of the ROYAL NAVY
Under the control of the New Zealand Navy Board

Light cruisers
• *ACHILLES*
• *LEANDER*

Escort sloops
• *LEITH*
• *WELLINGTON*

USSR Southwestern Front, June 22, 1941

SOUTHWESTERN FRONT, JUNE 22, 1941
    A Red Army front was the equivalent of a German Army Group.

FIFTH ARMY (destroyed September 1941, reformed October 1941)
    15th Rifle Corps (45th, 62d Rifle Divisions); 27th Rifle Corps (87th, 124th, 135th Rifle Divisions); 2d Fortified Region; 1st Antitank Artillery Brigade; 21st, 231st, 264th, 460th Corps Artillery Regiments; 23rd, 243rd Separate Antiaircraft Artillery Battalions; 9th Mechanized Corps (20th, 35th Tank Divisions, 131st Motorized Division, 32d Motorcycle Regiment); 22d Mechanized Corps (19th, 41st Tank Divisions, 215th Motorized Division, 23rd Motorcycle Regiment); 5th Pontoon Bridge Regiment

SIXTH ARMY (disbanded in August 1941 due to losses, then reformed)
    6th Rifle Corps (41st, 97th, 159th Rifle Divisions); 37th Rifle Corps (80th, 139th, 141st Rifle Divisions); 5th Cavalry Corps (3rd, 14th Cavalry Divisions); 4th, 6th Fortified Regions; 3rd Antitank Artillery Brigade; 209th, 229th, 441st, 445th Corps Artillery Regiments; 135th Gun Artillery Regiment; 17th, 307th Separate Antiaircraft Artillery Battalions; 4th Mechanized Corps (8th, 32d Tank Divisions, 81st Motorized Division, 3rd Motorcycle Regiment); 15th Mechanized Corps (10th, 37th Tank Divisions, 212th Motorized Division); 9th Pontoon Bridge Regiment

TWELFTH ARMY
    13th Rifle Corps (44th, 58th, 192d Mountain Rifle Divisions); 17th Rifle Corps (60th, 96th Mountain Rifle Divisions, 164th Rifle Division); 10th, 11th, 12th Fortified Regions; 4th Antitank Artillery Brigade; 269th, 274th, 283rd, 468th Corps Artillery Regiments; 20th, 30th Separate Antiaircraft Artillery Battalions; 16th Mechanized Corps (15th, 39th Tank Divisions, 240th Motorized Division, 19th Motorcycle Regiment); 37th Engineer Regiment; 19th Pontoon Bridge Regiment

TWENTY-SIXTH ARMY (destroyed September 1941, reformed November 1941)
    8th Rifle Corps (99th, 173rd Rifle Divisions, 72d Mountain Rifle Division); 8th Fortified Region; 2d Antitank Artillery Brigade; 233rd, 236th Corps Artillery Regiments; 28th Separate Antiaircraft Artillery Battalion; 8th Mechanized Corps (12th, 34th Tank Divisions, 7th Motorized Division, 2d Motorcycle Regiment); 17th Pontoon Bridge Regiment

FRONT UNITS
    31st Rifle Corps (193rd, 195th, 200th Rifle Divisions); 36th Rifle Corps (140th, 146th, 228th Rifle Divisions); 49th Rifle Corps (190th, 197th, 199th Rifle Divisions); 55th Rifle Corps (130th, 169th, 189th Rifle Divisions); 1st Airborne Corps (1st, 204th, 211th Airborne Brigades); 1st, 3rd, 5th, 7th, 13th, 15th, 17th Fortified Regions; 5th Antitank Artillery Brigade; 205th, 207th, 368th, 437th, 458th, 507th, 543rd, 646th Corps Artillery Regiments; 305th, 555th Gun Artillery Regiments; 4th, 168th, 324th, 330th, 526th High-Power Artillery Regiments; 331st, 376th, 529th, 538th, 589th Howitzer Artillery Regiments; 34th, 245th, 315th, 316th Separate Special-Power Artillery Battalions; 263rd Separate Antiaircraft Artillery Battalion; 3rd, 4th, 11th PVO Brigades; five PVO brigade regions; 19th Mechanized Corps (40th, 43rd Tank Divisions, 213th Motorized Division, 21st Motorcycle Regiment); 24th Mechanized Corps (45th, 49th Tank Divisions, 216th Motorized Division, 17th Motorcycle Regiment); 44th, 64th Fighter Aviation Divisions; 19th, 62d Bomber Aviation Divisions; 14th, 15th, 16th, 17th, 63rd Mixed Aviation Divisions; 315th, 316th Reconnaissance Aviation Regiments; 45th Engineer Regiment; 1st Pontoon Bridge Regiment

USSR Southwestern Front, June 22, 1941

NINTH SEPARATE ARMY

14th Rifle Corps (25th, 51st Rifle Divisions); 35th Rifle Corps (95th, 176th Rifle Divisions); 48th Rifle Corps (74th, 150th Rifle Divisions, 30th Mountain Rifle Division); 2nd Cavalry Corps (5th, 9th Cavalry Divisions); 80th, 81st, 82d, 84th, 86th Fortified Regions; 320th Gun Artillery Regiments; 430th High-Power Howitzer Artillery Regiment; 265th, 266th, 374th, 648th Corps Artillery Regiments; 317th Separate Special-Power Artillery Battalion; 26th, 268th Separate Antiaircraft Artillery Battalions; one brigade PVO region; 2d Mechanized Corps (11th, 16th Tank Divisions, 15th Motorized Division, 6th Motorcycle Regiment); 18th Mechanized Corps (44th, 47th Tank Divisions, 218th Motorized Division, 26th Motorcycle Regiment); 20th, 21st, 45th Mixed Aviation Divisions; 131st Fighter Aviation Division PVO; 317th Reconnaissance Aviation Regiment; 65th, 66th Fighter Aviation Divisions; 8th, 16th Separate Engineer Battalions; 121st Motorized Engineer Battalion

Authorized Red Army unit strengths in 1941:

- Cavalry Corps: *21,000 men*
- Cavalry Division: *6,000 men*
- Tank Army: *48,000 men, 450–560 tanks*
- Tank Corps: *7,800 men, 168 tanks (opposite, top)*
- Tanks Corps (January 1944): *11,000 men*
- Tank Brigade (November 1943): *1,400 men, 53 tanks*
- Mechanized Corps (January 1944): *16,500 men, 246 tanks and self-propelled guns*
- Motorized Rifle Brigade (November 1943): *3,500 men; rifle corps: 40,000 men*
- Guards Rifle and Rifle Divisions: *10,700 men (guards), 9,400 (rifle) (opposite, bottom)*
- Mountain Rifle Division: *9,400 men*
- Destroyer Division: *4,000 men*
- Ski Brigade: *3,800 men*
- Airborne Brigade: *3,600 men*
- Naval Infantry Brigade: *4,300 men*
- Artillery Division: *9,200 men*

USSR Rifle Division

The majority of Red Army formations throughout World War II consisted of rifle divisions. The infantry units of the Red Army were in a constant state of flux during the first two years of the war on the Eastern Front. Huge losses required constant reorganization to keep the units in some sort of fighting order. The reasons for these massive losses are not hard to find: during 1941–1942, units were quickly formed and often thrown into battle with little or no training. Stalin's purges in the 1930s meant that thousands of inexperienced officers were promoted beyond their level of competence. This resulted in poor leadership on the battlefield. To compound problems, each rifle division had an inadequate number of radios, which made coordinating artillery support all but impossible (German observers during Operation Barbarossa noted the almost total absence of artillery support for the attacking Red Army infantry).

On the eve of Barbarossa, the Red Army had 200 rifle and mountain rifle divisions; by the end of December 1941, this had risen to 400, peaking at 430 in July 1943. Of these, 216 were reformed at least once due to battle losses, and 52 were reformed three or four times! Some 117 rifle divisions earned the Guards distinction for outstanding performance on the battlefield.

The army's rifle divisions on the eve of Barbarossa were under strength, having 8,000–9,000 men, or even 5,000–6,000 men, as opposed to the authorized strength of 9,500 (and many rifle divisions in the western military districts had only 50 percent of their vehicle allocation). As stated, one reason for their poor performance in 1941 was a dire lack of radios. Indeed, the divisions relied mainly on cable for communications which, especially during Barbarossa, were often cut by German infiltration squads, Luftwaffe bombs, or German Army artillery. Very quickly, regiments, divisions, even armies, became "blind," a situation made worse by German aerial superiority, which acted as the "eyes and ears" of army units, pinpointing stranded Red Army infantry formations.

A rifle division was divided into three infantry regiments, an artillery regiment, headquarters company, reconnaissance battalion, antitank battalion, engineer battalion, signals battalion, and services. A rifle division numbered, on paper, approximately 9,400 troops, but, like many wartime establishments, it could fluctuate wildly. Guards rifle divisions numbered 10,700 troops.

When it came to mobility and firepower, rifle divisions were at a disadvantage compared to their German rivals. A December 1941 rifle division had 213 trucks and 1,613 horses, but by July 1942 these had dropped to 117 trucks and 601 horses. The December 1941 rifle division could deploy 120 machine guns, 184 sub-machine guns and 24 artillery pieces, but by July 1942 these had dropped to 41 machine guns, 164 submachine guns, and 16 artillery pieces.

Typical organization of a 1943 Soviet rifle division was as follows:

- Reconnaissance Company
- Three Rifle Regiments, *each with three Battalions*
- Artillery Regiment
- Antitank Battalion
- Engineer Battalion
- Signals Company

Total strength: 9,500

Divisional firepower
- Machine guns: *647*

Antitank weapons
- Antitank rifles: *212*
- 45mm antitank guns: *50*

Mortars
- 50mm mortars: *56*
- 82mm mortars: *83*
- 120mm mortars: *21*

Infantry guns
- 76mm: *32*

Artillery
- 122mm howitzers: *12*

Transport
- Assorted motor vehicles: *180*
- Horsedrawn vehicles :*640*

USSR Tanks Corps

At the start of World War II, the Red Army had no answer to the German panzer group. Its mechanized corps, each one numbering 36,000 men and 1,031 tanks, were scattered along the frontier—not concentrated, as they were in Wehrmacht army groups. On paper, the Soviet armored force in 1941 was very impressive: 29,484 vehicles. However, of this number, 29 percent of the tanks required a major overhaul; 44 percent required a rebuild. This left 7,000 as combat worthy. Tank crew training was poor, leadership was even worse, and the tanks themselves were mechanically unreliable. A lack of radios in individual tanks meant it was impossible to coordinate tank units on the battlefield. In addition, at the start of Barbarossa there was a shortage of 76.2mm ammunition, which adversely affected the performance of the Red Army's two best tanks, the KV-1 and T-34. The result was that by the end of 1941, the German offensive had destroyed a staggering 90 percent of the USSR's tank force.

Typical organization of a 1944 Soviet tank corps was as follows:

- Reconnaissance Battalion
- Three Tank Brigades
- Motorized Rifle Brigade, *with three Battalions*
- Artillery Regiment, Mortar Regiment, and Rocket Battalion
- Antitank Regiment and an Antitank Battalion
- Engineer Battalion
- Signals Battalion

Total strength: 10,980

Divisional firepower
- Machine guns: *517*

Antitank weapons
- 45mm antitank guns: *46*
- 76mm antitank guns: *36*
- Antitank rifles: *207*

Mortars
- 82mm mortars: *52*
- 120mm mortars: *42*

Infantry guns
- 85mm: *21*

Artillery
- 152mm howitzers: *21*
- Rocket launchers: *8*

Tanks
- T-34s: *208*

Transport
- Assorted motor vehicles: *1,610*

Soviet tank armies
- By Kursk in 1943, the Red Army had created so-called tank armies to combat the German panzer corps. The creation of the first two armies—the Third and Fifth—was ordered on May 25, 1942. In theory, each tank army was made up of two tank corps, one mechanized corps, and supporting units—a strength of 560 tanks and 45,000 men. In January 1945, the Third Guards Tank Army had 670 tanks, 43,400 troops, 254 assault guns, 24 BM-13 rocket launchers, and 368 artillery pieces.

- A tank corps in January 1943 was made up of three tank brigades, a motorized rifle brigade, a mortar battalion, and various support units. The assault guns were usually grouped in their own units. Thus, a tank brigade had up to 65 tanks, giving a tank corps up to 230 tanks. The assault guns were grouped into heavy, medium, and light regiments. Thus, the heavy units comprised 12 SU-152s, the medium units 16 SU-122s, and 1 T-34 tank, and the light regiments were composed of 21 SU-76s or 16 SU-85s, and 1 T-34 tank. The regiments made up of SU-152s were usually assigned to armies for breakthrough operations.

USSR Mechanized, Cavalry, and Artillery Divisions

 On October 31, 1942, the Stavka ordered the raising of 26 Red Army artillery divisions in recognition of the Soviet doctrine that artillery was the basic strike force of the Red Army. The original divisional organization was three howitzer regiments (each with 20 x 122mm howitzers), two gun regiments (each with 18 x 122mm or 152mm gun-howitzers), three tank-destroyer artillery regiments (each with 24 x 76mm guns), and an observation battalion. In April 1943, five artillery corps headquarters were created to control the groupings of artillery divisions. Also, breakthrough artillery divisions were created.

Typical organization of a 1944 Soviet mechanized corps was as follows:

- Reconnaissance Battalion
- Tank Brigade
- Three Motorized Rifle Regiments
- Artillery Regiment, Motor Regiment, and Rocket Battalion
- Antitank Regiment and Antitank Battalion
- Engineer Battalion
- Signals Battalion

Total Strength: 15,020

Divisional firepower
- Machine guns: *895*

Antitank guns
- 45mm antitank guns: *52*
- 76mm antitank guns: *16*
- Antitank rifles: *375*

Mortars
- 82mm mortars: *100*
- 120mm mortars: *42*

Artillery
- Rocket launchers: *8*

Tanks
- T-70s: *21*

Transport:
- 2,120 assorted motor vehicles

Typical organization of a 1943 Soviet cavalry division was as follows:

- Reconnaissance Battalion
- Three Cavalry Regiments
- Artillery Regiment
- Antitank Company
- Engineer Battalion
- Signals Company

Total strength: 4,600

Divisional firepower
- Machine guns: *230*

Antitank weapons
- 37mm antitank guns: *6*
- 45mm antitank guns: *12*
- Antitank rifles: *112*

Mortars
- 82mm mortars: *36*
- 120mm mortars: *12*

Artillery
- 76mm gun howitzers: *24*

Transport
- Assorted motor vehicles: *100*
- Horsedrawn vehicles: *404*

Typical organization of a 1944 Soviet artillery division was as follows:
- Mortar Brigade
- Light Artillery Brigade
- Medium Artillery Brigade
- Howitzer Brigade
- Fire Control Battalion
- Signals Battalion

Total strength: 9,700

Divisional firepower
- Machine guns: *230*

Antitank weapons
- Antitank rifles: *288*

Mortars
- 120mm mortars: *108*

Artillery
- 76mm guns :*72*
- 122mm gun/howitzers: *60*
- 152mm gun/howitzers: *48*

Transport
- Assorted motor vehicles: *1,530*

USSR Air Army and Fleet

On paper, the Red Air Force in 1941 was impressive, with 19,533 aircraft, 7,133 of which were located in the western USSR. However, many of its aircraft were obsolete, its pilots lacked flying experience, few aircraft had radios, and three successive air force commanders plus many senior officers had been shot in the purges, which further diluted its effectiveness. The losses suffered by the Red Air Force during the first week of Barbarossa resulted in the Germans retaining air superiority over the Eastern Front until the end of 1942!

However, one of the most dramatic and impressive accomplishments of the war was the grandiose maneuver of shifting most of the aviation fuselage and engine production to new production facilities in the east. From the spring of 1942, production of the Yak-1 was in Novosibirsk, the Il-2 Stormovik plant was moved to the Volga region, and the MiG-3 factory moved to the Urals, near Kuibyshev. Production accelerated swiftly, increasing to a maximum rate of 35,000 aircraft in 1943 and almost 40,000 in 1944. This allowed the Soviets to build air armies that finally gained air superiority over the Eastern Front from the end of 1942 onward.

During the early months of the war, the Soviet Navy's primary task was to assist land forces where they could, as well as to protect sea lines of communication and disrupt enemy ones. Soviet ships, along with other branches of the navy, took an active part in the defense of the naval bases at Hanko, Libava, Odessa, and Sevastopol, and in exhausting battles for Leningrad,

where naval artillery played a very significant role. It was used, mainly, for combating enemy heavy artillery, which bombarded the city between 1941 until its relief in 1944.

At the beginning of 1942, the Black Sea Fleet conducted the Kerch landing operation. Two armies of the Caucasus Front, naval units, more than 250 ships and vessels, together with 600 aircraft, were engaged. Submarines of the Black Sea Fleet operated against enemy lines of communication and evacuated people and valuable property from Sevastopol.

The Northern Fleet played a key role on the Murmansk Front by protecting its own lines of communication and constantly undermining the enemy ones situated along the northern Norway coast. With Lend-Lease supplies, the USSR started to receive military weaponry, equipment, and food supplies from the Allies. During the first war period, 20 convoys numbering 288 vessels left the ports of Britain and Iceland and took the Northern Route to Arkhangel and Murmansk. Soviet transport vessels also sailed from the USSR to the West carrying traditional Soviet export goods, first and foremost, strategic raw materials.

During the war, the navy sank 708 enemy warships, as well as 791 transport vessels. During the war against Japan in August and September 1945, the Pacific Ocean Fleet successfully landed a number of operational and tactical landing bodies. In close cooperation with Soviet Army units, the fleet liberated South Sakhalin, the Kuril Islands, ports along the Korea eastern coast, and Port Arthur.

Soviet Fourth Air Army. In May 1942 it had 208 aircraft and 437 crews, and consisted of:

- 216th Fighter Division (*Commander V. I. Shevchenko*)
- 217th Fighter Division (*Commander D.P. Galunov*)
- 229th Fighter Division (*Commander P.G. Stepanovich*)
- 230th Storm Division (*Commander S.G. Get'man*)
- 219th Bomber Division (*Commander I.T. Batygin*)
- 218th Night Bomber Division (*Commander D.D. Popov*)
- one training regiment, seven separate mixed aviation regiments, one communication squadron, one long-range reconnaissance squadron

Ships of the Baltic Fleet, 1940
- Battleships: *2*
- Cruisers: *1*
- Fleet command and destroyers: *13*
- Submarines: *29*
- Gunboats: *3*
- Escort ships (*or frigates*): *12*
- Minelayers and net laying ships: *3*
- Minesweepers: *28*
- Torpedo boats: *62*
- Other naval boats: *33*

Aircraft
- Fighters: *246*
- Bombers: *111*

Belgian, Chinese, Danish, and Finnish Divisions

The armies of many Allied nations suffered two major problems when compared to divisions of the German Army: lack of firepower and lack of transport. The fact that most Allied infantry divisions marched on foot to the battlefield did not necessarily put them at a disadvantage in combat. However, their deficiencies in antitank weaponry and machine guns resulted in them being outgunned by the Germans. This invariably resulted in them suffering heavy casualties and then being unable to hold their positions. Once forced to retreat, their lack of transport made them vulnerable to being quickly surrounded and forced to surrender. Chinese infantry divisions were threadbare throughout the war, both in weapons and ammunition. They were always short of weapons and ammunition. (Finland is classed as an Allied nation, because that was its status in 1939; Finland later joined Germany against the Soviet Union in 1941.)

Typical organization of a Belgian infantry division was as follows:

- Three Infantry Regiments, *each with three Battalions*
- Three Antitank Companies
- Three Machine Gun Companies
- Weapons Battalion

Total strength: 10,000

Divisional firepower
- Light machine guns: *324*
- Heavy machine guns: *156*

Antitank weapons
- 47mm antitank guns: *18*

Mortars
- Heavy mortars: *27*
- Light mortars: *324*

Artillery
- 105mm howitzers: *8*
- 120mm field guns: *8*
- 155mm howitzers: *16*

Typical organization of a Chinese infantry division was as follows:

- Two Infantry Brigades, *each with an Artillery Battalion, Engineer Battalion, and Quartermaster Battalion*
- Two Infantry Regiments

Total strength 10,923

Divisional firepower
- Light machine guns: *274*
- Heavy machine guns: *54*

Artillery
- Pack howitzers: *16*
- Assorted artillery: *30*

Typical organization of a Danish infantry division was as follows:

- Four Infantry Regiments
- Cavalry Regiment
- Antiaircraft Battalion
- Engineer Battalion

Total strength of infantry regiments: 4,200

Divisional firepower
- Light machine guns: *1,024*
- Heavy machine guns: *96*

Antitank weapons
- 37mm antitank guns: *24*

Artillery:
- 50mm howitzers
- 75mm field guns
- 105mm field guns

Typical organization of a Finnish infantry division was as follows:

- Three Infantry Regiments
- Artillery Regiment
- Signals Company
- Pioneer Company

Total strength: 14,200

Divisional firepower
- Heavy machine guns: *116*
- Submachine guns: *250*

Mortars
- 81mm: *18*

Artillery
- 36 pieces, assorted calibers

Netherlands, Norwegian, and Polish Divisions

Of the Dutch, Polish, and Norwegian armies, the Poles were the most effective. The Polish Army in 1939, like its German opponent, remained predominantly an infantry force organized in 30 infantry divisions, plus the equivalent of 18 less effective second-echelon divisions. The Poles were well-trained soldiers, but their divisions suffered from a lack of firepower and mobility compared to German units. For example, a Polish infantry division had 320 light machine guns, whereas a German infantry division possessed over 500. A Polish infantry division had 6,937 horses and 76 vehicles, whereas a German equivalent had 5,375 horses, 938 vehicles, and 530 motorcycles.

Next to the infantry, the cavalry was the second most important arm of the Polish Army. The Poles organized their cavalry into 11 brigades. Each brigade (7,000 troops) had three regiments, a horse artillery section, which included 37mm antitank guns, a bicycle squadron, engineer and communications sections, and a supply element with a large number of wagons.

Typical organization of a Netherlands infantry corps was as follows:

- Light Brigade, *with an Armored Car Squadron, Cyclist Regiment and Hussar Regiment, Horse Artillery Regiment, and a Signals Battalion*
- Infantry Division, *with three Infantry Regiments and a Field Artillery Regiment*
- Heavy Artillery Regiment
- Antiaircraft Regiment
- Independent Artillery Battalion
- Signals Battalion

Total strength: 2,691

Corps firepower
- Light machine guns: *72*
- Heavy machine guns: *36*

Antitank weapons
- Antitank guns: *4*

Mortars
- Heavy mortars: *6*

Typical organization of a Norwegian infantry division was as follows:

- Three Infantry Regiments
- Field Artillery Regiment, *with three Field Artillery Battalions or a Mountain Artillery Battalion*

Total strength: 3,750

Divisional firepower
- Light machine guns: *96*
- Heavy machine guns: *36*

Mortars
- Heavy mortars: *8*

Infantry guns
- 75mm: *9*

Artillery
- 120mm howitzers: *8–12*

Typical organization of a 1939 Polish infantry division was as follows:

- Cavalry Regiment
- Cycle Company
- Three Infantry Regiments, *each with three Infantry Battalions, each with an Infantry Company*
- Reconnaissance Company
- Antitank Company
- Heavy Machine Gun Company

Total strength: 16,492

Divisional firepower
- Light machine guns: *320*
- Heavy machine guns: *132*

Antitank weapons
- 37mm antitank guns: *27*
- Antitank rifles: *92*

Mortars
- 46mm mortars: *81*
- 81mm mortars: *20*

Infantry guns:
- 100mm: *12*
- 105mm: *3*

Artillery
- 75mm field guns: *30*
- 155mm howitzers: *3*

BATTLES

Invasion of Poland

LOCATION Poland
DATE September 1–October 6, 1939
COMMANDERS AND FORCES
GERMAN: Army Group North (Third and Fourth Armies, Colonel General Fedor von Bock); Army Group South (Eighth, Tenth, and Fourteenth Armies, Colonel General Gerd von Rundstedt); **POLISH:** Modlin Army (General Emil Krukowicz-Przedrzymirski), Narew Special Operational Group (General Czeslaw Mlot-Fijalkowski), Pomorze Army (General Wladyslaw Bortnowski), Poznan Army (General Tadeusz Kutrzeba), Lodz Army (General Juliusz Rommel), Cracow Army (General Antoni Szylling), Carpathian Army (General Kazimierz Fabrycy), Prusy Army (High Command)
LAND FORCES
GERMAN: 1,250,000 troops, 2,511 tanks, 5,805 artillery pieces, and 4,019 antitank guns; **POLISH:** 1,000,000 troops, 2,800 artillery pieces, 500 tanks
AIRCRAFT
GERMAN: 2,085; **POLISH:** 360
CASUALTIES
GERMAN: 10,500 killed; **POLISH:** 50,000 killed, 750,000 taken prisoner
KEY ACTIONS The Battle of the Bzura, September 11–20, 1939, saw the the German Eighth and Tenth Armies trap and then destroy the Polish Poznan Army, which amounted to around 25 percent of the entire Polish field force.
KEY EFFECTS In the swift defeat of Polish forces in 1939, Germany had won the first of what would become a series of devastating Blitzkrieg attacks—from the Low Countries and France to the Soviet Union—that shattered the military balance of power in Europe between 1939 and 1941. However, following his successful invasion of Poland, Adolf Hitler now faced Britain and France's declarations of war.

Battle of the Atlantic

LOCATION Atlantic Ocean
DATE September 1939–May 1943
COMMANDERS AND FORCES
GERMAN: 1,000 U-boats (Rear Admiral Karl Dönitz); **BRITISH:** 9 battleships, 4 aircraft carriers, 35 cruisers, 95 destroyers, 25 submarines (Admiral Sir Charles Forbes)
CASUALTIES
GERMAN: 19,000 killed (U-boat crews); **ALLIED:** 85,000 killed
KEY ACTIONS After taking heavy losses in the first part of the war, from early 1943 onward British strategy and equipment improved. More aggressive antisubmarine tactics, better depth charges, and the fitting of long-range aircraft with improved radar ensured that U-boat losses rose. A total of 45 German submarines were destroyed in April and May 1943. Dönitz, seeing that such losses could not be tolerated, called off the battle on May 23, 1943. Although the German U-boat threat did not completely disappear, after this time it was greatly diminished.
KEY EFFECTS The U-boat threat was probably the single most serious threat to Britain during the war. If the Germans had been able to deploy more U-boats in 1940 and 1941, the course of World War II would have been very different, with Britain perhaps starved into submission.

JAN **FEB** **MAR** **APR** **MAY** **JUN**

1939

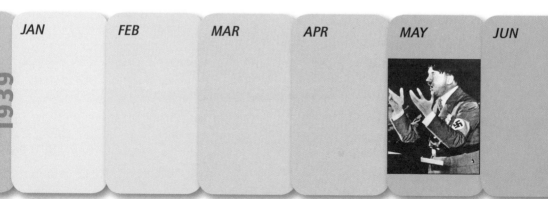

EASTERN FRONT

Winter War

LOCATION Finland
DATE November 30, 1939–March 13, 1940
COMMANDERS AND FORCES
FINNISH: Isthmus Army (Lieutenant General H. Österman), IV Corps (Major General J. Hägglund), Reserve (Major General V. Tuompo). Total: 337,000; **SOVIET:** Seventh Army (General V. F. Jakolev), Eighth Army (General I. N. Habarov), Ninth Army (General M. P. Duhanov), Fourteenth Army (General V. A. Frolov). Total: 600,000
CASUALTIES
FINNISH: 25,000 killed and 45,500 wounded; **SOVIET:** 126,875 killed and 391,783 wounded
KEY ACTIONS On February 1, 1940, the Red Army began its offensive in Karelia. Some 600,000 men were committed to the attack. The Finns had six divisions in the front line and three in reserve. Finnish positions were

pounded by 300,000 artillery shells on the first day, with Soviet artillery mustering 440 guns in the Summa sector alone. The Soviets also deployed close air support all along the front. The Red Army attacked for three days non-stop, paused for a day, then resumed the offensive for a further three days. Finnish forces were gradually worn down by the onslaught.
KEY EFFECTS The Red Army learned some valuable lessons from the Winter War: infantry tactics needed to be flexible; there needed to be greater coordination between different units; battle training should be realistic; and winter clothing was imperative for winter warfare. Absorbing these lessons, the Red Army would become a more effective force in the run-up to Operation Barbarossa in June 1941.

WAR AT SEA

Battle of the River Plate

LOCATION South Atlantic Ocean
DATE December 13, 1939
COMMANDERS AND FORCES
GERMAN: Pocket battleship *Admiral Graf Spee* (Captain Langsdorff); **BRITISH:** cruisers *Exeter*, *Achilles*, and *Ajax* (Commodore Harwood)
CASUALTIES
GERMAN: 36 killed, 60 wounded; **BRITISH:** 72 killed, 28 wounded

KEY ACTIONS After badly damaging HMS *Exeter* and scoring hits on HMS *Ajax*, Langsdorff, who had been wounded twice, ordered the lightly damaged pocket battleship *Admiral Graf Spee* to seek safety in the neutral harbor of Montevideo, Uruguay, instead of remaining at sea and finishing off the British warships. Later, when he thought he had no choice, Langsdorff ordered that the *Admiral Graf Spee* be scuttled.
KEY EFFECTS The scuttling of the *Admiral Graf Spee* was the first real Allied success of World War II, which had begun with the German invasion of Poland in September 1939. Adolf Hitler was furious with Captain Langsdorff's decision to sink his own warship.

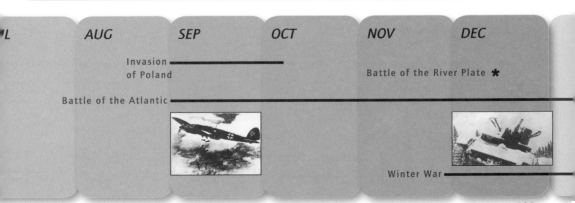

L   AUG   SEP   OCT   NOV   DEC

Invasion of Poland

Battle of the River Plate ✱

Battle of the Atlantic

Winter War

WESTERN FRONT

Invasion of Norway

LOCATION Norway
DATE April 9–June 9, 1940
COMMANDERS AND FORCES
GERMAN: 10,000 troops initially, rising to 100,000, 1,060 aircraft, and 24 warships (General Nikolaus von Falkenhorst); **NORWEGIAN:** 12,000 troops plus 120,000 reservists, 102 aircraft (King Haakon). From April, the Norwegians were reinforced by 25,000 British and French troops, who were landed at Namsos, Åndalsnes, and Narvik
CASUALTIES
GERMAN: 5,100; **NORWEGIAN:** 850; **BRITISH AND FRENCH:** 4,900
KEY ACTIONS From April 9, German aircraft achieved air superiority over Norway and the Baltic Sea.
KEY EFFECTS Norwegian bases proved useful for the Germans in the Battle of Britain, against the USSR from 1941, and for attacks on Allied sea convoys. However, Norway drained German resources because Hitler continually reinforced the German occupying forces against a British invasion that never came.

WESTERN FRONT

Invasion of the West

LOCATION France, Belgium, and Holland
DATE May 10–June 4, 1940
COMMANDERS AND FORCES
GERMAN: 2,350,000 troops, 2,700 tanks, 3,200 aircraft (Hitler); **BRITAIN:** 237,000 troops (Gort); **FRENCH:** 2 million troops (Gamelin); **BELGIAN:** 375,000 troops (King Leopold III); **DUTCH:** 250,000 troops (Winkelman). Total Allied tanks: 3,000. Total Allied aircraft: 1,700
CASUALTIES
GERMAN: 10,200 killed, 42,500 wounded, 8,400 missing; **ALLIED:** 150,000 killed and wounded, 1,200,000 captured
KEY ACTIONS German victory at the Battle of Sedan on May 13–15 allowed German tanks to strike west into northern France. With the French and British armies lured north, there was nothing to stop the Germans reaching the English Channel and cutting off the Allied armies from the rest of France.
KEY EFFECTS The success of the German "Blitzkrieg" advance allowed the German Army to quickly regroup for the conquest of the whole of France.

WESTERN FRONT

Battle of France

LOCATION France
DATE June 5–21, 1940
COMMANDERS AND FORCES
GERMAN: Army Group A (von Rundstedt), Army Group B (von Bock), Army Group C (von Leeb); **FRENCH:** Army Group 2 (Pretelat), Army Group 3 (Besson), Army Group 4 (Huntziger)
CASUALTIES
GERMAN: 95,000 killed and wounded; **FRENCH:** 150,000 killed and wounded, 800,000 taken prisoner
KEY ACTIONS German Army Group B quickly destroyed the French forces and German victory was assured.
KEY EFFECTS Hitler was now the master of continental Europe and could focus on forcing Britain out of the war.

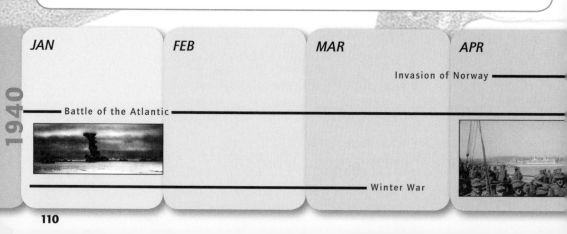

JAN

FEB

MAR

APR

Invasion of Norway

Battle of the Atlantic

Winter War

1940

WESTERN FRONT

Battle of Britain

LOCATION Britain
DATE July–October, 1940
COMMANDERS AND FORCES
GERMAN: Air Fleet 2 (Kesselring), Air Fleet 3 (Sperrle), Air Fleet 5 (Stumpff); **BRITISH:** Fighter Command (Dowding)
TOTAL GERMAN AIR STRENGTH 2,800 aircraft
TOTAL BRITISH FIGHTER STRENGTH 715 plus 424 in storage
CASUALTIES
GERMAN AIRCRAFT LOST: 1,733; **BRITISH AIRCRAFT LOST:** 915
KEY ACTIONS The turning point came on September 7, when the German Luftwaffe switched its attention from British airfields to London itself. This tactical blunder allowed Fighter Command to recover its strength and show the Germans the battle could not be won. On September 15, 56 German aircraft were shot down.
KEY EFFECTS The Germans realized that the RAF could not be defeated in 1940. Germany was also preparing to attack the Soviet Union, so the plan to invade Britain, Operation Sealion, was cancelled indefinitely and eventually abandoned altogether.

AIR WAR

The Blitz

LOCATION Britain
DATE September 7, 1940–May 11, 1941
COMMANDERS AND FORCES
GERMAN: Luftwaffe (Goering); **BRITISH:** RAF Fighter Command (Dowding)
CASUALTIES
GERMAN: 518 aircraft destroyed; **BRITISH:** 43,000 killed, 1.4 million made homeless
KEY ACTIONS Bombing British cities caused heavy civilian casualties, but did not break British morale.
KEY EFFECTS An undefeated Britain in the West in the spring of 1941 meant Germany would be faced with a war on two fronts when Hitler's invasion of the Soviet Union was launched in June 1941. Also, heavy losses of skilled Luftwaffe aircrews over Britain would be keenly felt during the German attack on the USSR.

NORTH AFRICA

Italian Offensive in North Africa

LOCATION North Africa
DATE September 13, 1940–February 7, 1941
COMMANDERS AND FORCES
BRITISH: Western Desert Force (Major General Richard O'Connor), 30,000 troops, 120 field guns, 275 tanks; **ITALIAN:** Tenth Army (Marshal Rodolfo Graziani), 250,000 troops, 1,500 field guns, 300 tanks, 390 aircraft
CASUALTIES
BRITISH: 500 killed, 1,373 wounded; **ITALIAN:** 130,000 taken prisoner
KEY ACTIONS The Italians halted at Sidi Barrani on September 16, allowing the British to launch a counterattack on December 9. Assisted by aircraft and naval gunfire, the British expelled the Italians from Egypt.
KEY EFFECTS The Italian collapse in North Africa forced Hitler to send German forces to bolster the Axis war effort, including the Afrika Korps under Erwin Rommel. The war in North Africa would continue until 1943.

JUN   JUL   AUG

Invasion of the West

Battle of France

Battle of Britain

MEDITERRANEAN

Italian Attack on Greece

LOCATION Greece
DATE October 28, 1940–March 9, 1941
COMMANDERS AND FORCES
ITALIAN: part of Ninth and Eleventh Armies (General Sebastiano Visconti Prasca), 163,000 troops; **GREEK:** Greek Army (General Alexander Papagos), 150,000 troops
CASUALTIES
ITALIAN: 63,000 killed, 100,000 wounded, 23,000 taken prisoner; **GREEK:** 13,000 killed, 42,000 wounded, 1,500 taken prisoner
KEY ACTIONS Italian leader Benito Mussolini made an error in never authorizing the use of his navy or air force to assist in the attack on Greece. Also, the invasion coincided with the Greek rainy season when the weather dropped below freezing, and many Italian soldiers did not possess winter boots or suitable winter clothing. As a result, the Italians could make little headway against determined Greek counterattacks.
KEY EFFECTS Italy's failure in Greece resulted in Adolf Hitler having to invade Greece and Yugoslavia in April 1941 to secure his southern flank before he could invade the Soviet Union. The loss of time, troops, and vehicles would have major consequences for the Germans during the invasion of the USSR in June 1941.

MEDITERRANEAN

Taranto

LOCATION Italy
DATE November 11–12, 1940
COMMANDERS AND FORCES
BRITISH: Mediterranean Fleet (Admiral Cunningham); **ITALIAN:** Italian Fleet (Vice Admiral Inigo Campioni)
CASUALTIES
BRITISH: 2 aircraft destroyed; **ITALIAN:** the battleship *Conte di Cavour* was sunk and the Italian battleships *Littorio* and *Caio Duilio* were heavily damaged. In addition to these setbacks, 2 Italian cruisers were badly damaged and 2 fleet auxiliaries were sunk
KEY ACTIONS The British plan called for their warplanes to attack in two waves about an hour apart.
KEY EFFECTS As a result of the British strike, the Italians withdrew the bulk of their fleet farther north to Naples. The Taranto Raid changed many naval experts' thoughts regarding air-launched torpedo attacks. Prior to the Taranto Raid, many military planners believed that deep water (100 ft/30 m) was needed to successfully drop torpedoes. To compensate for the shallow water of Taranto harbor (40 ft/12 m), the British specially modified their torpedoes and dropped them from very low altitude. This solution, as well as other aspects of the raid, was heavily studied by Japanese military commanders as they planned their attack on the U.S. naval base at Pearl Harbor, Hawaii, which took place in December 1941.

SEP	OCT	NOV	DEC

1940

The Blitz

Battle of the Atlantic

Italian attack on Greece

Battle of Britain

Taranto ✱

EAST AFRICA

Italian East Africa

LOCATION Eritrea, Somaliland, and Ethiopia
DATE January 19-May 18, 1941
COMMANDERS AND FORCES
BRITISH: 70,000 troops, 100 aircraft (Cunningham and Platt); **ITALIAN:** 100,000 troops, 103 tanks, 325 aircraft (Duke Amedeo of Aosta)
CASUALTIES
BRITISH: 3,100 killed and wounded; **ITALIAN:** 55,000 killed and wounded
KEY ACTIONS Platt's defeat of the Italians at Agordat on January 31 and Keren on March 27 cost Aosta 55,000 killed and wounded. These losses, combined with Cunningham's capture of Addis Ababa, resulted in the total collapse of the Italian war effort in East Africa.
KEY EFFECTS In a daring campaign, the British had eliminated any threat to the Suez Canal and had secured the Red Sea as an Allied supply route.

NORTH AFRICA

Rommel's 1st Offensive

LOCATION North Africa
DATE March 24-May 30, 1941
COMMANDERS AND FORCES
GERMAN: Afrika Korps (Major General Erwin Rommel); **BRITISH:** 2nd Armoured Division and 9th Australian Infantry Division, 3 Indian Motor Brigade, 50 aircraft (Lieutenant General Philip Neame)
CASUALTIES Unknown
KEY ACTIONS Rommel's failure to capture Tobruk in Libya meant that the German Afrika Korps could not advance eastward into Egypt.
KEY EFFECTS Rommel's first offensive in North Africa was the beginning of the myth of the "Desert Fox." His boldness and willingness always to attack indicated that the war in North Africa would not be over quickly. In addition, the desert war was no longer one-sided: the British now faced an enemy commander who led highly mobile and capable mechanized forces.

MEDITERRANEAN

Cape Matapan

LOCATION Aegean Sea
DATE March 28, 1941
COMMANDERS AND FORCES
BRITISH: Mediterranean Fleet (Cunningham), 19 warships
ITALIAN: Italian Fleet (Iachino), 9 warships
CASUALTIES
BRITISH: 1 aircraft lost, 3 aircrew killed; **ITALIAN:** 5 ships

lost, 2,400 sailors killed
KEY ACTIONS Late in the day on March 28, the Italian naval commander, Admiral Iachino, ordered two cruisers and four destroyers to go the aid of the stricken cruiser *Pola*. This allowed Admiral Cunningham's Royal Navy warships to close with the Italian vessels and engage them in a night battle. As a result, the Italians lost five ships sunk, with the loss of 2,400 sailors.
KEY EFFECTS The defeat at Cape Matapan dealt another crushing blow to the Italian Navy's morale as much as to its fleet of warships.

JAN   FEB   MAR

Italian offensive in North Africa

Italian East Africa

Greece & Yugoslavia

LOCATION Greece and Yugoslavia
DATE April 6-27, 1941
COMMANDERS AND FORCES
GERMAN: Second Army (von Weichs), Twelfth Army (von List); Total German forces: 680,000 troops, 1,200 tanks, 700 aircraft. **ITALIAN:** Second Army (General Vittorio Ambrosio, 565,000 troops). **YUGOSLAV:** Yugoslav Army (King Peter II, 1 million men, 700 aircraft). **GREEK:** Greek Army (Marshal Alexander Papagos, 430,000 troops, 50 aircraft). **BRITISH:** 62,000 troops, 100 tanks, 200 aircraft (Field Marshal Henry Maitland Wilson)

CASUALTIES GERMAN: 5,600; **YUGOSLAV:** 100,000 killed and wounded, 300,000 captured; **GREEK:** 70,000 killed and wounded, 270,000 captured; **BRITISH:** 11,840 killed and wounded, 7,000 captured, 200 aircraft destroyed
KEY ACTIONS In Yugoslavia, German air attacks paralyzed the enemy high command, while German ground attacks sliced through Yugoslav forces. In Greece in the first three days, the Germans penetrated the Metaxas Line, forcing the surrender of the Greek Second Army, allowing German panzers to get through to the center of the country.
KEY EFFECTS Although successful, the Balkan campaign delayed two panzer divisions from joining the invasion of the Soviet Union in June. Also, the German Army was forced to deploy forces to guard the coastlines and to central Yugoslavia to combat partisan guerrilla groups.

Battle for Crete

LOCATION Crete
DATE May 20-31, 1941
COMMANDERS AND FORCES
GERMAN: XI Air Corps (Student, 10,000 troops, 500 aircraft), VIII Air Corps (610 fighters and bombers); **BRITISH:** 27,500 British/Commonwealth troops, plus 14,000 Greeks (Major General Bernard Freyberg)
CASUALTIES
GERMAN: 7,000 killed and wounded; **BRITISH:** 17,000 killed and wounded, plus 11,800 taken prisoner
KEY ACTIONS The German capture of Máleme airfield enable Germany to land reinforcements there.
KEY EFFECTS High losses on Crete meant that the day of the large-scale German air assault was over.

Battle of the Denmark Strait

LOCATION Denmark Strait
DATE May 23-27, 1941
COMMANDERS AND FORCES
GERMAN: Ships *Bismarck* and *Prinz Eugen* (Vice Admiral Lütjens); **BRITISH:** Task force including ships *Suffolk*, *Norfolk*, *Ark Royal*, *Rodney*, *King George V*, *Hood*, *Prince of Wales*, (Vice Admiral Holland)
CASUALTIES GERMAN: 1,995; **BRITISH:** 1,500
KEY ACTIONS Though the *Bismarck* sank the *Hood*, the German battleship was also sunk on May 27.
KEY EFFECTS After losing their prize warship, the Germans focused on the U-boat war in the Atlantic.

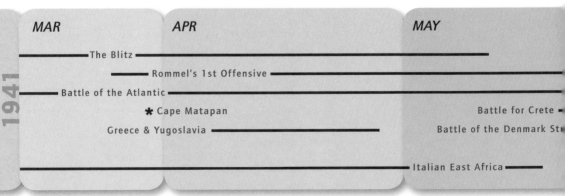

MAR	APR	MAY
The Blitz		
	Rommel's 1st Offensive	
Battle of the Atlantic		
	✱ Cape Matapan	Battle for Crete ◄
	Greece & Yugoslavia	Battle of the Denmark St
		Italian East Africa

1941

MIDDLE EAST

Invasion of Syria

LOCATION Syria
DATE June 8–July 14, 1941
COMMANDERS AND FORCES
BRITISH, COMMONWEALTH, FREE FRENCH (ALLIED):
General Henry Maitland Wilson, 20,000 troops;
VICHY FRENCH: General Henri Dentz, 35,000 troops
CASUALTIES
ALLIED: 3,900 killed and wounded; **VICHY FRENCH:**
3,300 killed and wounded, plus 3,000 captured
KEY ACTIONS Well-armed Allied forces mounted
continuous attacks that wore down the Vichy French,
exhausting their reserves and forcing their eventual
surrender.
KEY EFFECTS Allied control of Syria was secure, thus
increasing the security of Palestine and Egypt.

NORTH AFRICA

Operation Battleaxe

LOCATION North Africa
DATE June 15–17, 1941
COMMANDERS AND FORCES
GERMAN: 13,000 troops, plus 170 tanks and 210
aircraft (Rommel); **BRITISH:** 20,000 troops, plus 200
tanks and 203 aircraft (General Sir Archibald Wavell)
CASUALTIES
GERMAN: 700 killed and 70 tanks destroyed;
BRITISH: 900 killed and 100 tanks destroyed
KEY ACTIONS On June 15, German guns destroyed
dozens of British tanks at Halfaya Pass, effectively
deciding the outcome of the British offensive.
KEY EFFECTS The morale of the Afrika Korps soared,
while British spirits sank. Winston Churchill relieved
Wavell of his command on June 21. Wavell was
replaced by General Sir Claude Auchinleck.

EASTERN FRONT

Operation Barbarossa

LOCATION USSR
DATE June 22–September 30, 1941
COMMANDERS AND FORCES, GERMAN: Army of Norway
(von Falkenhorst), Army Group North (von Leeb), Army
Group Center (von Bock), Army Group South (von
Rundstedt); Finnish Army (Mannerheim)
FORCE LEVELS German: 3 million troops, 3,350 tanks,
7,200 field guns, 2,770 aircraft
COMMANDERS AND FORCES, SOVIET: Northern Front
(Popov), Northwestern Front (Kuznetsov), Western Front
(Pavlov), Southwestern Front (Kirponos), Southern Front
(Tiulenev), Reserve (six armies and four mechanized corps)
FORCE LEVELS: 5.5 million troops, 24,000 tanks, 9,500
aircraft
CASUALTIES
GERMAN: 680,000; **SOVIET:** 2.8 million
KEY ACTIONS The German Blitzkrieg destroyed hundreds
of Soviet aircraft on the ground, and the speed of the
German tank advance created vast pockets of trapped
Soviet armies. At Kiev alone, 665,000 Red Army troops
were killed or captured by German forces.
KEY EFFECTS The decision by Hitler to divert armored
forces from Army Group Center south to destroy Soviet
forces in the Ukraine in July fatally delayed the advance
on Moscow, the Soviet capital. This would have disastrous
consequences in the fall and winter of 1941.

JUN   **JUL**   **AUG**

Invasion of Syria ──────────────────────────

★ Operation Battleaxe

Operation Barbarossa ──────

EASTERN FRONT

Operation Typhoon

LOCATION USSR
DATE September 30–December 8, 1941
COMMANDERS AND FORCES
GERMAN: Army Group Center (von Bock), 1,929,000 troops, 14,000 artillery pieces, 1,000 tanks, and 1,390 aircraft.
SOVIET: Western Front (Konev), Reserve Front (Budenny), Bryansk Front (Eremenko), 1,250,000 troops, 7,600 artillery pieces, 990 tanks, and 670 aircraft
CASUALTIES
GERMAN: 250,000; **SOVIET:** 650,000
KEY ACTIONS Soviet leader Joseph Stalin deployed 100,000 troops from the east to the Moscow Front to confront the Germans, who were being hampered by a lack of supplies and the increasingly severe winter weather.
KEY EFFECTS The end of Typhoon in December marked the start of a Soviet counteroffensive all along the Eastern Front.

NORTH AFRICA

Operation Crusader

LOCATION North Africa
DATE November 18, 1941–January 31, 1942
COMMANDERS AND FORCES
GERMAN: Germany: Panzergruppe Afrika (Rommel), 100,000 troops, 410 tanks, 320 aircraft; **BRITISH:** Eighth Army (Cunningham), 150,000 troops, 700 tanks, 1,000 aircraft
CASUALTIES
GERMAN: 33,000 men and 300 tanks; **BRITISH:** 18,000 men and 278 tanks
KEY ACTIONS In the Allied operation to relieve the besieged port of Tobruk, the British Eighth Army eventually suceeded in driving Rommel's forces back.
KEY EFFECTS The Allied operation had saved the vital Suez Canal from falling into German hands.

PACIFIC WAR

Pearl Harbor

LOCATION Oahu, Hawaii
DATE December 7, 1941
COMMANDERS AND FORCES
U.S.: Pacific Fleet (Kimmel, 70 warships and 24 auxiliaries), U.S. Army (Short). Total number of U.S. aircraft: 300; **JAPANESE:** Carrier Striking Task Force (Nagumo), 18 warships, 3 submarines, 423 aircraft
CASUALTIES
U.S.: In total, 21 vessels sunk or damaged, 3,000 navy personnel killed, 876 wounded, 226 army personnel killed, and 396 wounded, 200 aircraft destroyed; **JAPANESE:** 29 aircraft destroyed, 5 midget submarines lost
KEY ACTIONS Strict radio silence allowed the Japanese fleet to approach Hawaii undetected. On December 7, the U.S. battleships in Pearl Harbor were not protected by antisubmarine nets, there were no barrage balloons over the harbor, and there was no equipment to put up a smoke screen over the anchored ships.
KEY EFFECTS The damage to the U.S Pacific Fleet was not fatal, as all three fleet carriers were absent from Pearl Harbor. The surprise attack outraged the U.S. public, who rallied behind their government. The United States had now entered World War II, and would become a military and economic giant in the next four years.

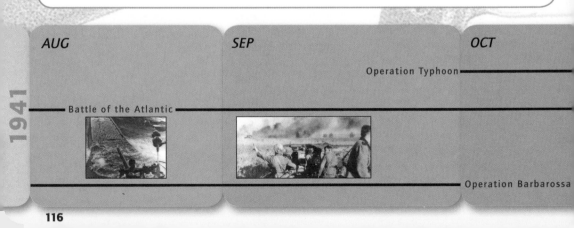

1941

AUG

SEP

OCT

Operation Typhoon

Battle of the Atlantic

Operation Barbarossa

WAR AT SEA

U.S. Submarine Campaign

LOCATION Pacific Ocean
DATE December 1941–August 1945
FORCES AND COMMANDERS
U.S.: Submarine Force Pacific, 288 submarines (Lockwood);
JAPANESE: Combined Fleet, 166 warships, 68 submarines
(Admiral Isoruku Yamamoto). Merchant fleet, 2,337 ships
CASUALTIES
U.S.: 52 submarines; **JAPANESE:** 5.6 million tons (5.7 million tonnes) of shipping

KEY ACTIONS In August 1942, U.S. submarines were fitted with radar, and in mid-1943, U.S. torpedoes were fitted with a more effective detonator mechanism. Both measures increased the number of Japanese ships sunk.
KEY EFFECTS The U.S. submarine fleet made a critical contribution to the Allied victory over Japan. Merchant marine losses crippled Japanese war industries, and the destruction of Japanese naval forces reduced Japan's ability to project their military power throughout the Pacific. Finally, the deployment of its submarine force enabled the U.S. Navy to take the offensive in Japanese-controlled waters and to inflict heavy losses relative to the number of U.S. submarines that were available.

PACIFIC WAR

Malaya

LOCATION Malaya
DATE December 8, 1941–February 6, 1942
COMMANDERS AND FORCES
BRITISH: Malaya Command (Percival), 100,000 troops,
158 aircraft; **JAPANESE:** Twenty-Fifth Army (Yamashita),
100,000 troops, 568 aircraft, 200 tanks
CASUALTIES
BRITISH: 10,500 killed and wounded, 40,000 taken
prisoner; **JAPANESE:** 4,200 killed and wounded
KEY ACTIONS The Japanese made a number of amphibious landings from the sea to penetrate behind British lines.
KEY EFFECTS As 1941 ended, the British and their allies were pushed south toward Singapore by the invading Japanese. They were demoralized, while Japanese morale was high. Also, Japanese aircraft had sunk the British warships *Prince of Wales* and *Repulse* on December 10, further weakening the British war effort around Malaya.

PACIFIC WAR

Fall of the Philippines

LOCATION Luzon, Philippines
DATE December 8, 1941–May 6, 1942
COMMANDERS AND FORCES
U.S.: U.S. Army Forces Far East, 130,000 troops,
120 aircraft (MacArthur); **JAPANESE:** Fourteenth
Army, 43,000 troops, 200 aircraft (Homma)
CASUALTIES
U.S.: 2,000 killed and wounded, 11,500 taken
prisoner; **JAPANESE:** 4,000 killed
KEY ACTIONS On December 22, Japanese landings in the Lingayen Gulf forced MacArthur to withdraw his forces to the Bataan Peninsula. Besieged, the Americans surrendered on May 6, 1942.
KEY EFFECTS The fight for Bataan forced the Japanese to commit more troops than planned to capture an objective far less important than Malaya or the Dutch East Indies.

NOV

DEC

Operation Crusader

Pearl Harbor ✱

U.S. Submarine Campaign

Malaya

Fall of the Philippines

PACIFIC WAR

Fall of Burma

LOCATION Burma
DATE January 12–May, 1942
COMMANDERS AND FORCES
BRITISH: Two British divisions, plus Chinese Fifth and Sixth Armies (Lieutenant General Thomas Hutton); **JAPANESE:** Fifteenth Army (Lieutenant General Iida)
CASUALTIES
BRITISH: 30,000; **JAPANESE:** 7,000; **CHINESE:** 80,000
KEY ACTIONS With the loss of Rangoon, Burma, to the Japanese on March 7, the British Army in Burma was now isolated from its main base in India and dependent for its supplies on the stocks that had been so carefully built up by General Hutton in the Mandalay area. Japanese air attacks between March 23–27 resulted in the withdrawal of all Allied aircraft from Burma to India. The rout of the Chinese Sixth Army by the Japanese between April 18–23 and the fall of Lashio on April 29 resulted in the Allies being forced to begin their retreat from Burma.
KEY EFFECTS The Japanese had now conquered 80 percent of Burma and had cut off the Chinese from their British and U.S. allies.

PACIFIC WAR

Fall of Singapore

LOCATION Singapore Island
DATE February 8–15, 1942
COMMANDERS AND FORCES
BRITISH: Malay Command (Lieutenant General Arthur Percival), 85,000 troops; **JAPANESE:** part of Twenty-Fifth Army (Lieutenant General Tomoyukai Yamashita), 30,000 troops
CASUALTIES
BRITISH: 100,000, mostly prisoners;
JAPANESE: 4,500
KEY ACTIONS On February 8, the Japanese carried out a number of successful landings on Singapore Island, and by February 11 they had captured most of the Allied ammunition and fuel supplies, and taken control of the main water supply. Also by this time, Japanese aircraft had seized total control of the airspace over Singapore.
KEY EFFECTS The conquest of the important British base of Singapore gave the Japanese a relatively safe martime passage from the Pacific Ocean into the Indian Ocean.

PACIFIC WAR

Battle of the Java Sea

LOCATION Java Sea, Pacific Ocean
DATE February 27, 1942
COMMANDERS AND FORCES
ALLIED: Eastern Striking Force, 14 warships (Rear Admiral Karel Doorman); **JAPANESE:** Eastern Invasion Force, 17 warships (Admiral Sokichi Takagi)
CASUALTIES
ALLIED: 5 warships and 5 cruisers sunk;
JAPANESE: 1 cruiser sunk and 6 destroyers damaged
KEY ACTIONS Admiral Doorman was killed and his flagship, *De Ruyter*, was sunk.
KEY EFFECTS The Allied defeat meant that no Allied warships remained in the Java Sea, which made the Japanese invasion of Java inevitable.

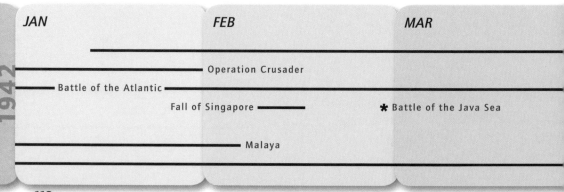

PACIFIC WAR

Battle of the Coral Sea

LOCATION Southwest of Solomon Islands, Pacific Ocean
DATE May 7–8, 1942
COMMANDERS AND FORCES
U.S.: Task Force 17 (Fletcher), Task Force 44 (Crace);
JAPANESE: Carrier Striking Force (Takagi), Port Moresby Invasion Group (Hara)
CASUALTIES
U.S.: 1 aircraft carrier destroyed, 1 damaged, 1 oiler and

1 destroyer sunk, 66 aircraft lost, and 543 men killed or wounded; JAPANESE: 1 small carrier destroyed, 1 carrier severely damaged, 1 destroyer and 3 small naval ships sunk, 77 aircraft lost, and 1,074 men killed or wounded.
KEY ACTIONS On May 8, U.S. carrier *Lexington* was scuttled after being seriously damaged. Also, the Japanese carrier *Shokaku* from the Carrier Striking Force was seriously damaged, to the extent that it was removed from the battle and sent back to its base in Truk.
KEY EFFECTS This was the first time that the Japanese had experienced failure in a major operation. The U.S. victory stopped the Japanese seaborne invasion of Port Moresby.

NORTH AFRICA

Battle of Gazala

LOCATION North Africa
DATE May 28–June 13, 1942
COMMANDERS AND FORCES
GERMAN: Panzer Army Afrika, 113,000 troops, 570 tanks, 500 aircraft (Rommel); BRITISH: Eighth Army, 125,000 troops, 740 tanks, 700 aircraft (Ritchie)
CASUALTIES
GERMAN: 40,000; BRITISH: 75,000 (33,000 taken prisoner at Tobruk)
KEY ACTIONS On May 28–29, Axis forces got behind the British lines and created a fortress called the "Cauldron." Then, on June 10, Rommel launched attacks from the Cauldron, and his tanks and antitank guns worked in close cooperation to knock out most of the British tanks. On June 13, facing defeat, General Ritchie ordered a British withdrawal.
KEY EFFECTS The British retreated to Egypt, followed by Rommel's forces. This left the port of Tobruk isolated, and it fell to the Germans on June 21.

PACIFIC WAR

Battle of Midway

LOCATION Pacific Ocean
DATE June 4–7, 1942
COMMANDERS AND FORCES
U.S.: Pacific Fleet, 3 carriers, 8 cruisers, 15 destroyers, 360 aircraft (Nimitz); JAPANESE: Combined Fleet, 4 large aircraft carriers, 7 battleships, 11 cruisers, 41 destroyers, 272 aircraft (Nagumo)
CASUALTIES
U.S.: 1 carrier and 1 destroyer sunk, 147 aircraft destroyed, 307 men killed; JAPANESE: 4 carriers and 1 cruiser sunk, 272 aircraft destroyed, 3,500 men killed
KEY ACTIONS On June 4, U.S. carrier aircraft sank three Japanese carriers (*Akagi*, *Kaga*, and *Soryu*). The fourth Japanese carrier, *Hiryu*, was sunk later that day.
KEY EFFECTS Midway was one of the most decisive sea battles of the war. Afterward, Japan was on the defensive and the United States grew ever stronger militarily. Japanese morale also suffered as a result of the defeat and the loss of four aircraft carriers.

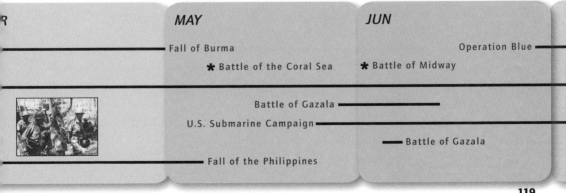

MAY — JUN

Fall of Burma

Operation Blue

★ Battle of the Coral Sea   ★ Battle of Midway

Battle of Gazala

U.S. Submarine Campaign

Battle of Gazala

Fall of the Philippines

EASTERN FRONT

Operation Blue

LOCATION Caucasus, USSR
DATE June 28–August 19, 1942
COMMANDERS AND FORCES
GERMAN: Army Group South (von Bock): Sixth Army (330,000 troops and 300 tanks and assault guns); Second Army (95,000 troops); Seventeenth Army (150,000 troops and 180 tanks and assault guns); First Panzer Army (220,000 troops and 480 tanks and assault guns); Fourth Panzer Army (200,000 troops and 480 tanks), plus the Hungarian Second and Italian Eighth Armies. Luftwaffe: 2,690 aircraft; **SOVIET:** Bryansk Front (169,000 troops), Southwestern Front (610,000 troops) and Southern Front (522,500 troops); tank total of 3,470
CASUALTIES
SOVIET: 250,000 killed or missing, 175,000 wounded; **GERMAN:** 40,000 killed.
KEY ACTIONS On July 13, Hitler decided to advance on Stalingrad and the Caucasus at the same time. In early August, he ordered the Fourth Panzer Army from the Caucasus back to the Stalingrad Front.
KEY EFFECTS The decision by Hitler to switch the Fourth Panzer Army from Stalingrad to the Caucasus on July 13 allowed the Soviets to reinforce the city, which would have dire consequences for the Germans later in the year.

PACIFIC WAR

Guadalcanal

LOCATION Guadalcanal Island, Solomon Islands
DATE August 7, 1942–February 9, 1943
COMMANDERS AND FORCES
U.S.: 1st Marine Division (Vandegrift); **JAPANESE:** Seventeenth Army (General Haruyoshi Hyakutake)
CASUALTIES
U.S.: 1,600 killed, 4,200 wounded; **JAPANESE:** 14,000 killed, 9,000 dead from disease, 1,000 taken prisoner
KEY ACTIONS U.S. Marines defeated Japanese attacks on the Henderson Field air base between September 12 and 14, and again in October and November. The base was crucial to the U.S. plan to deny Japanese planes the means to attack Allied sea lanes.
KEY EFFECTS Victory on Guadalcanal was the first U.S. land victory in the Pacific theater and paved the way for further victories in the Solomon Islands.

PACIFIC WAR

Eastern Solomons

LOCATION North of Santa Isabel, Solomon Islands
DATE August 24–25, 1942
COMMANDERS AND FORCES
U.S.: 2 aircraft carriers, 16 warships, 176 aircraft (Fletcher); **JAPANESE:** K Naval Force: 13 warships (Tanaka), 3 aircraft carriers (Nagumo), 6 warships (Abe), 6 warships (Kondo). Total aircraft: 170
CASUALTIES U.S.: 90 killed, 25 aircraft lost:
JAPANESE: 1 aircraft carrier, 1 light cruiser, 1 destroyer, 1 troop ship sunk, 90 aircraft lost
KEY ACTIONS On August 24, American aircraft sank the Japanese carrier *Ryujo* and Japanese aircraft badly damaged the U.S. carrier *Enterprise*.
KEY EFFECTS The loss of 90 aircraft, valuable pilots, and an aircraft carrier was a severe blow to the Japanese Imperial Navy.

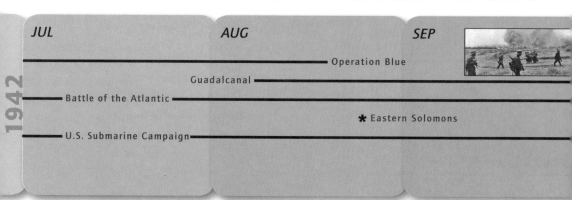

1942

JUL — AUG — SEP

Operation Blue
Guadalcanal
Battle of the Atlantic
★ Eastern Solomons
U.S. Submarine Campaign

NORTH AFRICA

Battle of El Alamein

LOCATION Egypt
DATE October 23–November 5, 1942
COMMANDERS AND FORCES
GERMAN: Panzer Army Afrika, 100,000 troops, 500 tanks (Rommel); **BRITISH:** Eighth Army, 195,000 troops, 1,000 tanks (Montgomery)
CASUALTIES
GERMAN: 59,000 killed, wounded, and captured, 500 tanks destroyed; **BRITISH:** 13,000 killed and wounded, 432 tanks destroyed
KEY ACTIONS On the night of November 1/2 British armored divisions broke through the last line of Axis defenses, and Axis forces retreated westward.
KEY EFFECTS The battle signaled the end of the Axis war effort in North Africa. The Suez Canal—a vital sea route for the Allies—had been saved, and the triumph was the first British land victory over the Germans in World War II. Allied morale rose, as that of the Axis nations dipped.

PACIFIC WAR

Battle of Santa Cruz

LOCATION Santa Cruz Island, Solomons, Pacific Ocean
DATE October 26, 1942
COMMANDERS AND FORCES
U.S.: Task Force 61—two aircraft carriers, 21 warships, 136 aircraft (Kinkaid); **JAPANESE:** four aircraft carriers, 39 warships, 11 submarines, 200 aircraft (Kondo)
CASUALTIES
U.S.: 1 carrier sunk, 1 destroyer sunk, 81 aircraft destroyed, 266 killed; **JAPANESE:** 2 carriers heavily damaged, 1 cruiser heavily damaged, 100 aircraft destroyed, 500 killed
KEY ACTIONS A coordinated Japanese dive-bombing and torpedo-plane attack left the carrier USS *Hornet* so severely damaged that it had to be abandoned. After losing this carrier, the U.S. ships retreated to the southeast. Kondo failed to pursue them.
KEY EFFECTS U.S. losses of the carrier USS *Hornet* and also of a destroyer were more severe than those of the Japanese, who lost no ships in the engagement. However, after the battle both sides were left with several badly damaged warships and the Japanese had lost another 100 aircraft and their irreplaceable pilots.

WAR AT SEA

Battle of the Barents Sea

LOCATION Barents Sea, north of North Cape, Norway
DATE December 30–31, 1942
COMMANDERS AND FORCES
GERMAN: 7 warships (Vice Admiral Oskar Kummetz); **BRITISH:** Force R, plus convoy escorts, 13 warships (Rear Admiral Robert L. Burnett)

CASUALTIES
GERMAN: 1 warship sunk, 330 men killed; **BRITISH:** 2 warships sunk, 250 men killed
KEY ACTIONS When Kummetz in the *Hipper* came under fire from three British ships, he ordered a ceasefire and a withdrawal of all units, and the Allied convoy was saved.
KEY EFFECTS Adolf Hitler was furious and ordered the German battle fleet to be scrapped, but this was later rescinded. However, henceforth, the German maritime war effort would be carried out by the U-boat force.

T | NOV | DEC

Battle of El Alamein ———————

✱ Battle of Santa Cruz

Battle of the Barents Sea ✱

EASTERN FRONT

Stalingrad

LOCATION USSR
DATE November 1942–January 1943
COMMANDERS AND FORCES
GERMAN: Sixth Army, 300,000 troops, 2,000 tanks (Paulus): **SOVIET:** 1.1 million troops, 3,500 tanks (Zhukov)
CASUALTIES
GERMAN: 207,000 killed or wounded, 93,000 taken prisoner: **SOVIET:** 480,000 killed and missing

KEY ACTIONS The failure of the Luftwaffe to supply German troops trapped in the Stalingrad Pocket resulted in food and ammunition shortages. The failure of the German relief attempt in December, Operation Winter Storm, doomed the Stalingrad garrison.
KEY EFFECTS German forces in the south of the USSR were never again able to mount a large-scale offensive. The Soviet Red Army, on the other hand, was able to launch an offensive along the whole of the Eastern Front that involved 4.5 million troops. This resulted in the Soviets regaining most of the territory they had lost to the German advance in 1942.

NORTH AFRICA

Battle of Kasserine Pass

LOCATION Tunisia
DATE February 19–25, 1943
COMMANDERS AND FORCES GERMAN: Panzer Army Africa (Rommel), Fifth Panzer Army (von Arnim). Total German forces: 22,000 troops;
U.S.: II Corps, 30,000 troops (Fredendall)
CASUALTIES
GERMAN: 2,000 killed and 34 tanks destroyed; **U.S.:** 5,200 killed and 183 tanks destroyed
KEY ACTIONS The German attack was at first successful, but then U.S. forces counterattacked, supported by Allied aircraft.
KEY EFFECTS Kasserine was the last successful Axis offensive in North Africa. With U.S. forces advancing from the west and the British from the east, Axis forces were trapped in a pocket around Tunis. In May 1943, they surrendered and 230,000 Axis troops were taken prisoner.

PACIFIC WAR

Battle of the Bismarck Sea

LOCATION Bismarck Sea, near Lae, New Guinea
DATE March 2–4, 1943
COMMANDERS AND FORCES
U.S./AUSTRALIAN: Fifth Air Force (Kenney);
JAPANESE: 8 destroyers, 8 transport ships, 6,900 troops
CASUALTIES
ALLIED: 2 bombers and 3 fighters shot down;
JAPANESE: 2,890 killed, 8 transports and 4 destroyers sunk
KEY ACTIONS Kenney had modified his bomber aircraft to carry 500 lb (227 kg) bombs with delayed-action fuses. The aircraft also had eight machine guns installed in the nose. Throughout the battle, the bombers made a series of devastating wave-level attacks against the Japanese ships.
KEY EFFECTS Japan never again risked large convoys to reinforce their army on New Guinea. This gave U.S. General MacArthur time to build up his forces for an assault on the Japanese base at Rabaul. Kenney's aircraft established air superiority over the Japanese in the region.

JAN

FEB

MAR

APR

1943

———————————————— Stalingrad
—————————————————— Guadalcanal

———————— Battle of Kasserine Pass

—— U.S. Submarine Campaign ——————————

* Battle of the Bismarck Sea

PACIFIC WAR

Operation Cartwheel

LOCATION Solomon Islands and New Guinea, Pacific
DATE June 1943–March, 1944
FORCES AND COMMANDERS
ALLIED: Allied Forces, Southwest Pacific Area (MacArthur);
JAPANESE: Eighth Army Area, 123,000 troops, 500 aircraft (Imamaru), Southeastern Fleet (Kusaka)

KEY ACTIONS A series of naval operations carried out by U.S. forces to isolate the key Japanese base at Rabaul. It was successful in its aims.
KEY EFFECTS Operation Cartwheel became the model for Allied Pacific commanders throughout the rest of the war. The strategy was to advance quickly using air superiority and to bypass major Japanese strongpoints, leaving them isolated and impotent. It also involved attacking Japanese weak spots, avoiding frontal assaults wherever possible, and using techniques of deception and surprise.

EASTERN FRONT

Battle of Kursk

LOCATION USSR
DATE July 5–13, 1943
FORCES AND COMMANDERS
GERMAN: Ninth Army, 335,000 troops, (Colonel General Model); Fourth Panzer Army & Army Detachment Kempf, 350,000 troops, (Field Marshal von Manstein);
SOVIET: Western Front, 211,458 troops (Sokolovsky); Bryansk Front, 433,616 troops (Popov); Central Front, 711,575 troops (Rokossovsky); Voronezh Front, 625,591 troops (Vatutin); Steppe Military District , 573,195 troops, (Konev); Southwestern Front, 65,000 troops (Malinovsky)
CASUALTIES
GERMAN: 50,000 killed, 323 tanks destroyed;
SOVIET: 177,800 killed, 1,614 tanks destroyed
KEY ACTIONS On July 12, a mass tank battle took place, but a counterattack by the Soviet Fifth Guards Tank Army eventually stopped the German advance.
KEY EFFECTS The German defeat at Kursk was a major turning point. Soon, the Red Army would be pushing the Germans back all along the Eastern Front.

MEDITERRANEAN

Invasion of Sicily

LOCATION Sicily
DATE July 9–August 17, 1943
COMMANDERS AND FORCES
AXIS: Italian Sixth Army, 300,000 Italian and 30,000 German troops (Guzzoni); **ALLIED:** U.S. Seventh Army (Patton), British Eighth Army (Montgomery), 500,000 troops, airmen, and sailors
CASUALTIES
AXIS: 29,000 killed and 140,000 taken prisoner: **U.S.:** 2,237 killed, 6,544 wounded; **BRITISH:** 12,843 killed and wounded
KEY ACTIONS By July 24, the U.S. Seventh Army had taken control of the entire western half of Sicily, capturing 53,000 dispirited Italian soldiers and 400 vehicles, for the loss of 272 men.
KEY EFFECTS Axis forces were driven from Sicily and the Mediterranean was opened to Allied shipping. Hitler had been forced to transfer German troops to Sicily from elsewhere, while the Italian leader Benito Mussolini had been toppled from power.

JUN   *JUL*   *AUG*

The Ukraine ━━━━━━━━━━

 Operation Cartwheel ━━━━━━━━━

━━━━ Battle of the Atlantic ━━━━━

━━━━━━ Battle of Kursk

Invasion of Sicily ━━━━━━━━

EASTERN FRONT

The Ukraine

LOCATION USSR
DATE July–November 1943
COMMANDERS AND FORCES
GERMAN: 2.5 million troops (Adolf Hitler);
SOVIET: Red Army, 6 million troops (Joseph Stalin)
CASUALTIES
GERMAN: 213,000 killed and wounded; **SOVIET:**
430,000 killed and wounded
KEY ACTIONS After the Battle of Kursk, the Red
Army swept westward, driving back the Germans.
KEY EFFECTS Vast areas of the central and southern
Soviet Union were liberated by the Red Army. The
German Army faced ultimate defeat. The Germans
had lost thousands of tanks and vehicles, which
meant that they had to rely more and more on
horses for their transportation.

WESTERN FRONT

Invasion of Italy

LOCATION Italy
DATE September 3–December 31, 1943
COMMANDERS AND FORCES
GERMAN: Supreme Commander South (Kesselring); **ALLIED:**
British Eighth Army (Montgomery), U.S. Fifth Army (Clark)
CASUALTIES
GERMAN: 15,000 killed and wounded; **ALLIED:** 21,000
killed and wounded
KEY ACTIONS After landing at Salerno, it took the Allies
five days of desperate defending to repulse the Germans.
KEY EFFECTS The Allies now had bases in southern Italy
from which to launch strategic air attacks on the Balkans
and on Germany; the Mediterranean was now secure;
and German divisions were tied down in Italy opposing
the Allied 15th Army Group and holding those areas
in northern Italy, France, and the Balkans previously
garrisoned by their former Italian allies.

PACIFIC WAR

Gilbert Islands

LOCATION Central Pacific Ocean
DATE November 20-23, 1943
COMMANDERS AND FORCES
U.S.: Task Force 54 (Turner); **JAPANESE:** Betio, 4,800
(Shibasaki); Makin: 800 troops (Ishikawa)
CASUALTIES
U.S.: 3,407 killed and wounded (Betio); 66 killed and
152 wounded (Makin); **JAPANESE:** 4,690 killed, 17 taken
prisoner (Betio); 550 killed, 105 taken prisoner (Makin)
KEY ACTIONS Betio: On November 20, the U.S. Marines

went ashore on a low tide that stranded their landing
craft on reefs. Many troops had to wade ashore under
Japanese machine-gun fire. At the end of the day, 75
percent of the islet of Betio was still in Japanese hands.
KEY EFFECTS For the first time in military history, a
seaborne assault was launched against a heavily-
defended coral atoll, and U.S. planners concluded that
the preparatory bombing and shelling to be delivered on
enemy-defended islands similar to Betio would have to be
increased to destroy Japanese weapons and fortifications.
The battle also highlighted the need for naval gunfire and
air bombardments to coincide with the initial movements
of the landing craft taking the first waves of assault
troops ashore.

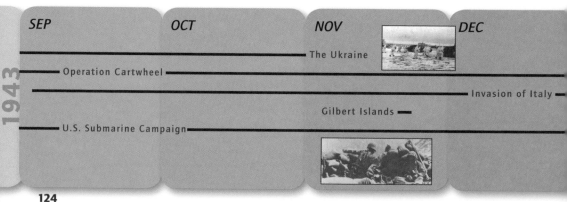

SEP   OCT   NOV   DEC

1943

The Ukraine

Operation Cartwheel

Invasion of Italy

Gilbert Islands

U.S. Submarine Campaign

Monte Cassino

LOCATION Italy
DATE January 17–May 19, 1944
COMMANDERS AND FORCES
GERMAN: Tenth Army (Vietinghoff);
U.S; Fifth Army (Clark); **BRITISH:** Eighth Army (Lieutenant General Oliver Leese)
CASUALTIES
GERMAN: 25,000 killed; **ALLIED:** 54,000 killed and wounded
KEY ACTIONS When the Allies broke through the Gustav Line defenses and also broke through either side of Monte Cassino, the Germans evacuated the entire Cassino Front.
KEY EFFECTS By May 25, with the German Tenth Army in full retreat, the Allies could have captured it. However, they changed their line of attack and headed directly toward Rome instead. The Germans escaped to fight another day.

Anzio

LOCATION West coast of Italy
DATE January 22–May 25, 1944
COMMANDERS AND FORCES
GERMAN: Fourteenth Army, 135,000 troops (von Mackensen); **U.S.:** VI Corps: 100,000 troops (Lucas), 2,000 aircraft; Task Force 81, 250 naval vessels; Task Force X-Ray, 74 vessels (Lowry); **BRITISH:** Task Force Peter, 52 vessels (Admiral Thomas H. Troubridge)
CASUALTIES
ALLIED: 4,400 killed, 18,000 wounded, 6,800 taken prisoner; **GERMAN:** 5,500 killed, 17,500 wounded, 4,500 taken prisoner
KEY ACTIONS On January 22, Lucas made no attempt to drive inland from Anzio, despite there being no German forces in the area. The Allied forces were then pinned down within a small beachhead. Between February 28 and March 4, the Germans launched a series of heavy attacks against the Anzio beachhead.
KEY EFFECTS The presence of a major Allied military force behind the German main line of resistance in Italy represented a constant threat. The Germans could not ignore Anzio and the 135,000 troops of the Fourteenth Army surrounding Anzio could not be moved elsewhere, nor could they be deployed to make the already formidable Gustav Line defenses virtually impregnable.

Operation Flintlock

LOCATION Marshall Islands, Pacific Ocean
DATE January 29–February 21, 1944
COMMANDERS AND FORCES
U.S.: Fifth Amphibious Force, 41,000 troops (Admiral Turner); **JAPANESE:** Marshall Islands Garrison, 28,000 troops (Admiral Masashi Kobayashi)

CASUALTIES
U.S.: 3,000 killed and wounded: **JAPANESE:** 18,800 killed
KEY ACTIONS The U.S. invasion of Kwajalein Atoll on February 1 and Eniwetok Island on February 17.
KEY EFFECTS Rapid victory for U.S. forces in the Marshall Islands added momentum to their Central Pacific drive and put Japanese positions in the Carolines and the Marianas within range of U.S. reconnaissance and bombing aircraft. In addition, new bases were acquired for the U.S. Navy.

JAN   FEB   MAR

Monte Cassino

Kohima & Imphal

Anzio

Operation Flintlock

PACIFIC WAR

Kohima & Imphal

LOCATION India
DATE March 6–June 22, 1944
COMMANDERS AND FORCES
BRITISH: Fourteenth Army (Lieutenant General William Slim); **JAPANESE:** Fifteenth Army (Lieutenant General Renya Mutaguchi)

CASUALTIES
BRITISH: 17,500 killed and wounded; **JAPANESE:** 55,000 killed and wounded
KEY ACTIONS By May 1, the Japanese had still failed to capture Kohima and Imphal. On June 22, the battle at Milestone 109 was won by British and Indian troops, and the siege of Imphal was lifted.
KEY EFFECTS In July, August, and September, the Japanese retreated south, pursued by the British. By the end of September, the Japanese force had almost ceased to exist.

WESTERN FRONT

D-Day

LOCATION Normandy, France
DATE June 6, 1944
FORCES
GERMAN: Total German strength: 850,000 troops, 1,552 tanks, 800 aircraft. **ALLIED:** Total Allied strength: 176,000 troops, 4,000 ships and landing craft, 600 warships, 2,500 heavy bombers, 7,000 fighters
CASUALTIES
GERMAN: 9,000 killed and wounded; **ALLIED:** 3,000 killed and 7,000 wounded
KEY ACTIONS The massive Allied invasion of Western Europe, codenamed Operation Overlord, began on D-Day, June 6, 1944, and would change the course of Wold War II in Europe.
KEY EFFECTS By failing to defeat the bold and meticulously planned Allied invasion within the first 24 hours, the Germans had, in effect, lost the entire battle for Normandy. The war was entering its final phase.

PACIFIC WAR

The Marianas

LOCATION Marianas Islands
DATE June 15–August 10, 1944
COMMANDERS AND FORCES
U.S.: Joint Expeditionary Force—110 transport vessels, 88 fire support ships (Turner), V Amphibious Corps—106,000 troops (Smith); **JAPANESE:** 57,500 (Saito)
CASUALTIES
SAIPAN: U.S.: 14,111 killed and wounded; **JAPANESE:** 30,000 killed; **GUAM: U.S.:** 7,800 killed and wounded; **JAPANESE:** 18,500 killed and taken prisoner; **TINIAN: U.S.:** 1,899 killed and wounded; **JAPANESE:** 6,056 killed, 236 taken prisoner
KEY ACTIONS On Saipan, the Japanese used caves as defensive systems but U.S. flamethrowing tanks proved effective against these caves.
KEY EFFECTS Victory in the Marianas Islands brought U.S. Army and Navy forces one step closer to the Philippine Islands and to the Japanese home islands. American forces were now in a better position to hit Japan's vital East Indies oilfields, as well as to strike at key targets in the Philippines and in Japan itself.

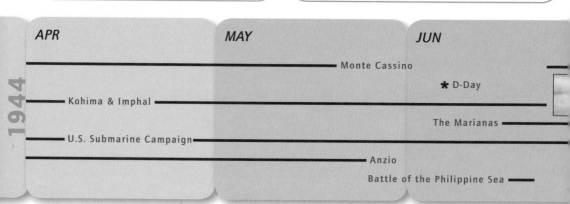

1944

APR — MAY — JUN

Monte Cassino

Kohima & Imphal

✱ D-Day

The Marianas

U.S. Submarine Campaign

Anzio

Battle of the Philippine Sea

PACIFIC WAR

Battle of the Philippine Sea

LOCATION The Philippine Sea
DATE June 19-20, 1944
FORCES AND COMMANDERS
U.S.: Task Force 58 (Mitscher); **JAPANESE:** Mobile Fleet (Ozawa)
CASUALTIES
U.S.: 76 killed, 126 aircraft destroyed;
JAPANESE: Two fleet carriers sunk, 445 pilots killed, 476 aircraft destroyed
KEY ACTIONS On June 19, four waves of Japanese aircraft were decimated by U.S. aircraft and antiaircraft gunfire, and 225 planes were destroyed. Also, two Japanese carriers were sunk by U.S. submarines.
KEY EFFECTS The Battle of the Philippine Sea was the greatest carrier aircraft battle in history, with the result that Japanese naval air power was all but destroyed. The loss of planes, and experienced pilots, proved crucial in the battles that followed.

EASTERN FRONT

Operation Bagration

LOCATION Belorussia, USSR
DATE June 22-August 29, 1944
COMMANDERS AND FORCES GERMAN: Army Group Center, 580,000 troops (Busch); **SOVIET:** 1st Baltic Front (Bagramyan); 3rd Belorussian Front (Chernyakhovsky); 2d Belorussian Front (Zakharov); 1st Belorussian Front (Rokossovsky). Total Red Army strength: 2.5 million troops
CASUALTIES
GERMAN: 190,000 killed and wounded, 160,000 taken prisoner; **SOVIET:** 178,000 dead, 587,000 wounded
KEY ACTIONS On July 3, Soviet forces captured the city of Minsk, cutting off the German Fourth Army to the east. Five days later, the Fourth Army had been wiped out.
KEY EFFECTS Operation Bagration, combined with the Lvov–Sandomierz Offensive in the Ukraine (launched on July 13), dramatically turned the tide of war against the Third Reich. The irreplaceable German losses in Belorussia, taken in conjunction with the Allied landings on the beaches of Normandy on June 6, and the July 20 bomb attempt on Adolf Hitler's life, spread demoralization throughout the Wehrmacht's high command.

WESTERN FRONT

The Liberation of France

LOCATION France
DATE July 25-August 25, 1944
COMMANDERS AND FORCES
ALLIED: 12th Army Group (Bradley), 21st Army Group (Montgomery), 1.5 million troops; **GERMAN:** Commander-in-Chief West (von Kluge), 600,000 troops

CASUALTIES
GERMAN: 500,00 killed, wounded, and taken prisoner; **ALLIED:** 40,000 killed, 165,000 wounded
KEY ACTIONS Between August 13 and 19, 50,000 German troops were captured in the Falaise Pocket. The Allies then raced westward and liberated the French capital, Paris, on August 25.
KEY EFFECTS Although the German Army had suffered a massive defeat, it still retained good leadership and tight discipline. The war in the West would not end in 1944.

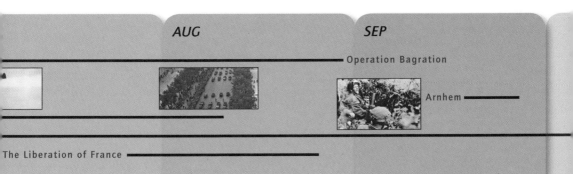

AUG

SEP

Operation Bagration

Arnhem

The Liberation of France

WESTERN FRONT

Arnhem

LOCATION Holland
DATE September 17-26, 1944
COMMANDERS AND FORCES
GERMAN: II SS Panzer Corps (Bittrich); **ALLIED:**
1st Airborne Corps, 35,000 troops—Brereton
(U.S. 82nd Airborne Division & 101st Airborne
Division, British 1st Airborne Division, Polish
1st Parachute Brigade), British XXX Corps
(Lieutenant General Horrocks)
CASUALTIES
GERMAN: 10,000 killed and wounded; **ALLIED:**
17,200 killed, wounded, and taken prisoner
KEY ACTIONS On September 17, at Arnhem,
British paratroopers failed to hold the bridge
because of German resistance. On September
21, British troops were overwhelmed.
KEY EFFECTS The German defense in the West
was still intact. The war would not end in
1944, and the Allies would still have to cross
the Rhine River to enter Germany itself.

PACIFIC WAR

Battle of Leyte Gulf

LOCATION Leyte Gulf, The Philippines
DATE October 23-26, 1944
FORCES AND COMMANDERS
U.S.: Third Fleet (Halsey), Seventh Fleet (Kinkaid). Total U.S.
strength: 1,500 aircraft, 32 aircraft carriers, 12 battleships,
23 cruisers; **JAPANESE:** Northern Force (Ozawa), Southern
Force (Nishimura), Center Force (Kurita), Second Striking
Force (Shima). Total Japanese strength: 130 aircraft, 4
aircraft carriers, 2 hybrid aircraft carriers, 7 battleships, 19
cruisers, 33 destroyers
CASUALTIES
U.S.: 10 ships sunk; **JAPANESE:** 35 ships sunk
KEY ACTIONS October 25-26: Battle off Cape Engaño.
Aircraft of the U.S Third Fleet engaged the aircraft carriers
of the Northern Force. Ozawa lost all four of his aircraft
carriers, all of his 130 aircraft, one cruiser, and two
destroyers.
KEY EFFECTS The Americans had eliminated the threat that
Japanese warships had posed to amphibious operations in
the Philippines, and had effectively isolated the Japanese
garrisons on the Philippines for the duration of the war.

WESTERN FRONT

The Ardennes Offensive

LOCATION Ardennes, Belgium
DATE December 16, 1944-January 16, 1945
FORCES AND COMMANDERS GERMAN: Army Group B
(Model); German strength (on December 16): 200,000
troops. **U.S.:** First Army (Hodges), Third Army (Patton). U.S.
strength (on December 16): 83,000 troops

CASUALTIES
GERMAN: 100,000 killed, wounded, and taken prisoner;
U.S.: 81,000 killed, wounded, and taken prisoner
KEY ACTIONS The German planned to have their panzers
at the Meuse River four days after the attack began. The
stubborn American defense at Bastogne and St. Vith
made this impossible.
KEY EFFECTS Massive German losses in the "Battle of the
Bulge," as the offensive became known, brought about a
more rapid end to the war in Europe.

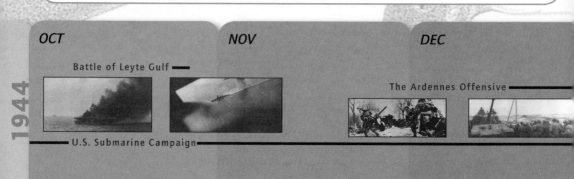

OCT   NOV   DEC

Battle of Leyte Gulf —

1944

— U.S. Submarine Campaign —

The Ardennes Offensive —

PACIFIC WAR

Battle for Luzon

LOCATION Luzon, the Philippines
DATE January 9–August 15, 1945
COMMANDERS AND FORCES
U.S.: Sixth Army (General Krueger), Eighth Army (General Eicheberger); **JAPANESE:** Fourteenth Army, 250,000 troops (General Yamashita)

CASUALTIES
U.S.: 7,933 killed; **JAPANESE:** 192,000 killed
KEY ACTIONS Between February 3 and March 4, U.S. troops captured Manila after fierce fighting in which 16,600 Japanese troops were killed. Then U.S. forces captured the fortress of Corregidor by February 27.
KEY EFFECTS General Douglas MacArthur had fulfilled the promise he had made two years before ("I will return") when he was forced to leave the Philippines when the Japanese invaded.

EASTERN FRONT

The Vistula–Oder Offensive

LOCATION Germany and Poland
DATE January 12–February 3, 1945
COMMANDERS AND FORCES
GERMAN: Army Group Center—Third Panzer Army, Fourth Army, Second Army (Reinhardt); Army Group A—Ninth Army, Fourth Panzer Army, Seventeenth Army, First Panzer Army (Harpe); **SOVIET:** 3rd Belorussian Front (Cherniakovsky); 2d Belorussian Front (Rokossovsky); 1st Belorussian Front (Zhukov); 1st Ukrainian Front (Konev); 4th Ukrainian Front (Petrov). Total: 4 million troops
CASUALTIES GERMAN: 500,000 killed and taken prisoner; **SOVIET:** 43,000 killed, 149,000 wounded
KEY ACTIONS The Soviet offensive was so powerful all along the front that by January 31, 1945, Red Army tanks had reached the Oder River, 250 miles (400 km) from their starting positions just two weeks earlier.
KEY EFFECTS At the end of the offensive, the Red Army was only 37.5 miles (60 km) from the German capital, Berlin. The Soviets would now amass more than two million troops for their attack on the city.

PACIFIC WAR

Iwo Jima

LOCATION Iwo Jima, Pacific Ocean
DATE February 19–March 26, 1945
FORCES AND COMMANDERS
U.S.: V Amphibious Corps—3rd Marine Division, 4th Marine Division, 5th Marine Division, 70,000 troops (Smith); U.S. Navy Fifth Fleet, 485 surface ships (Spruance); **JAPANESE:** 23,000 troops (Lieutenant General Tadamichi Kuribayashi)
CASUALTIES
U.S.: 6,821 killed, 19,217 wounded;
JAPANESE: 20,867 killed, 1,083 taken prisoner
KEY ACTIONS Mount Suribachi fell to the U.S. Marines on February 23. Five days later, they had captured two-thirds of the island.
KEY EFFECTS The capture of Iwo Jima breached the Japanese inner defensive ring around their homeland. In order to keep up the momentum, the Americans next planned to move even closer to the Japanese home islands to capture Okinawa, only 360 miles (576 km) from Japan.

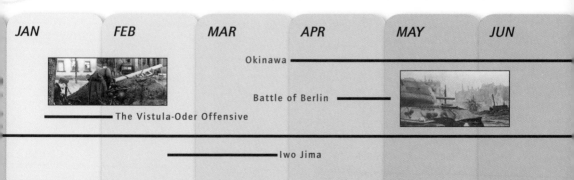

JAN FEB MAR APR MAY JUN

Okinawa

Battle of Berlin

The Vistula-Oder Offensive

Iwo Jima

Okinawa

LOCATION Ryukyu Island chain, Pacific Ocean
DATE April 1–June 30, 1945
FORCES AND COMMANDERS
U.S.: Fifth Fleet, 1,300 ships (Admiral Raymond A. Spruance); Tenth Army, 183,000 troops (Lieutenant General Simon Bolivar Buckner); **JAPANESE:** Thirty-Second Army, 140,000 troops (General Ushijima)
CASUALTIES
U.S.: 12,000 killed, 36,000 wounded, 763 aircraft destroyed, 36 ships sunk, 368 ships damaged.
JAPANESE: 107,539 soldiers killed and 23,764 sealed in caves or buried, 10,755 taken prisoner, 42,000 civilians killed, 7,830 aircraft destroyed, and 16 warships sunk
KEY ACTIONS The battle for the island was split into four phases: first, the advance to the eastern coast (April 1–4); second, the clearing of the northern part of the island (April 5–18); third, the occupation of the outlying islands (April 10–June 26); and fourth, the main battle against the dug-in elements of the Japanese Thirty-Second Army, which began on April 6 and did not end until June 30. On April 7, the Japanese battleship *Yamato* was sunk on its way to Okinawa by U.S. aircraft. Ushijima committed suicide on June 16.
KEY EFFECTS The military value of Okinawa to U.S. forces was great. The island was sufficiently large to house great numbers of troops; it provided numerous airfield sites close to the enemy's homeland; and it also furnished fleet anchorage, which would help the U.S. Navy to keep its operations active. However, the scale of losses suffered on Iwo Jima and Okinawa convinced the U.S. president, Harry S. Truman, and his military chiefs that an American-led invasion of Japan's home islands would result in unacceptably high losses. The historic decision was then taken to use atomic bombs on Japanese cities in order to hasten the end of the war.

Battle of Berlin

LOCATION Germany
DATE April 16–May 2, 1945
FORCES AND COMMANDERS
GERMAN: Army Group Vistula, Third Panzer and Ninth Armies, with LVI Panzer Corps in reserve, 200,000 troops, 750 tanks and assault guns, 1,500 artillery pieces (Generaloberst Gotthard Heinrici); Army Group Center, Fourth Panzer Army, 100,000 troops and 200 tanks and assault guns (Field Marshal Ferdinand Schörner);
SOVIET: 1st Belorussian Front (Marshal Georgi Zhukov), 2d Belorussian Front (Marshal Konstantin Rokossovsky), 1st Ukrainian Front (Marshal Ivan Konev). Total Soviet strength:
2.5 million troops, 41,000 artillery pieces, 6,200 tanks and assault guns, 100,000 motor vehicles, 7,200 aircraft
CASUALTIES
GERMAN: 500,000 killed and taken prisoner;
SOVIET: 81,000 killed, 272,000 wounded
KEY ACTIONS April 21: the artillery of the 1st Belorussian Front began shelling Berlin's eastern suburbs. The next day, Soviet troops broke into the city's northeastern and eastern suburbs. On April 28, Soviet troops were only 1 mile (1.6 km) from Hitler's bunker. Hitler shot himself on April 30.
KEY EFFECTS The fall of Berlin brought World War II in Europe to an end.

World War II in the Pacific formally ended with the Japanese surrender to General Douglas MacArthur on September 2, 1945. The surrender followed the almost total destruction of two Japanese cities (Hiroshima and Nagasaki) by U.S. atomic bombs in August 1945.

JUL · AUG · SEP · OCT · NOV · DEC

1945

U.S. Submarine Campaign

HARDWARE

HEAVY MACHINE GUNS

The purpose of heavy machine guns in World War II was to pin down attacking infantrymen in the open, making them easy targets for small arms and preplanned indirect fires. Light machine guns and machine pistols supplemented the fire of the heavy machine guns and were emplaced in other firing positions to the front and flanks of the attackers. The long range and high rate of fire of heavy machine guns made them formidable battlefield weapons.

MG 1907/12

TYPE: **Heavy Water-Cooled Machine Gun**
CALIBER: **8mm**
LENGTH: **42 in (1.066 m)**
LENGTH OF BARREL: **20.75 in (0.526 m)**
WEIGHT: **44 lb (19.9 kg) for gun and 43.75 lb (19.8 kg) for tripod**
MUZZLE VELOCITY: **2,034 ft (620 m) per second**
FEED: **250-round fabric belt (400rpm)**

HOTCHKISS M1914

TYPE: **Heavy Water-Cooled Machine Gun**
CALIBER: **8mm**
LENGTH: **42 in (1.066 m)**
LENGTH OF BARREL: **20.75 in (0.526 m)**
WEIGHT: **44 lb (19.9 kg) for gun and 43.75 lb (19.8 kg) for tripod**
MUZZLE VELOCITY: **2,034 ft (620 m) per second**
FEED: **250-round fabric belt (400rpm)**

The Schwere Maschinengewehr 08 (specification at right) was one of Germany's most important weapons of World War I, and numbers remained in service up to the outbreak of World War II in 1939, as there were insufficient MG 34 weapons to replace them. However, by 1942 the MG 08 had been retired to second-line duties.

MG 08

TYPE: **Heavy Water-Cooled Machine Gun**
CALIBER: **7.92mm**
LENGTH: **46.25 in (1.175 m)**
LENGTH OF BARREL: **28.3 in (0.719 m)**
WEIGHT: **136.7 lb (62 kg) with spares**
MUZZLE VELOCITY: **2,953 ft (900 m) per second**
FEED: **250-round fabric belt (300–450rpm)**

VICKERS .303 MK I

TYPE: **Heavy Water-Cooled Machine Gun**
CALIBER: **0.303in**
LENGTH: **45.5 in (1.156 m)**
LENGTH OF BARREL: **28.4 in (0.721 m)**
WEIGHT: **40 lb (18.1 kg) for the gun with cooling water**
MUZZLE VELOCITY: **2,440 ft (744 m) per second**
FEED: **250-round fabric belt (450–500rpm)**

BREDA M37

TYPE: **Heavy Air-Cooled Machine Gun**
CALIBER: **8mm**
LENGTH: **50 in (1.27 m)**
LENGTH OF BARREL: **29.1 in (0.74 m)**
WEIGHT: **42.8 lb (19.3 kg) gun; 41.5 lb (18.7 kg) tripod mounting**
MUZZLE VELOCITY: **2,592 ft (790 m) per second**
FEED: **20-round strip (450rpm)**

The Heavy Machine Gun (HMG) Type 3 was adopted by Japan in 1914 as a development of a French weapon. The Type 3 was the standard heavy machine gun of the Japanese Army for many years, and large numbers were still in use in 1941. It was a reliable weapon, but its drawbacks were its poor range and the limited stopping power of its 6.5mm round. In 1932, the Japanese developed a more powerful 7.7mm round offering greater range and hitting power. Of the new weapons produced to exploit the capabilities of the new round, one was the Heavy Machine Gun Type 92. The Type 92 became the Japanese Army's standard heavy machine gun and remained in service throughout World War II. It was robust and reliable, and gave frontline troops sound machine-gun support.

HMG TYPE 3

TYPE: **Heavy Air-Cooled Machine Gun**
CALIBER: **6.5mm**
LENGTH: **45.5 in (1.156 m)**
LENGTH OF BARREL: **29.2 in (0.745 m)**
WEIGHT: **62 lb (28.1 kg) gun; 60 lb (27.2 kg) tripod mounting**
MUZZLE VELOCITY: **2,444 ft (745 m) per second**
FEED: **30-round metal strips (400–500rpm)**

HMG TYPE 92

TYPE: **Heavy Air-Cooled Machine Gun**
CALIBER: **7.7mm**
LENGTH: **45.5 in (1.156 m)**
LENGTH OF BARREL: **29.5 in (0.749 mm)**
WEIGHT: **122 lb (55.3 kg) with tripod mounting**
MUZZLE VELOCITY: **2,395 ft (730 m) per second**
FEED: **30-round metal strip (450–500rpm)**

The Model 1921 and Model 1921A machine guns were subsequently developed into the Machine Gun, Caliber .50in, M2 that was itself the basis for a family of heavy machine guns, all using the same mechanism. The M2 series was manufactured in very large numbers (greater than any other American machine gun), and in 1944 a development of the M2 with a higher rate of fire was introduced as the M3 for aircraft installations.

M2

TYPE: **Heavy Air-Cooled Machine Gun**
CALIBER: **0.5in**
LENGTH: **65.1 in (1.65 m)**
LENGTH OF BARREL: **45 in (1.14 m)**
WEIGHT: **84 lb (38.1 kg) gun; 44 lb (19.95 kg) tripod mounting**
MUZZLE VELOCITY: **2,840 ft (866 m) per second**
FEED: **110-round metal link belt (450–550rpm)**

Based on the Maxim gun, the PM1910 was first produced in 1910, and production continued until 1943. The weapon was immensely strongly built and could be installed on many types of mounting, of which the most common was the Sokolov, in essence a small artillery carriage. For the antiaircraft role, the PM1910 was mounted on a special tripod. The PM1910 was used right through World War II. In 1939, the DShK38 entered Soviet service. It was an extremely capable and robust weapon and was used on Soviet tanks, as well as on armored trains and fast attack craft. However, it was in the ground role that the DShK38 played its most important part in the ultimate Soviet victory over the Germans.

PM1910

TYPE: **Heavy Water-Cooled Machine Gun**
CALIBER: **7.62mm**
LENGTH: **43.6 in (1.107 m)**
LENGTH OF BARREL: **28.4 in (0.72 m)**
WEIGHT: **52.5 lb (23.8 kg) gun; 99.7 lb (45.2 kg) with shield**
MUZZLE VELOCITY: **2,838 ft (865 m) per second**
FEED: **250-round fabric belt (520–600rpm)**

DSHK38

TYPE: **Heavy Water-Cooled Machine Gun**
CALIBER: **12.7mm**
LENGTH: **62.3 in (1.602 m)**
LENGTH OF BARREL: **39.4 in (1.002 m)**
WEIGHT: **73.5 lb (33.3 kg)**
MUZZLE VELOCITY: **2,772 ft (845 m) per second**
FEED: **250-round belt (550–600rpm)**

MEDIUM MACHINE GUNS

Lighter and more mobile than their heavy counterparts, medium machine guns gave infantry units heavy firepower suppport when attacking.

HOTCHKISS M1914
TYPE: Medium Air-Cooled Machine Gun
CALIBER: 8mm
LENGTH: 50 in (1.27 m)
LENGTH OF BARREL: 30.5 in (0.775 m)
WEIGHT: 52 lb (23.6 kg) excluding tripod
MUZZLE VELOCITY: 2,379 ft (725 m) per second
FEED: 24 or 30-round strips, or 349-round belt
(450–600rpm)

FIAT M14
TYPE: Medium Air-Cooled Machine Gun
CALIBER: 8mm
LENGTH: 49.75 in (1.2635 m)
LENGTH OF BARREL: 25.75 in (0.654 m)
WEIGHT: 39.75 lb (17.9 kg) gun; 41.5 lb (18.7 kg)
for the tripod
MUZZLE VELOCITY: 2,592 ft (790 m) per second
FEED: 300-round non-disintegrating belt (500rpm)

Unlike other Browning weapons of its era, the Machine Gun, Caliber .30in, M1917 was designed from the late 1890s with recoil rather than gas operation, and this was so successful that all subsequent Browning automatic weapons used the same system. 68,000 were built, and the M1917 gave good service to its users.

M1917
TYPE: Medium Water-Cooled Machine Gun
CALIBER: 0.3in
LENGTH: 38.64 in (0.981 m)
LENGTH OF BARREL: 23.9 in (0.607 m)
WEIGHT: 32.6 lb (14.7 kg) without cooling water
MUZZLE VELOCITY: 2,800 ft (854 m) per second
FEED: 250-round belt (450–600rpm)

LIGHT MACHINE GUNS

Light machine guns could be operated by a single soldier and were a significant force multiplier for infantry sections.

ZB VZ/26
TYPE: Light Air-Cooled Machine Gun
CALIBER: 7.92mm
LENGTH: 45.75 in (1.161 m)
BARREL LENGTH: 23.7 in (0.672 m)
WEIGHT: 21.3 lb (9.6 kg)
MUZZLE VELOCITY: 2,493 ft (760 m) per second
FEED: 20- or 30-round detachable box magazine
(550rpm)

MADSEN
TYPE: Light Air-Cooled Machine Gun
CALIBER: 7.7mm
LENGTH: 45 in (1.143 m)
BARREL LENGTH: 23 in (0.584 m)
WEIGHT: 20 lb (9.07 kg)
MUZZLE VELOCITY: 2,346 ft (715 m) per second
FEED: 20-, 25-, 30-, and 40-round box magazines
(450rpm)

Arguably the first light machine gun to enter large-scale service anywhere, the Fusil Mitrailleur Hotchkiss modèle 1909 was based on features employed in the larger Hotchkiss machine guns. In World War I, it was used by the French, as well as Britain and the USA. The Chatellerault modèle 1924 was based on the Browning Automatic Rifle, but included two triggers: the front and rear triggers controlled single-shot and automatic fire respectively. Development resulted in the modèle 1924/29, which was the French Army's standard light machine gun at the start of World War II.

HOTCHKISS M1909

TYPE: **Light Air-Cooled Machine Gun**
CALIBER: **7.92mm**
LENGTH: **48 in (1.22 m)**
LENGTH OF BARREL: **21.65 in (0.55 m)**
WEIGHT: **19.8 lb (9 kg)**
MUZZLE VELOCITY: **2,444 ft (745 m) per second**
FEED: **25-round metal strip (500rpm)**

CHATELLERAULT

TYPE: **Light Air-Cooled Machine Gun**
CALIBER: **7.5mm**
LENGTH: **39.65 in (1.007 m)**
LENGTH OF BARREL: **19.7 in (0.50 m)**
WEIGHT: **19.7 lb (8.93 kg)**
MUZZLE VELOCITY: **2,690 ft (820 m) per second**
FEED: **25-round detachable box magazine (450–600rpm)**

The Bren Gun, the most famous light machine gun of World War II, had its origins in a Czechoslovak weapon. The Bren Gun entered production in 1937 and saw extensive service in World War II. The Bren Gun was widely used by resistance forces in Europe, as its light weight, accuracy, reliability, and ease of maintenance were invaluable. The Vickers-Berthier light machine gun, first bult by Vickers for export in 1925, was largely used by the Indian Army, but also by British special forces in World War II. The Lewis Gun was first manufactured prior to World War I, but also saw service in World War II.

BREN GUN

TYPE: **Light Air-Cooled Machine Gun**
CALIBER: **0.303in**
LENGTH: **45.5 in (1.156 m)**
LENGTH OF BARREL: **25 in (0.635 m)**
WEIGHT: **22.12 lb (9.95 kg)**
MUZZLE VELOCITY: **2,440 ft (744 m) per second**
FEED: **30-round detachable curved box magazine (500rpm)**

VICKERS-BERTHIER

TYPE: **Light Air-Cooled Machine Gun**
CALIBER: **0.303in**
LENGTH: **45.5 in (1.156 m)**
LENGTH OF BARREL: **23.6 in (0.60 m)**
WEIGHT: **24.4 lb (10.9 kg)**
MUZZLE VELOCITY: **2,450 ft (747 m) per second**
FEED: **30-round round curved box magazine (450–600rpm)**

LEWIS GUN

TYPE: **Light Air-Cooled Machine Gun**
CALIBER: **0.303in**
LENGTH: **49.2 in (1.25 m)**
LENGTH OF BARREL: **26.04 in (0.661 m)**
WEIGHT: **27 lb (12.15 kg)**
MUZZLE VELOCITY: **2,440 ft (744 m) per second**
FEED: **47- or 97-round overhead drum magazine (450rpm)**

The Fucile Mitriagliatori Breda modello 30 was a light machine gun that served in World War II as the Italian Army's standard light machine gun. In many ways, the M30 was a poor weapon, but for lack of any viable alternative it was retained in service and saw extensive use, especially in the see-saw campaign waged in North Africa. Poor design meant it was prone to jamming and it often became inoperable due to becoming clogged with dust and dirt.

BREDA M30

TYPE: **Light Air-Cooled Machine Gun**
CALIBER: **6.5mm**
LENGTH: **48.5 in (1.232 m)**
LENGTH OF BARREL: **20.5 in (0.520 m)**
WEIGHT: **22.75 lb (10.24 kg)**
MUZZLE VELOCITY: **2,067 ft (630 m) per second**
FEED: **20-round fixed straight box magazine (450–500rpm)**

The Light Machine Gun Type 11 entered service with the Imperial Japanese Army in 1922, and was still the infantry's standard light machine gun when Japan entered World War II in December 1941. It remained in service, even though superior machine guns were created to replace it. The LMG Type 96 entered service in 1936. It was a more modern design, with an overhead box magazine and the facility to use either drum or telescopic sights. Another feature was the provision for a bayonet. The Light Machine Gun Type 99 was the best Japanese machine gun used in World War II. Introduced in 1939, production figures never reached a level where it could entirely replace the older Types 11 and 96.

LMG TYPE 11
TYPE: **Light Air-Cooled Machine Gun**
CALIBER: **6.5mm**
LENGTH: **43.5 in (1.105 m)**
LENGTH OF BARREL: **19 in (0.483 m)**
WEIGHT: **22.5 lb (10.1 kg)**
MUZZLE VELOCITY: **2,297 ft (700 m) per second**
FEED: **30-round hopper using six 5-round clips (500rpm)**

LMG TYPE 96
TYPE: **Light Air-Cooled Machine Gun**
CALIBER: **6.5mm**
LENGTH: **41.5 in (1.055 m)**
BARREL LENGTH: **21.65 in (0.55 m)**
WEIGHT: **20 lb (9.07 kg)**
MUZZLE VELOCITY: **2,395 ft (730 m) per second**
FEED: **30-round detachable curved magazine (550rpm)**

LMG TYPE 99
TYPE: **Light Air-Cooled Machine Gun**
CALIBER: **7.7mm**
LENGTH: **46.75 in (1.19 m)**
LENGTH OF BARREL: **21.5 in (0.545 m)**
WEIGHT: **23 lb (10.4 kg)**
MUZZLE VELOCITY: **2,346 ft (715 m) per second**
FEED: **30-round detachable box magazine (850rpm)**

While to U.S. forces the classic Browning Automatic Rifle, or BAR, was just that, to others the weapon was a light machine gun. The BAR was introduced to give U.S. infantry in World War I a weapon to bolster their firepower, and in World War II it was the standard squad support weapon. The Machine Gun, Caliber .30in, M1919 was one of the definitive machine guns of World War II, and almost 440,000 were produced for service with most Allied nations. The M1919 was also the basis for the M2 series of machine guns used as U.S. warplanes' armament in the period before and into World War II.

BAR
TYPE: **Light Machine Gun**
CALIBER: **0.3in**
LENGTH: **47.8 in (1.214 m)**
LENGTH OF BARREL: **24.07 in (0.611 m)**
WEIGHT: **19.4 lb (8.73 kg)**
MUZZLE VELOCITY: **2,650 ft (808 m) per second**
FEED: **20-round detachable box magazine (300–350rpm)**

M1919
TYPE: **Light Air-Cooled Machine Gun**
CALIBER: **0.3in**
LENGTH: **41 in (1.041 m)**
LENGTH OF BARREL: **24 in (0.61 m)**
WEIGHT: **31 lb (13.95 kg)**
MUZZLE VELOCITY: **2,800 ft (854 m) per second**
FEED: **250-round fabric or metal link belt (400–500rpm)**

The Pulemet Degtyareva Pekhotnii (DP) light machine gun was the first of wholly Soviet design to enter service. Designed in the early 1920s, the DP quickly proved to be a superb weapon, light in weight and with a simple mechanism that contained only six moving parts. It was also very strong and reliable under even the most adverse geographic and climatic extremes. The Soviets used the DP in large numbers right through their involvement in World War II.

DP
TYPE: **Light Air-Cooled Machine Gun**
CALIBER: **7.62mm**
LENGTH: **49.8 in (1.265 m)**
LENGTH OF BARREL: **23.8 in (0.605 m)**
WEIGHT: **26.8 lb (12.2 kg)**
MUZZLE VELOCITY: **2,772 ft (845 m) per second**
FEED: **47-round detachable drum magazine (520–580rpm)**

GENERAL PURPOSE MACHINE GUNS

Reliable, mobile, and having high rates of fire, the German MG 34 and MG 42 heralded a new generation of infantry support weapons.

The MG 34 was the world's first general purpose machine gun, introduced in 1936 and seeing service until 1945. The MG 42, with its high rate of fire, was one of the most feared weapons of World War II.

MG 34

TYPE: General-Purpose Air-Cooled Machine Gun
CALIBER: 7.92mm
LENGTH: 48 in (1.219 m)
LENGTH OF BARREL: 24.75 in (0.627 m)
WEIGHT: 23.1 lb (10.5 kg) with bipod
MUZZLE VELOCITY: 2,477 ft (755 m) per second
FEED: 50-round belt, 50- or 75-round magazine (900rpm)

MG 42

TYPE: General-Purpose Air-Cooled Machine Gun
CALIBER: 7.92mm
LENGTH: 48 in (1.22 m)
LENGTH OF BARREL: 21 in (0.533 m)
WEIGHT: 25.3 lb (11.5 kg) with bipod
MUZZLE VELOCITY: 2,477 ft (755 m) per second
FEED: 50-round belt, 50- or 75-round magazine (1500rpm)

SUBMACHINE GUNS

Combining the high rates of fire of a machine gun with the portability of a rifle, the submachine gun was an excellent weapon for close-quarters infantry work.

The Machine Carbine, 9mm Owen submachine gun was built between 1940 and 1944, by which time 45,000 units had been produced. In service with Australian troops in World War II, the Owen soon showed itself to be a sturdy, reliable, and effective (and therefore a very popular) weapon.

9MM OWEN

TYPE: Submachine Gun
CALIBER: 9mm Parabellum
LENGTH: 32 in (0.813 m)
LENGTH OF BARREL: 9.85 in (0.25 m)
WEIGHT: 8.8 lb (4 kg)
MUZZLE VELOCITY: 1,375 ft (419 m) per second
FEED: 33-round detachable box magazine (680–700rpm)

ZK VZ.383

TYPE: Submachine Gun
CALIBER: 9mm Parabellum
LENGTH: 35.4 in (0.90 m)
LENGTH OF BARREL: 12.8 in (0.325 m)
WEIGHT: 9.4 lb (4.27 kg)
MUZZLE VELOCITY: 1,247 ft (380 m) per second
FEED: 30-round detachable box magazine (500–700rpm)

KONEPISTOOLI M/31

TYPE: Submachine Gun
CALIBER: 9mm Parabellum
LENGTH: 34.25 in (0.87 m)
LENGTH OF BARREL: 12.5 in (0.3175 m)
WEIGHT: 10.3 lb (4.68 kg)
MUZZLE VELOCITY: 1,312 ft (400 m) per second
FEED: 20-, 50-, and 71-round box or drum magazine (450rpm)

The Maschinenpistole 28/II submachine gun was in essence a 1928 development of the MP 18/I, which entered service in 1918. The MP 28/II had a fire selector (single-shot or automatic) rather than the MP 18/I's automatic fire only. It was aimed at the export market and was produced in a number of calibers with features to suit its buyers. It sold well to South American markets, as well as to Belgium, China, and Japan. License-made in Spain and Belgium, the MP 28/II saw extensive service in the Spanish Civil War. When World War II broke out in 1939, all German production went to the German armed forces. The Maschinenpistole Erma (or MPE) was designed in the early 1930s for the Erfurter Maschinenfabrik company, hence the weapon's name. The Erma was a development of a Vollmer design of the mid-1920s, which featured a main spring enclosed in a telescopic tube to keep out dirt and other matter that might otherwise have jammed the action: this system became standard in subsequent German submachine guns, such as the MP 38 and MP 40. The MPE was adopted by the German Army after the Nazis' rise to power in 1933, and remained a first-line German weapon until 1942. The Maschinenpistole 38 introduced a number of unusual and innovative features: the main spring was contained within a telescopic sleeve, the butt could be folded, and the weapon was entirely of steel and plastic construction. Initially created for airborne and motorized troops (and thus with a folding butt), the MP 38 was a technical and tactical success, but was also expensive to manufacture in terms of materials and time. The MP 38 was therefore redesigned as the Maschinenpistole 40 that was generally similar, but easier to manufacture. The MP 40 thus inaugurated the era of the swift and cheap production of basic small arms, and was one of the most important submachine guns of World War II. In contrast to the MP 40, the Maschinenpistole 41 demanded greater manufacturing resources for a weapon that offered little operational advantage over its predecessors, something that Germany really could not afford, so it is uncertain why it entered production. As it was, only small numbers were manufactured, and the MP 41 seems to have been a complete waste of time, manpower, and precious German resources at a crucial stage of World War II.

MP 28/II

TYPE: Submachine Gun
CALIBER: 9mm Parabellum
LENGTH: 32 in (0.81 m)
LENGTH OF BARREL: 7.9 in (0.20 m)
WEIGHT: 8.8 lb (4 kg)
MUZZLE VELOCITY: 1,247 ft (380 m) per second
FEED: 20-, 32-, or 50-round detachable magazine (500rpm)

ERMA

TYPE: Submachine Gun
CALIBER: 9mm Parabellum
LENGTH: 35.5 in (0.90 m)
LENGTH OF BARREL: 9.9 in (0.25 m)
WEIGHT: 9.2lb (4.15 kg)
MUZZLE VELOCITY: 1,247 ft (380 m) per second
FEED: 20- or 32-round detachable box magazine (500rpm)

MP 38

TYPE: Submachine Gun
CALIBER: 9mm Parabellum
LENGTH: 32.8 in (0.833 m), butt extended
LENGTH OF BARREL: 9.9 in (0.252 m)
WEIGHT: 9 lb (4.086 kg)
MUZZLE VELOCITY: 1,247 ft (380 m) per second
FEED: 32-round detachable box magazine (500rpm)

MP 40

TYPE: Submachine Gun
CALIBER: 9mm Parabellum
LENGTH: 32.8 in (0.833 m), butt extended
LENGTH OF BARREL: 9.9 in (0.252 m)
WEIGHT: 8.88 lb (4.027 kg)
MUZZLE VELOCITY: 1,247 ft (380 m) per second
FEED: 32-round detachable box magazine (500rpm)

MP 41

TYPE: Submachine Gun
CALIBER: 9mm Parabellum
LENGTH: 34 in (0.865 m)
LENGTH OF BARREL: 9.9 in (0.25 m)
WEIGHT: 8.15 lb (3.7 kg)
MUZZLE VELOCITY: 1,247 ft (380 m) per second
FEED: 32-round detachable magazine (500rpm)

After its expulsion from mainland Europe in June 1940, the British Army needed a submachine gun that was cheap and easy to make. The result was the Sten Mk I, which entered service in 1941.

Then came the Mk II (see specifications right) that was reliable and easy to maintain. The Sten was simple to conceal and was favored by resistance forces. Several later variants were produced.

STEN GUN

TYPE: **Submachine Gun**
CALIBRE: **9mm Parabellum**
LENGTH: **30 in (0.762 m)**
LENGTH OF BARREL: **7.75 in (0.197 m)**
WEIGHT: **6.625 lb (3 kg)**
MUZZLE VELOCITY: **1,200 ft (366 m) per second**
FEED: **32-round detachable box magazine (540rpm)**

The celebrated Pietro Beretta SpA company of Italy produced several submachine guns for the Italian armed forces. The Beretta M1918 was developed toward the end of World War I, and had an overhead magazine. It was manufactured in two variants. The well-designed M38 and M38/42 submachine guns were among the company's most successful later products.

BERETTA M1918

TYPE: **Submachine Gun**
CALIBER: **9mm Glisenti**
LENGTH: **33.5 in (0.85 m)**
LENGTH OF BARREL: **12.5 in (0.317 m)**
WEIGHT: **7.2 lb (3.27 kg)**
MUZZLE VELOCITY: **1,280 ft (390 m) per second**
FEED: **25-round detachable box magazine (900rpm)**

BERETTA M38

TYPE: **Submachine Gun**
CALIBER: **9mm**
LENGTH: **37.3 in (0.947 m)**
LENGTH OF BARREL: **12.6 in (0.32 m)**
WEIGHT: **8.7 lb (3.945 kg)**
MUZZLE VELOCITY: **1,476 ft (450 m) per second**
FEED: **10-, 20-, or 40-round box magazine (550–600rpm)**

BERETTA M38/42

TYPE: **Submachine Gun**
CALIBER: **9mm Parabellum**
LENGTH: **31.5 in (0.80 m)**
LENGTH OF BARREL: **7.87 in (0.20 m)**
WEIGHT: **7.2 lb (3.27 kg)**
MUZZLE VELOCITY: **1,476 ft (450 m) per second**
FEED: **20- or 40-round detachable box magazine (550rpm)**

Japan was less keen on the submachine gun than other nations, yet in 1940 the Japanese built the Sub-Machine Gun Type 100. Use of the weapon in combat was hampered by the poor quality of the ammunition.

Designed in World War I by J.T. Thompson, the Model 1921 submachine gun was later modifed as the Model 1928. The drum magazine model entered folklore as the weapon of 1930s' American gangsters.

SMG TYPE 100

TYPE: **Submachine Gun**
CALIBER: **8mm**
LENGTH: **34 in (0.867 m) butt extended; 22.2 in (0.564 m) folded**
LENGTH OF BARREL: **9 in (0.228 m)**
WEIGHT: **8.5 lb (3.83 kg)**
MUZZLE VELOCITY: **1,099 ft (335 m) per second**
FEED: **30-round detachable box magazine (450rpm)**

THOMPSON M1928

TYPE: **Submachine Gun**
CALIBER: **0.45in**
LENGTH: **33.75 in (0.857 m)**
LENGTH OF BARREL: **10.52 in (0.267 m)**
WEIGHT: **10.75 lb (4.88 kg)**
MUZZLE VELOCITY: **920 ft (280 m) per second**
FEED: **20- or 30-round box, or 50-round drum (600–725rpm)**

In the 1930s, efforts were made to reduce the complexity and cost of the Model 1928. This resulted in the Gun, Sub-machine, Caliber .45, M1, of which more than one million were built by 1945. It was delivered in large numbers to the forces of other Allied powers, and the Chinese produced their own version. It was a robust, reliable weapon, and easily maintained in the field. Another simple design, the SMG M3, was built in 1942, based on the Sten gun. It was very effective, reliable, and could be easily mass produced. 600,000 units were completed by the end of World War II in 1945.

SMG M1

TYPE: Submachine Gun
CALIBER: 0.45in
LENGTH: 32 in (0.813 m)
LENGTH OF BARREL: 10.52 in (0.267 m)
WEIGHT: 10.45 lb (4.74 kg)
MUZZLE VELOCITY: 920 ft (280 m) per second
FEED: 20- or 30-round detachable box magazine (700rpm)

SMG M3

TYPE: Submachine Gun
CALIBER: 0.45in
LENGTH: 29 in (0.757 m) extended; 22.8 in (0.579 m) retracted
LENGTH OF BARREL: 8 in (0.203 m)
WEIGHT: 8.15 lb (3.7 kg)
MUZZLE VELOCITY: about 920 ft (280 m) per second
FEED: 30-round detachable box magazine (350–450rpm)

Designed for service from 1934, PPD 1934/38 submachine guns derived some features from a pair of foreign weapons, the Finnish m/1931 and the German MP 28/II. In 1941 and 1942, the Germans captured large numbers of PPD submachine guns, which they placed in service, firing either captured Soviet ammunition or the Mauser 7.63mm pistol round that was dimensionally identical to the Soviet type. The PPD38/40 was produced from high-quality materials in the fashion typical of peacetime rather than wartime planning, and so was taken out of production in 1941 after the German invasion of the Soviet Union, which cost the USSR not only vast amounts of territory and personnel, but much industrial capability. The need was for a submachine gun that could be produced quickly and cheaply. This PPSH41 entered service in 1942, and was so easy to make that more than five million had been delivered by the end of World War II in 1945. Similarly, the PPS43 was a simple weapon to build and played a crucial role in the Soviet fightback on the Eastern Front from 1943.

PPD34/38

TYPE: Submachine Gun
CALIBER: 7.62mm
LENGTH: 30.6 in (0.777 m)
LENGTH OF BARREL: 10.75 in (0.273 m)
WEIGHT: 8.25 lb (3.74 kg)
MUZZLE VELOCITY: 1,608 ft (490 m) per second
FEED: 71-round drum or 25-round box magazine (800rpm)

PPD38/40

TYPE: Submachine Gun
CALIBER: 7.62mm
LENGTH: 31 in (0.787 m)
LENGTH OF BARREL: 10.5 in (0.26 m)
WEIGHT: 8 lb (3.63 kg)
MUZZLE VELOCITY: 1,608 ft (490 m) per second
FEED: 71-round detachable drum magazine (800rpm)

PPSH41

TYPE: Submachine Gun
CALIBER: 7.62mm
LENGTH: 33.1 in (0.840 m)
LENGTH OF BARREL: 10.6 in (0.269 m)
WEIGHT: 7.7 lb (3.5 kg)
MUZZLE VELOCITY: 1,608 ft (490 m) per second
FEED: 35-round box magazine or 71-drum (900–1,000rpm)

PPS43

TYPE: Submachine Gun
CALIBER: 7.62mm
LENGTH: 35.7 in (0.907 m) extended; 25.25 in (0.641 m) folded
LENGTH OF BARREL: 10.75 in (0.273 m)
WEIGHT: 7.34 lb (3.33 kg)
MUZZLE VELOCITY: 1,608 ft (490 m) per second
FEED: 35-round detachable box magazine (700rpm)

BOLT-ACTION RIFLES

Throughout World War II the bolt-action rifle was the standard infantry weapon for the majority of armies that took part in the conflict.

FN 1924

Belgium's main constructor of small arms, the Fabrique Nationale (FN) d'Armes de Guerre located in Herstal, license-manufactured Mauser bolt-action rifles from 1889 for the Belgian Army and also for export. From 1919, the year after Germany's defeat in World War I, FN built an updated version of the definitive Mauser Gewehr 1898 rifle, designated the Fusil Mauser FN, modèle 1924, which provided FN with one of its greatest export successes.

TYPE: **Bolt-Action Rifle**
CALIBER: **7, 7.65, and 7.92mm**
LENGTH: **43 in (1.10 m)**
LENGTH OF BARREL: **23.2 in (0.589 m)**
WEIGHT: **8.5 lb (3.85 kg) without bayonet**
MUZZLE VELOCITY: **2,461 ft (750 m) per second with 7.5mm ammunition**
FEED: **5-round box magazine**

ROSS RIFLE MK III

The first Ross rifle was made in 1896, and thereafter there were many service models. In World War I, the Canadian weapon was shown to lack strength and reliability, but it was still used as a sniping rifle. In 1940, 70,000 Ross rifles were sold to the UK, primarily for use by the Home Guard, at a time when Britain was desperate for weapons.

TYPE: **Bolt-Action Rifle**
CALIBER: **7.7mm**
LENGTH: **50.56 in (1.285 m)**
LENGTH OF BARREL: **30.15 in (0.775 m)**
WEIGHT: **9.75 lb (4.48 kg)**
MUZZLE VELOCITY: **2,600 ft (792 m) per second**
FEED: **5-round box magazine**

By the middle of World War I, the French Army ordered a revision of the Fusil modèle 07/15 with a larger magazine. The resulting weapon was the Fusil d'Infanterie modèle 1916. The 07/15 M34 was created in 1934 by shortening the modèle 07/15 and installing a new barrel. The weapon that resulted bore only a limited resemblance to the modèle 07/15 weapon. Production of the modèle 07/15 M34 ended in 1940, when France was invaded by Nazi Germany. In 1936, the definitive Fusil MAS 36 was created. The MAS 36 was the last bolt-action rifle adopted by a major power, and by 1939 was in full production. From 1940, the Germans used it in their own forces.

FUSIL M1916

TYPE: **Bolt-Action Rifle**
CALIBER: **8mm**
LENGTH: **51.4 in (1.306 m)**
LENGTH OF BARREL: **31.4 in (0.797 m)**
WEIGHT: **9.25 lb (4.2 kg)**
MUZZLE VELOCITY: **2,379 ft (725 m) per second**
FEED: **5-round fixed box magazine**

FUSIL M07/1915

TYPE: **Bolt-Action Rifle**
CALIBER: **7.5mm**
LENGTH: **42.7 in (1.084 m)**
LENGTH OF BARREL: **22.8 in (0.58 m)**
WEIGHT: **7.85 lb (3.56 kg)**
MUZZLE VELOCITY: **2,707 ft (825 m) per second**
FEED: **5-round fixed box magazine**

FUSIL MAS 36

TYPE: **Bolt-Action Rifle**
CALIBER: **7.5mm**
LENGTH: **40.13 in (1.019 m)**
LENGTH OF BARREL: **22.6 in (0.574 m)**
WEIGHT: **8.29 lb (3.67 kg)**
MUZZLE VELOCITY: **2,707 ft (825 m) per second**
FEED: **5-round fixed box magazine**

During World War I, the German Army had decided that its standard rifle, the Gewehr 98, was too long for effective use. By 1924, Mauser had developed a shorter rifle, but it did not enter full production until 1935 as the Karabiner 98k. Millions of these weapons in several variants were made before Germany's defeat in 1945.

KARABINER 98K

TYPE: Bolt-Action Rifle
CALIBER: 7.92mm
LENGTH: 43.6 in (1.1075 m)
LENGTH OF BARREL: 23.6 in (0.739 m)
WEIGHT: 8.6 lb (3.9 kg)
MUZZLE VELOCITY: 2,477 ft (755 m) per second
FEED: 5-round fixed box magazine

Teething problems with the Rifle No 1, introduced in 1907, led to consideration of a replacement. The P.13 development model of 1913 was based on a modified Mauser bolt action, but further work of the P.14 definitive model was postponed until 1915, when a variant in 0.303in caliber was ordered from American manufacturers for service as the Rifle No 3 Mk I (see specification). In 1940, British-made No 3 rifles were converted for sniper use, and this saw limited service up to 1943. Work on the design of a newer rifle started during 1924. The new weapon was the Rifle No 4 Mk I that first appeared in 1931, although the UK's straitened financial circumstances of the period meant that full-scale manufacture did not start until 1940. The No 4 Mk I was more accurate than earlier models due to its heavier barrel and longer sight base. However, it was rushed into production in 1940, which led to several teething problems when it entered full-scale service the following year.

RIFLE NO 3 MK I

TYPE: Bolt-Action Rifle
CALIBER: 0.303in
LENGTH: 46.25 in (1.175 m)
LENGTH OF BARREL: 26 in (0.66 m)
WEIGHT: 9.62 lb (4.37 kg)
MUZZLE VELOCITY: 2,500 ft (762 m) per second
FEED: 5-round fixed box magazine

RIFLE NO 4 MK I

TYPE: Bolt-Action Rifle
CALIBER: 0.303in
LENGTH: 44.43 in (1.129 m)
LENGTH OF BARREL: 25.2 in (0.64 m)
WEIGHT: 9.125 lb (4.14 kg)
MUZZLE VELOCITY: 2,465 ft (751 m) per second
MAGAZINE: 10-round detachable box magazine

The Fucile modello 91 was the first rifle of the Mauser-Paravicino or Mannlicher-Carcano type to be taken into service with the Italian Army. This took place in 1892, and the bolt action was that of the Mauser Gewehr 1889 modified with a Carcano bolt-sleeve safety mechanism. The modello 91 was the Italian Army's standard rifle in World War I and was still in use when Italy entered World War II, when Italian leader Mussolini invaded France in 1940.

The Fucile modello 38 was the first rifle created for a new Italian 7.35mm cartridge. The rifle was in fact a straightforward development of the 6.5mm modello 91 weapon with a larger-caliber barrel and modified sights. The weapon entered service in 1938, but was revised to fire the older 6.5mm cartridge (most existing rifles were fitted with a new barrel). After Italy's exit from World War II in 1943, the Germans took over stocks of the weapons.

FUCILE M91

TYPE: Bolt-Action Rifle
CALIBER: 6.5mm
LENGTH: 50.6 in (1.285 m)
LENGTH OF BARREL: 30.7 in (0.78 m)
WEIGHT: 8.4 lb (3.8 kg)
MUZZLE VELOCITY: 2,067 ft (630 m) per second
FEED: 6-round fixed box magazine

FUCILE M38

TYPE: Bolt-Action Rifle
CALIBER: 6.5mm and 7.35mm
LENGTH: 40.2 in (1.02 m)
LENGTH OF BARREL: 21.1 in (0.54 m)
WEIGHT: 7.6 lb (3.45 kg)
MUZZLE VELOCITY: 2,320 ft (707 m) per second
FEED: 6-round fixed straight box magazine

The Rifle Type 38 was a development of the Rifle Type 30. The Type 30 (and thus the Type 38) was based on the Mauser bolt action as exemplified in the Gewehr 98. The Type 38 fired a relatively low-powered cartridge, and, in combination with a long barrel, this resulted in low recoil forces, which suited the generally small size and light weight of the average Japanese infantryman. However, the length of the rifle made the Type 38 difficult to handle, especially after the long Type 30 bayonet had been fitted. The Type 38 was the standard Japanese Army rifle from 1905, and remained in service to the end of World War II. Overall, it was a reliable and robust weapon. An exact contemporary of the Rifle Type 38, being introduced in 1905, the Carbine Type 38 was basically similar and differed significantly only in the length of its barrel. It was intended for service with mounted troops, but with the decline of this branch of the Imperial Japanese Army in the 1930s, the Carbine Type 38 was by 1941 the weapon mainly of second-line forces and also of the garrisons of fixed installations. Like the Rifle Type 38, the Carbine Type 38 was also captured in large enough numbers by the Chinese to equip several formations. The shorter length and lower weight of the Carbine Type 38 by

comparison with the Rifle Type 38 also commended the Carbine Type 38 for use by Japanese airborne forces, which received limited numbers of a version with a butt that was hinged to fold to the right as a means of reducing length still further. From 1932, Japanese forces gradually adopted a heavier 7.7mm cartridge for use in the Type 92 machine gun, and in 1939 a rimless derivative of this cartridge was introduced as the ammunition for an improved Rifle Type 99 version of the Type 38 rifle, despite the fact that the higher recoil forces were difficult for the average Japanese soldier to handle. The chance was taken to introduce other changes, including a rear sight designed to provide antiaircraft capability through the addition of folding lateral arms marked off for speed "lead", a folding wire monopod, and alterations designed to ease production. As the effects of World War II on Japanese war industries became more acute, further changes were introduced to simplify production with poorer materials and less skilled manpower, and from 1943 the weapon was crude in its finish. There were two models which differed only in barrel length (the specification below applies to the shorter-barrel model), and another model was made for airborne troops.

RIFLE TYPE 38

TYPE: **Bolt-Action Rifle**

CALIBER: **6.5mm**

LENGTH: **50.2 in (1.275 m)**

LENGTH OF BARREL: **31.4 in (0.7975 m)**

WEIGHT: **9.25 lb (4.2 kg)**

MUZZLE VELOCITY: **2,395 ft (730 m) per second**

FEED: **5-round fixed box magazine**

CARBINE TYPE 38

TYPE: **Bolt-Action Carbine**

CALIBER: **6.5mm**

LENGTH: **34.2 in (0.869 m)**

LENGTH OF BARREL: **19.9 in (0.506 m)**

WEIGHT: **7.3 lb (3.3 kg)**

MUZZLE VELOCITY: **2,297 ft (700 m) per second**

FEED: **5-round fixed box magazine**

RIFLE TYPE 99

TYPE: **Bolt-Action Rifle**

CALIBER: **7.7mm**

LENGTH: **50.1 in (1.275 m)**

LENGTH OF BARREL: **25.8 in (0.655 m)**

WEIGHT: **8.6 lb (3.9 kg)**

MUZZLE VELOCITY: **2,395 ft (730 m) per second**

FEED: **5-round fixed box magazine**

The first service rifle based on the indigenous Krag-Jorgensen bolt action to enter Norwegian service was the Gevaer M/1894 firing a Mauser 6.5mm rimless cartridge. Production was initially undertaken both in Austria-Hungary and in Norway, but the majority of the rifles were made in Norway. The M/1894 was a reliable weapon that was excellently made of high-quality materials, and was still the Norwegian Army's standard rifle at the time Germany overran Norway between April and June 1940.

GEVAER M/1894

TYPE: **Bolt-Action Rifle**

CALIBER: **6.5mm**

LENGTH: **49.9 in (1.27 m)**

LENGTH OF BARREL: **30.1 in (0.765 mm)**

WEIGHT: **8.9 lb (4.05 kg)**

MUZZLE VELOCITY: **about 2,625 ft (800 m) per second**

FEED: **5-round detachable straight box magazine**

In 1903, the U.S. Army standardized as its infantry rifle a modified version of the short Mauser rifle, and this was generally known as the "Springfield" for the arsenal in which it was first manufactured. The Model 1903 had the look of a typical Mauser rifle, but, being of the short type, could also be used by cavalry. The M1903 was the U.S.'s standard rifle in World War I and remained in large-scale service right up to end of World War II in 1945.

SPRINGFIELD M1903

TYPE: **Bolt-Action Rifle**
CALIBER: **0.3in**
LENGTH: **43.5 in (1.105 m)**
LENGTH OF BARREL: **24 in (0.61 m)**
WEIGHT: **9 lb (4.1 kg)**
MUZZLE VELOCITY: **2,805 ft (855 m) per second**
FEED: **5-round fixed box magazine**

In 1891, the Imperial Russian Army standardized the Mosin-Nagant rifle that combined features created by the Belgian Nagin brothers (magazine) and the Russian Colonel N.I. Mosin (action). The 1891 model (see specification) was the standard Russian rifle of World War I in a form with updated sights and improved ammunition, and remained in service to the USSR's involvement in World War II. Although the Germans captured large numbers of these rifles in 1941, the calibration of their sights in non-metric units meant that only a limited distribution was made of what was now known as the 7.62mm Gewehr 252(r). The vintovka obrazets 1891/30 was a shortened development of the obrazets 1891 rifle with more modern sights and changes to facilitate mass production. The obrazets 1891/30 (see specification) was the Soviet Army's standard rifle through World War II, and was also produced in a sniper model that could be fitted with either the PU x3.5 or PE x4 telescopic sight, and had a turned-down bolt handle to avoid hitting the telescopic sight. These weapons entered service in 1937, and became a major component in the Soviets' World War II propaganda extolling the courage and skill of snipers. The Germans captured large numbers of obrazets 1891/30 rifles in 1941 and 1942, and these were issued with the revised designation 7.62mm Gewehr 254(r) to German second-line forces as well as anti-Soviet units raised from prisoners of war. As was inevitable at a time when horsed cavalry was considered as important as the infantry, the Soviets needed a shorter version of its long infantry rifle. The first genuine carbine version of the Mosin-Nagant rifle was the karabin obrazets 1910. Only limited production was undertaken of this weapon, which was a truncated version of the obrazets 1891 rifle and could not be fitted with a bayonet. Cavalry continued to be important to the Soviets before World War II, and this led to the development of the karabin obrazets 1938 (see specification), which was basically the karabin obrazets 1910 upgraded to vintovka 1891/30 standard. The final version was the karabin obrazets 1944, which was the last Mosin-Nagant weapon to enter production. This differed from the obrazets 1938 weapon only in its permanently attached folding bayonet. The German Army used some captured weapons with the designation Karabiner 457(r).

MOSIN-NAGANT M1891

TYPE: **Bolt-Action Rifle**
CALIBER: **7.62mm**
LENGTH: **51.37 in (1.305 m)**
LENGTH OF BARREL: **31.2 in (0.802 m)**
WEIGHT: **9.62 lb (4.37 kg)**
MUZZLE VELOCITY: **2,660 ft (810 m) per second**
FEED: **5-round fixed box magazine**

MOSIN-NAGANT M1891/30

TYPE: **Bolt-Action Rifle**
CALIBER: **7.62mm**
LENGTH: **48.5 in (1.232 m)**
LENGTH OF BARREL: **28.7 in (0.729 m)**
WEIGHT: **8.8 lb (4 kg)**
MUZZLE VELOCITY: **2,657 ft (810 m) per second**
FEED: **5-round fixed box magazine**

MOSIN-NAGANT M1938

TYPE: **Bolt-Action Carbine**
CALIBER: **7.62mm**
LENGTH: **40 in (1.016 m)**
LENGTH OF BARREL: **20 in (0.508 m)**
WEIGHT: **7.6 lb (3.47 kg)**
MUZZLE VELOCITY: **2,510 ft (765 m) per second**
FEED: **5-round fixed box magazine**

SEMI–AUTOMATIC RIFLES

Semi-automatic rifles differ from bolt-action models in that they use an amount of the energy generated by each shot fired to commence the reloading cycle (extract and eject the spent case, feed a live round and lock the action, and cock the hammer or striker). Due to this mechanical sequence, semi-automatic rifles are often referred to as self-loading rifles.

 In 1940, Germany needed a semi-automatic rifle to succeed the Gewehr 98 series. The Gewehr 41 was less successful than the Gewehr 43, but both saw service until the end of World War II in 1945.

GEWEHR 41
TYPE: **Semi-Automatic Rifle**
CALIBER: **7.92mm**
LENGTH: **46.25 in (1.175 m)**
LENGTH OF BARREL: **21.75 in (0.5525 m)**
WEIGHT: **11.25 lb (5.1 kg)**
MUZZLE VELOCITY: **2,543 ft (775 m) per second**
FEED: **10-round fixed straight box magazine**

GEWEHR 43
TYPE: **Semi-Automatic Rifle**
CALIBER: **7.92mm**
LENGTH: **44 in (1.117 m)**
LENGTH OF BARREL: **21.6 in (0.55 m)**
WEIGHT: **9.56 lb (4.4 kg)**
MUZZLE VELOCITY: **2,543 ft (775 m) per second**
FEED: **10-round detachable straight box magazine**

 The M1 Rifle was the first semi-automatic rifle to enter full service with the U.S. Army in 1932. The M1 Carbine was one of the great weapons of World War II. 6.3 million units were made during the war.

M1 RIFLE
TYPE: **Semi-Automatic Rifle**
CALIBER: **0.3in**
LENGTH: **43.6 in (1.107 m)**
LENGTH OF BARREL: **24 in (0.609 m)**
WEIGHT: **9.5 lb (4.31 kg)**
MUZZLE VELOCITY: **2,805 ft (855 m) per second**
FEED: **8-round fixed magazine**

M1 CARBINE
TYPE: **Semi-Automatic Carbine**
CALIBER: **0.3in**
LENGTH: **35.6 in (0.904 m)**
LENGTH OF BARREL: **18 in (0.457 m)**
WEIGHT: **5.2 lb (2.36 kg)**
MUZZLE VELOCITY: **1,970 ft (600 m) per second**
FEED: **15- or 30-round detachable straight box magazine**

The Simonov 1936 was the first semi-automatic rifle placed in service by the Soviet Army. The Tokarev M1940 was, like most Soviet weapons, a sturdy design that could withstand a lot of punishment.

SIMONOV 1936
TYPE: **Semi-Automatic Rifle**
CALIBER: **7.62mm**
LENGTH: **48.6 in (12.34 m)**
LENGTH OF BARREL: **24.16 in (0.614 m)**
WEIGHT: **8.93 lb (4.05 kg) without the magazine**
MUZZLE VELOCITY: **2,756 ft (840 m) per second**
FEED: **5-round detachable straight box magazine**

TOKAREV M1940
TYPE: **Semi-Automatic Rifle**
CALIBER: **7.62mm**
LENGTH: **48.1 in (1.222 m)**
LENGTH OF BARREL: **24.6 in (0.625 m)**
WEIGHT: **8.56 lb (3.89 kg)**
MUZZLE VELOCITY: **2,723 ft (830 m) per second**
FEED: **10-round detachable straight box magazine**

ASSAULT RIFLES

These all-purpose guns were developed and used by the German Army as a result of studies that showed that the ordinary rifle's range was in fact much longer than required, since the soldiers almost always engaged enemies at short ranges.

 Designed for use by German paratroopers, the FG 42 was one of the most remarkable weapons developed during World War II, incorporating both a permanently attached bipod and a fixed folding bayonet. However, it was expensive to manufacture and only 7,000 units were made. The Sturmgewehr 44 assault rifle was a development of the MP 43 series of weapons, which were very effective in combat, and which paved the way for assault rifle design in the years following World War II.

FG 42
TYPE: Airborne Forces Assault Rifle
CALIBER: 7.92mm
LENGTH: 37 in (0.94 m)
LENGTH OF BARREL: 19.75 in (0.502 m)
WEIGHT: 9.94 lb (4.53 kg)
MUZZLE VELOCITY: 2,493 ft (760 m) per second
FEED: 20-round magazine (750–800rpm)

STURMGEWEHR 44
TYPE: Assault Rifle
CALIBER: 7.92mm
LENGTH: 37 in (0.94 m)
LENGTH OF BARREL: 16.5 in (0.419 m)
WEIGHT: 11.5 lb (5.22 kg)
MUZZLE VELOCITY: 2,133 ft (650 m) per second
FEED: 30-round detachable box magazine (500rpm)

SEMI–AUTOMATIC PISTOLS

Pistols are generally not suitable for the battlefield. With their very short effective range and little ammunition, they are carried in combat by soldiers who are not expected to use them as their main fighting weapon, such as senior officers and noncombatants.

FN HIGH POWER
TYPE: Semi-Automatic Pistol
CALIBER: 9mm Parabellum
LENGTH: 7.75 in (0.197 m)
LENGTH OF BARREL: 4.65 in (0.118 m)
WEIGHT: 2.44 lb (1.01 kg) loaded
MUZZLE VELOCITY: 1,150 ft (351 m) per second
FEED: 13-round detachable box magazine

One of the best pistols ever produced, the High Power design incorporated a positive breech lock. The construction was sturdy and featured an unusual 13-round magazine, which resulted in a bulky but still easily holdable butt. FN's licensed production began in 1935, and, due to its excellent design and build, this weapon is still in service today.

PISTOLE M1935S
TYPE: Semi-Automatic Pistol
CALIBER: 7.65mm Long
LENGTH: 7.4 in (0.188 m)
LENGTH OF BARREL: 4.1 in (0.104 m)
WEIGHT: 1.75 lb (0.79 kg)
MUZZLE VELOCITY: 1,132 ft (345 m) per second
FEED: 8-round box magazine

In 1935, the French Army fixed on its first automatic pistol of indigenous design, the Pistole Automatique modèle 1935A. Derived from the Colt M1911A1, the modèles 1935A and 1935S (specification at right) were both in service when France was invaded by Germany in 1940. German armed forces subsequently adopted both weapons.

Generally known as the "Luger", the Pistole 08 is among the most celebrated pistols ever placed in production. The first Luger pistols for military service were manufactured in 1900 to meet a Swiss order, and the type was also adopted by the German Navy in 1904 and then by the German Army in 1908. It was this last order that led to the designation P 08, which became the most important of some 35 or more Luger pistol variants. The P 08 was the standard German service pistol until 1938, when the P 38 was introduced as its successor, but even so the P 08 remained in production to 1943 and at the end of World War II in 1945 remained in full service for lack of adequate numbers of the P 38. Oddly enough, the P 08 was not a first-class weapon for military use as it was susceptible to jamming when its open toggle mechanism was clogged by dirt. On the other side of the coin, however, the P 08 was a very "pointable" weapon and was therefore fairly accurate. A semi-automatic pistol that was first delivered in 1929, the Walther Model PP had been designed for police use as indicated by its full designation, Polizei Pistole (police pistol). The pistol used the Walther double-action trigger mechanism that was also used on the later P 38, and other features included a lightweight receiver and, next to the hammer, a signal button that protruded when the weapon was loaded. In overall terms, the design was light and slim. The Model PPK was chambered for the same caliber as the Model PP, the magazine holding seven 7.65mm or six 9mm rounds. Like most German small arms, the PP was manufactured to a high standard. The Pistole 38 entered service with the German armed forces in 1938 as successor to the P 08. The P 38 was reliable and in service was a popular weapon, being able to withstand extremes of temperature and inhospitable terrain (especially in the USSR), but was never produced in numbers large enough to allow complete replacement of the P 08.

PISTOLE 08

TYPE: **Semi-Automatic Pistol**
CALIBER: **9mm Parabellum**
LENGTH: **8.75 in (0.222 m)**
LENGTH OF BARREL: **4.06 in (0.103 m)**
WEIGHT: **1.93 lb (0.876 kg)**
MUZZLE VELOCITY: **1,050 ft (320 m) per second**
FEED: **8-round detachable straight box magazine**

WALTHER PP

TYPE: **Semi-Automatic Pistol**
CALIBER: **7.65mm or 9mm**
LENGTH: **6.38 in (0.162 m)**
LENGTH OF BARREL: **3.35 in (0.085 m)**
WEIGHT: **1.56 lb (0.708 kg)**
MUZZLE VELOCITY: **951 ft (290 m) per second with 7.65mm ammunition**
FEED: **8-round detachable straight box magazine**

WALTHER P38

TYPE: **Semi-Automatic Pistol**
CALIBER: **9mm Parabellum**
LENGTH: **8.6 in (0.2185 m)**
LENGTH OF BARREL: **4.9 in (0.1245 m)**
WEIGHT: **2.1 lb (0.95 kg)**
MUZZLE VELOCITY: **1,115 ft (340 m) per second**
FEED: **8-round detachable straight box magazine**

The Beretta M1934 was taken into large-scale service as the Italian Army's standard semi-automatic pistol of World War II. This gun was generally manufactured in 9mm caliber, the round being of the 9mm modello 1934 *corto* (short) type, but small numbers were completed in 7.65mm caliber. The modello 1934 was finished to a high standard, and after their seizure of northern Italy in 1943, the Germans took into service all the weapons they could with the revised designation 9mm Pistole 671 (i).

BERETTA M1934

TYPE: **Semi-Automatic Pistol**
CALIBER: **9mm modello 1934**
LENGTH: **6 in (0.152 m)**
LENGTH OF BARREL: **3.4 in (0.0865 m)**
WEIGHT: **1.36 lb (0.617 kg)**
MUZZLE VELOCITY: **804 ft (245 m) per second**
FEED: **7-round detachable straight box magazine**

Introduced in 1925, the Pistol Type 14 pistol was designed by Colonel Kijiro Nambu and manufactured by the Kayoba Factory Co. Ltd. as the specifically military version of Nambu's 8mm Pistol Type 1904. The 1904 model had been created for the commercial market, but even so had secured major sales to Japanese officers wanting a pistol more advanced than the Type 26 revolver. Basically, the Type 14 was a modfied version of the Type 1904, and the construction was beefed up for service use. However, the Type 14 was, at best, an indifferent pistol prone to reliability problems. Arguably one of the worst, if not actually the worst, semi-automatic pistol ever placed in full military service, the Type 94 pistol was introduced in 1934 and, securing virtually no civil sales, was manufactured in the Japanese Army's own arsenals as the sidearm of the Imperial Japanese Army's officers. Service use very rapidly revealed the extent of the weapon's deficiencies, which included an acute lack of "pointability", a sear that was exposed on the left-hand side of the receiver in a fashion that allowed it to be jolted and so discharge the weapon, and a locking mechanism that allowed the weapon to be fired without the receiver being locked, especially if poor maintenance had allowed the relevant parts to be worn down. All these factors were bad enough when the pistol was manufactured under peace-time conditions, but the situation got worse after Japan's 1941 entry into World War II resulted in a steady degradation of quality control, to the extent that late-production examples of the Type 14 were as dangerous to the firer as the target it was being aimed at! Work on the design of a replacement pistol was launched in 1942 and resulted in the Type 11 pistol, but progress was slow and only 500 of these guns had been completed before Japan's defeat in 1945.

PISTOL TYPE 14

TYPE: **Semi-Automatic Pistol**
CALIBER: **8mm**
LENGTH: **9 in (0.23 m)**
LENGTH OF BARREL: **4.75 in (0.12 m)**
WEIGHT: **2 lb (0.91 kg)**
MUZZLE VELOCITY: **1,066 ft (325 m) per second**
FEED: **8-round detachable straight box magazine**

PISTOL TYPE 94

TYPE: **Semi-Automatic Pistol**
CALIBER: **8mm**
LENGTH: **7.2 in (0.183 m)**
LENGTH OF BARREL: **3.8 in (0.096 m)**
WEIGHT: **1.69 lb (0.766 kg)**
MUZZLE VELOCITY: **1,066 ft (325 m) per second**
FEED: **6-round detachable straight box magazine**

The M1911 semi-automatic was first produced in 1911 by Colt to a classic design by John M. Browning, who created it as a short-range pistol capable of halting a charging man. After that, the pistol became one of the most important military sidearms ever produced. The definitive 1926 variant, the M1911A1 (see specifications right), was used by the USA and many Allied armed forces in World War II.

PISTOL M1911A1

TYPE: **Semi-Automatic Pistol**
CALIBER: **0.45 in**
LENGTH: **8.6 in (0.218 m)**
LENGTH OF BARREL: **5.03 in (0.128 m)**
WEIGHT: **2.44 lb (1.1 kg)**
MUZZLE VELOCITY: **860 ft (262 m) per second**
FEED: **7-round detachable straight box magazine**

The two versions of the Soviets' Pistolet Tula-Tokareva were best known as the TT30 and TT33. Both were based on well-established Browning pistol designs. The TT33 was manufactured in larger numbers than the TT30, in a production life that lasted until after World War II, and, despite the decline in production standards, the TT33 remained an effective, sturdy, and reliable sidearm.

TULA-TOKAREVA 30-33

TYPE: **Semi-Automatic Pistol**
CALIBER: **7.62mm**
LENGTH: **7.68 in (0.195 m)**
LENGTH OF BARREL: **4.57 in (0.116 m)**
WEIGHT: **1.88 lb (0.854 kg)**
MUZZLE VELOCITY: **1,378 ft (420 m) per second**
FEED: **8-round detachable straight box magazine**

REVOLVERS

By the end of the 19th century, the revolver had reached its definitive form and its highest possible effectiveness as a military weapon. Indeed, from the 1880s through World War II, British officers carried such revolvers as the Webley. However, by the 1940s the revolver was totally outdated, but remained in service in some armies until the 1990s.

 During World War I, the British found that their No 1 revolver was too heavy for battlefield use (though the weapon was very accurate). What was needed, the British decided, was a lighter pistol. This resulted in a new pistol that entered service in 1932 as the Pistol, Revolver, No 2 Mk I. It replaced the huge 0.455in Webley revolver that had entered service with the British Army in 1887 after being designed as a powerful "man stopper" for use in colonial warfare. The final version of this series was introduced in 1915, and became the Pistol, Revolver, .455 No 1 Mk VI. By the start of World War II, there were large numbers of the 0.455in revolver still in service.

REVOLVER NO 2 MK I
TYPE: **Revolver Pistol**
CALIBER: **0.38in**
LENGTH: **10.25 in (0.26 m)**
LENGTH OF BARREL: **5 in (0.127 m)**
WEIGHT: **1.68 lb (0.766 kg)**
MUZZLE VELOCITY: **600 ft (183 m) per second**
FEED: **6-round revolving cylinder**

REVOLVER NO 1 MK VI
TYPE: **Revolver Pistol**
CALIBER: **0.455in**
LENGTH: **11.25 in (0.29 m)**
LENGTH OF BARREL: **6 in (0.15 m)**
WEIGHT: **2.4 lb (1.09 kg)**
MUZZLE VELOCITY: **620 ft (189 m) per second**
FEED: **6-round revolving cylinder**

 The Italian Pistola a Rotazione modello 1889 was one of the oldest types of pistol still in service in 1940, when Italy entered World War II. Although the weapon was introduced to Italian service in 1889, it was derived from a revolver first issued to the Italian Army in 1872. The modello 1889 was sturdy and reliable rather than being an inspired revolver.

PISTOLA M1889
TYPE: **Revolver Pistol**
CALIBER: **10.35mm**
LENGTH: **9.07 in (0.23 m)**
LENGTH OF BARREL: **4.79 in (0.122 m)**
WEIGHT: **2 lb (0.91 kg)**
MUZZLE VELOCITY: **837 ft (255 m) per second**
FEED: **6-round revolving cylinder**

PISTOL TYPE 26
TYPE: **Revolver Pistol**
CALIBER: **9mm**
LENGTH: **9.4 in (0.24 m)**
LENGTH OF BARREL: **4.7 in (0.12 m)**
WEIGHT: **2 lb (0.9 kg)**
MUZZLE VELOCITY: **902 ft (75 m) per second**
FEED: **6-round cylinder**

NAGANT 1895
TYPE: **Revolver Pistol**
CALIBER: **7.62mm**
LENGTH: **9.055 in (0.23 m)**
LENGTH OF BARREL: **4.35 in (0.11 m)**
WEIGHT: **1.75 lb (0.795 kg)**
MUZZLE VELOCITY: **892 ft (272 m) per second**
FEED: **7-round cylinder**

BATTLESHIPS

The battleship was the most heavily armed ship in any fleet. Bristling with large and small guns, the battleship was the manifestation of a country's naval power. And yet, as World War II was to prove, the battleship was very vulnerable to enemy aircraft and submarines. In fact, the aircraft carrier would replace the battleship as the most important surface vessel of the fleet.

Dunkerque was one of two new fast battleships built by France in the 1930s, the other being the *Strasbourg*. In World War II, *Dunkerque* was an convoy escort vessel. She was scuttled in Toulon harbor on November 27, 1942, when German forces occupied the port. The fast, modern battleship *Richelieu* was launched in 1935, and during World War II she served with the British Royal Navy. After World War II, *Richelieu* continued to serve the French Navy. She was broken up in 1968.

DUNKERQUE

TYPE: Battleship
LENGTH: 703.75 ft (214.5 m)
BEAM: 102.25 ft (31.16 m)
DRAUGHT: 28.5 ft (8.68 m)
DISPLACEMENT (NORMAL): 26,500 t (26,924 tnes)
DISPLACEMENT (FULL LOAD): 35,500 t (36,068 tnes)
MACHINERY: Steam Turbines
ARMOR (BELT): 9.5 in (241.3 mm)
ARMOR (DECK): 5.5 in (139.7 mm)
ARMOR (TURRETS): 13.2 in (355.26 mm)
GUNS: 8x13in; 16x5.1in
AA GUNS: 8x37mm; 32x13.2mm
AIRCRAFT: 2
CREW: 1,431
LAUNCHED: October 1935
SPEED: 30 knots

RICHELIEU

TYPE: Battleship
LENGTH: 813.25 ft (247.87 m)
BEAM: 108.75 ft (33.14 m)
DRAUGHT: 31.75 ft (9.67 m)
DISPLACEMENT (NORMAL): 38,500 t (39,116 tnes)
DISPLACEMENT (FULL LOAD): 47,500 t (48,260 tnes)
MACHINERY: Steam Turbines
ARMOR (BELT): 13.6 in (345.44 mm)
ARMOR (DECK): 6.7 in (170.18 mm)
ARMOR (TURRETS): 16.9 in (429.26 mm)
GUNS: 8x15in; 9x6in; 12x3.9in
AA GUNS: 16x37mm; 8x13.2mm
AIRCRAFT: 3
CREW: 1,670
LAUNCHED: January 1940
SPEED: 32 knots

BISMARCK

TYPE: Battleship
LENGTH: 823.5 ft (251 m)
BEAM: 118 ft (35.96 m)
DRAUGHT: 31.3 ft (9.54 m)
DISPLACEMENT (NORMAL): 45,200 t (46,923 tnes)
DISPLACEMENT (FULL LOAD): 50,950 t (51,763 tnes)
MACHINERY: Steam Turbines
ARMOR (BELT): 12.6 in (68 mm)
ARMOR (DECK): 3.15 in (80 mm)
ARMOR (TURRETS): 14.2 in (360 mm)
GUNS: 8x15in; 12x5.9in
AA GUNS: 14x4.1in; 16x37mm
AIRCRAFT: 6
CREW: 2,100
LAUNCHED: February 1939
SPEED: 30 knots

TIRPITZ

TYPE: Battleship
LENGTH: 823.5 ft (251 m)
BEAM: 118 ft (36 m)
DRAUGHT: 31 ft (9.45 m)
DISPLACEMENT (NORMAL): 45,200 t (45,923 tnes)
DISPLACEMENT (FULL LOAD): 50,950 t (51,765 tnes)
MACHINERY: Steam Turbines
ARMOR (BELT): 12.6 in (320 mm)
ARMOR (DECK): 3.15 in (80 mm)
ARMOR (TURRETS): 14.2 in (360.68 mm)
GUNS: 8x15in; 12x5.9in; 16x4.1in
AA GUNS: 16x37mm
AIRCRAFT: 6
CREW: 2,100
LAUNCHED: April 1939
SPEED: 30 knots

HMS *Barham* was a fast battleship launched in December 1914. *Barham* served throughout World War I and saw action at Jutland, where she received six hits. Reconstructed in 1927–28, she served in the Mediterranean in World War II and was damaged by enemy air attack off Crete in May 1941. On November 25, 1941, she was torpedoed three times by a German U-boat, capsized, and blew up off Sollum, Egypt. HMS *Centurion*, launched in 1911, saw action in the Battle of Jutland in World War I. Reconfigured several times, *Centurion* was scuttled off Normandy in June 1944 to form part of an artificial harbor for Allied troops landing there

after D-Day. HMS *Duke of York* was launched in 1940. From 1942, she was a convoy escort ship, and in 1943 she was engaged in the action that destroyed the German battlecruiser *Scharnhorst*. She survived World War II and was broken up in 1958. HMS *King George V* was launched in 1939, and, famously, in May 1941 she took part in the hunt for the German battleship *Bismarck*, playing a key role in sinking the fearsome Nazi vessel. She later served in the Mediterranean and the Pacific. HMS *Nelson* performed escort duties in the Mediterranean in World War II. It was on the *Nelson* in 1943 that the Allies' armistice agreement with Italy was signed.

BARHAM

TYPE: **Battleship**
LENGTH: **643 ft (196 m)**
BEAM: **104 ft (31.7 m)**
DRAUGHT: **34.1 ft (10.41 m)**
DISPLACEMENT (NORMAL): **29,150 t (29,616 tnes)**
DISPLACEMENT (FULL LOAD): **33,000 t (33,528 tnes)**
MACHINERY: **Steam Turbines**
ARMOR (BELT): **13 in (330.2 mm)**
ARMOR (DECK): **3 in (76.2 mm)**
ARMOR (TURRETS): **13 in (330.2 mm)**
GUNS: **8x15in; 4x6in**
AA GUNS: **2x4in**
AIRCRAFT: **2–3**
CREW: **1,297**
LAUNCHED: **December 1914**
SPEED: **25 knots**

CENTURION

TYPE: **Battleship**
LENGTH: **597.6 ft (181.2 m)**
BEAM: **89 ft (27.1 m)**
DRAUGHT: **28.75 ft (8.7 m)**
DISPLACEMENT (NORMAL): **23,000 t (23,369 tnes)**
DISPLACEMENT (FULL LOAD): **25,700 t (26,112 tnes)**
MACHINERY: **Four Turbines**
ARMOR (BELT): **12 in (305 mm)**
ARMOR (DECK): **4 in (102 mm)**
ARMOR (TURRETS): **11 in (279 mm)**
GUNS: **10x343mm**
AA GUNS: **4x102mm**
AIRCRAFT: **none**
CREW: **782**
LAUNCHED: **November 1911**
SPEED: **21.75 knots**

DUKE OF YORK

TYPE: **Battleship**
LENGTH: **745 ft (227 m)**
BEAM: **103 ft (31.39 m)**
DRAUGHT: **31.5 ft (9.6 m)**
DISPLACEMENT (NORMAL): **38,000 t (38,608 tnes)**
DISPLACEMENT (FULL LOAD): **44,800 t (45,517 tnes)**
MACHINERY: **Steam Turbines**
ARMOR (BELT): **15 in (381 mm)**
ARMOR (DECK): **6 in (152.4 mm)**
ARMOR (TURRETS): **13 in (330.2 mm)**
GUNS: **10x14in; 15x5.25in**
AA GUNS: **64x2pdr**
AIRCRAFT: **2**
CREW: **1,900**
LAUNCHED: **February 1940**
SPEED: **29 knots**

KING GEORGE V

TYPE: **Battleship**
LENGTH: **745 ft (227 m)**
BEAM: **103 ft (31.39 m)**
DRAUGHT: **31.5 ft (9.6 m)**
DISPLACEMENT (NORMAL): **35,990 t (36,566 tnes)**
DISPLACEMENT (FULL LOAD): **40,990 t (41,646 tnes)**
MACHINERY: **Boilers & Steam Turbines**
ARMOR (BELT): **16 in (406.4 mm)**
ARMOR (DECK): **6 in (152.6 mm)**
ARMOR (TURRETS): **13 in (330.2 mm)**
GUNS: **10x14in; 8x5.25in**
AA GUNS: **32x2pdr; 6x20mm**
AIRCRAFT: **3**
CREW: **2,000**
LAUNCHED: **February 1939**
SPEED: **28.5 knots**

NELSON

TYPE: **Battleship**
LENGTH: **710 ft (216.4 m)**
BEAM: **106 ft (32.3 m)**
DRAUGHT: **35.4 ft (10.79 m)**
DISPLACEMENT (NORMAL): **36,000 t (36,576 tnes)**
DISPLACEMENT (FULL LOAD): **43,140 t (43,830 tnes)**
MACHINERY: **Boilers & Geared Turbines**
ARMOR (BELT): **14 in (355.6 mm)**
ARMOR (DECK): **6 in (152.4 mm)**
ARMOR (TURRETS): **16 in (406.4 mm)**
GUNS: **9x16in; 12x6in**
AA GUNS: **6x4.7in; 8x2pdr**
AIRCRAFT: **none**
CREW: **1,314**
LAUNCHED: **September 1925**
SPEED: **23 knots**

HMS *Prince of Wales* was damaged in the battle with the German warship *Bismarck* in 1941, and later that year was sunk by Japanese bombs and torpedoes in the Pacific. HMS *Vanguard*, launched in 1944, became known as Britain's last battleship. She took no part in World War II and was broken up in 1960. HMS *Warspite* saw action off Norway in 1940 and in the Mediterranean in 1941. In 1944, *Warspite* took part in the bombardment of German defenses in Normandy during the D-Day landings.

PRINCE OF WALES

TYPE: **Battleship**
LENGTH: **745 ft (227.07 m)**
BEAM: **103 ft (31.39 m)**
DRAUGHT: **31.5 ft (9.6 m)**
DISPLACEMENT (NORMAL):
35,990 t (35,565 tnes)
DISPLACEMENT (FULL LOAD):
40,990 t (41,646 tnes)
MACHINERY: **Steam Turbines**
ARMOR (BELT): **16 in (406.4 mm)**
ARMOR (DECK): **6 in (152.4 mm)**
ARMOR (TURRETS): **13 in (330.2 mm)**
GUNS: **10x14in; 8x5.25in**
AA GUNS: **32x2pdr; 16x.5in**
AIRCRAFT: **2**
CREW: **2,000**
LAUNCHED: **March 1941**
SPEED: **29 knots**

VANGUARD

TYPE: **Battleship**
LENGTH: **800 ft (243.84 m)**
BEAM: **108 ft (32.91 m)**
DRAUGHT: **30.25 ft (9.22 m)**
DISPLACEMENT (NORMAL):
44,500 t (45,212 tnes)
DISPLACEMENT (FULL LOAD):
51,420 t (52,243 tnes)
MACHINERY: **Steam Turbines**
ARMOR (BELT): **16 in (406.4 mm)**
ARMOR (DECK): **6 in (152.4 mm)**
ARMOR (TURRETS): **15 in (381 mm)**
GUNS: **8x15in; 16x5.25in**
AA GUNS: **71x40mm**
AIRCRAFT: **none**
CREW: **2,000**
LAUNCHED: **November 1944**
SPEED: **29.5 knots**

WARSPITE

TYPE: **Battleship**
LENGTH: **645.5 ft (196.74 m)**
BEAM: **104 ft (31.7 m)**
DRAUGHT: **33 ft (10.05 m)**
DISPLACEMENT (NORMAL):
31,315 t (31,816 tnes)
DISPLACEMENT (FULL LOAD):
36450 t (37,037 tnes)
MACHINERY: **Steam Turbines**
ARMOR (BELT): **13 in (330.2 mm)**
ARMOR (DECK): **3 in (76.2 mm)**
ARMOR (TURRETS): **13 in (330.2 mm)**
GUNS: **8x15in; 12x6in**
AA GUNS: **8x4.5in; 32x2pdr**
AIRCRAFT: **3**
CREW: **1,200**
LAUNCHED: **November 1913**
SPEED: **25 knots**

 One of the most powerful warships in the Italian Navy in World War II, *Vittorio Veneto* was interned when Italy surrendered to the Allies in 1943.

Japan's battleship *Mutsu* saw action in the Battle of Midway in 1942. She was later destroyed when her ammunition magazine exploded accidentally.

VITTORIO VENETO

TYPE: **Battleship**
LENGTH: **780 ft (237.8 m)**
BEAM: **107.93 ft (32.9 m)**
DRAUGHT: **34.49 ft (10.5 m)**
DISPLACEMENT (NORMAL): **40,517 t (41,167 tnes)**
DISPLACEMENT (FULL LOAD): **45,752 t (46,484 tnes)**
MACHINERY: **Boilers**
ARMOR (BELT): **13.79 in (350 mm)**
ARMOR (DECK): **.39 in (10 mm)**
ARMOR (TURRETS): **13.79 in (350 mm)**
GUNS: **9x12in; 12x6in; 12x90mm**
AA GUNS: **20x37mm**
AIRCRAFT: **3**
CREW: **1,920**
LAUNCHED: **July 1937**
SPEED: **30 knots**

MUTSU

TYPE: **Battleship**
LENGTH: **700 ft (213.36 m)**
BEAM: **95 ft (28.95 m)**
DRAUGHT: **30 ft (9.14 m)**
DISPLACEMENT (NORMAL): **33,800 t (34,431 tnes)**
DISPLACEMENT (FULL LOAD): **38,500 t (39,116 tnes)**
MACHINERY: **Steam Turbines**
ARMOR (BELT): **12 in (304.8 mm)**
ARMOR (DECK): **3 in (76.2 mm)**
ARMOR (TURRETS): **14 in (355.6 mm)**
GUNS: **8x16in; 20x5.5in; 4x3in**
AA GUNS: **20x25mm**
AIRCRAFT: **3**
CREW: **1,333**
LAUNCHED: **May 1920**
SPEED: **25 knots**

The *Alabama* saw action in most of the U.S. Navy's main operations in the Pacific in World War II. The *Maryland* was damaged at Pearl Harbor in 1941, but went on to serve in the Pacific in 1944 and 1945. The *Missouri* saw action in World War II, the Korean War, and in the Persian Gulf War of 1991.

ALABAMA
TYPE: **Battleship**
LENGTH: **680 ft (207.26 m)**
BEAM: **108 ft (32.91 m)**
DRAUGHT: **29.25 ft (8.91 m)**
DISPLACEMENT (NORMAL):
35,400 t (35,966 tnes)
DISPLACEMENT (FULL LOAD):
45,200 t (45,923 tnes)
MACHINERY: **Steam Turbines**
ARMOR (BELT): **12.2 in (309.88 mm)**
ARMOR (DECK): **1.5 in (38.1 mm)**
ARMOR (TURRETS): **18 in (457 mm)**
GUNS: **9x16in; 36x5in**
AA GUNS: **28x1.1in; 24x40mm**
AIRCRAFT: **3**
CREW: **1,793**
LAUNCHED: **February 1942**
SPEED: **27 knots**

MARYLAND
TYPE: **Battleship**
LENGTH: **624.5 ft (190.34 m)**
BEAM: **97.5 ft (29.71 m)**
DRAUGHT: **35.1 ft (10.69 m)**
DISPLACEMENT (NORMAL):
32,500 t (33,020 tnes)
DISPLACEMENT (FULL LOAD):
37,500 t (38,100 tnes)
MACHINERY: **Geared Turbines**
ARMOR (BELT): **13.5 in (342.9 mm)**
ARMOR (DECK): **3.5 in (88.9 mm)**
ARMOR (TURRETS): **18 in (457.2 mm)**
GUNS: **8x16in; 12x5in; 4x3in**
AA GUNS: **8x.5in**
AIRCRAFT: **none**
CREW: **1,500**
LAUNCHED: **March 1920**
SPEED: **21 knots**

MISSOURI
TYPE: **Battleship**
LENGTH: **887 ft (270.35 m)**
BEAM: **108 ft (32.91 m)**
DRAUGHT: **37 ft (11.27 m)**
DISPLACEMENT (NORMAL):
45,000 t (45,720 tnes)
DISPLACEMENT (FULL LOAD):
59,331 t (60,280 tnes)
MACHINERY: **Geared Turbines**
ARMOR (BELT): **12.2 in (309.88 mm)**
ARMOR (DECK): **5 in (127 mm)**
ARMOR (TURRETS): **17 in (431.8 mm)**
GUNS: **9x16in; 20x5in**
AA GUNS: **80x40mm; 60x20mm**
AIRCRAFT: **3**
CREW: **1,851**
LAUNCHED: **January 1944**
SPEED: **33 knots**

NAGATO
TYPE: **Battleship**
LENGTH: **700 ft (213.36 m)**
BEAM: **95 ft (28.95 m)**
DRAUGHT: **30 ft (9.14 m)**
DISPLACEMENT (NORMAL):
33,800 t (34,341 tnes)
DISPLACEMENT (FULL LOAD):
38,500 t (39,116 tnes)
MACHINERY: **Steam Turbines**
ARMOR (BELT): **12 in (304.8 mm)**
ARMOR (DECK): **3 in (76.2 mm)**
ARMOR (TURRETS): **14 in (355.6 mm)**
GUNS: **8x16in; 20x5.5in**
AA GUNS: **20x25mm**
AIRCRAFT: **3**
CREW: **1,333**
LAUNCHED: **November 1919**
SPEED: **27 knots**

YAMATO
TYPE: **Battleship**
LENGTH: **862.5 ft (262.89 m)**
BEAM: **121 ft (36.88 m)**
DRAUGHT: **34 ft (10.36 m)**
DISPLACEMENT (NORMAL):
63,000 t (64,008 tnes)
DISPLACEMENT (FULL LOAD):
71,659 t (72,806 tnes)
MACHINERY: **Steam Turbines**
ARMOR (BELT): **16.1 in (409 mm)**
ARMOR (DECK): **7.8 in (198.12 mm)**
ARMOR (TURRETS): **25 in (635 mm)**
GUNS: **19x18in; 12x6in; 12x5in**
AA GUNS: **24x25mm; 1x13.2mm**
AIRCRAFT: **5**
CREW: **2,500**
LAUNCHED: **August 1940**
SPEED: **27 knots**

SOUTH DAKOTA
TYPE: **Battleship**
LENGTH: **680 ft (207.26 m)**
BEAM: **108 ft (32.91 m)**
DRAUGHT: **36.3 ft (11.06 m)**
DISPLACEMENT (NORMAL):
34,563 t (35,116 tnes)
DISPLACEMENT (FULL LOAD):
46,218 t (46,957 tnes)
MACHINERY: **Geared Turbines**
ARMOR (BELT): **12.2 in (309.88 mm)**
ARMOR (DECK): **1.5 in (38.1 mm)**
ARMOR (TURRETS): **18 in (457.2 mm)**
GUNS: **9x16in; 20x5in**
AA GUNS: **24x40mm; 35x20mm**
AIRCRAFT: **none**
CREW: **1,793**
LAUNCHED: **June 1941**
SPEED: **27.8 knots**

POCKET BATTLESHIPS/BATTLECRUISERS

Officially classed as a *Panzerschiff* (Armored Ship), but more popularly known as a "pocket battleship", the *Admiral Graf Spee* was a fast commerce raider. In 1939, in the South Atlantic, she sank or captured nine British merchant vessels. In December 1939, she was scuttled by her captain to prevent the ship falling into British hands. Originally named *Deutschland*, the *Lützow* saw action off Norway and in the Atlantic in World War II. On April 16, 1945, the *Lützow* was bombed and sunk in shallow water at Swinemunde by British aircraft, which were roaming the undefended skies of Germany at will.

ADMIRAL GRAF SPEE

TYPE: **Pocket Battleship**
LENGTH: **616.5 ft (187.9 m)**
BEAM: **71 ft (21.64 m)**
DRAUGHT: **24 ft (7.31 m)**
DISPLACEMENT (NORMAL): **13,600 t (13,818 tnes)**
DISPLACEMENT (FULL LOAD): **16,023 t (16,279 tnes)**
MACHINERY: **Diesel**
ARMOR (BELT): **2.3 in (58.42 mm)**
ARMOR (DECK): **1.6 in (40.64 mm)**
ARMOR (TURRETS): **5.5 in (139.7 mm)**
GUNS: **6x11in; 8x5.9in; 6x3.5in**
AA GUNS: **none**
AIRCRAFT: **2**
CREW: **1,150**
LAUNCHED: **June 1934**
SPEED: **26 knots**

LÜTZOW

TYPE: **Pocket Battleship**
LENGTH: **616.5 ft (187.9 m)**
BEAM: **70 ft (21.33 m)**
DRAUGHT: **23.75 ft (7.23 m)**
DISPLACEMENT (NORMAL): **13,600 t (13,817 tnes)**
DISPLACEMENT (FULL LOAD): **15,423 t (15,670 tnes)**
MACHINERY: **Diesel**
ARMOR (BELT): **2.3 in (58.42 mm)**
ARMOR (DECK): **1.6 in (40.64 mm)**
ARMOR (TURRETS): **5.5 in (139.7 mm)**
GUNS: **6x11in; 8x5.9in**
AA GUNS: **6x3.46in**
AIRCRAFT: **2**
CREW: **1,150**
LAUNCHED: **May 1931**
SPEED: **26 knots**

German battlecruisers *Gneisenau* and *Scharnhorst* made their first Atlantic sortie in November 1939, sinking the British ship *Rawalpindi*, and in 1940 they sank the British aircraft carrier *Glorious* and her escorting destroyers *Ardent* and *Acasta*. In February 1942, the two German battlecruisers and the heavy cruiser *Prinz Eugen* made the famous dash through the English Channel from Brest in France back home to Germany. In late December 1943, *Scharnhorst* was intercepted off Norway's North Cape by a strong force of British warships and was sunk. *Gneisenau* was scuttled in March 1945.

GNEISENAU

TYPE: **Battlecruiser**
LENGTH: **753.75 ft (229.74 m)**
BEAM: **98.3 ft (30 m)**
DRAUGHT: **28.5 ft (8.68 m)**
DISPLACEMENT (NORMAL): **34,850 t (35,407 tnes)**
DISPLACEMENT (FULL LOAD): **38,900 t (39522 tnes)**
MACHINERY: **Steam Turbines**
ARMOR (BELT): **13.8 in (350.5 mm)**
ARMOR (DECK): **2 in (50.8 mm)**
ARMOR (TURRETS): **14.2 in (360.68 mm)**
GUNS: **9x11in; 12x5.9in; 14x4in**
AA GUNS: **16x37mm; 8x20mm**
AIRCRAFT: **3**
CREW: **1,670**
LAUNCHED: **December 1936**
SPEED: **31.5 knots**

SCHARNHORST

TYPE: **Battlecruiser**
LENGTH: **757.75 ft (230.96 m)**
BEAM: **898.4 ft (30 m)**
DRAUGHT: **28.5 ft (8.68 m)**
DISPLACEMENT (NORMAL): **34,850 t (35,408 tnes)**
DISPLACEMENT (FULL LOAD): **38,900 t (39,522 tnes)**
MACHINERY: **Steam Turbines**
ARMOR (BELT): **13.8 in (350.5 mm)**
ARMOR (DECK): **2 in (50.8 mm)**
ARMOR (TURRETS): **14.2 in (360.68 mm)**
GUNS: **9x11in; 12x5.9in; 14x4in**
AA GUNS: **16x37mm**
AIRCRAFT: **3**
CREW: **1,670**
LAUNCHED: **October 1936**
SPEED: **31.5 knots**

When HMS *Hood* was launched in 1918, she was the largest warship in the world, and remained so until World War II. With a speed of 32 knots, she was also one of the fastest, deck armor having been sacrificed to produce a higher speed. In May 1941, along with several other British warships, *Hood* sailed to intercept the German battleship *Bismarck* and the heavy cruiser *Prinz Eugen* in the Denmark Strait. In the running battle that followed, a salvo from the *Bismarck* penetrated one of *Hood*'s ammunition magazines. She blew up at once and sank with the loss of 1,415 crew. HMS *Repulse* served in both World War I and World War II. In May 1941, she took part in the search for the *Bismarck*. Later in 1941, together with the *Prince of Wales*, *Repulse* deployed to the Far East to strengthen the defenses of Singapore. It was a fatal decision, for on December 10, while sailing to operate against Japanese forces, both ships were sunk off the east coast of Malaya by Japanese air attack.

HOOD

TYPE: **Battlecruiser**
LENGTH: **860.5 ft (262.2 m)**
BEAM: **105 ft (32 m)**
DRAUGHT: **33.3 ft (10.14 m)**
DISPLACEMENT (NORMAL): **42,100 t (42,774 tnes)**
DISPLACEMENT (FULL LOAD): **46,200 t (46,939 tnes)**
MACHINERY: **Boilers & Steam Turbines**
ARMOR (BELT): **12 in (304.8 mm)**
ARMOR (DECK): **3 in (76.2 mm)**
ARMOR (TURRETS): **11 in (279.4 mm)**
GUNS: **8x15in**
AA GUNS: **14x4in; 24x2pdr; 8x.5in**
AIRCRAFT: **none**
CREW: **1,418**
LAUNCHED: **August 1918**
SPEED: **28.8 knots**

REPULSE

TYPE: **Battlecruiser**
LENGTH: **794.25 ft (242 m)**
BEAM: **90 ft (27.43 m)**
DRAUGHT: **31.75 ft (9.67 m)**
DISPLACEMENT (NORMAL): **32,000 t (32,512 tnes)**
DISPLACEMENT (FULL LOAD): **37,400 t (38,000 tnes)**
MACHINERY: **Steam Turbines**
ARMOR (BELT): **9 in (228.6 mm)**
ARMOR (DECK): **3.5 in (88.9 mm)**
ARMOR (TURRETS): **11 in (279.4 mm)**
GUNS: **6x15in; 9x4in**
AA GUNS: **24x2pdr; 16x.5in**
AIRCRAFT: **4**
CREW: **1,309**
LAUNCHED: **August 1916**
SPEED: **32 knots**

The battlecruiser *Haruna* and her three sister-ships, *Hiei*, *Kirishima*, and *Kongo*, were designed by an Englishman, Sir George Thurston. *Hiei* was launched in 1912 and *Haruna* in 1913. In December 1941, *Haruna* served in Malaya and the East Indies, and in 1942 took part in the Battle of Midway. Later, she participated in the Battles of Guadalcanal, Santa Cruz, Philippine Sea, and Leyte Gulf. On July 28, 1945, she was sunk by U.S. carrier aircraft. *Hiei* was fully modernized by 1941, and was part of the Japanese task force for the attack on Pearl Harbor. She was sunk by American forces in 1942.

HARUNA

TYPE: **Battlecruiser**
LENGTH: **704 ft (215 m)**
BEAM: **92 ft (28.04 m)**
DRAUGHT: **27.5 ft (8.38 m)**
DISPLACEMENT (NORMAL): **27,500 t (27,940 tnes)**
DISPLACEMENT (FULL LOAD): **32,300 t (32,817 tnes)**
MACHINERY: **Steam Turbines**
ARMOR (BELT): **8 in (203.2 mm)**
ARMOR (DECK): **2.2 in (55.88 mm)**
ARMOR (TURRETS): **9 in (228.6 mm)**
GUNS: **8x14in; 16x6in; 8x3in**
AA GUNS: **none**
AIRCRAFT: **3**
CREW: **1,221**
LAUNCHED: **December 1913**
SPEED: **27 knots**

HIEI

TYPE: **Battlecruiser**
LENGTH: **704 ft (214.57 m)**
BEAM: **92 ft (28.04 m)**
DRAUGHT: **27.5 ft (8.38 m)**
DISPLACEMENT (NORMAL): **27,500 t (27,940 tnes)**
DISPLACEMENT (FULL LOAD): **32,300 t (32,817 tnes)**
MACHINERY: **Boilers & Steam Turbines**
ARMOR (BELT): **8 in (203.2 mm)**
ARMOR (DECK): **2.2 in (55.88 mm)**
ARMOR (TURRETS): **9 in (228.6 mm)**
GUNS: **8x14in; 16x6in; 8x3in**
AA GUNS: **none**
AIRCRAFT: **3**
CREW: **1,201**
LAUNCHED: **November 1912**
SPEED: **27 knots**

DREADNOUGHTS

HMS Dreadnought, *launched in 1906, represented one of the most notable design transformations of the armored warship era and created a whole new class of battleships.*

Schleswig-Holstein was launched in 1906 and served with the German High Seas Fleet, seeing action in the Battle of Jutland in 1916. After World War I, she was one of the small force of warships that Germany was permitted to retain by the Versailles Treaty for coastal defense in the post-war years. After reconstruction, she was used as a cadet training ship. In 1939, she was brought back into firstline service to provide fire support for German forces invading Poland, and, on September 1, her four 11 in (280 mm) guns fired the opening shots of World War II when she shelled the Polish fortress of Westerplatte. She later led a battle group covering troop transports to Norway in 1940. On December 18, 1944, she was severely damaged in an RAF bombing raid on Gdynia, and she was finally scuttled on March 21, 1945.

SCHLESWIG-HOLSTEIN

TYPE: **Pre-Dreadnought**
LENGTH: **418.5 ft (127.55 m)**
BEAM: **72.6 ft (22.12 m)**
DRAUGHT: **27 ft (8.22 m)**
DISPLACEMENT (NORMAL): **13,190 t (13,400 tnes)**
DISPLACEMENT (FULL LOAD): **14,220 t (14,441 tnes)**
MACHINERY: **Boilers**
ARMOR (BELT): **9 in (228.6 mm)**
ARMOR (DECK): **1.5 in (38.1 mm)**
ARMOR (TURRETS): **11 in (280 mm)**
GUNS: **4x11in; 14x6.7in; 20x3.5in**
AA GUNS: **none**
AIRCRAFT: **none**
CREW: **745**
LAUNCHED: **December 1906**
SPEED: **18 knots**

In World War I, *Queen Elizabeth* was the Grand Fleet flagship from 1916 to 1918. She served in the Mediterranean between the two world wars, and in 1941 was based at Alexandria, Egypt, where she was damaged in a daring attack by three Italian "human torpedo" teams, who placed explosive charges under her. She later returned to service, but was broken up in 1948. In World War II, *Royal Sovereign* operated in the Mediterranean and the Indian Ocean. In 1944, she was loaned to the Soviet Union for convoy escort duties. She returned to Britain in 1949 and was sent to the breaker's yard.

QUEEN ELIZABETH

TYPE: **Dreadnought**
LENGTH: **643 ft (195.98 m)**
BEAM: **104 ft (31.69 m)**
DRAUGHT: **33.5 ft (10.21 m)**
DISPLACEMENT (NORMAL): **29,150 t (29,616 tnes)**
DISPLACEMENT (FULL LOAD): **33,000 t (33,528 tnes)**
MACHINERY: **Steam Turbines**
ARMOR (BELT): **13 in (330.2 mm)**
ARMOR (DECK): **2.5 in (63.5 mm)**
ARMOR (TURRETS): **13 in (330.2 mm)**
GUNS: **8x15in; 4x6in**
AA GUNS: **2x4in**
AIRCRAFT: **none**
CREW: **951**
LAUNCHED: **October 1913**
SPEED: **30 knots**

ROYAL SOVEREIGN

TYPE: **Dreadnought**
LENGTH: **624 ft (191.19 m)**
BEAM: **88.5 ft (26.97 m)**
DRAUGHT: **28.5 ft (8.68 m)**
DISPLACEMENT (NORMAL): **28,000 t (28,448 tnes)**
DISPLACEMENT (FULL LOAD): **31,000 t (31,496 tnes)**
MACHINERY: **Steam Turbines**
ARMOR (BELT): **13 in (330.2 mm)**
ARMOR (DECK): **2 in (50.8 mm)**
ARMOR (TURRETS): **13 in (330.2 mm)**
GUNS: **8x15in; 12x6in**
AA GUNS: **8x4in; 16x2pdr**
AIRCRAFT: **1**
CREW: **910**
LAUNCHED: **April 1915**
SPEED: **32 knots**

A Dreadnought of the "Ise" class, *Hyuga* was launched in 1917. In 1934–36, in common with other capital ships of the Imperial Japanese Navy, she underwent a complete reconstruction, improvements that included thicker deck armor. In 1942, she formed part of Japan's escort force at the Battle of Midway. As a result of the carrier losses sustained by the Japanese in this battle, *Hyuga* and others of her class were converted as "battleship-carriers" in 1943, being fitted with a hangar to house 22 seaplanes. All the aircraft would be catapult-launched, landing on the sea on their return and then hoisted back aboard by cranes. The scheme was not tested in combat because of a shortage of aircraft and pilots, but, by this stage of the war, the Americans had such a superiority in carriers and aircraft that it would have made little difference. *Hyuga* saw action in the Battle of Leyte Gulf in 1944. She was sunk near Kure by U.S. aircraft in July 1945. *Hyuga* was refloated and broken up in 1952.

HYUGA

TYPE: **Dreadnought**
LENGTH: **675 ft (205.74 m)**
BEAM: **94 ft (28.65 m)**
DRAUGHT: **29 ft (8.83 m)**
DISPLACEMENT (NORMAL): **31,260 t (31,760 tnes)**
DISPLACEMENT (FULL LOAD): **36,500 t (37,084 tnes)**
MACHINERY: **Boilers & Steam Turbines**
ARMOR (BELT): **12 in (304.8 mm)**
ARMOR (DECK): **3 in (76.2 mm)**
ARMOR (TURRETS): **12 in (304.8 mm)**
GUNS: **12x14in; 20x5.5in; 4x3in**
AA GUNS: **none**
AIRCRAFT: **none**
CREW: **1,360**
LAUNCHED: **January 1917**
SPEED: **23 knots**

The USS *Texas* (BB-35) was a Dreadnought-type battleship of the "New York" class, laid down in 1911. She was launched on May 18, 1912, and completed in March 1914. During World War I, she was attached to the Royal Navy's Grand Fleet for convoy protection duty in the North Atlantic, operating from Scapa Flow naval base in the Orkneys, and while she was in British waters *Texas* became the first U.S. battleship to be fitted with a flying-off platform for spotter aircraft. From 1919 to 1925, she served with the Pacific Fleet, rejoining the Atlantic Fleet in 1927 after undergoing a period of reconstruction. During World War II, by which time she was obsolete, *Texas* again served on convoy protection duty in the Atlantic, and provided fire support for the landings in North Africa in November 1942, and for the D-Day landings in Normandy in June 1944. During the latter operations, *Texas* was damaged by gunfire from a shore battery at Cherbourg, France. After supporting the Allied landings in the south of France in August 1944, she was transferred to the Pacific Ocean, where she provided gunfire support for the American landings on the islands of Iwo Jima and Okinawa. *Texas* was

TEXAS

TYPE: **Dreadnought**
LENGTH: **573 ft (174.65 m)**
BEAM: **97.2 ft (29.62 m)**
DRAUGHT: **31.5 ft (9.6 m)**
DISPLACEMENT (NORMAL): **27,000 t (27,432 tnes)**
DISPLACEMENT (FULL LOAD): **28,500 t (28,956 tnes)**
MACHINERY: **Boilers**
ARMOR (BELT): **12 in (304.8 mm)**
ARMOR (DECK): **2.5 in (63.5 mm)**
ARMOR (TURRETS): **14 in (355.6 mm)**
GUNS: **10x14in; 37x5in**
AA GUNS: **8x3in; 8x.5in**
AIRCRAFT: **none**
CREW: **1,054**
LAUNCHED: **May 1912**
SPEED: **21 knots**

decommissioned in April 1948, and then preserved as a memorial at the port of Galveston, Texas.

CRUISERS

Fast and relatively heavily armed, the cruiser was the backbone of the fleet. Cruisers were also designed for long-range missions.

In World War II, *Jeanne D'Arc* took part in operations off Corsica and also carried out many transport operations, ferrying French troops from North Africa to the French Riviera after the Allied landings there in August 1944. *Montcalm* was one of six light cruisers of the "La Galissonniere" class. The ships were very well designed and mounted an excellent main armament of nine 6in (152mm) guns. They were among the best in the French Navy, which was a world leader in military ships, at the outbreak of World War II. *Montcalm* survived the war.

JEANNE D'ARC

TYPE: **Light Cruiser**
LENGTH: **557.6 ft (170 m)**
BEAM: **57.4 ft (17.5 m)**
DRAUGHT: **20.6 ft (6.3 m)**
DISPLACEMENT (NORMAL): **6,496 t (6,600 tnes)**
DISPLACEMENT (FULL LOAD): **8,950 t (9,094 tnes)**
MACHINERY: **Geared Turbines**
ARMOR (BELT): **4.75 in (120 mm)**
ARMOR (DECK): **3 in (76 mm)**
ARMOR (TURRETS): **3.75 in (95 mm)**
GUNS: **8x155mm; 4x75mm**
AA GUNS: **4x37mm; 12x13.2mm**
AIRCRAFT: **1**
CREW: **505**
LAUNCHED: **February 1930**
SPEED: **25 knots**

MONTCALM

TYPE: **Light Cruiser**
LENGTH: **587 ft (179 m)**
BEAM: **57.3 ft (17.48 m)**
DRAUGHT: **17.3 ft (5.28 m)**
DISPLACEMENT (NORMAL): **8,214 t (8,342 tnes)**
DISPLACEMENT (FULL LOAD): **9,120 t (9,266 tnes)**
MACHINERY: **Boilers & Turbines**
ARMOR (BELT): **4.7 in (120 mm)**
ARMOR (DECK): **2 in (50.8 mm)**
ARMOR (TURRETS): **5 in (130 mm)**
GUNS: **9x152mm**
AA GUNS: **8x90mm; 8x13.2mm**
AIRCRAFT: **2**
CREW: **540**
LAUNCHED: **October 1935**
SPEED: **31 knots**

The heavy cruiser *Blücher* took part in the German invasion of Norway in April 1940, carrying troops bound for Oslo. While sailing through the Drobak Narrows, Norwegian gunners opened fire and quickly set her ablaze. She later sank with the loss of more than 1,000 men. In World War II, *Prinz Eugen*, *Blücher*'s sister-ship, served in the Atlantic and the Baltic. On October 15, 1944, she was badly damaged in collision with the light cruiser *Leipzig*. At the end of the war, she was anchored in Copenhagen, where she surrendered to the Allies.

BLÜCHER

TYPE: **Heavy Cruiser**
LENGTH: **675.3 ft (205.83 m)**
BEAM: **69.75 ft (21.25 m)**
DRAUGHT: **19 ft (5.79 m)**
DISPLACEMENT (NORMAL): **14,247 t (14,474 tnes)**
DISPLACEMENT (FULL LOAD): **18,208 t (18,499 tnes)**
MACHINERY: **Boilers & Steam Turbines**
ARMOR (BELT): **3 in (76.2 mm)**
ARMOR (DECK): **2 in (50.8 mm)**
ARMOR (TURRETS): **4 in (101.6 mm)**
GUNS: **8x8in; 12x4.1in**
AA GUNS: **12x40mm; 8x37mm**
AIRCRAFT: **3**
CREW: **1,600**
LAUNCHED: **June 1937**
SPEED: **32.5 knots**

PRINZ EUGEN

TYPE: **Heavy Cruiser**
LENGTH: **697 ft (212.44 m)**
BEAM: **71.5 ft (21.8 m)**
DRAUGHT: **23.5 ft (7.16 m)**
DISPLACEMENT (NORMAL): **14,271 t (14,500 tnes)**
DISPLACEMENT (FULL LOAD): **18,700 t (19,000 tnes)**
MACHINERY: **Boilers & Steam Turbines**
ARMOR (BELT): **3 in (76.2 mm)**
ARMOR (DECK): **2 in (50.8 mm)**
ARMOR (TURRETS): **4 in (101.6 mm)**
GUNS: **8x8in; 12x4.1in**
AA GUNS: **12x40mm; 8x37mm**
AIRCRAFT: **3**
CREW: **1,600**
LAUNCHED: **August 1938**
SPEED: **33 knots**

Launched in 1941, HMS *Argonaut* saw service with the British Home Fleet, and then was transferred to Gibraltar for service with Force H. She took part in Operation Torch, the Allied landings in North Africa in November 1942, and the Normandy D-Day landings on June 6, 1944. From late 1944, she was operational in the Pacific for the remainder of the war. HMS *Ajax* was in the South Atlantic on anti-commerce raider duty in September 1939. In December 1939, with other British warships, *Ajax* engaged the German pocket battleship *Admiral Graf Spee*, being severely damaged in the action. After repairs, she deployed to the Mediterranean. *Ajax* later provided fire support for the D-Day landings. The cruiser HMS *Belfast*, launched in 1938, was the largest cruiser ever built for the Royal Navy. In December 1943, she took part in the Battle of North Cape, which culminated in the destruction of the German Navy battlecruiser *Scharnhorst*.

On June 6, 1944, she supported the Allied landings on "Juno" Beach in Normandy. *Belfast* continued to serve for many years postwar. In 1971, she was preserved as a permanent memorial on the River Thames in London, where she continues to be a popular tourist attraction. HMS *Dunedin* was launched in 1918 and was loaned to the Royal New Zealand Navy between 1924 and 1937. Reassigned to the Royal Navy before World War II, she formed part of the Northern Patrol from September 6, 1939, searching for enemy vessels attempting to reach Germany. In 1940, *Dunedin* was assigned to convoy escort duty, and in June 1941 she captured a German supply ship, *Lothringen*, off Freetown, Sierra Leone. In November 1941, *Dunedin* was sighted by the German submarine *U124*, which torpedoed and sank her. HMS *Dunedin* was the only one of her class to be lost through enemy action in the whole of World War II.

ARGONAUT

TYPE: **Light Cruiser**
LENGTH: **512 ft (156 m)**
BEAM: **50 ft (15.24 m)**
DRAUGHT: **17 ft (5.18 m)**
DISPLACEMENT
(NORMAL): **5,840 t
(5,933 tnes)**
DISPLACEMENT (FULL
LOAD): **7,080 t
(7,193 tnes)**
MACHINERY: **Steam
Turbines**
ARMOR (BELT): **1.5 in
(38.1 mm)**
ARMOR (DECK): **2 in
(50.8 mm)**
ARMOR (TURRETS): **1.5 in
(38.1 mm)**
GUNS: **10x5.25in**
AA GUNS: **8x2pdr; 8x.5in**
AIRCRAFT: **none**
CREW: **487**
LAUNCHED: **September
1941**
SPEED: **31.75 knots**

AJAX

TYPE: **Light Cruiser**
LENGTH: **554 ft (168.85 m)**
BEAM: **55 ft (16.76 m)**
DRAUGHT: **19.8 ft (6.03 m)**
DISPLACEMENT
(NORMAL): **7,430 t
(7,549 tnes)**
DISPLACEMENT (FULL
LOAD): **9,350 t
(9,500 tnes)**
MACHINERY: **Steam
Turbines**
ARMOR (BELT): **3.5 in
(88.9 mm)**
ARMOR (DECK): **2 in
(50.8 mm)**
ARMOR (TURRETS): **1 in
(25.4 mm)**
GUNS: **8x6in; 4x4in**
AA GUNS: **12x.5in**
AIRCRAFT: **1**
CREW: **570**
LAUNCHED: **September
1932**
SPEED: **32.5 knots**

BELFAST

TYPE: **Heavy Cruiser**
LENGTH: **613 ft (186.8 m)**
BEAM: **63 ft (19.2 m)**
DRAUGHT: **20 ft (6 m)**
DISPLACEMENT
(NORMAL): **10,635 t
(10,805 tnes)**
DISPLACEMENT (FULL
LOAD): **13,175 t
(13,386 tnes)**
MACHINERY: **Steam
Turbines**
ARMOR (BELT): **4.88 in
(123.9 mm)**
ARMOR (DECK): **3 in
(76.2 mm)**
ARMOR (TURRETS): **4 in
(101.6 mm)**
GUNS: **12x6in; 12x4in**
AA GUNS: **16x2pdr;
8x.5in**
AIRCRAFT: **3**
CREW: **780**
LAUNCHED: **March 1938**
SPEED: **33 knots**

DUNEDIN

TYPE: **Light Cruiser**
LENGTH: **472 ft (143.8 m)**
BEAM: **46 ft (14 m)**
DRAUGHT: **16 ft (4.87 m)**
DISPLACEMENT
(NORMAL): **4,590 t
(4,663 tnes)**
DISPLACEMENT (FULL
LOAD): **5,720 t
(5,811 tnes)**
MACHINERY: **Steam
Turbines**
ARMOR (BELT): **3 in
(76.2 mm)**
ARMOR (DECK): **1 in
(25.4 mm)**
ARMOR (TURRETS): **1 in
(25.4 mm)**
GUNS: **6x6in; 2x3in**
AA GUNS: **2x2pdr**
AIRCRAFT: **none**
CREW: **450**
LAUNCHED: **November
1918**
SPEED: **30 knots**

In 1940, the cruiser HMS *Edinburgh*'s main role was convoy protection, but, in May 1941, she took part in the hunt for the German battleship *Bismarck*. In 1942, while *Edinburgh* was sailing the Arctic route to Russia, she was hit by German torpedoes and later sank. In World War II, the cruiser HMS *Newcastle* served in the Mediterranean and the South Atlantic. In 1944, she was transferred to the Indian Ocean for escort protection duties. In 1940,

HMS *Sheffield* transported troops to Norway, and in 1941 she was part of the British naval group that sank the *Bismarck*. In 1942, she was involved in the Battle of the Barents Sea, in which her gunfire sank the German destroyer *Friedrich Eckholdt*. HMS *Trinidad* was launched in 1940, and, while on Arctic convoy duties in 1942, she was attacked by German dive bombers. Hit amidships, she was abandoned and she was then sunk by HMS *Matchless*.

EDINBURGH

TYPE: **Cruiser**
LENGTH: **613 ft (18.7 m)**
BEAM: **63 ft (19.2 m)**
DRAUGHT: **29 ft (8.83 m)**
DISPLACEMENT
(NORMAL): **10,635 t
(10,805 tnes)**
DISPLACEMENT (FULL
LOAD): **13,175 t
(13,386 tnes)**
MACHINERY: **Steam
Turbines**
ARMOR (BELT): **4.88 in
(124 mm)**
ARMOR (DECK): **3 in
(76.2 mm)**
ARMOR (TURRETS): **4 in
(101.6 mm)**
GUNS: **12x6in; 12x4in**
AA GUNS: **16x2pdr;
8x.5in**
AIRCRAFT: **3**
CREW: **780**
LAUNCHED: **March 1938**
SPEED: **33 knots**

NEWCASTLE

TYPE: **Cruiser**
LENGTH: **591 ft
(180.13 m)**
BEAM: **64 ft (19.5 m)**
DRAUGHT: **20 ft (6.09 m)**
DISPLACEMENT
(NORMAL): **9,320 t
(9,469 tnes)**
DISPLACEMENT (FULL
LOAD): **11,540 t
(11,725 tnes)**
MACHINERY: **Steam
Turbines**
ARMOR (BELT): **4.88 in
(123.95 mm)**
ARMOR (DECK): **2 in
(50.8 mm)**
ARMOR (TURRETS): **1 in
(25.4 mm)**
GUNS: **12x6in; 8x4in**
AA GUNS: **8x2pdr; 8x.5in**
AIRCRAFT: **3**
CREW: **750**
LAUNCHED: **January
1936**
SPEED: **32.5 knots**

SHEFFIELD

TYPE: **Cruiser**
LENGTH: **591.5 ft
(180.29 m)**
BEAM: **61.75 ft (18.82 m)**
DRAUGHT: **17 ft (5.18 m)**
DISPLACEMENT
(NORMAL): **9,100 t
(9,246 tnes)**
DISPLACEMENT (FULL
LOAD): **11,350 t
(11,532 tnes)**
MACHINERY: **Steam
Turbines**
ARMOR (BELT): **4.5 in
(114.3 mm)**
ARMOR (DECK): **1.5 in
(38.1 mm)**
ARMOR (TURRETS): **1 in
(25.4 mm)**
GUNS: **12x6in; 8x4in**
AA GUNS: **8x2pdr; 8x.5in**
AIRCRAFT: **2**
CREW: **750**
LAUNCHED: **August 1937**
SPEED: **32 knots**

TRINIDAD

TYPE: **Light Cruiser**
LENGTH: **555 ft
(169.16 m)**
BEAM: **62 ft (18.9 m)**
DRAUGHT: **19 ft (5.79 m)**
DISPLACEMENT
(NORMAL): **8,900 t
(9,042 tnes)**
DISPLACEMENT (FULL
LOAD): **10,725 t
(10,897 tnes)**
MACHINERY: **Steam
Turbines**
ARMOR (BELT): **3.5 in
(88.9 mm)**
ARMOR (DECK): **2 in
(50.8 mm)**
ARMOR (TURRETS): **2 in
(50.8 mm)**
GUNS: **12x6in; 8x4in**
AA GUNS: **8x2pdr**
AIRCRAFT: **2**
CREW: **730**
LAUNCHED: **March 1940**
SPEED: **32 knots**

The *Bande Nere* was launched on October 31, 1928, and completed in April the following year. On July 19, 1940, she and her sister-ship, the *Bartolomeo Colleoni*, were engaged by the Australian cruiser HMAS *Sydney* and five destroyers in what became known as the Battle of Cape Spada; the *Colleoni* was sunk, 525 of her crew being rescued by the British destroyers, and *Bande Nere* got away after registering a hit on the *Sydney*. During subsequent naval operations, *Bande Nere* was assigned to the 4th Division, which acted directly under the orders of the Italian Admiralty. Most of the 4th Division's activities involved convoy escort, although it did operate offensively against British Mediterranean convoys. It also undertook some minelaying, mainly in the Sicilian Channel. *Bande Nere* met her end on April 1, 1942, being torpedoed and sunk by the British submarine *Urge* off Stromboli. Though the *Bande Nere* was a fast vessel, it was relatively lightly armed and its antiaircraft defenses were poor. The *Fiume*, *Gorizia*, *Pola*, and *Zara* were heavy cruisers of the "Zara" class. All four warships were assigned to the Italian Navy's 1st Division at the time of Italy's entry into World War II in June 1940, but all were destroyed during the conflict. *Zara*, *Fiume*, and *Pola* were all sunk in the Battle of Matapan in 1941.

BANDE NERE

TYPE: **Light Cruiser**
LENGTH: **554.46 ft (169 m)**
BEAM: **50.85 ft (15.5 m)**
DRAUGHT: **17.38 ft (5.3 m)**
DISPLACEMENT (NORMAL): **5,200 t (5,283 tnes)**
DISPLACEMENT (FULL LOAD): **6,954 t (7,065 tnes)**
MACHINERY: **Turbines**
ARMOR (BELT): **.78 in (20 mm)**
ARMOR (DECK): **.95 in (24 mm)**
ARMOR (TURRETS): **.9 in (23 mm)**
GUNS: **8x152mm; 6x100mm**
AA GUNS: **3x37mm; 8x13.2mm**
AIRCRAFT: **none**
CREW: **507**
LAUNCHED: **October 1928**
SPEED: **37 knots**

FIUME

TYPE: **Heavy Cruiser**
LENGTH: **600 ft (182.8 m)**
BEAM: **67.58 ft (20.6 m)**
DRAUGHT: **23.62 ft (7.2 m)**
DISPLACEMENT (NORMAL): **11,500 t (11,685 tnes)**
DISPLACEMENT (FULL LOAD): **14,530 t (14,762 tnes)**
MACHINERY: **8 Boilers**
ARMOR (BELT): **2.75 in (70 mm)**
ARMOR (DECK): **2.75 in (70 mm)**
ARMOR (TURRETS): **5.9 in (150 mm)**
GUNS: **8x203mm; 16x100mm**
AA GUNS: **4x40mm; 8x12.7mm**
AIRCRAFT: **none**
CREW: **841**
LAUNCHED: **April 1930**
SPEED: **27 knots**

GORIZIA

TYPE: **Heavy Cruiser**
LENGTH: **600 ft (182.8 m)**
BEAM: **67.58 ft (20.6 m)**
DRAUGHT: **23.62 ft (7.2 m)**
DISPLACEMENT (NORMAL): **11,500 t (11,685 tnes)**
DISPLACEMENT (FULL LOAD): **14,530 t (14,762 tnes)**
MACHINERY: **8 Boilers**
ARMOR (BELT): **2.75 in (70 mm)**
ARMOR (DECK): **2.75 in (70 mm)**
ARMOR (TURRETS): **5.9 in (150 m)**
GUNS: **8x203mm; 16x100mm**
AA GUNS: **4x40mm; 8x12.7mm**
AIRCRAFT: **none**
CREW: **841**
LAUNCHED: **December 1930**
SPEED: **27 knots**

POLA

TYPE: **Heavy Cruiser**
LENGTH: **600 ft (182.8 m)**
BEAM: **67.58 ft (20.6 m)**
DRAUGHT: **23.62 ft (7.2 m)**
DISPLACEMENT (NORMAL): **11,500 t (11,685 tnes)**
DISPLACEMENT (FULL LOAD): **14,530 t (14,762 tnes)**
MACHINERY: **8 Boilers**
ARMOR (BELT): **2.75 in (70 mm)**
ARMOR (DECK): **2.75 in (70 mm)**
ARMOR (TURRETS): **5.9 in (150 mm)**
GUNS: **8x203mm; 16x100mm**
AA GUNS: **4x40mm; 8x12.7mm**
AIRCRAFT: **none**
CREW: **841**
LAUNCHED: **December 1931**
SPEED: **27 knots**

ZARA

TYPE: **Heavy Cruiser**
LENGTH: **600 ft (182.8 m)**
BEAM: **67.58 ft (20.6 m)**
DRAUGHT: **23.62 ft (7.2 m)**
DISPLACEMENT (NORMAL): **11,500 t (11,685 tnes)**
DISPLACEMENT (FULL LOAD): **14,530 t (14,762 tnes)**
MACHINERY: **8 Boilers**
ARMOR (BELT): **2.75 in (70 mm)**
ARMOR (DECK): **2.75 in (70 mm)**
ARMOR (TURRETS): **5.9 in (150 mm)**
GUNS: **8x203mm; 16x100mm**
AA GUNS: **4x40mm; 8x12.7mm**
AIRCRAFT: **none**
CREW: **841**
LAUNCHED: **April 1930**
SPEED: **27 knots**

MOGAMI

TYPE: Cruiser
LENGTH: 656.16 ft (200 m)
BEAM: 65.61 ft (20.5 m)
DRAUGHT: 35.76 ft (10.9 m)
DISPLACEMENT (NORMAL):
12,400 t (12,599 tnes)
DISPLACEMENT (FULL LOAD):
12,980 t (13,188 tnes)
MACHINERY: Geared Turbines
ARMOR (BELT): 3.93 in (100 mm)
ARMOR (DECK): 1.5 in (38 mm)
ARMOR (TURRETS): 5 in (127 mm)
GUNS: 15x155mm; 8x127mm
AA GUNS: 8x25mm
AIRCRAFT: 3
CREW: 930
LAUNCHED: March 1934
SPEED: 36 knots

MYOKO

TYPE: Cruiser
LENGTH: 679.13 ft (207 m)
BEAM: 62.33 ft (19 m)
DRAUGHT: 20.75 ft (6.3 m)
DISPLACEMENT (NORMAL):
12,370 t (12,568 tnes)
DISPLACEMENT (FULL LOAD):
13,380 t (13,594 tnes)
MACHINERY: Geared Turbines
ARMOR (BELT): 4.01 in (102 mm)
ARMOR (DECK): 5 in (127 mm)
ARMOR (TURRETS): 3 in (76.2 mm)
GUNS: 10x203mm; 6x120mm
AA GUNS: 8x25mm
AIRCRAFT: 2
CREW: 792
LAUNCHED: April 1927
SPEED: 33 knots

TAKAO

TYPE: Cruiser
LENGTH: 671.58 ft (204.7 m)
BEAM: 62.33 ft (19 m)
DRAUGHT: 35.76 ft (10.9 m)
DISPLACEMENT (NORMAL):
41,217 t (41,878 tnes)
DISPLACEMENT (FULL LOAD):
47,000 t (47,754 tnes)
MACHINERY: Geared Turbines
ARMOR (BELT): 4.01 in (102 mm)
ARMOR (DECK): 3 in (76.2 mm)
ARMOR (TURRETS): 3 in (76.2 mm)
GUNS: 10x203mm; 4x120mm
AA GUNS: 2x40mm
AIRCRAFT: 3
CREW: 762
LAUNCHED: May 1930
SPEED: 35 knots

ATLANTA

TYPE: Antiaircraft Cruiser
LENGTH: 543 ft (165.5 m)
BEAM: 54.3 ft (16.55 m)
DRAUGHT: 20 ft (6.09 m)
DISPLACEMENT
(NORMAL): 6,000 t
(6,096 tnes)
DISPLACEMENT (FULL
LOAD): 8,500 t
(8,666 tnes)
MACHINERY: Steam
Turbines
ARMOR (BELT): 3.5 in
(88.9 mm)
ARMOR (DECK): 1.2 in
(30.48 mm)
ARMOR (TURRETS): 1.2 in
(30.48 mm)
GUNS: 16x5in
AA GUNS: 3x1.1in; 24x40
& 14x20m
CREW: 590
LAUNCHED: September
1941
SPEED: 32.5 knots

AUGUSTA

TYPE: Heavy Cruiser
LENGTH: 600 ft (182.88 m)
BEAM: 66.25 ft (20.91 m)
DRAUGHT: 23 ft (7.01 m)
DISPLACEMENT (NORMAL):
9,050 t (9,195 tnes)
DISPLACEMENT (FULL
LOAD): 12,300 t
(12,497 tnes)
MACHINERY: Geared
Turbines
ARMOR (BELT): 3 in
(76.2 mm)
ARMOR (DECK): 3 in
(76.2 mm)
ARMOR (TURRETS): 1.5 in
(38.1 mm)
GUNS: 9x8in; 8x5in
AA GUNS: 32x40mm;
27x20mm
AIRCRAFT: Four
CREW: 872
LAUNCHED: February
1930
SPEED: 32.7 knots

USS *Chicago* escaped the Japanese attack on Pearl Harbor in 1941, and in 1942 she was present at the Battle of the Coral Sea. While serving in the Pacific, in early 1943 she was damaged in a torpedo attack by Japanese aircraft, and sunk the next day. From 1944 onward, USS *Denver* lent her fire support to Pacific operations, from Leyte Gulf to Japanese mainland targets on Southern Honshu in July 1945.

USS *Houston* also operated in the Pacific in World War II, but was sunk by Japanese warships in 1942 in the Battle of the Java Sea. Battle honours for the USS *Indianapolis* included the Coral Sea, Midway, Iwo Jima, the Marianas, and Okinawa. She was sunk in July 1945. USS *Pittsburgh* saw action in the Pacific in World War II. USS *Tuscaloosa* took part in Allied D-Day operations at Utah beach in 1944.

CHICAGO

TYPE: **Heavy Cruiser**
LENGTH: **600 ft (182.88 m)**
BEAM: **66.25 ft (20.19 m)**
DRAUGHT: **23 ft (7.01 m)**
DISPLACEMENT (NORMAL):
9,050 t (9,195 tnes)
DISPLACEMENT (FULL LOAD):
12,300 t (12,497 tnes)
MACHINERY: **Geared Turbines**
ARMOR (BELT): **3 in (76.2 mm)**
ARMOR (DECK): **3 in (76.2 mm)**
ARMOR (TURRETS): **1.5 in (38.1 mm)**
GUNS: **9x8in; 8x5in**
AA GUNS: **32x40mm; 27x20mm**
AIRCRAFT: **4**
CREW: **872**
LAUNCHED: **April 1930**
SPEED: **32.7 knots**

DENVER

TYPE: **Light Cruiser**
LENGTH: **608 ft (185.31 m)**
BEAM: **63.5 ft (19.35 m)**
DRAUGHT: **22 ft (6.7 m)**
DISPLACEMENT (NORMAL):
10,000 t (10,160 tnes)
DISPLACEMENT (FULL LOAD):
13,887 t (14,109 tnes)
MACHINERY: **Steam Turbines**
ARMOR (BELT): **5 in (127 mm)**
ARMOR (DECK): **3 in (76.2 mm)**
ARMOR (TURRETS): **5 in (127 mm)**
GUNS: **12x6in; 12x5in**
AA GUNS: **8x40mm; 19x20mm**
AIRCRAFT: **3**
CREW: **900**
LAUNCHED: **April 1942**
SPEED: **33 knots**

HOUSTON

TYPE: **Heavy Cruiser**
LENGTH: **600 ft (182.88 m)**
BEAM: **66.25 ft (20.19 m)**
DRAUGHT: **23 ft (7.01 m)**
DISPLACEMENT (NORMAL):
9,050 t (9,195 tnes)
DISPLACEMENT (FULL LOAD):
12,300 t (12,497 tnes)
MACHINERY: **Geared Turbines**
ARMOR (BELT): **3 in (76.2 mm)**
ARMOR (DECK): **3 in (76.2 mm)**
ARMOR (TURRETS): **1.5 in (38.1 mm)**
GUNS: **9x8in; 8x5in**
AA GUNS: **32x40mm; 27x20mm**
AIRCRAFT: **4**
CREW: **872**
LAUNCHED: **September 1929**
SPEED: **32.7 knots**

INDIANAPOLIS

TYPE: **Heavy Cruiser**
LENGTH: **610 ft (185.92 m)**
BEAM: **66 ft (20.11 m)**
DRAUGHT: **22 ft (6.7 m)**
DISPLACEMENT (NORMAL):
9,850 t (10,008 tnes)
DISPLACEMENT (FULL LOAD):
13,750 t (13,970 tnes)
MACHINERY: **Geared Turbines**
ARMOR (BELT): **5 in (127 mm)**
ARMOR (DECK): **4 in (101.6 mm)**
ARMOR (TURRETS): **2.5 in (63.5 mm)**
GUNS: **9x8in; 8x5in**
AA GUNS: **24x40mm; 28x20mm**
AIRCRAFT: **2**
CREW: **876**
LAUNCHED: **November 1931**
SPEED: **32.7 knots**

PITTSBURGH

TYPE: **Heavy Cruiser**
LENGTH: **673 ft (205.13 m)**
BEAM: **69.75 ft (21.25 m)**
DRAUGHT: **21.5 ft (6.55 m)**
DISPLACEMENT (NORMAL):
13,620 t (13,838 tnes)
DISPLACEMENT (FULL LOAD):
17,200 t (17,475 tnes)
MACHINERY: **Steam Turbines**
ARMOR (BELT): **6.08 in (154.43 mm)**
ARMOR (DECK): **2.56 in (65 mm)**
ARMOR (TURRETS): **8 in (211 mm)**
GUNS: **9x8in; 12x5in**
AA GUNS: **48x40mm; 26x20mm**
AIRCRAFT: **4**
CREW: **1,200**
LAUNCHED: **February 1944**
SPEED: **33 knots**

TUSCALOOSA

TYPE: **Heavy Cruiser**
LENGTH: **588 ft (179.22 m)**
BEAM: **61.25 ft (18.66 m)**
DRAUGHT: **23 ft (7.01 m)**
DISPLACEMENT (NORMAL):
9,950 t (10,109 tnes)
DISPLACEMENT (FULL LOAD):
13,200 t (13,411 tnes)
MACHINERY: **Geared Turbines**
ARMOR (BELT): **5 in (127 mm)**
ARMOR (DECK): **5 in (127 mm)**
ARMOR (TURRETS): **6 in (152.4 mm)**
GUNS: **9x8in; 8x5in**
AA GUNS: **16x40mm; 19x20mm**
AIRCRAFT: **4**
CREW: **876**
LAUNCHED: **November 1933**
SPEED: **30 knots**

AIRCRAFT CARRIERS

Aircraft carriers had a decisive impact on naval warfare in World War II. In the Pacific, for example, U.S. carrier aircraft at the battles of the Philippines Sea in June 1944 and Leyte Gulf in October 1944 destroyed Japanese naval aviation. By the end of the war, the U.S. Navy had 40 carriers, while the Royal Navy possessed 59.

The *Ark Royal*, launched in 1937, incorporated all the best of previous aircraft carrier design, including a full-length deck overhanging the stern. In 1940, her aircraft gave cover for the evacuation of Allied forces from Norway. In April 1941, she was involved in the hunt for the *Bismarck*. In November 1941, while in the Mediterranean, *Ark Royal* was sunk after being attacked by a German U-boat, *U81*.

ARK ROYAL
TYPE: **Aircraft Carrier**
LENGTH: **800 ft (243.84 m)**
BEAM: **94 ft (28.65 m)**
DRAUGHT: **28 ft (8.53 m)**
DISPLACEMENT (NORMAL):
23,600 t (23,978 tnes)
DISPLACEMENT (FULL LOAD):
28,480 t (28,936 tnes)
MACHINERY: **Steam Turbines**
ARMOR (BELT): **4.5 in (24.3 mm)**
ARMOR (DECK): **3.5 in (88.9 mm)**
ARMOR (TURRETS): **n/a**
GUNS: **16x4.5in**
AA GUNS: **32x2pdr; 32x.5in**
AIRCRAFT: **60**
CREW: **1,600**
LAUNCHED: **April 1937**
SPEED: **32 knots**

AUDACITY
TYPE: **Escort Carrier**
LENGTH: **467 ft (142.3 m)**
BEAM: **56 ft (17.06 m)**
DRAUGHT: **27.5 ft (8.38 m)**
DISPLACEMENT (NORMAL):
unknown
DISPLACEMENT (FULL LOAD):
11,000 t (11,172 tnes)
MACHINERY: **Diesel Turbines**
ARMOR (BELT): **none**
ARMOR (DECK): **none**
ARMOR (TURRETS): **n/a**
GUNS: **1x4in**
AA GUNS: **6x20mm**
AIRCRAFT: **Eight**
CREW: **650**
LAUNCHED: **March 1939**
SPEED: **16 knots**

FORMIDABLE
TYPE: **Fleet Carrier**
LENGTH: **740 ft (225.55 m)**
BEAM: **95 ft (28.96 m)**
DRAUGHT: **28 ft (8.54 m)**
DISPLACEMENT (NORMAL):
23,580 t (23,957 tnes)
DISPLACEMENT (FULL LOAD):
28,620 t (29,078 tnes)
MACHINERY: **Steam Turbines**
ARMOR (BELT): **4.5 in (114.3 mm)**
ARMOR (DECK): **2 in (50.8 mm)**
ARMOR (TURRETS): **n/a**
GUNS: **16x4.5in**
AA GUNS: **42x2pdr**
AIRCRAFT: **36**
CREW: **1,230**
LAUNCHED: **August 1939**
SPEED: **32 knots**

FURIOUS
TYPE: **Fleet Carrier**
LENGTH: **786 ft (239.57 m)**
BEAM: **89 ft (27.12 m)**
DRAUGHT: **27 ft (8.23 m)**
DISPLACEMENT (NORMAL): **22,600 t (23,165 tnes)**
DISPLACEMENT (FULL LOAD): **26,800 t (27,229 tnes)**
MACHINERY: **Steam Turbines**
ARMOR (BELT): **3 in (76.2 mm)**
ARMOR (DECK): **2 in (50.8 mm)**
ARMOR (TURRETS): **n/a**
GUNS: **10x5.5in; 2x4in**
AA GUNS: **4x2pdr**
AIRCRAFT: **36**
CREW: **1,218**
LAUNCHED: **August 1916**
SPEED: **31 knots**

HERMES
TYPE: **Fleet Carrier**
LENGTH: **600 ft (182.8 m)**
BEAM: **70.25 ft (21.41 m)**
DRAUGHT: **21.5 ft (6.55 m)**
DISPLACEMENT (NORMAL): **10,850 t (11,024 tnes)**
DISPLACEMENT (FULL LOAD): **13,000 t (13,208 tnes)**
MACHINERY: **Boilers & Steam Turbines**
ARMOR (BELT): **3 in (76.2 mm)**
ARMOR (DECK): **1 in (25.4 mm)**
ARMOR (TURRETS): **n/a**
GUNS: **6x5.5in**
AA GUNS: **3x4in; 6x20mm; 8x.5in**
AIRCRAFT: **20**
CREW: **700**
LAUNCHED: **September 1919**
SPEED: **25 knots**

HMS *Indomitable* was launched in 1940. In late 1941, she went aground off Jamaica, delaying her deployment to the Indian Ocean. In 1942, she joined in the Allied attack on the Vichy French garrison on Madagascar, and in 1943 she gave air cover for the Sicily invasion force. In 1944, she rejoined the Eastern Fleet and began a series of attacks on enemy communications in Sumatra. In 1945, she sailed for Sydney, Australia, and in April saw action off Okinawa, where she was damaged in a kamikaze attack. On her final mission of World War II, she led the task force that reoccupied Hong Kong. She underwent a major refit after the war and was broken up in 1955.

HMS *Victorious* saw action in every theater of World War II. She differed from previous carriers in having an armored hangar, which reduced the number of aircraft that could be carried, but greatly increased the vessel's damage resistance level. *Victorious* was involved in the hunt for the *Bismarck* in 1941, and in 1942–43 she was assigned to convoy protection duty in the Arctic. In 1944, she deployed to the Indian Ocean, her aircraft attacking Japanese oil refineries at Palembang and Sabang, and in early 1945 she sailed for the Pacific, seeing action off Okinawa during the desperate Japanese defense of the island. She saw considerable service in the postwar years, and she was broken up in 1969.

INDOMITABLE

TYPE: **Fleet Carrier**
LENGTH: **800 ft (243.8 m)**
BEAM: **94.75 ft (28.8 m)**
DRAUGHT: **27.75 ft (8.45 m)**
DISPLACEMENT (NORMAL): **22,352 t (22,709 tnes)**
DISPLACEMENT (FULL LOAD): **28,143 t (28,593 tnes)**
MACHINERY: **Boilers & Steam Turbines**
ARMOR (BELT): **4 in (101.6 mm)**
ARMOR (DECK): **3 in (76.2 mm)**
ARMOR (TURRETS): **n/a**
GUNS: **16x4.5in**
AA GUNS: **16x2pdr; 10x20mm**
AIRCRAFT: **55**
CREW: **1,600**
LAUNCHED: **March 1940**
SPEED: **31 knots**

VICTORIOUS

TYPE: **Fleet Carrier**
LENGTH: **800 ft (243.8 m)**
BEAM: **94.75 ft (28.88 m)**
DRAUGHT: **27.75 ft (8.3 m)**
DISPLACEMENT (NORMAL): **22,352 t (22,709 tnes)**
DISPLACEMENT (FULL LOAD): **28,143 t (28,593 tnes)**
MACHINERY: **Steam Turbines**
ARMOR (BELT): **4 in (101.6 mm)**
ARMOR (DECK): **3 in (76.2 mm)**
ARMOR (TURRETS): **n/a**
GUNS: **none**
AA GUNS: **8x4.5in; 16x2pdr**
AIRCRAFT: **50**
CREW: **900**
LAUNCHED: **September 1939**
SPEED: **31 knots**

In December 1941, *Akagi* was part of the Japanese task force that attacked Pearl Harbor. Later, her aircraft attacked Rabaul, Java, Ceylon, and Darwin in Australia. On June 4, 1942, *Akagi* was damaged by U.S. aircraft in the Battle of Midway and had to be sunk by Japanese destroyers. *Hosho* was Japan's first dedicated aircraft carrier, launched in 1921. She saw active service in the Battle of Midway in 1942. On March 19, 1945, she was severely damaged in an air attack on the naval base at Kure and was disarmed. At the war's end, *Hosho* was used to repatriate prisoners of war.

AKAGI

TYPE: **Aircraft Carrier**
LENGTH: **856 ft (261 m)**
BEAM: **103 ft (31.4 m)**
DRAUGHT: **28.54 ft (8.7 m)**
DISPLACEMENT (NORMAL): **36,500 t (37,084 tnes)**
DISPLACEMENT (FULL LOAD): **41,300 t (41,961 tnes)**
MACHINERY: **Steam Turbines**
ARMOR (BELT): **6 in (152.4 mm)**
ARMOR (DECK): **3 in (76.2 mm)**
ARMOR (TURRETS): **n/a**
GUNS: **6x102mm; 12x127mm**
AA GUNS: **28x25mm**
AIRCRAFT: **91**
CREW: **2,000**
LAUNCHED: **April 1925**
SPEED: **31.5 knots**

HOSHO

TYPE: **Aircraft Carrier**
LENGTH: **813.64 ft (248 m)**
BEAM: **107 ft (32.6 m)**
DRAUGHT: **31.17 ft (9.5 m)**
DISPLACEMENT (NORMAL): **7,470 t (7,590 tnes)**
DISPLACEMENT (FULL LOAD): **9,630 t (9,785 tnes)**
MACHINERY: **Steam Turbines**
ARMOR (BELT): **none**
ARMOR (DECK): **none**
ARMOR (TURRETS): **n/a**
GUNS: **4x140mm**
AA GUNS: **8x25mm**
AIRCRAFT: **21**
CREW: **550**
LAUNCHED: **November 1921**
SPEED: **25 knots**

Kaga was laid down as a battleship and launched in 1920. Under the 1921 Washington Treaty, she was to have been scrapped, but, instead, the Imperial Japanese Navy decided to complete her as an aircraft carrier. Her career in World War II was short but spectacular. In December 1941, her aircraft attacked Pearl Harbor, and then operated over Rabaul, Darwin, and Java. At the Battle of Midway in 1942, *Kaga*, along with two other Japanese carriers, *Akagi* and *Soryu*, was sunk.

KAGA

TYPE: **Aircraft Carrier**
LENGTH: **789 ft (240.48 m)**
BEAM: **108 ft (32.91 m)**
DRAUGHT: **31 ft (9.44 m)**
DISPLACEMENT (NORMAL):
26,000 t (26,417 tnes)
DISPLACEMENT (FULL LOAD):
33,693 t (34,233 tnes)
MACHINERY: **Boilers & Steam Turbines**
ARMOR (BELT): **11 in (279.4 mm)**
ARMOR (DECK): **2.3 in (58.42 mm)**
GUNS: **none**
AA GUNS: **25x20mm; 30x13.2mm**
AIRCRAFT: **85**
CREW: **1,340**
LAUNCHED: **November 1920**
SPEED: **27.5 knots**

ZUIHO

TYPE: **Aircraft Carrier**
LENGTH: **712 ft (217 m)**
BEAM: **59.05 ft (18 m)**
DRAUGHT: **21.65 ft (6.6 m)**
DISPLACEMENT (NORMAL):
11,266 t (11,446 tnes)
DISPLACEMENT (FULL LOAD):
14,200 t (14,427 tnes)
MACHINERY: **Steam Turbines**
ARMOR (BELT): **none**
ARMOR (DECK): **none**
ARMOR (TURRETS): **n/a**
GUNS: **8x127mm**
AA GUNS: **15x25mm**
AIRCRAFT: **30**
CREW: **785**
LAUNCHED: **June 1936**
SPEED: **28 knots**

ZUIKAKU

TYPE: **Aircraft Carrier**
LENGTH: **844.81 ft (257.5 m)**
BEAM: **91.86 ft (28 m)**
DRAUGHT: **29.19 ft (8.9 m)**
DISPLACEMENT (NORMAL):
25,675 t (26,086 tnes)
DISPLACEMENT (FULL LOAD):
32,105 t (32,618 tnes)
MACHINERY: **Steam Turbines**
ARMOR (BELT): **6.5 in (165.1 mm)**
ARMOR (DECK): **5.1 in (129.54 mm)**
ARMOR (TURRETS): **n/a**
GUNS: **16x127mm**
AA GUNS: **36x25mm**
AIRCRAFT: **84**
CREW: **1,660**
LAUNCHED: **November 1939**
SPEED: **34.2 knots**

USS *Enterprise* was at sea when the Japanese attacked Pearl Harbor in 1941. In April 1942, she escorted USS *Hornet* on the famous Tokyo raid, when *Hornet* flew off B-25 bombers to attack the Japanese capital. During the Battle of Midway, *Enterprise*'s dive bombers helped to sink three Japanese carriers, changing the course of the war. *Enterprise* survived World War II. In April 1942, USS *Hornet* leapt to fame as the carrier that launched 16 B-25 bombers, led by Lt-Col Jimmy Doolittle, to attack Tokyo. *Hornet* also saw action at the Battle of Midway, and later escorted convoys resupplying Guadalcanal. In October 1942, during the Battle of Santa Cruz, *Hornet* was hit by Japanese bombs and torpedoes and she was abandoned. She was later sunk by Japanese destroyers.

ENTERPRISE

TYPE: **Aircraft Carrier**
LENGTH: **809 ft (246.58 m)**
BEAM: **95.5 ft (29.1 m)**
DRAUGHT: **21.4 ft (6.52 m)**
DISPLACEMENT (NORMAL): **19,900 t (20,218 tnes)**
DISPLACEMENT (FULL LOAD): **25,484 t (25,892 tnes)**
MACHINERY: **Geared Turbines**
ARMOR (BELT): **4 in (101.6 mm)**
ARMOR (DECK): **none**
GUNS: **8x5in; 40x40mm**
AA GUNS: **16x1.1in; 25x.5in**
AIRCRAFT: **100**
CREW: **2,702**
LAUNCHED: **October 1936**
SPEED: **34 knots**

HORNET

TYPE: **Aircraft Carrier**
LENGTH: **809 ft (246.58 m)**
BEAM: **83.34 ft (25.4 m)**
DRAUGHT: **21.4 ft (6.52 m)**
DISPLACEMENT (NORMAL): **19,900 t (20,218 tnes)**
DISPLACEMENT (FULL LOAD): **25,484 t (25,892 tnes)**
MACHINERY: **Geared Turbines**
ARMOR (BELT): **4 in (101.6 mm)**
ARMOR (DECK): **none**
ARMOR (TURRETS): **n/a**
GUNS: **8x5in**
AA GUNS: **16x1.1in; 24x40mm**
AIRCRAFT: **100**
CREW: **2,702**
LAUNCHED: **December 1940**
SPEED: **34 knots**

America's second aircraft carrier, the USS *Lexington* was originally ordered as a battlecruiser named *Constitution*, but was later renamed and reordered as an aircraft carrier. Her career in World War II was to prove that aircraft carriers could be vulnerable to enemy aircraft. After the Japanese attack on Pearl Harbor, her air group was involved in the battle for Wake Island, followed by convoy escort duty. In May 1942, she was operating as part of Task Force 11, a joint Allied naval force formed to prevent a Japanese landing at Port Moresby, New Guinea. In the Battle of the Coral Sea, *Lexington* was hit by Japanese torpedoes and bombs and was abandoned, being sunk later by the destroyer USS *Phelps*. The only large carrier in the Atlantic Fleet, USS *Ranger* led the task force that provided air superiority during the Allied amphibious invasion of French Morocco in November 1942. She joined the British Home Fleet at Scapa Flow in 1943 and patrolled with the British Second Battle Squadron until the end of the year. In 1944, she was used for training and then underwent a major refit. Operating out of San Diego, she continued training air groups and squadrons along the peaceful California coast for the rest of the war. USS *Saratoga*, sister-ship to the *Lexington*, was originally laid down as a battlecruiser in 1920, but was reordered as an aircraft carrier in 1922. In January 1942, she was torpedoed by a Japanese submarine southwest of Oahu, but was repaired. *Saratoga*'s battle honors in World War II included the Battle of the Eastern Solomons, the Rabaul raids, the Gilbert Islands, Kwajalein, and Eniwetok. In July 1946, her hulk was destroyed in U.S. atomic tests at Bikini. In World War II, USS *Yorktown* served in both the Atlantic and the Pacific. In June 1942, aircraft from the Japanese carrier *Hiryu* hit *Yorktown* with torpedoes and bombs, and she sank two days later.

LEXINGTON

TYPE: Aircraft Carrier
LENGTH: 888 ft (270.6 m)
BEAM: 106 ft (32.3 m)
DRAUGHT: 24.1 ft (7.34 m)
DISPLACEMENT (NORMAL): 33,000 t (33,528 tnes)
DISPLACEMENT (FULL LOAD): 43,400 t (44,094 tnes)
MACHINERY: Express Boilers
ARMOR (BELT): 6 in (152.4 mm)
ARMOR (DECK): 3 in (76.2 mm)
ARMOR (TURRETS): n/a
GUNS: 8x8in; 12x5in
AA GUNS: 16x1.1in; 16x.5in
AIRCRAFT: 80–90
CREW: 1,899
LAUNCHED: October 1925
SPEED: 33 knots

RANGER

TYPE: Aircraft Carrier
LENGTH: 769 ft (234.3 m)
BEAM: 80.2 ft (24.44 m)
DRAUGHT: 19.5 ft (5.94 m)
DISPLACEMENT (NORMAL): 14,500 t (14,732 tnes)
DISPLACEMENT (FULL LOAD): 18,000 t (18,288 tnes)
MACHINERY: Geared Turbines
ARMOR (BELT): 1 in (25.4 mm)
ARMOR (DECK): 1 in (25.4 mm)
ARMOR (TURRETS): n/a
GUNS: 8x5in
AA GUNS: 16x1.1in; 16x.5in
AIRCRAFT: 70
CREW: 1,788
LAUNCHED: February 1933
SPEED: 30.36 knots

SARATOGA

TYPE: Aircraft Carrier
LENGTH: 888 ft (270.6 m)
BEAM: 106 ft (32.3 m)
DRAUGHT: 24.1 ft (7.34 m)
DISPLACEMENT (NORMAL): 33,000 t (33,528 tnes)
DISPLACEMENT (FULL LOAD): 43,400 t (44,094 tnes)
MACHINERY: Electric Turbines
ARMOR (BELT): 6 in (152.4 mm)
ARMOR (DECK): 3 in (76.2 mm)
ARMOR (TURRETS): n/a
GUNS: 8x8in; 18x5in; 12x5in
AA GUNS: 16x1.1in; 30x20mm
AIRCRAFT: 80–90
CREW: 1,890
LAUNCHED: April 1925
SPEED: 33 knots

YORKTOWN

TYPE: Aircraft Carrier
LENGTH: 809.5 ft (246.73 m)
BEAM: 83.34 ft (25.4 m)
DRAUGHT: 21.4 ft (6.52 m)
DISPLACEMENT (NORMAL): 19,900 t (20,218 tnes)
DISPLACEMENT (FULL LOAD): 25,484 t (25,892 tnes)
MACHINERY: Geared Turbines
ARMOR (BELT): 4 in (101.6 mm)
ARMOR (DECK): none
ARMOR (TURRETS): n/a
GUNS: 8x5in
AA GUNS: 16x1.1in; 24x.5in
AIRCRAFT: 100
CREW: 2,702
LAUNCHED: April 1936
SPEED: 34 knots

SUBMARINES

In World War II, submarines were widely used by both sides as the ultimate weapon of naval blockade, sinking large numbers of both merchant ships and warships. They had quite limited underwater speed, range, and endurance. They usually sailed on the surface, especially at night, and submerged only in order to avoid being detected and attacked. German U-boats almost starved Britain into submission in the Battle of the Atlantic.

Argonaute was based at Oran when France fell to Nazi Germany in 1940. She was handed over to the Vichy French Navy, and was sunk by British warships off Oran on November 8. One of four Circe-class submarines, *Calypso* was well armed and well constructed, but with poor crew conditions. *Calypso* was seized by Axis forces in December 1942 and then was destroyed in an Allied air attack in January 1943. On December 8, 1942, *Espadon* was one of four boats captured by the Italians at Bizerta; she was subsequently commissioned by the Italian Navy as the *FR114*, and in September 1943 she was scuttled by the Germans. Before the French collapse in 1940, *Junon* managed to escape across the English Channel to Plymouth. She then served with the Free French Naval Forces, carrying out patrols in the Norwegian Sea and in the Arctic.

ARGONAUTE

DISPLACEMENT SURFACED: **630 t (640 tnes)**
DISPLACEMENT SUBMERGED: **798 t (811 tnes)**
MACHINERY: **two screws, diesel/electric motors; 1,300/1,000 hp**
LENGTH: **208 ft 11 in (63.4 m)**
BEAM: **17 ft (5.2 m)**
DRAUGHT: **11 ft 9 in (3.61 m)**
PERFORMANCE SURFACED: **13.5 knots**
PERFORMANCE SUBMERGED: **7.5 knots**
ARMAMENT: **six 550mm TT; one 75mm gun**
SURFACE RANGE: **2,300 nm (4,260 km) at 7.5 knots**
CREW: **41**
LAUNCH DATE: **May 23, 1929**

CALYPSO

DISPLACEMENT SURFACED: **615 t (625 tnes)**
DISPLACEMENT SUBMERGED: **776 t (788 tnes)**
MACHINERY: **two screws, diesel-electric motors, 1,250/1,000 hp**
LENGTH: **205 ft (62.48 m)**
BEAM: **17 ft 9 in (5.40 m)**
DRAUGHT: **12 ft 9 in (3.90 m)**
PERFORMANCE SURFACED: **14 knots**
PERFORMANCE SUBMERGED: **7.5 knots**
ARMAMENT: **seven 550 mm TT; one 75mm gun**
SURFACE RANGE: **3,500 nm (6,482 km) at 10 knots**
CREW: **41**
LAUNCH DATE: **January 15, 1926**

ESPADON

DISPLACEMENT SURFACED: **1,150 t (1,168 tnes)**
DISPLACEMENT SUBMERGED: **1,441 t (1,464 tnes)**
MACHINERY: **twin screws, diesel/electric motors; 2,900/1,800 hp**
LENGTH: **256 ft 9 in (78.2 m)**
BEAM: **22 ft 5 in (6.8 m)**
DRAUGHT: **16 ft 9 in (5 m)**
PERFORMANCE SURFACED: **15 knots**
PERFORMANCE SUBMERGED: **9 knots**
ARMAMENT: **10 533mm TT; one 100mm gun**
SURFACE RANGE: **5,650 nm (10,469 km) at 10 knots**
CREW: **54**
LAUNCH DATE: **May 28, 1926**

JUNON

DISPLACEMENT SURFACED: **662 t (672 tnes)**
DISPLACEMENT SUBMERGED: **856 t (869 tnes)**
MACHINERY: **two screws, diesel/electric motors; 1,800/1,230 hp**
LENGTH: **223 ft 5 in (68.10 m)**
BEAM: **18ft 5 in (5.62 m)**
DRAUGHT: **13 ft 3 in (4.03 m)**
PERFORMANCE SURFACED: **15 knots**
PERFORMANCE SUBMERGED: **9.3 knots**
ARMAMENT: **six 550mm and three 400mm TT; one 75mm gun**
SURFACE RANGE: **4,000 nm (7,400 km) at 10 knots**
CREW: **42**
LAUNCH DATE: **September 15, 1935**

The French submarine *Minerve* began operatiing off Norway in February 1941, and on April 19, while attacking an enemy convoy, she was heavily depth-charged by German escorts and narrowly escaped being sunk. In May 1941, *Minerve* took part in the hunt for the German warships *Bismarck* and *Prinz Eugen*. Together with the British submarine *Uproar*, she was sent north to search for the *Bismarck*, but neither submarine could locate the elusive battleship. Later in 1941, *Minerve* operated in concert with another French submarine, *Rubis*, and in July 1942 she operated in the Arctic with eight British submarines south of Bear Island to protect the ill-fated convoy PQ.17, which was later virtually destroyed by air and U-boat attacks.

MINERVE

DISPLACEMENT SURFACED: 662 t (672 tnes)
DISPLACEMENT SUBMERGED: 856 t (869 tnes)
MACHINERY: two screws, diesel/electric motors; 1,800/1,230 hp
LENGTH: 223 ft 5 in (68.10 m)
BEAM: 18 ft 5 in (5.62 m)
DRAUGHT: 13 ft 3 in (4.03 m)
PERFORMANCE SURFACED: 15 knots
PERFORMANCE SUBMERGED: 9.3 knots
ARMAMENT: six 550mm and three 400mm TT; one 75mm gun
SURFACE RANGE: 4,000 nm (7,400 km) at 10 knots
CREW: 42
LAUNCH DATE: October 23, 1934

NARVAL

DISPLACEMENT SURFACED: 990 t (974 tnes)
DISPLACEMENT SUBMERGED: 1,441 t (1,464 tnes)
MACHINERY: twin screws, diesel/electric motors; 2,900/1,800 hp
LENGTH: 256 ft 7 in (78.25 m)
BEAM: 22 ft 6 in (6.84 m)
DRAUGHT: 16 ft 9 in (5.10 m)
PERFORMANCE SURFACED: 15 knots
PERFORMANCE SUBMERGED: 9 knots
ARMAMENT: 10 550mm TT; one 100mm gun
SURFACE RANGE: 2,300 nm (4,262 km) at 7.5 knots
CREW: 54
LAUNCH DATE: May 9, 1925

ORPHEE

DISPLACEMENT SURFACED: 571 t (580 tnes)
DISPLACEMENT SUBMERGED: 809 t (822 tnes)
MACHINERY: twin screws, diesel/electric motors; 1,300/1,800 hp
LENGTH: 211 ft 4 in (64.4 m)
BEAM: 20 ft 4 in (6.2 m)
DRAUGHT: 14 ft 1 in (4.3 m)
PERFORMANCE SURFACED: 13.7 knots
PERFORMANCE SUBMERGED: 9.2 knots
ARMAMENT: six 550mm TT; one 75mm gun
SURFACE RANGE: 4,000 nm (7,400 km) at 10 knots
CREW: 41
LAUNCH DATE: November 10, 1931

PONCELET

DISPLACEMENT SURFACED: 1,570 t (1,595 tnes)
DISPLACEMENT SUBMERGED: 2084 t (2,117 tnes)
MACHINERY: twin screws, diesel/electric motors; 2,900/1,800 hp
LENGTH: 210 ft (92.3 m)
BEAM: 18 ft 7 in (8.2 m)
DRAUGHT: 10 ft 9 in (4.7 m)
PERFORMANCE SURFACED: 17–20 knots
PERFORMANCE SUBMERGED: 10 knots
ARMAMENT: nine 550mm and two 400mm TT; one 100mm gun
SURFACE RANGE: 10,000 nm (18,530 km) at 10 knots
CREW: 61
LAUNCH DATE: February 2, 1935

REQUIN

DISPLACEMENT SURFACED: 1,150 t (1,168 tnes)
DISPLACEMENT SUBMERGED: 1,441 t (1,464 tnes)
MACHINERY: twin screws, diesel/electric motors; 2,900/1,800 hp
LENGTH: 56 ft 9 in (78.2 m)
BEAM: 22 ft 5 in (6.8 m)
DRAUGHT: 16 ft 9 in (5 m)
PERFORMANCE SURFACED: 15 knots
PERFORMANCE SUBMERGED: 9 knots
ARMAMENT: 10 533mm TT; one 100mm gun
SURFACE RANGE: 5,650 nm (10,469 km) at 10 knots
CREW: 54
LAUNCH DATE: July 19, 1926

The Type VIIA U-boat *U-30* was among the first wave of German submarines to be deployed to their operational areas in the North Atlantic just prior to the outbreak of World War II. *U-30* survived the war, but was scuttled at Flensburg, Germany, on May 5, 1945.

U-30

DISPLACEMENT SURFACED: **630 t (640 tnes)**
DISPLACEMENT SUBMERGED: **745 t (757 tnes)**
MACHINERY: **two screws, diesel/electric motors; 2,100/750 hp**
LENGTH: **211 ft 6 in (64.5 m)**
BEAM: **19 ft 3 in (5.8 m)**
DRAUGHT: **14 ft 6 in (4.4 m)**
PERFORMANCE SURFACED: **16 knots**
PERFORMANCE SUBMERGED: **8 knots**
ARMAMENT: **five 533mm TT; one 88mm gun; one 20 mm AA gun**
SURFACE RANGE: **3,732 nm (6,916 km) at 12 knots**
CREW: **44**
LAUNCH DATE: **1937**

U-32

DISPLACEMENT SURFACED: **626 t (636 tnes)**
DISPLACEMENT SUBMERGED: **745 t (757 tnes)**
MACHINERY: **two screws, diesel/electric motors; 2,100/750 hp**
LENGTH: **211 ft 6 in (64.5 m)**
BEAM: **19 ft 3 in (5.8 m)**
DRAUGHT: **14ft 6 in (4.4 m)**
PERFORMANCE SURFACED: **16 knots**
PERFORMANCE SUBMERGED: **8 knots**
ARMAMENT: **five 533mm TT; one 88mm gun; one 20 mm AA gun**
SURFACE RANGE: **3,732 nm (6,916 km) at 12 knots**
CREW: **44**
LAUNCH DATE: **1937**

U-39

DISPLACEMENT SURFACED: **630 t (640 tnes)**
DISPLACEMENT SUBMERGED: **745 t (757 tnes)**
MACHINERY: **two screws, diesel/electric motors; 2,100/750 hp**
LENGTH: **211 ft 6 in (64.5 m)**
BEAM: **19 ft 3 in (5.8 m)**
DRAUGHT: **14 ft 6 in (4.4 m)**
PERFORMANCE SURFACED: **16 knots**
PERFORMANCE SUBMERGED: **8 knots**
ARMAMENT: **five 533mm TT; one 88mm gun; one 20 mm AA gun**
SURFACE RANGE: **3,732 nm (6,916 km) at 12 knots**
CREW: **44**
LAUNCH DATE: **1937**

RUBIS

DISPLACEMENT SURFACED: **630 t (640 tnes)**
DISPLACEMENT SUBMERGED: **745 t (757 tnes)**
MACHINERY: **two screws, diesel/electric motors; 1,300/1,000 hp**
LENGTH: **208 ft 11 in (63.4 m)**
BEAM: **17 ft (5.2 m)**
DRAUGHT: **11 ft 9 in (3.61 m)**
PERFORMANCE SURFACED: **13.5 knots**
PERFORMANCE SUBMERGED: **7.5 knots**
ARMAMENT: **10 533mm TT; one 100mm gun**
SURFACE RANGE: **2,300 nm (4,262 km) at 7.5 knots**
CREW: **41**
LAUNCH DATE: **May 23, 1929**

SURCOUF

DISPLACEMENT SURFACED: **3,250 t (3,302 tnes)**
DISPLACEMENT SUBMERGED: **4,304 t (4,373 tnes)**
MACHINERY: **twin screws, diesel/electric motors; 7,600/3,400 hp**
LENGTH: **360 ft 10 in (110 m)**
BEAM: **29 ft 9 in (9.1 m)**
DRAUGHT: **9.07 m (29 ft 9 in)**
PERFORMANCE SURFACED: **18 knots**
PERFORMANCE SUBMERGED: **8.5 knots**
ARMAMENT: **eight 551mm and four 400mm TT; two 203mm**
SURFACE RANGE: **10,000 nm (18,530 km)**
CREW: **118**
LAUNCH DATE: **October 18, 1929**

U-47

DISPLACEMENT SURFACED: **753 t (765 tnes)**
DISPLACEMENT SUBMERGED: **857 t (871 tnes)**
MACHINERY: **two shafts, diesel/electric motors; 2,800/750 hp**
LENGTH: **218 ft (66.5 m)**
BEAM: **20 ft 3 in (6.2 m)**
DRAUGHT: **15 ft 6 in (4.7 m)**
PERFORMANCE SURFACED: **17.25 knots**
PERFORMANCE SUBMERGED: **8 knots**
ARMAMENT: **10 533mm TT; one 100mm gun**
SURFACE RANGE: **2,300 nm (4,262 km) at 7.5 knots**
CREW: **44**
LAUNCH DATE: **1938**

The British aircraft carrier *Ark Royal* was sunk by German torpedoes in November 1941, and the submarine that launched the missile was the *U-81*. Under the command of Lt-Cdr Guggenberger, this Type VIIC U-boat began operations in the Arctic in July 1941 and narrowly escaped being sunk by a Soviet patrol vessel on her first sortie. She continued to operate in the Arctic, before deploying to the Mediterranean in October of that year. On November 13, 1941, *Ark Royal* was returning to Gibraltar after flying off reinforcement fighters for Malta, when she was attacked by *U-81*, being hit by one torpedo from a salvo of four. Despite desperate attempts to tow her to safety, she sank the following day, fortunately with the loss of only one life. *U-81* continued to operate in the Mediterranean, but did not enjoy any further success until November 1942, when she sank a transport vessel during the Allied landings in North Africa. The boat now had a new commander, Lt Krieg, but failed to achieve any major successes, her principal victims being sailing vessels, which were sunk by gunfire. On January 9, 1944, *U-81* was destroyed in an air attack on Pola, her main operating base.

U-81

DISPLACEMENT SURFACED: 781 t (793 tnes)
DISPLACEMENT SUBMERGED: 871 t (879 tnes)
MACHINERY: two shafts, diesel/electric motors; 2,800/750 hp
LENGTH: 218 ft (66.5 m)
BEAM: 20 ft 3 in (6.2 m)
DRAUGHT: 15 ft 6 in (4.7 m)
PERFORMANCE SURFACED: 17 knots
PERFORMANCE SUBMERGED: 7.5 knots
ARMAMENT: five 533mm TT; one 37mm gun; one 20mm AA guns
SURFACE RANGE: 5,642 nm (10,454 km) at 12 knots
CREW: 44
LAUNCH DATE: 1939

U-106

DISPLACEMENT SURFACED: 1,051 t (1,068 tnes)
DISPLACEMENT SUBMERGED: 1,178 t (1,197 tnes)
MACHINERY: two shafts, diesel/electric motors; 4,400/1,000 hp
LENGTH: 251 ft (76.5 m)
BEAM: 22 ft 3 in (6.8 m)
DRAUGHT: 15 ft (4.6 m)
PERFORMANCE SURFACED: 18.25 knots
PERFORMANCE SUBMERGED: 7.25 knots
ARMAMENT: six 533mm TT; one 102mm gun
SURFACE RANGE: 7,552 nm (13,993 km)
CREW: 48
LAUNCH DATE: 1939

U-110

DISPLACEMENT SURFACED: 1,051 t (1,068 tnes)
DISPLACEMENT SUBMERGED: 1,178 t (1,197 tnes)
MACHINERY: two shafts, diesel/electric motors; 4,400/1,000 hp
LENGTH: 251 ft (76.5 m)
BEAM: 22 ft 3 in (6.8 m)
DRAUGHT: 15 ft (4.6 m)
PERFORMANCE SURFACED: 18.25 knots
PERFORMANCE SUBMERGED: 7.25 knots
ARMAMENT: six 533mm TT; one 102m gun; one 20mm AA gun
SURFACE RANGE: 7,552 nm (13,993 km)
CREW: 48
LAUNCH DATE: 1939

U-112

DISPLACEMENT SURFACED: 3,140 t (3,190 tnes)
DISPLACEMENT SUBMERGED: 3,630 t (3,688 tnes)
MACHINERY: two shafts, diesel/electric motors
LENGTH: 377 ft (115 m)
BEAM: 31 ft (9.5 m)
DRAUGHT: 20 ft (6 m)
PERFORMANCE SURFACED: 23 knots
PERFORMANCE SUBMERGED: 7 knots
ARMAMENT: eight 533mm TT; four 127mm guns; two 30mm and two 20 mm AA guns
SURFACE RANGE: 13,635 nm (25,266 km) at 12 knots
CREW: 110
LAUNCH DATE: Projected only

U-570

DISPLACEMENT SURFACED: 781 t (793 tnes)
DISPLACEMENT SUBMERGED: 871 t (879 tnes)
MACHINERY: two shafts, diesel/electric motors; 2,800/750 hp
LENGTH: 218 ft (66.5 m)
BEAM: 20 ft 3 in (6.2 m)
DRAUGHT: 15 ft 6 in (4.7 m)
PERFORMANCE SURFACED: 17 knots
PERFORMANCE SUBMERGED: 7.5 knots
ARMAMENT: five 533mm TT; one 37mm gun; one 20mm AA gun
SURFACE RANGE: 5,642 nm (10,454 km) at 12 knots
CREW: 44
LAUNCH DATE: 1939

In the 1930s, German engineer Helmuth Walter began work on a circuit motor that would function independently of oxygen derived from the atmosphere. The turbine he developed used concentrated hydrogen peroxide, which was heated via a catalyst to produce the required oxygen and high-pressure steam. The first submarine fitted with this reached a submerged speed of 28 knots. Other experimental boats followed, culminating in the submarine *U-791*, built in 1943. However, work proceeded slowly, and the project was given low priority. By 1943, when conventional U-boats were being defeated in the Atlantic and Mediterranean, work was accelerated, but it was too late to help Nazi Germany; it was calculated that the development of an operational long-range Walter-propelled submarine would have taken at least two years.

U-791

DISPLACEMENT SURFACED: **600 t (609 tnes)**
DISPLACEMENT SUBMERGED: **645 t (655 tnes)**
MACHINERY: **single screw, two diesels and two Walter turbines and two electric motors; 150/2, 180/75 hp**
LENGTH: **170 ft 11 in (52.10 m)**
BEAM: **13 ft 1 in (4.00 m)**
DRAUGHT: **70 ft (21 m)**
PERFORMANCE SURFACED: **9.3 knots**
PERFORMANCE SUBMERGED: **19 knots**
ARMAMENT: **two 533mm TT**
SURFACE RANGE: **not known**
CREW: **25**
LAUNCH DATE: **1943**

U-1405

DISPLACEMENT SURFACED: **314 t (319 tnes)**
DISPLACEMENT SUBMERGED: **357 t (363 tnes)**
MACHINERY: **single screw, two diesels and two Walter turbines and two electric motors; 150/2,180/75 hp**
LENGTH: **129 ft 7 in (39.5 m)**
BEAM: **11 ft 2 in (3.4 m)**
DRAUGHT: **15 ft 5 in (4.7 m)**
PERFORMANCE SURFACED: **8.5 knots (estimated)**
PERFORMANCE SUBMERGED: **23 knots**
ARMAMENT: **Two 533mm TT**
SURFACE RANGE: **2,604 nm (4,825 km) (estimated)**
CREW: **19**
LAUNCH DATE: **Project cancelled**

U-2321

DISPLACEMENT SURFACED: **232 t (236 tnes)**
DISPLACEMENT SUBMERGED: **256 t (260 tnes)**
POWERPLANT: **single-shaft diesel/electric motors plus silent creeping electric motor; 580/580/35 hp**
LENGTH: **112 ft (34 m)**
BEAM: **9 ft 9 in (2.9 m)**
DRAUGHT: **12 ft 3 in (3.7 m)**
PERFORMANCE SURFACED: **9.75 knots**
PERFORMANCE SUBMERGED: **12.5 knots**
ARMAMENT: **two 533mm TT**
SURFACE RANGE: **1,172 nm (2,171 km)**
CREW: **14**
LAUNCH DATE: **not known**

U-2501

DISPLACEMENT SURFACED: **1,621 t (1,647 tnes)**
DISPLACEMENT SUBMERGED: **2,067 t (2,100 tnes)**
POWERPLANT: **twin screws, diesel/electric motors, silent creeping motors; 4,000/5,000/226 hp at 15/15/5 knots**
LENGTH: **251 ft 8 in (77 m)**
BEAM: **26 ft 3 in (8 m)**
DRAUGHT: **20 ft 4 in (6.2 m)**
PERFORMANCE SURFACED: **15.5 knots**
PERFORMANCE SUBMERGED: **16 knots**
ARMAMENT: **six 533 mm TT; four 30mm AA guns**
SURFACE RANGE: **9,678 nm (17,934 km)**
CREW: **57**
LAUNCH DATE: **1944**

U-2511

DISPLACEMENT SURFACED: **1,621 t (1,647 tnes)**
DISPLACEMENT SUBMERGED: **2,067 t (2,100 tnes)**
MACHINERY: **twin screws, diesel/electric motors, silent creeping motors; 4,000/5,000/226 hp at 15/15/5 knots**
LENGTH: **251 ft 8 in (77 m)**
BEAM: **26 ft 3 in (8 m)**
DRAUGHT: **20 ft 4 in (6.2 m)**
PERFORMANCE SURFACED: **15.5 knots**
PERFORMANCE SUBMERGED: **16 knots**
ARMAMENT: **six 533mm TT; four 30mm AA guns**
SURFACE RANGE: **9,678 nm (17,934 km)**
CREW: **57**
LAUNCH DATE: **1944**

HMS *Clyde* was one of three Thames-class combined fleet and patrol type submarines laid down between 1932 and 1933, and completed between 1932 and 1935. There were originally to have been 20 boats in this class, but the order was drastically reduced following a policy change. The submarines featured a double hull with welded external fuel tanks, eliminating the leakage problems that had plagued earlier classes. *Clyde, Thames,* and the third boat, *Severn*, were assigned to the 2nd Submarine Flotilla on the outbreak of World War II, beginning operations against enemy shipping in the North Sea and off the coast of Norway.

On June 20, 1940, *Clyde*, under Lt-Cdr Ingram, achieved a torpedo hit on the German battlecruiser *Gneisenau*, which had left Trondheim to make a sortie into the Iceland-Faeroes passage. The warship limped back to Trondheim and, after repairs, sailed for Kiel, where she remained until early 1941. This was a major success, as the German vessel was a fast and powerfully armed ship. *Clyde*'s sister-boat *Thames* fell victim to a mine off Norway on July 23, 1940. After many successful forays against enemy shipping in northern waters, both boats deployed to the Eastern Fleet via the Mediterranean in 1944, and they were both scrapped in India in 1946.

CLYDE

DISPLACEMENT SURFACED: **1,805 t (1,834 tnes)**
DISPLACEMENT SUBMERGED: **2,723 t (2,680 tnes)**
MACHINERY: **two screws, diesel/electric motors; 10,000/2,500 hp**
LENGTH: **325 ft (99.1 m)**
BEAM: **28 ft (8.5 m)**
DRAUGHT: **13 ft 6 in (4.1 m)**
PERFORMANCE SURFACED: **21.75 knots**
PERFORMANCE SUBMERGED: **10 knots**
ARMAMENT: **eight 21 in TT; one 4in gun**
SURFACE RANGE: **5,000 nm (9,265 km) at 10 knots**
CREW: **61**
LAUNCH DATE: **January 26, 1932**

OBERON

DISPLACEMENT SURFACED: **1,490 t (1,513 tnes)**
DISPLACEMENT SUBMERGED: **1,892 t (1,922 tnes)**
MACHINERY: **twin screws, diesel/electric motors; 3,000/1,350 hp**
LENGTH: **273 ft 8 in (83.4 m)**
BEAM: **27 ft 3 in (8.3 m)**
DRAUGHT: **15 ft (4.6 m)**
PERFORMANCE SURFACED: **15.5 knots**
PERFORMANCE SUBMERGED: **9 knots**
ARMAMENT: **eight 21 in TT; one 4in gun**
SURFACE RANGE: **5,633 nm (9,500 km)**
CREW: **54**
LAUNCH DATE: **September 24, 1926**

ORPHEUS

DISPLACEMENT SURFACED: **1,490 t (1,513 tnes)**
DISPLACEMENT SUBMERGED: **1,892 t (1,922 tnes)**
MACHINERY: **twin screws, diesel/electric motors; 4,400/1,320 hp**
LENGTH: **273 ft 8 in (83.4 m)**
BEAM: **27 ft 3 in (8.3 m)**
DRAUGHT: **15 ft (4.6 m)**
PERFORMANCE SURFACED: **15.5 knots**
PERFORMANCE SUBMERGED: **9 knots**
ARMAMENT: **eight 21 in TT; one 4in gun**
SURFACE RANGE: **5,633 nm (9,500 km)**
CREW: **54**
LAUNCH DATE: **February 26, 1929**

PROTEUS

DISPLACEMENT SURFACED: **1,760 t (1,788 tnes)**
DISPLACEMENT SUBMERGED: **2,040 t (2,072 tnes)**
MACHINERY: **two screws, diesel/electric motors; 4,640/1,635 hp**
LENGTH: **289 ft 2 in (88.14 m)**
BEAM: **29 ft 11 in (9.12 m)**
DRAUGHT: **15 ft 11 in (4.85 m)**
PERFORMANCE SURFACED: **17.5 knots**
PERFORMANCE SUBMERGED: **8.6 knots**
ARMAMENT: **10 21 in TT; one 3.9in gun**
SURFACE RANGE: **2,300 nm (4,262 km) at 7.5 knots**
CREW: **53**
LAUNCH DATE: **July 23, 1929**

SEAL

DISPLACEMENT SURFACED: **1,500 t (1,524 tnes)**
DISPLACEMENT SUBMERGED: **2,053 t (2,086 tnes)**
MACHINERY: **twin screws, diesel/electric motors; 3,300/1,630 hp**
LENGTH: **267 ft (81.5 m)**
BEAM: **29 ft 9 in (9 m)**
DRAUGHT: **13 ft 9 in (13.75 m)**
PERFORMANCE SURFACED: **15 knots**
PERFORMANCE SUBMERGED: **8.75 knots**
ARMAMENT: **six 21 in TT; one 4in gun**
SURFACE RANGE: **5,500 nm (10,191 km) at 10 knots**
CREW: **61**
LAUNCH DATE: **September 7, 1938**

One of 33 S-class submarines laid down under a British war emergency programme initiated in 1941, *Seraph* and her sisters were improved and enlarged developments of the Shark class of the late 1930s. Though they were rushed into service, the class served the Royal Navy well during World War II. The S-class submarines, originally intended for service in the North Sea theater of operations, were offensively employed in all three main theaters of warfare, and proved to be a most successful design. *Seraph*'s area of operations was the Mediterranean, where, in addition to normal war patrols, she carried out many special missions, such as inserting agents along enemy coastlines, which was dangerous but

necessary work. During the Allied invasion of Sicily in July 1943, *Seraph* acted as beacon submarine for Task Force 85. In July/September 1944, *Seraph* was converted at Devonport to the high-speed target role, with a streamlined hull and casing, higher-capacity batteries, uprated motors, and new propellers. This revised configuration increased the submarine's speed at periscope depth by some three knots. Nine of the S-class submarines were lost during World War II, and two more submarines, *Safari* and *Sportsman*, were lost as a result of post-war accidents, which was an average loss rate compared to other classes of submarines. *Seraph* was eventually broken up in 1965.

SERAPH

DISPLACEMENT SURFACED: 872 t (886 tnes)
DISPLACEMENT SUBMERGED: 990 t (1,005 tnes)
MACHINERY: twin screws, diesel/electric motors; 1,900/1,300 hp
LENGTH: 216 ft 10 in (66.1 m)
BEAM: 23 ft 8 in (7.2 m)
DRAUGHT: 11 ft 2 in (3.4 m)
PERFORMANCE SURFACED: 14.75 knots
PERFORMANCE SUBMERGED: 9 knots
ARMAMENT: six 21in TT; one 3 in gun
SURFACE RANGE: 6,144 nm (11,400 km)
CREW: 44
LAUNCH DATE: October 25, 1941

SPLENDID

DISPLACEMENT SURFACED: 872 t (886 tnes)
DISPLACEMENT SUBMERGED: 990 t (1,005 tnes)
MACHINERY: twin screws, diesel/electric motors; 1,900/1,300 hp
LENGTH: 216 ft 10 in (66.1 m)
BEAM: 23 ft 8 in (7.2 m)
DRAUGHT: 11 ft 2 in (3.4 m)
PERFORMANCE SURFACED: 14.75 knots
PERFORMANCE SUBMERGED: 9 knots
ARMAMENT: six 21in TT; one 3 in gun
SURFACE RANGE: 6,144 nm (11,400 km)
CREW: 48
LAUNCH DATE: January 19, 1942

SWORDFISH

DISPLACEMENT SURFACED: 640 t (650 tnes)
DISPLACEMENT SUBMERGED: 927 t (942 tnes)
MACHINERY: twin shafts, diesel/electric motors; 1,550/1,440 hp
LENGTH: 193 ft (58.8 m)
BEAM: 24 ft (7.3 m)
DRAUGHT: 10 ft 6 in (3.2 m)
PERFORMANCE SURFACED: 15 knots
PERFORMANCE SUBMERGED: 10 knots
ARMAMENT: six 21in TT; one 3in gun
SURFACE RANGE: 4,000 nm (7,412 km)
CREW: 38
LAUNCH DATE: January 8, 1932

THUNDERBOLT

DISPLACEMENT SURFACED: 1,090 t (1,107 tnes)
DISPLACEMENT SUBMERGED: 1,575 t (1,600 tnes)
MACHINERY: twin screws, diesel/electric motors; 2,500/1,450 hp
LENGTH: 265 ft (80.8 m)
BEAM: 26 ft 6 in (8 m)
DRAUGHT: 14 ft 9 in (4.5 m)
PERFORMANCE SURFACED: 15.25 knots
PERFORMANCE SUBMERGED: 9 knots
ARMAMENT: 10 21in TT; one 4in gun
SURFACE RANGE: 3,800 nm (7,041km) at 10 knots
CREW: 59
LAUNCH DATE: June 29, 1938

UNBROKEN

DISPLACEMENT SURFACED: 545 t (554 tnes)
DISPLACEMENT SUBMERGED: 740 t (752 tnes)
MACHINERY: twin screws, diesel/electric motors; 825/615 hp
LENGTH: 180 ft (54.9 m)
BEAM: 16 ft (4.8 m)
DRAUGHT: 12 ft 9 in (3.8 m)
PERFORMANCE SURFACED: 11.25 knots
PERFORMANCE SUBMERGED: 9 knots
ARMAMENT: four 21in TT; one 3in gun
SURFACE RANGE: 3,800 nm (7,041 km)
CREW: 31
LAUNCH DATE: November 4, 1941

A famous British U-class submarine, but one that unfortunately did not survive the war, was HMS *Upholder*. She served with the Malta-based 10th Submarine Flotilla, whose boats sank 49 troop transports and supply ships, (a total of 150,000 tons/152,400 tonnes) from the start of June to the end of September 1941. Much more success followed, but *Upholder*'s run of luck ran out in April 1942, when she was sunk by the Italian torpedo boat *Pegaso* while on her 24th war mission.

UPHOLDER

DISPLACEMENT SURFACED:
545 t (554 tnes)
DISPLACEMENT SUBMERGED:
740 t (752 tnes)
MACHINERY: **two screws, diesel/electric motors; 825/615 hp**
LENGTH: **180 ft (54.9 m)**
BEAM: **16 ft (4.8 m)**
DRAUGHT: **12 ft 9 in (3.8 m)**
PERFORMANCE SURFACED: **11.25 knots**
PERFORMANCE SUBMERGED: **9 knots**
ARMAMENT: **four 21 in TT; one 3 in gun**
SURFACE RANGE: **3,800 nm (7,041 km)**
CREW: **31**
LAUNCH DATE: **July 8, 1940**

UTMOST

DISPLACEMENT SURFACED:
545 t (554 tnes)
DISPLACEMENT SUBMERGED:
740 t (752 tnes)
MACHINERY: **two screws, diesel/electric motors; 825/615 hp**
LENGTH: **180 ft (54.9 m)**
BEAM: **16 ft (4.8 m)**
DRAUGHT: **12 ft 9 in (3.8 m)**
PERFORMANCE SURFACED: **11.25 knots**
PERFORMANCE SUBMERGED: **9 knots**
ARMAMENT: **four 21 in TT; one 3 in gun**
SURFACE RANGE: **3,800 nm (7,041 km)**
CREW: **31**
LAUNCH DATE: **April 20, 1940**

X-CRAFT

DISPLACEMENT SURFACED:
25.4 t (27 tnes)
DISPLACEMENT SUBMERGED:
29.5 t (30 tnes)
MACHINERY: **single screw, diesel/electric motors; 42/30 hp**
LENGTH: **51 ft 6 in (15.7 m)**
BEAM: **6 ft (1.8 m)**
DRAUGHT: **8 ft 6 in (2.6 m)**
PERFORMANCE SURFACED: **6.5 knots**
PERFORMANCE SUBMERGED: **5 knots**
ARMAMENT: **Explosive charges**
SURFACE RANGE: **not recorded**
CREW: **4**
LAUNCH DATE: **1942**

The Italian submarine *Adua* was leader of a class of 17 short-range submarines completed between 1936 and 1937, at a time when Italy and France were striving to establish naval supremacy in the Mediterranean. In fact, these two nations built more submarines in the inter-war years than any other country. The Adua-class boats, although not endowed with a particularly fast surface speed, were highly maneuverable and structurally strong, both considerable advantages when evasive action was needed during battle. All of the Adua-class boats gave excellent service during World War II.

ADUA

DISPLACEMENT SURFACED: **680 t (691 tnes)**
DISPLACEMENT SUBMERGED: **866 t (880 tnes)**
MACHINERY: **two shaft, diesel/electric motors; 1,200/800 hp**
LENGTH: **197 ft 6 in (60.2 m)**
BEAM: **21 ft 4 in (6.5 m)**
DRAUGHT: **15 ft (4.6 m)**
PERFORMANCE SURFACED: **14 knots**
PERFORMANCE SUBMERGED: **7 knots**
ARMAMENT: **eight 21 in TT; one 3.9 in gun**
SURFACE RANGE: **10,000 nm (18,530 km) at 10 knots**
CREW: **58**
LAUNCH DATE: **April 3, 1938**

BRIN

DISPLACEMENT SURFACED: **1,016 t (1,032 tnes)**
DISPLACEMENT SUBMERGED: **1,266 t (1,286 tnes)**
MACHINERY: **two screws, diesel/electric motors; 3,400/1,300 hp**
LENGTH: **231 ft 4 in (70 m)**
BEAM: **22 ft 6 in (7 m)**
DRAUGHT: **13 ft 6 in (4.2 m)**
PERFORMANCE SURFACED: **17 knots**
PERFORMANCE SUBMERGED: **8 knots**
ARMAMENT: **eight 21 in TT; one 3.9 in gun**
SURFACE RANGE: **10,000 nm (18,530 km) at 10 knots**
CREW: **58**
LAUNCH DATE: **April 3, 1938**

Completed in September 1938, *Barbarigo* enjoyed a longer operational life than many of her 10 sister-boats, most of which had been sunk by the end of 1942. *Barbarigo* deployed to Bordeaux in the late summer of 1940 for operations in the Central Atlantic, which began in October. The boat had little success, apart from sinking a neutral Spanish ship, the *Navemar*. On October 6, 1942, she added farce to her record when she attacked the British corvette *Petunia*, which she mistook for an American battleship. A new skipper, Lt-Cdr Rigoli, brought a measure of success to the boat, sinking three ships in early March 1943. *Barbarigo* was subsequently converted as a supply submarine for service on the France-Japan route, but was sunk by Allied aircraft in the Bay of Biscay at the start of her first trip out in June 1943.

BARBARIGO

DISPLACEMENT SURFACED: **1,043 t (1,059 tnes)**
DISPLACEMENT SUBMERGED: **1,290 t (1,310 tnes)**
MACHINERY: **twin screws, diesel/electric motors; 3,600/1,100 hp**
LENGTH: **239 ft 6 in (73 m)**
BEAM: **23 ft (7 m)**
DRAUGHT: **16 ft 6 in (5 m)**
PERFORMANCE SURFACED: **17.4 knots**
PERFORMANCE SUBMERGED: **8 knots**
ARMAMENT: **eight 533mm TT**
SURFACE RANGE: **768 nm (1,425 km) at 10 knots**
CREW: **58**
LAUNCH DATE: **June 13, 1938**

CAGNI

DISPLACEMENT SURFACED: **1,504 t (1,528 tnes)**
DISPLACEMENT SUBMERGED: **1,680 t (1,707 tnes)**
MACHINERY: **twin screws, diesel/electric motors; 4,370/1,800 hp**
LENGTH: **200 ft 5 in (87.9 m)**
BEAM: **17 ft 7 in (7.76 m)**
DRAUGHT: **13 ft (5.72 m)**
PERFORMANCE SURFACED: **17 knots**
PERFORMANCE SUBMERGED: **9 knots**
ARMAMENT: **14 450mm TT; two 100mm guns**
SURFACE RANGE: **12,000 nm (22,236 km) at 11 knots**
CREW: **85**
LAUNCH DATE: **July 20, 1940**

CALVI

DISPLACEMENT SURFACED: **1,500 t (1,574 tnes)**
DISPLACEMENT SUBMERGED: **2,060 t (2,092 tnes)**
MACHINERY: **twin screws, diesel/electric motors; 4,400/1,800 hp**
LENGTH: **276 ft 6 in (84.3 m)**
BEAM: **25 ft 3 in (7.7 m)**
DRAUGHT: **17 ft (5.2 m)**
PERFORMANCE SURFACED: **17 knots**
PERFORMANCE SUBMERGED: **8 knots**
ARMAMENT: **eight 533mm TT; two 120mm guns**
SURFACE RANGE: **10,409 nm (19,311 km) at 10 knots**
CREW: **77**
LAUNCH DATE: **March 31, 1935**

DANDOLO

DISPLACEMENT SURFACED: **1,063 t (1,080 tnes)**
DISPLACEMENT SUBMERGED: **1,317 t (1,338 tnes)**
MACHINERY: **two screws, diesel/electric motors; 2,880/1,250 hp**
LENGTH: **239 ft 6 in (73 m)**
BEAM: **23 ft 8 in (7.2 m)**
DRAUGHT: **16 ft 5 in (5 m)**
PERFORMANCE SURFACED: **17.4 knots**
PERFORMANCE SUBMERGED: **8 knots**
ARMAMENT: **eight 533mm TT; two 100mm guns**
SURFACE RANGE: **2,560 nm (4,750 km) at 17 knots**
CREW: **57**
LAUNCH DATE: **November 20, 1937**

FOCA

DISPLACEMENT SURFACED: **1,333 t (1,354 tnes)**
DISPLACEMENT SUBMERGED: **1,659 t (1,685 tnes)**
MACHINERY: **twin screws, diesel/electric motors; 2,880/1,250 hp**
LENGTH: **271 ft 8 in (82.8 m)**
BEAM: **23 ft 6 in (7.2 m)**
DRAUGHT: **17 ft 5 in (5.3 m)**
PERFORMANCE SURFACED: **15.2 knots**
PERFORMANCE SUBMERGED: **7.4 knots**
ARMAMENT: **six 533mm TT; one 100mm gun**
SURFACE RANGE: **2,500 nm (4,632 nm) at 17 knots**
CREW: **60**
LAUNCH DATE: **June 26, 1937**

The *Flutto* was the class leader of the first of three planned groups of submarines that would have reached a total of 49 boats, all embodying the lessons absorbed by the Italian Navy since it entered the war in 1940. The plan called for the boats to be completed by the end of 1944, but production was overtaken by the armistice of 1943, and only a few of the first group, including *Flutto*, saw active service. *Flutto* was sunk by Royal Navy MTBs 640, 651, and 670 in the Straits of Messina on July 11, 1943. Of her sister-boats, *Gorgo* and *Tritone* were sunk by the Allies in 1943. Others were sunk in harbor after being seized by the Germans, or destroyed in various stages of construction by Allied air attacks. The *Nautilo* was refloated and handed over to the Yugoslav Navy; the *Murea* went to the USSR in 1949 and was redesignated the *Z13*.

FLUTTO

DISPLACEMENT SURFACED: 958 t (973 tnes)
DISPLACEMENT SUBMERGED: 1,170 t (1,189 tnes)
MACHINERY: twin screws, diesel/electric motors
LENGTH: 207 ft (63.2 m)
BEAM: 23 ft (7 m)
DRAUGHT: 16 ft (4.9 m)
PERFORMANCE SURFACED: 16 knots
PERFORMANCE SUBMERGED: 7 knots
ARMAMENT: six 533mm TT
SURFACE RANGE: 3,200 nm (5,297 km)
CREW: 50
LAUNCH DATE: November 1942

GALILEI

DISPLACEMENT SURFACED: 985 t (1,000 tnes)
DISPLACEMENT SUBMERGED: 1,259 t (1,279 tnes)
MACHINERY: twin screws, diesel/electric motors; 3,000/1,300 hp
LENGTH: 231 ft 4 in (70.5 m)
BEAM: 22 ft 4 in (6.8 m)
DRAUGHT: 13 ft 5 in (4 m)
PERFORMANCE SURFACED: 17 knots
PERFORMANCE SUBMERGED: 8.5 knots
ARMAMENT: eight 533mm TT; two 100mm guns
SURFACE RANGE: 3,600 nm (6,670 km)
CREW: 55
LAUNCH DATE: March 19, 1934

MAMELI

DISPLACEMENT SURFACED: 830 t (843 tnes)
DISPLACEMENT SUBMERGED: 1,010 t (1,026 tnes)
MACHINERY: twin screws, diesel/electric motors; 3,000/1,100 hp
LENGTH: 212 ft (64.6 m)
BEAM: 21 ft 4 in (6.5 m)
DRAUGHT: 14 ft (4.3 m)
PERFORMANCE SURFACED: 17 knots
PERFORMANCE SUBMERGED: 7 knots
ARMAMENT: six 533mm TT; one 102mm gun
SURFACE RANGE: 3,200 nm (5,930 km) at 10 knots
CREW: 49
LAUNCH DATE: December 9, 1926

PERLA

DISPLACEMENT SURFACED: 696 t (707 tnes)
DISPLACEMENT SUBMERGED: 852 t (865 tnes)
MACHINERY: two screws, diesel/electric motors; 1,400/800 hp
LENGTH: 196 ft 9 in (60 m)
BEAM: 21 ft 2 in (6.5 m)
DRAUGHT: 15ft 3 in (5 m)
PERFORMANCE SURFACED: 14 knots
PERFORMANCE SUBMERGED: 8 knots
ARMAMENT: six 533mm TT; one 100mm gun
SURFACE RANGE: 3,595 nm (6,670 km) at 10 knots
CREW: 45
LAUNCH DATE: May 3, 1936

SQUALO

DISPLACEMENT SURFACED: 933 t (948 tnes)
DISPLACEMENT SUBMERGED: 1,142 t (1,160 tnes)
MACHINERY: two diesel/electric motors; 3,000/1,300 hp
LENGTH: 229 ft (70 m)
BEAM: 23 ft 7 in (7 m)
DRAUGHT: 23ft 7 in (7 m)
PERFORMANCE SURFACED: 15 knots
PERFORMANCE SUBMERGED: 8 knots
ARMAMENT: eight 533mm TT; one 102mm gun
SURFACE RANGE: 4,000 nm (7,412 km) at 10 knots
CREW: 52
LAUNCH DATE: January 15, 1930

The J3-class submarine *I-7* and her sister boat *I-8*, were among the first submarines of pure Japanese design and, at the time of their commissioning, were the largest in the Imperial Japanese Navy. They would begin a trend for large submarines in the Japanese Navy, a trend that was to prove futile in serving Japan's wartime needs, as large submarines used lots of fuel and had short endurance at sea. Approved in 1934, their design was based on a submarine cruiser concept, developed from earlier designs, and they had provision for a Yokosuka E14Y1 reconnaissance seaplane (codenamed "Glen" by the Allies). The aircraft made its operational debut on December 17, 1941, when *I-7* launched its Glen on a dawn reconnaissance mission over Pearl Harbor to assess the damage done by carrier-based attack aircraft. *I-7* had an endurance of 60 days and a diving depth of 325 ft (99 m). *I-7* and her sister sank seven Allied merchant vessels (41,902 tons / 42,574 tonnes) during the Pacific War. *I-7* was sunk by the American destroyer *Monaghan* off the Aleutian islands on June 22, 1943, while *I-8* was sunk by the destroyers USS *Morrison* and USS *Stockton* off Okinawa on March 30, 1945.

I-7

DISPLACEMENT SURFACED: 2,525 t (2,565 tnes)
DISPLACEMENT SUBMERGED: 3,583 t (3,640 tnes)
MACHINERY: twin screws, diesel/electric motors; 11,200/2,800 hp
LENGTH: 358 ft 7 in (109.3 m)
BEAM: 29 ft 6 in (9 m)
DRAUGHT: 17 ft (5.2 m)
PERFORMANCE SURFACED: 23 knots
PERFORMANCE SUBMERGED: 8 knots
ARMAMENT: six 533mm TT; one 140mm gun
SURFACE RANGE: 14,337 nm (26,600 km) at 16 knots
CREW: 100
LAUNCH DATE: July 3, 1935

I-15

DISPLACEMENT SURFACED: 2,584 t (2,625 tnes)
DISPLACEMENT SUBMERGED: 3,654 t (3,713 tnes)
MACHINERY: two screws, diesel/electric motors; 12,400/2,000 hp
LENGTH: 336 ft (102.5 m)
BEAM: 30 ft 6 in (9.3 m)
DRAUGHT: 16 ft 9 in (5.1 m)
PERFORMANCE SURFACED: 23.5 knots
PERFORMANCE SUBMERGED: 8 knots
ARMAMENT: six 533mm TT; one 140mm and two 25mm AA guns
SURFACE RANGE: 16,000 nm (29,648 km)
CREW: 100
LAUNCH DATE: March 7, 1939

I-16

DISPLACEMENT SURFACED: 2,554 t (2,595 tnes)
DISPLACEMENT SUBMERGED: 3,561 t (3,618 tnes)
MACHINERY: two screws, diesel/electric motors; 12,400/2,000 hp
LENGTH: 340 ft 7 in (103.80 m)
BEAM: 29 ft 10 in (9.10 m)
DRAUGHT: 17 ft 7 in (5.35 m)
PERFORMANCE SURFACED: 23.6 knots
PERFORMANCE SUBMERGED: 8 knots
ARMAMENT: eight 533mm TT; one 140mm and two 25mm AA guns
SURFACE RANGE: 14,000 nm (25,942 km)
CREW: 100
LAUNCH DATE: July 28, 1938

I-52

DISPLACEMENT SURFACED: 2,564 t (2,605 tnes)
DISPLACEMENT SUBMERGED: 3,561 t (3,618 tnes)
MACHINERY: two screws, diesel/electric motors; 4,700/1,200 hp
LENGTH: 335 ft 11 in (102.4 m)
BEAM: 30 ft 6 in (9.3 m)
DRAUGHT: 16 ft 10 in (5.12 m)
PERFORMANCE SURFACED: 17.7 knots
PERFORMANCE SUBMERGED: 6.5 knots
ARMAMENT: six 533mm TT; two 140mm and two 25mm AA guns
SURFACE RANGE: 21,000 nm (38,913 km) at 16 knots
CREW: 101
LAUNCH DATE: 1943

I-58

DISPLACEMENT SURFACED: 2,564 t (2,605 tnes)
DISPLACEMENT SUBMERGED: 3,561 t (3,618 tnes)
MACHINERY: two screws, diesel/electric motors; 4,700/1,200 hp
LENGTH: 335 ft 11 in (102.40 m)
BEAM: 30 ft 6 in (9.30 m)
DRAUGHT: 16 ft 10 in (5.12 m)
PERFORMANCE SURFACED: 17.7 knots
PERFORMANCE SUBMERGED: 6.5 knots
ARMAMENT: six 533mm TT; two 140mm and two 25mm AA guns
SURFACE RANGE: 21,000 nm (38,913 km) at 16 knots
CREW: 101
LAUNCH DATE: 1944

The *Kaiten* midget submarines, deployed in the closing months of World War II, were the Imperial Japanese Navy's equivalent of the kamikaze suicide aircraft. They were built onto the body of a Type 93 torpedo engine and air chamber, and early models were provided with a small hatch under the hull to enable the pilot to escape as soon as the craft was locked on to its target. This escape facility was later removed, and the *Kaiten* became a true suicide weapon. The *Kaiten* 1 was powered by petrol and oxygen. The next version, the *Kaiten* 2, was powered by a hydrogen peroxide engine, but only a few examples were built, as insufficient engines of this type were available. As a consequence, a *Kaiten* 4 was built, using the conventional petrol and oxygen engine and carrying a heavier warhead to ensure penetration of enemy hulls. The *Kaiten* 3 was an experimental unit which never entered production. The *Kaiten* 2 and 4 carried a two-man crew. Hundreds of *Kaiten* craft were built, and were intended to be used primarily for coastal defense in opposition to the expected invasion of Japan, although many were deployed against Allied naval forces elsewhere, and were first used in the battle for the Philippines in November 1944. The specifications table (below left) is for the *Kaiten* 1.

KAITEN

DISPLACEMENT SURFACED: **unknown**
DISPLACEMENT SUBMERGED: **8.5 t (8.6 tnes)**
MACHINERY: **one 550 hp petrol-oxygen engine**
LENGTH: **48 ft (14.73 m)**
BEAM: **3 ft 4 in (0.99 m)**
DRAUGHT: **3 ft 3 in (3.61 m)**
PERFORMANCE SURFACED: **30 knots maximum**
PERFORMANCE SUBMERGED: **unknown**
ARMAMENT: **one 1,550 kg (3,416 lb) HE warhead**
SURFACE RANGE: **50 nm (92 km) at 12 knots/14 nm (25 km) at 30 knots**
CREW: **1**
LAUNCH DATE: **1944–45**

I-121

DISPLACEMENT SURFACED: **1,383 t (1,405 tnes)**
DISPLACEMENT SUBMERGED: **1,768 t (1,796 tnes)**
MACHINERY: **two screws, diesel/electric motors; 2,400/1,100 hp**
LENGTH: **269 ft (82 m)**
BEAM: **24 ft 8 in (7.52 m)**
DRAUGHT: **14 ft 6 in (4.42 m)**
PERFORMANCE SURFACED: **14.5 knots**
PERFORMANCE SUBMERGED: **7 knots**
ARMAMENT: **four 533mm TT; one 140mm gun, two mines**
SURFACE RANGE: **10,500 nm (19,456 km) at 8 knots**
CREW: **75**
LAUNCH DATE: **unknown**

I-153

DISPLACEMENT SURFACED: **1,800 t (1,828 tnes)**
DISPLACEMENT SUBMERGED: **2,300 t (2,337 tnes)**
MACHINERY: **two screws, diesel/electric motors; 6,800/1,800 hp**
LENGTH: **310 ft (94.49 m)**
BEAM: **26 ft 2 in (7.98 m)**
DRAUGHT: **15 ft 10 in (4.83 m)**
PERFORMANCE SURFACED: **20 knots**
PERFORMANCE SUBMERGED: **8 knots**
ARMAMENT: **eight 533mm TT; one 105mm gun**
SURFACE RANGE: **10,000 nm (18,530 km) at 8 knots**
CREW: **60**
LAUNCH DATE: **August 5, 1925**

I-201

DISPLACEMENT SURFACED: **1,291 t (1,311 tnes)**
DISPLACEMENT SUBMERGED: **1,450 t (1,473 tnes)**
MACHINERY: **twin screws, diesel/electric motors; 2,750/5,000 hp**
LENGTH: **259 ft 2 in (79 m)**
BEAM: **19 ft (5.8 m)**
DRAUGHT: **17 ft 9 in (5.4 m)**
PERFORMANCE SURFACED: **15.7 knots**
PERFORMANCE SUBMERGED: **19 knots**
ARMAMENT: **four 533mm TT; two 25mm AA guns**
SURFACE RANGE: **5,800 nm (10,747 km) at 14 knots**
CREW: **100**
LAUNCH DATE: **1944**

I-351

DISPLACEMENT SURFACED: **3,512 t (3,568 tnes)**
DISPLACEMENT SUBMERGED: **4,290 t (4,358 tnes)**
MACHINERY: **twin screws, diesel/electric motors**
LENGTH: **361 ft (110 m)**
BEAM: **33 ft 6 in (10.2 m)**
DRAUGHT: **20 ft (6 m)**
PERFORMANCE SURFACED: **15.7 knots**
PERFORMANCE SUBMERGED: **19 knots**
ARMAMENT: **four 533mm TT**
SURFACE RANGE: **13,000 nm (24,089 km)**
CREW: **90**
LAUNCH DATE: **1944**

In 1942, the Japanese Imperial Navy investigated the feasibility of mounting a torpedo attack on the locks of the Panama Canal, using aircraft launched from a submarine. 19 large submarines capable of carrying two or three aircraft were planned, known as the I-400 Type STo. In the event, only two, *I-400* and *I-401*, were completed, each with a hangar to take three floatplanes. The aircraft were intended to be launched down a 85 ft (26 m) catapult rail on deck. The Panama mission was never carried out, and the two boats were surrendered in 1945. They were scrapped by the U.S. Navy in 1946.

I-400

DISPLACEMENT SURFACED: **5,233 t (5,316 tnes)**
DISPLACEMENT SUBMERGED: **6,560 t (6,665 tnes)**
MACHINERY: **twin screws, diesel/electric motors; 7,700/2,400 hp**
LENGTH: **380 ft 7 in (116 m)**
BEAM: **39 ft 4 in (12 m)**
DRAUGHT: **23 ft (7 m)**
PERFORMANCE SURFACED: **18.7 knots**
PERFORMANCE SUBMERGED: **6.5 knots**
ARMAMENT: **eight 533mm TT; one 140mm gun**
SURFACE RANGE: **37,000 nm (68,561 km) at 14 knots**
CREW: **100**
LAUNCH DATE: **1944**

RO-100

DISPLACEMENT SURFACED: **601 t (611 tnes)**
DISPLACEMENT SUBMERGED: **782 t (795 tnes)**
MACHINERY: **twin screws, diesel/electric motors; 1,100/760 hp**
LENGTH: **1,88ft 3 in (57.4 m)**
BEAM: **20 ft (6.1 m)**
DRAUGHT: **11 ft 6 in (3.5 m)**
PERFORMANCE SURFACED: **14 knots**
PERFORMANCE SUBMERGED: **8 knots**
ARMAMENT: **four 533mm TT; one 76mm gun**
SURFACE RANGE: **3,500 nm (6,485 km) at 12 knots**
CREW: **75**
LAUNCH DATE: **December 6, 1941**

The *Jastrzab* (Hawk) was the former American submarine *S25*, which had been scheduled for delivery to the Royal Navy. Instead, for propaganda reasons, she was commissioned in 1941 as the Polish *Jastrzab*, flying the White Ensign of the Royal Navy, as well as the flag of Poland and carrying the pennant number P.551. (Poland had been overrun by Hitler's Nazi Germany in 1939.)

JASTRZAB

DISPLACEMENT SURFACED: **850 t (864 tnes)**
DISPLACEMENT SUBMERGED: **1,090 t (1,107 tnes)**
MACHINERY: **two screws, diesel/electric motors; 1,200/1,500 hp**
LENGTH: **211 ft (64.3 m)**
BEAM: **20 ft 6 in (6.25 m)**
DRAUGHT: **4.6 m (15ft 3 in)**
PERFORMANCE SURFACED: **14.5 knots**
PERFORMANCE SUBMERGED: **11 knots**
ARMAMENT: **four 533mm TT; one 102mm gun**
SURFACE RANGE: **4,200 nm (7,782 km)**
CREW: **42**
LAUNCH DATE: **May 29, 1922**

ORZEL

DISPLACEMENT SURFACED: **1,100 t (1,117 tnes)**
DISPLACEMENT SUBMERGED: **1,473 t (1,496 tnes)**
MACHINERY: **twin screws, diesel/electric motors; 4,740/1,100 hp**
LENGTH: **275 ft 7 in (84 m)**
BEAM: **22 ft (6.7 m)**
DRAUGHT: **13 ft 8 in (4 m)**
PERFORMANCE SURFACED: **15 knots**
PERFORMANCE SUBMERGED: **8 knots**
ARMAMENT: **12 550mm TT; one 105mm gun**
SURFACE RANGE: **7,169 nm (13,300 km) at 10 knots**
CREW: **56**
LAUNCH DATE: **January 15, 1938**

WILK

DISPLACEMENT SURFACED: **980 t (996 tnes)**
DISPLACEMENT SUBMERGED: **1,250 t (1,270 tnes)**
MACHINERY: **two screws, diesel/electric motors; 1,800/1,200 hp**
LENGTH: **257 ft 6 in (78.5 m)**
BEAM: **19 ft 4 in (5.9 m)**
DRAUGHT: **13 ft 9 in (4.2 m)**
PERFORMANCE SURFACED: **14 knots**
PERFORMANCE SUBMERGED: **9 knots**
ARMAMENT: **six 550mm TT; one 100mm gun; 40 mines**
SURFACE RANGE: **2,500 nm (4,632 km)**
CREW: **54**
LAUNCH DATE: **April 12, 1929**

The US submarine *Angler* was one of the massive Gato-class ocean-going submarines that played havoc with Japan's maritime commerce in World War II. *Angler* opened her score in January 1944, when she sank a small freighter shortly after arriving in her operational area. Another freighter fell victim to *Angler's* torpedoes in May, while the submarine was operating in the area of the Mandate Islands. July 1944 found the boat operating off the Philippines and the Malay peninsula. After the war, *Angler* was rebuilt with increased engine power and converted to the hunter-killer role. At the end of her operational life in 1963, her propellers were removed, her torpedo tubes welded shut, and she became an immobilized dockside training vessel (AGSS), employed to train Naval Reserve personnel. She was used in this role until the 1970s.

ANGLER

DISPLACEMENT SURFACED: 1,825 t (1,854 tnes)
DISPLACEMENT SUBMERGED: 2,410 t (2,448 tnes)
MACHINERY: twin screws, diesels/electric motors; 5,400/2,740 hp
LENGTH: 311 ft 9 in (95 m)
BEAM: 27 ft 3 in (8.3 m)
DRAUGHT: 4.6 m (15ft 3 in)
PERFORMANCE SURFACED: 20 knots
PERFORMANCE SUBMERGED: 10 knots
ARMAMENT: 10 21in TT; one 3in gun
SURFACE RANGE: 12,000 nm (22,236 km) at 10 knots
CREW: 80
LAUNCH DATE: July 4, 1943

BARB

DISPLACEMENT SURFACED: 1,825 t (1,854 tnes)
DISPLACEMENT SUBMERGED: 2,410 t (2,448 tnes)
MACHINERY: twin screws, diesels/electric motors; 5,400/2,740 hp
LENGTH: 311 ft 9 in (95 m)
BEAM: 27 ft 3 in (8.3 m)
DRAUGHT: 15 ft 3 in (4.6 m)
PERFORMANCE SURFACED: 20 knots
PERFORMANCE SUBMERGED: 10 knots
ARMAMENT: 10 21in TT; one 3in gun
SURFACE RANGE: 12,000 nm (22,236 km) at 10 knots
CREW: 80
LAUNCH DATE: April 2, 1942

CUTLASS

DISPLACEMENT SURFACED: 1,860 t (1,570 tnes)
DISPLACEMENT SUBMERGED: 2,420 t (2,467 tnes)
MACHINERY: twin screws, diesel/electric motors; 5,400/2,740 hp
LENGTH: 307 ft (93.6 m)
BEAM: 27 ft 3 in (8.3 m)
DRAUGHT: 15 ft 3 in (4.6 m)
PERFORMANCE SURFACED: 20 knots
PERFORMANCE SUBMERGED: 10 knots
ARMAMENT: 10 21in torpedo tubes; two 5.9in guns
SURFACE RANGE: 12,152 nm (22,518 km) at 10 knots
CREW: 85
LAUNCH DATE: November 5, 1944

DACE

DISPLACEMENT SURFACED: 1,825 t (1,854 tnes)
DISPLACEMENT SUBMERGED: 2,410 t (2,448 tnes)
MACHINERY: twin screws, diesels/electric motors; 5,400/2,740 hp
LENGTH: 311 ft 9 in (95 m)
BEAM: 27 ft 3 in (8.3 m)
DRAUGHT: 15 ft 3 in (4.6 m)
PERFORMANCE SURFACED: 20 knots
PERFORMANCE SUBMERGED: 10 knots
ARMAMENT: 10 21in TT; one 3in gun
SURFACE RANGE: 12,000 nm (22,236 km) at 10 knots
CREW: 80
LAUNCH DATE: April 25, 1943

DRUM

DISPLACEMENT SURFACED: 1,825 t (1,854 tnes)
DISPLACEMENT SUBMERGED: 2,410 t (2,448 tnes)
MACHINERY: twin screws, diesels/electric motors; 5,400/2,740 hp
LENGTH: 311 ft 9 in (95 m)
BEAM: 27 ft 3 in (8.3 m)
DRAUGHT: 15 ft 3 in (4.6 m)
PERFORMANCE SURFACED: 20 knots
PERFORMANCE SUBMERGED: 10 knots
ARMAMENT: 10 21in TT; one 3in gun
SURFACE RANGE: 12,000 nm (22,236 km) at 10 knots
CREW: 80
LAUNCH DATE: May 15, 1941

Among the first of her class assigned to the U.S. Pacific Fleet, *Gato*'s first major mission was to form part of a submarine screen to the northwest of Midway Island, guarding against a possible Japanese landing there. In January 1943, she sank four ships of a total of 12,997 tons (13,205 tonnes) and damaged four more. She claimed her next victims in November and December 1943. In February 1944, during large-scale offensive air and sea operations around the Caroline Islands, *Gato* sank three more freighters and three small craft near the island of Truk. There were further successes in February 1945, when *Gato* sank a freighter and a corvette. *Gato*, along with all the early boats of her class, was laid up at the end of World War II to await disposal. *Gato* was discarded in 1960.

GATO

DISPLACEMENT SURFACED: **1,825 t (1,854 tnes)**
DISPLACEMENT SUBMERGED: **2,410 t (2,448 tnes)**
MACHINERY: **twin screws, diesels/electric motors; 5,400/2,740 hp**
LENGTH: **311 ft 9 in (95 m)**
BEAM: **27 ft 3 in (8.3 m)**
DRAUGHT: **15 ft 3 in (4.6 m)**
PERFORMANCE SURFACED: **20 knots**
PERFORMANCE SUBMERGED: **10 knots**
ARMAMENT: **10 21in TT; one 3in gun**
SURFACE RANGE: **12,000 nm (22,236 km) at 10 knots**
CREW: **80**
LAUNCH DATE: **August 21, 1941**

LIZARDFISH

DISPLACEMENT SURFACED: **1,825 t (1,854 tnes)**
DISPLACEMENT SUBMERGED: **2,410 t (2,448 tnes)**
MACHINERY: **twin screws, diesels/electric motors; 5,400/2,740 hp**
LENGTH: **311 ft 9 in (95 m)**
BEAM: **27 ft 3 in (8.3 m)**
DRAUGHT: **15 ft 3 in (4.6 m)**
PERFORMANCE SURFACED: **20 knots**
PERFORMANCE SUBMERGED: **10 knots**
ARMAMENT: **10 21in TT; one 3in gun**
SURFACE RANGE: **12,000 nm (22,236 km) at 10 knots**
CREW: **80**
LAUNCH DATE: **July 16, 1944**

MARLIN

DISPLACEMENT SURFACED: **940 t (955 tnes)**
DISPLACEMENT SUBMERGED: **1,140 t (1,158 tnes)**
MACHINERY: **two screws, diesel engines; 1,680 hp**
LENGTH: **238 ft 11 in (72.82 m)**
BEAM: **21 ft 8 in (6.60 m)**
DRAUGHT: **13 ft (3.96 m)**
PERFORMANCE SURFACED: **16.5 knots**
PERFORMANCE SUBMERGED: **8 knots**
ARMAMENT: **six 21in TT; one 3in gun**
SURFACE RANGE: **2,500 nm (4,632 km)**
CREW: **80**
LAUNCH DATE: **January 29, 1941**

NAUTILUS

DISPLACEMENT SURFACED: **2,730 t (2,773 tnes)**
DISPLACEMENT SUBMERGED: **3,900 t (3,962 tnes)**
MACHINERY: **twin screws, diesel/electric motors; 5,450/2,540 hp**
LENGTH: **370 ft (113 m)**
BEAM: **33 ft 3 in (10 m)**
DRAUGHT: **15 ft 9 in (4.8 m)**
PERFORMANCE SURFACED: **17 knots**
PERFORMANCE SUBMERGED: **8 knots**
ARMAMENT: **six 21in torpedo tubes, two 6in guns**
SURFACE RANGE: **10,000 nm (18,350 km)**
CREW: **90**
LAUNCH DATE: **March 15, 1930**

TANG

DISPLACEMENT SURFACED: **1,825 t (1,854 tnes)**
DISPLACEMENT SUBMERGED: **2,410 t (2,448 tnes)**
MACHINERY: **twin screws, diesel/electric motors; 5,400/2,740 hp**
LENGTH: **311 ft 9 in (95 m)**
BEAM: **27 ft 3 in (8.3 m)**
DRAUGHT: **15 ft 3 in (4.6 m)**
PERFORMANCE SURFACED: **20 knots**
PERFORMANCE SUBMERGED: **10 knots**
ARMAMENT: **10 21in TT; one 3in gun**
SURFACE RANGE: **12,000 nm (22,236 km) at 10 knots**
CREW: **80**
LAUNCH DATE: **August 17, 1943**

USS *Tautog* sank 26 ships during World War II, the biggest toll exacted by any U.S. submarine. She was at Pearl Harbor at the time of the Japanese attack in December 1941, but escaped undamaged. In April 1942, she sank two ships in Japanese waters and the submarine *I-28* off Truk. After further successes, in April 1943 she sank a Japanese merchant vessel and the destroyer *Isonami*. In 1945, she closed her wartime scoreboard by sinking three more enemy transport vessels. *Tautog* was scrapped in 1960, a somewhat ignominious end for a gallant submarine.

TAUTOG

DISPLACEMENT SURFACED: 1,475 t (1,498 tnes)
DISPLACEMENT SUBMERGED: 2,370 t (2,408 tnes)
MACHINERY: twin screws, diesel/electric motors; 5,400/2,740 hp
LENGTH: 302 ft 6 in (92.2 m)
BEAM: 27 ft 3 in (8.31 m)
DRAUGHT: 15 ft (4.57 m)
PERFORMANCE SURFACED: 20 knots
PERFORMANCE SUBMERGED: 8.7 knots
ARMAMENT: 10 21in TT; one 3in gun
SURFACE RANGE: 11,000 nm (20,383 km) at 10 knots
CREW: 85
LAUNCH DATE: January 27, 1940

TENCH

DISPLACEMENT SURFACED: 1,860 t (1,570 tnes)
DISPLACEMENT SUBMERGED: 2,420 t (2,467 tnes)
MACHINERY: twin screws, diesel/electric motors; 5,400/2,740 hp
LENGTH: 307 ft (93.6 m)
BEAM: 27 ft 3 in (8.3 m)
DRAUGHT: 15 ft 3 in (4.6 m)
PERFORMANCE SURFACED: 20 knots
PERFORMANCE SUBMERGED: 10 knots
ARMAMENT: 10 21in torpedo tubes; two 5.9in guns
SURFACE RANGE: 12,152 nm (22,518 km) at 10 knots
CREW: 85
LAUNCH DATE: July 7, 1944

The Soviet submarine *D3*, a Series I boat, was serving with the Northern Fleet at the time of Nazi Germany's attack on the Soviet Union in June 1941, and deployed to her war station off Norway's North Cape. On September 27, commanded by Lt-Cdr F.V. Konstantinov (and with the commander of the 2d Submarine Division, Capt 2d Class I.A. Kolyshkin on board) she began a series of attacks on German convoys off the Norwegian coast. All of her torpedoes missed their targets. The same thing happened in December 1941, by which time Konstantinov had been replaced Lt-Cdr N.A. Bibeyev. Bibeyev's aim against the German minelayer *Brummer*, which *D3* attacked on March 14, 1942, was equally as poor, and attacks on German convoys in June 1942 also met with no success. The submarine failed to return from a mission in July 1942, presumably sunk by a mine barrage. The Series I submarines were good seaboats, but their construction was of poor quality, and they had a number of design faults. For example, their diving time, originally, was three minutes, and a great deal of work had to be done on the ballast tanks before this was reduced to a more acceptable 30 seconds. Of the six boats in the class, four became casualties during World War II.

D3

DISPLACEMENT SURFACED: 933 t (948 tnes)
DISPLACEMENT SUBMERGED: 1,354 t (1,376 tnes)
MACHINERY: twin screws, diesel/electric motors; 2,600/1,600 hp
LENGTH: 249 ft 4 in (76 m)
BEAM: 21 ft 4 in (6.5 m)
DRAUGHT: 12 ft 6 in (3.8 m)
PERFORMANCE SURFACED: 14 knots
PERFORMANCE SUBMERGED: 9 knots
ARMAMENT: eight 533mm TT; one 100mm gun
SURFACE RANGE: 7,500 nm (13,897 km) at 12 knots
CREW: 80
LAUNCH DATE: July 12, 1929

D4

DISPLACEMENT SURFACED: 933 t (948 tnes)
DISPLACEMENT SUBMERGED: 1,354 t (1,376 tnes)
MACHINERY: twin screws, diesel/electric motors; 2,600/1,600 hp
LENGTH: 249 ft 4 in (76 m)
BEAM: 21 ft 4 in (6.5 m)
DRAUGHT: 12 ft 6 in (3.8 m)
PERFORMANCE SURFACED: 14 knots
PERFORMANCE SUBMERGED: 9 knots
ARMAMENT: eight 533mm TT; one 100mm gun
SURFACE RANGE: 7,500 nm (13,897 km) at 12 knots
CREW: 80
LAUNCH DATE: 1929

The Soviet Series XIV submarine *K3* was one of 12 K-class ocean-going submarines that were developed from several previous proposed designs. The boats were heavily armed, and were originally intended to carry a small dismantled reconnaissance floatplane, known as SPL (Samolet dlya Podvodnoi Lodki), which translates as "aircraft for submarines." The plane was actually built and test flown, but never entered service. *K3* was operating in the Baltic Sea at the time of the German invasion of the Soviet Union in June 1941, and in August she was transferred to the Northern Fleet via the Stalin (White Sea) Canal, reaching Molotovsk on September 25. In November of that year, she laid mine barrages off the Norwegian coast, after which she made a number of abortive attacks on German convoys. During one of these on November 26, she was attacked by German sub-chasers and depth-charged, after which *K3* was forced to surface. She managed to beat off the German craft in a gun duel, sinking one of them (*UJ1708*). In February 1943, *K3* sank another German sub-chaser, together with a large transport vessel. On March 21, 1943, after making two abortive attacks on enemy convoys, *K3* was herself attacked by a group of three enemy sub-chasers and sunk. Her commander throughout most of her operational career was Captain 3rd Class Malofeyev.

K3

DISPLACEMENT SURFACED: **1,490 t (1,514 tnes)**
DISPLACEMENT SUBMERGED: **2,104 t (2,138 tnes)**
MACHINERY: **twin screws, diesel/electric motors; 8,400/2,400 hp**
LENGTH: **320 ft 4 in (97.65 m)**
BEAM: **24 ft 3 in (7.4 m)**
DRAUGHT: **14 ft 10 in (4.51 m)**
PERFORMANCE SURFACED: **21 knots**
PERFORMANCE SUBMERGED: **10 knots**
ARMAMENT: **10 533mm TT; two 100mm guns; 20 mines**
SURFACE RANGE: **12,000 nm (22,236 km) at 9 knots**
CREW: **60**
LAUNCH DATE: **1938**

K21

DISPLACEMENT SURFACED: **1,490 t (1,514 tnes)**
DISPLACEMENT SUBMERGED: **2,104 t (2,138 tnes)**
MACHINERY: **twin screws, diesel/electric motors; 8,400/2,400 hp**
LENGTH: **320 ft 4 in (97.65 m)**
BEAM: **24 ft 3 in (7.4 m)**
DRAUGHT: **14 ft 10 in (4.51 m)**
PERFORMANCE SURFACED: **21 knots**
PERFORMANCE SUBMERGED: **10 knots**
ARMAMENT: **10 533mm TT; two 100mm guns; 20 mines**
SURFACE RANGE: **12,000 nm (22,236 km) at 9 knots**
CREW: **60**
LAUNCH DATE: **1938**

L3

DISPLACEMENT SURFACED: **1,200 t (1,219 tnes)**
DISPLACEMENT SUBMERGED: **1,550 t (1,574 tnes)**
POWERPLANT: **twin screws, diesel/electric motors; 2,200/1,050 hp**
LENGTH: **265 ft 9 in (81 m)**
BEAM: **24 ft 7 in (7.5 m)**
DRAUGHT: **15 ft 9 in (7.8 m)**
PERFORMANCE SURFACED: **15 knots**
PERFORMANCE SUBMERGED: **9 knots**
ARMAMENT: **six 533mm TT; one 100mm gun**
SURFACE RANGE: **5,000 nm (9,265 km)**
CREW: **54**
LAUNCH DATE: **July 1931**

M172

DISPLACEMENT SURFACED: **206 t (209 tnes)**
DISPLACEMENT SUBMERGED: **218 t (221 tnes)**
MACHINERY: **single screw, diesel/electric motors; 800/400 hp**
LENGTH: **146 ft (44.5 m)**
BEAM: **10 ft 10 in (3.3 m)**
DRAUGHT: **9 ft 10 in (3 m)**
PERFORMANCE SURFACED: **14 knots**
PERFORMANCE SUBMERGED: **8 knots**
ARMAMENT: **two 533mm TT; one 45 mm gun**
SURFACE RANGE: **1,880 nm (3,484 km) at 8 knots**
CREW: **20**
LAUNCH DATE: **1936**

M201

DISPLACEMENT SURFACED: **281 t (285 tnes)**
DISPLACEMENT SUBMERGED: **351 t (357 tnes)**
MACHINERY: **twin screws, diesel/electric motors; 1,600/875 hp**
LENGTH: **162 ft 5 in (49.5 m)**
BEAM: **14 ft 5 in (4.4 m)**
DRAUGHT: **9 ft (2.75 m)**
PERFORMANCE SURFACED: **15.7 knots**
PERFORMANCE SUBMERGED: **8 knots**
ARMAMENT: **one 533mm TT; one 45 mm gun**
SURFACE RANGE: **1,880 nm (3,484 km) at 8 knots**
CREW: **24**
LAUNCH DATE: **1940**

For the crew of the Soviet Series IXbis submarine *S7*, operations began on June 22, 1941, with a reconnaissance mission off Gotland. On September 26, under Capt 3rd Class L.P. Lisin, *S7* sank a small steamer off the Swedish coast. In November, she was involved in special operations, disembarking agents in Narva Bay, Estonia, and on convoy protection duty. Her first real success on offensive operations came in June and July 1942, when she sank four ships of a total of 9,164 tons (9,311 tonnes); three of these were Swedish, which the Soviets regarded as fair game, as they were transporting raw materials to Germany. In September 1942, having broken through enemy mine barrages with a number of other submarines, *S7* was operating in the Aaland Sea, between the Baltic and the Gulf of Bothnia. On October 21, 1942, she was sunk by the Finnish submarine *Vesihiisi*, under the command of Lt-Cdr Aittola. Four Soviet crewmen survived the attack, including Capt Lisin, and were taken prisoner. The S-class boats to which *S7* belonged were medium-sized submarines designed for open sea warfare, and were built in three progressively improved types. In general appearance, the third series, the Type XVI, resembled the German Type VIIC U-boat.

S7

DISPLACEMENT SURFACED: **856 t (870 tnes)**
DISPLACEMENT SUBMERGED: **1,090 t (1,107 tnes)**
MACHINERY: **twin screws, diesel/electric motors; 4,000/1,100 hp**
LENGTH: **255 ft 1 in (77.5 m)**
BEAM: **21 ft (6.4 m)**
DRAUGHT: **13 ft 4 in (4.06 m)**
PERFORMANCE SURFACED: **18.75 knots**
PERFORMANCE SUBMERGED: **8.8 knots**
ARMAMENT: **six 533mm TT; one 100mm gun**
SURFACE RANGE: **9,000 nm (16,677 km) at 10.5 knots**
CREW: **46**
LAUNCH DATE: **1937**

S13

DISPLACEMENT SURFACED: **856 t (870 tnes)**
DISPLACEMENT SUBMERGED: **1,090 t (1,107 tnes)**
MACHINERY: **two screws, diesel/electric motors; 4,000/1,100 hp**
LENGTH: **255 ft 1 in (77.5 m)**
BEAM: **21 ft (6.4 m)**
DRAUGHT: **13 ft 4 in (4.06 m)**
PERFORMANCE SURFACED: **18.75 knots**
PERFORMANCE SUBMERGED: **8.8 knots**
ARMAMENT: **six 533mm TT; one 100mm gun**
SURFACE RANGE: **9,000 nm (16,677 km) at 10.5 knots**
CREW: **46**
LAUNCH DATE: **1941**

S56

DISPLACEMENT SURFACED: **856 t (870 tnes)**
DISPLACEMENT SUBMERGED: **1,090 t (1,107 tnes)**
MACHINERY: **twin screws, diesel/electric motors; 4,000/1,100 hp**
LENGTH: **255 ft 1 in (77.5 m)**
BEAM: **21 ft (6.4 m)**
DRAUGHT: **13 ft 4 in (4.06 m)**
PERFORMANCE SURFACED: **18.75 knots**
PERFORMANCE SUBMERGED: **8.8 knots**
ARMAMENT: **six 533mm TT; one 100mm gun**
SURFACE RANGE: **9,000 nm (16,677 km) at 10.5 knots**
CREW: **46**
LAUNCH DATE: **December 1939**

SHCH 307

DISPLACEMENT SURFACED: **586 t (595 tnes)**
DISPLACEMENT SUBMERGED: **702 t (713 tnes)**
MACHINERY: **two screws; diesel/electric motors; 1,600/800 hp**
LENGTH: **191 ft 11 in (58.5 m)**
BEAM: **20 ft 4 in (6.2 m)**
DRAUGHT: **14 ft 1 in (4.3 m)**
PERFORMANCE SURFACED: **14 knots**
PERFORMANCE SUBMERGED: **8 knots**
ARMAMENT: **six 533mm TT; two 45mm guns**
SURFACE RANGE: **900 nm (1,667 km) at 8.5 knots**
CREW: **40**
LAUNCH DATE: **August 1, 1934**

SHCH 317

DISPLACEMENT SURFACED: **586 t (595 tnes)**
DISPLACEMENT SUBMERGED: **702 t (713 tnes)**
MACHINERY: **twin screws; diesel/electric motors; 1,600/800 hp**
LENGTH: **191 ft 11 in (58.5 m)**
BEAM: **20 ft 4 in (6.2 m)**
DRAUGHT: **14 ft 1 in (4.3 m)**
PERFORMANCE SURFACED: **14 knots**
PERFORMANCE SUBMERGED: **8 knots**
ARMAMENT: **six 533mm TT; two 45mm guns**
SURFACE RANGE: **900 nm (1,667 km) at 8.5 knots**
CREW: **40**
LAUNCH DATE: **September 25, 1935**

BOMBERS

The multi-engined aircraft designed to attack enemy military bases, as well as towns and cities.

The Blitz (Lightning) was the only turbojet-powered bomber to achieve operational status in World War II, and is a milestone in military aviation's development. Its evolution dates from 1940 and development resulted in 18 prototypes. A few were used from July 1944 by reconnaissance units. In addition, 210 Ar 234B-1 reconnaissance aircraft with drop tanks in place of bombs and Ar 234B-2 reconnaissance bombers were built. The type entered service in September 1944, and was complemented by just 14 examples of the Ar 234C with the revised powerplant of four BMW 109-003A-1 turbojets.

ARADO AR 234 BLITZ

MANUFACTURER: **Arado Flugzeugwerke**
TYPE: **Reconnaissance/Bomber**
LENGTH: **41 ft 5.5 in (12.65 m)**
SPAN: **47 ft 3.25 in (14.40 m)**
HEIGHT: **14 ft 1.25 in (4.3 m)**
MAXIMUM SPEED: **485 mph (780 km/h)**
SERVICE CEILING: **36,090 ft (16,370 m)**
RANGE: **1,243 miles (2,000 km)**
CREW: **1**
POWERPLANT: **2 or 4 x Jumo turbojets**
ARMAMENT: **2 x MG 151 cannon**
BOMB LOAD: **3,300 lb (1,500 kg)**
FIRST FLIGHT: **June 15, 1943**
INITIAL CLIMB: **not available**
WEIGHT (EMPTY): **10,580 lb (4,800 kg)**
WEIGHT (LOADED): **21,720 lb (9,850 kg)**

ARADO AR 95

MANUFACTURER: **Arado Flugzeugwerke**
TYPE: **Coast Patrol, Light Attack**
LENGTH: **36 ft 5 in (11.10 m)**
SPAN: **41 ft (12.5 m)**
HEIGHT: **11 ft 9.75 in (3.60 m)**
MAXIMUM SPEED: **193 mph (310 km/h)**
SERVICE CEILING: **23,945 ft (7,300 m)**
RANGE: **683 miles (1,100 km)**
CREW: **2**
POWERPLANT: **1 x BMW 132 radial**
ARMAMENT: **2 x 7.92mm MG15**
BOMB LOAD: **1,760 lb (800 kg)**
FIRST FLIGHT: **1937**
INITIAL CLIMB: **not available**
WEIGHT (EMPTY): **5,402 lb (2,450 kg)**
WEIGHT (LOADED): **7,870 lb (3,560 kg)**

DORNIER DO 17

MANUFACTURER: **Dornier-Werke GmbH**
TYPE: **Medium Bomber**
LENGTH: **51 ft 9.67 in (15.80 m)**
SPAN: **59 ft 0.5 in (18.00 m)**
HEIGHT: **15 ft 1 in (4.60 m)**
MAXIMUM SPEED: **255 mph (410 km/h)**
SERVICE CEILING: **26,905 ft (8,200 m)**
RANGE: **932 miles (1,500 km)**
CREW: **4**
POWERPLANT: **2 x BMW Bramo radials**
ARMAMENT: **1 or 2 7.92mm MG**
BOMB LOAD: **2,205 lb (1,000 kg)**
FIRST FLIGHT: **Fall 1934**
INITIAL CLIMB: **not available**
WEIGHT (EMPTY): **11,464 lb (5,200 kg)**
WEIGHT (LOADED): **18,937 lb (8,590 kg)**

DORNIER DO 217

MANUFACTURER: **Dornier-Werke GmbH**
TYPE: **Heavy Bomber**
LENGTH: **59 ft 8.5 in (18.20 m)**
SPAN: **62 ft 4 in (19.00 m)**
HEIGHT: **16 ft 6 in (5.03 m)**
MAXIMUM SPEED: **320 mph (515 km/h)**
SERVICE CEILING: **29,530 ft (9,000 m)**
RANGE: **1,740 miles (2,800 km)**
CREW: **4**
POWERPLANT: **2 x BMW 801ML radials**
ARMAMENT: **1 x cannon, 5 x MG**
BOMB LOAD: **8,818 lb (4,000 kg)**
FIRST FLIGHT: **August 1938**
INITIAL CLIMB: **708 ft (216 m) per min**
WEIGHT (EMPTY): **23,225 lb (10,535 kg)**
WEIGHT (LOADED): **36,299 lb (16,465 kg)**

FOCKE WULF FW 200

MANUFACTURER: **Focke Wulf Flugzeugbau**
TYPE: **Maritime Recon' Bomber**
LENGTH: **76 ft 11.5 in (23.46 m)**
SPAN: **107 ft 8 in (32.84 m)**
HEIGHT: **20 ft 8 in (6.30 m)**
MAXIMUM SPEED: **224 mph (360 km/h)**
SERVICE CEILING: **19,685 ft (6,000 m)**
RANGE: **2,759 miles (4,440 km)**
CREW: **5**
POWERPLANT: **4 x BMW-Bramo 323R-2**
ARMAMENT: **1 x cannon, 4 x MG**
BOMB LOAD: **4,630 lb (2,100 kg)**
FIRST FLIGHT: **not given**
INITIAL CLIMB: **not available**
WEIGHT (EMPTY): **28,549 lb (12,950 kg)**
WEIGHT (LOADED): **50,044 lb (22,700 kg)**

The Heinkel He 111 could carry 2,205 lb (1,000 kg) of bombs and was extensively used in World War II. The Junkers Ju 87 "Stuka" dive-bomber was perhaps the most famous German warplane of World War II, used in "Blitzkrieg" attacks. The Ju 88 was produced in many variants.

HEINKEL HE 111

MANUFACTURER: **Ernst Heinkel A.G.**
TYPE: **Medium Bomber**
LENGTH: **53 ft 9.5in (16.40 m)**
SPAN: **74 ft 1.75 in (22.60 m)**
HEIGHT: **13 ft 1.5 in (3.40 m)**
MAXIMUM SPEED: **252 mph (405 km/h)**
SERVICE CEILING: **27,890 ft (8,500 m)**
RANGE: **1,199 miles (1,930 km)**
CREW: **4 or 5**
POWERPLANT: **2 x Junkers Jumo 211F-2**
ARMAMENT: **7 x 7.92mm MG**
BOMB LOAD: **5,511 lb (2,500 kg)**
FIRST FLIGHT: **February 24, 1935**
INITIAL CLIMB: **558 ft (170 m) per min**
WEIGHT (EMPTY): **19,136 lb (8,680 kg)**
WEIGHT (LOADED): **30,865 lb (14,000 kg)**

JUNKERS JU 87

MANUFACTURER: **Junkers Flugzeug**
TYPE: **Dive-Bomber**
LENGTH: **36 ft 5 in (11.2 m)**
SPAN: **45 ft 3.33 in (13.80 m)**
HEIGHT: **13 ft 2 in (4.01 m)**
MAXIMUM SPEED: **238 mph (383 km/h)**
SERVICE CEILING: **26,245 ft (8,000 m)**
RANGE: **491 miles (790 km)**
CREW: **2**
POWERPLANT: **1 x Junkers Jumo 211Da**
ARMAMENT: **3 x 7.92mm MG**
BOMB LOAD: **2,205 lb (1,000 kg)**
FIRST FLIGHT: **November 1935**
INITIAL CLIMB: **1,515 ft (462 m) per min**
WEIGHT (EMPTY): **5,974 lb (2,710 kg)**
WEIGHT (LOADED): **9,568 lb (4,340 kg)**

JUNKERS JU 88

MANUFACTURER: **Junkers Flugzeug**
TYPE: **High Speed Bomber**
LENGTH: **47 ft 2.75 in (14.40 m)**
SPAN: **65 ft 7.5 in (20 m)**
HEIGHT: **15 ft 11 in (4.85 m)**
MAXIMUM SPEED: **292 mph (470 km/h)**
SERVICE CEILING: **26,900 ft (8,200 m)**
RANGE: **1,696 miles (2,730 km)**
CREW: **4**
POWERPLANT: **2 x Junkers Jumo 211J**
ARMAMENT: **7 x 7.92mm MG**
BOMB LOAD: **5,511 lb (2,500 kg)**
FIRST FLIGHT: **December 21, 1936**
INITIAL CLIMB: **770 ft (235 m) per min**
WEIGHT (EMPTY): **21,737 lb (9,860 kg)**
WEIGHT (LOADED): **30,865 lb (14,000 kg)**

The Lancaster was the most successful bomber used by the RAF in World War II. In service from 1942, it was a sturdy aeroplane with good defensive and offensive firepower. The Lincoln was a development of the Lancaster and could fly farther and higher, and carry heavier armament.

AVRO LANCASTER

MANUFACTURER: **A.V. Roe & Co., Ltd.**
TYPE: **Heavy Bomber**
LENGTH: **69 ft 6 in (21.18 m)**
SPAN: **102 ft (31.09 m)**
HEIGHT: **20 ft 6 in (6.25 m)**
MAXIMUM SPEED: **287 mph (462 km/h)**
SERVICE CEILING: **19,000 ft (5,790 m)**
RANGE: **1,730 miles (2,784 km)**
CREW: **7**
POWERPLANT: **4 x RR Merlin XX**
ARMAMENT: **9 x 0.303in MG**
BOMB LOAD: **18,000 lb (8,165 kg)**
FIRST FLIGHT: **January 9, 1941**
INITIAL CLIMB: **250 ft (76 m) per min**
WEIGHT (EMPTY): **37,000 lb (16,783 kg)**
WEIGHT (LOADED): **65,000 lb (29,484 kg)**

AVRO LINCOLN

MANUFACTURER: **A.V. Roe & Co. Ltd.**
TYPE: **Heavy Bomber**
LENGTH: **78 ft 3.5 in (23.86 m)**
SPAN: **120 ft (36.58 m)**
HEIGHT: **17 ft 3.5 in (5.27 m)**
MAXIMUM SPEED: **295 mph (475 km/h)**
SERVICE CEILING: **30,500 ft (9,295 m)**
RANGE: **1,470 miles (2,366 km)**
CREW: **7**
POWERPLANT: **4 x RR Merlin 85**
ARMAMENT: **6 x 0.50in MG**
BOMB LOAD: **14,000 lb (6,350 kg)**
FIRST FLIGHT: **June 9, 1944**
INITIAL CLIMB: **not available**
WEIGHT (EMPTY): **43,400 lb (19,686 kg)**
WEIGHT (LOADED): **75,000 lb (34,019 kg)**

During the inter-war period, the British Air Ministry concentrated much of its resources on building up a fleet of bombers, in line with the doctrine of the day on future offensive air operations. The Manchester Mk I became operational in 1940. The Blenheim was a militarized version of the Type 142 high-speed light transport Bristol. Undeniably one of the most important aircraft of the war, and matched only by the Junkers Ju 88 in terms of its versatility, the Mosquito was developed from October 1938 as a bomber. However, the Mosquito's versatility and high performance meant it was made in other forms. There were nine night-fighter versions, and also many unarmed photo-reconnaissance and bomber variants, with progressively improved armament, engines, and avionics.

AVRO MANCHESTER

MANUFACTURER: A.V. Roe & Co. Ltd.
TYPE: Medium Bomber
LENGTH: 69 ft 4.25 in (21.14 m)
SPAN: 90 ft 1 in (27.46 m)
HEIGHT: 19 ft 6 in (5.94 m)
MAXIMUM SPEED: 265 mph (426 km/h)
SERVICE CEILING: 19,200 ft (5,850 m)
RANGE: 1,630 miles (2,623 km)
CREW: 7
POWERPLANT: 2 x RR Vulture X-type
ARMAMENT: 8 x 0.303in MG
BOMB LOAD: 10,350 lb (4,695 kg)
FIRST FLIGHT: July 25, 1939
INITIAL CLIMB: not available
WEIGHT (EMPTY): 29,432 lb (13,350 kg)
WEIGHT (LOADED): 56,000 lb (25,402 kg)

BRISTOL BLENHEIM

MANUFACTURER: Bristol Aeroplane Co.
TYPE: Light Bomber
LENGTH: 39 ft 9 in (12.12 m)
SPAN: 56 ft 4 in (17.17 m)
HEIGHT: 9 ft 10 in (3.00 m)
MAXIMUM SPEED: 285 mph (459 km/h)
SERVICE CEILING: not given
RANGE: 1,125 miles (1,810 km)
CREW: 3
POWERPLANT: 2 x Bristol Mercury VIII
ARMAMENT: 2 x 0.303in MG
BOMB LOAD: 1,000 lb (454 kg)
FIRST FLIGHT: June 25, 1936
INITIAL CLIMB: 1,499 ft (457 m) per min
WEIGHT (EMPTY): 8,839 lb (4,013 kg)
WEIGHT (LOADED): 13,100 lb (5,947 kg)

DE HAVILLAND MOSQUITO

MANUFACTURER: De Havilland Aircraft Co.
TYPE: Light Bomber
LENGTH: 44 ft 6 in (13.56 m)
SPAN: 54 ft 2 in (16.51 m)
HEIGHT: 15 ft 3 in (4.65 m)
MAXIMUM SPEED: 415 mph (668 km/h)
SERVICE CEILING: 37,000 ft (11,280 m)
RANGE: 1,795 miles (2,888 km)
CREW: 2
POWERPLANT: 2 x RR Merlin
ARMAMENT: none
BOMB LOAD: 4,000 lb (1,814 kg)
FIRST FLIGHT: November 25, 1940
INITIAL CLIMB: 1,999 ft (609 m) per min
WEIGHT (EMPTY): 15,500 lb (7,031 kg)
WEIGHT (LOADED): 25,917 lb (11,766 kg)

FAIREY ALBACORE

MANUFACTURER: Fairey Aviation Co.
TYPE: Torpedo Bomber
LENGTH: 39 ft 11.75 in (12.18 m)
SPAN: 49 ft 11.75 in (15.23 m)
HEIGHT: 12 ft 6 in (3.81 m)
MAXIMUM SPEED: 161 mph (257 km/h)
SERVICE CEILING: 20,700 ft (6,310 m)
RANGE: 930 miles (1,497 km)
CREW: 3
POWERPLANT: 1 x Bristol Taurus XII
ARMAMENT: 3 x 0.303in MG
BOMB OR TORPEDO LOAD: 2,000 lb (907 kg)
FIRST FLIGHT: December 12, 1938
INITIAL CLIMB: 750 ft (228 m) per min
WEIGHT (EMPTY): 7,200 lb (3,269 kg)
WEIGHT (LOADED): 12,500 lb (5,670 kg)

FAIREY BARRACUDA

MANUFACTURER: Fairey Aviation Co.
TYPE: Naval Torpedo Bomber
LENGTH: 39 ft 9 in (12.12 m)
SPAN: 49 ft 2 in (15 m)
HEIGHT: 15 ft 1in (4.6 m)
MAXIMUM SPEED: 228 mph (367 km/h)
SERVICE CEILING: 16,600 ft (5,060 m)
RANGE: 684 miles (1,101 km)
CREW: 3
POWERPLANT: 1 x RR Merlin 32
ARMAMENT: 2 x 0.303in MG
BOMB LOAD: 1,617 lb (735 kg)
FIRST FLIGHT: December 7, 1940
INITIAL CLIMB: 950 ft (290 m) per min
WEIGHT (EMPTY): 9,350 lb (4,241 kg)
WEIGHT (LOADED): 14,100 lb (6,396 kg)

At the outbreak of World War II, the Fairey Battle was the RAF's most numerous day bomber, yet it suffered appalling losses at the hands of German fighters because it was completely unable to defend itself from them. It was relegated to second-line service in 1940. In contrast, the Fairey Swordfish proved to be superbly effective as a torpedo-carrying fleet spotter. Its most famous hour was the torpedo attack on the Italian fleet at Taranto in November 1940. Designed to the same specification as the Lancaster, the Halifax never achieved the fame of the Avro aircraft, despite making almost as great a contribution to the Allied war effort and in a greater diversity of roles, undertaking maritime reconnaissance, and playing a key role in transport and airborne forces work. It was also used for clandestine insertion of agents by parachute into enemy territory.

FAIREY BATTLE

MANUFACTURER: **Fairey Aviation Co.**
TYPE: **Light Day Bomber**
LENGTH: **42 ft 5 in (12.93 m)**
SPAN: **54 ft (16.45 m)**
HEIGHT: **15 ft (4.57 m)**
MAXIMUM SPEED: **252 mph (406 km/h)**
SERVICE CEILING: **26,000 ft (7,925 m)**
RANGE: **1,200 miles (1,931 km)**
CREW: **2 or 3**
POWERPLANT: **1 x RR Merlin II**
ARMAMENT: **1 x 0.303in MG**
BOMB LOAD: **1,500 lb (680 kg)**
FIRST FLIGHT: **March 10, 1936**
INITIAL CLIMB: **920 ft (280 m) per min**
WEIGHT (EMPTY): **7,410 lb (3,361 kg)**
WEIGHT (LOADED): **11,700 lb (5,307 kg)**

FAIREY SWORDFISH

MANUFACTURER: **Fairey Aviation Co.**
TYPE: **Torpedo Bomber Biplane**
LENGTH: **36 ft 4 in (11.12 m)**
SPAN: **45 ft 6 in (13.92 m)**
HEIGHT: **12 ft 10 in (3.93 m)**
MAXIMUM SPEED: **138 mph (222 km/h)**
SERVICE CEILING: **10,700 ft (3,260 m)**
RANGE: **550 miles (885 km)**
CREW: **3**
POWERPLANT: **1 x Bristol Pegasus III**
ARMAMENT: **2 x 0.303in MG**
BOMB LOAD: **1,610 lb (731 kg) torpedo**
FIRST FLIGHT: **April 17, 1934**
INITIAL CLIMB: **1,220 ft (372 m) per min**
WEIGHT (EMPTY): **5,200 lb (2,359 kg)**
WEIGHT (LOADED): **9,250 lb (4,196 kg)**

HANDLEY PAGE HALIFAX

MANUFACTURER: **Handley Page Ltd.**
TYPE: **Heavy Bomber**
LENGTH: **71 ft 4 in (21.74 m)**
SPAN: **98 ft 8 in (30.07 m)**
HEIGHT: **20 ft 1 in (6.12 m)**
MAXIMUM SPEED: **282 mph (454 km/h)**
SERVICE CEILING: **24,000 ft (7,315 m)**
RANGE: **1,985 miles (3,194 km)**
CREW: **7**
POWERPLANT: **4 x Bristol Hercules VI**
ARMAMENT: **9 x 0.303in MG**
BOMB LOAD: **14,500 lb (6,577 kg)**
FIRST FLIGHT: **October 25, 1939**
INITIAL CLIMB: **750 ft (229 m) per min**
WEIGHT (EMPTY): **42,500 lb (19,278 kg)**
WEIGHT (LOADED): **65,000 lb (29,484 kg)**

HANDLEY PAGE HAMPDEN

MANUFACTURER: **Handley Page Ltd.**
TYPE: **Medium Bomber**
LENGTH: **53 ft 7 in (16.33 m)**
SPAN: **69 ft 2 in (21.08 m)**
HEIGHT: **14 ft 11 in (4.55 m)**
MAXIMUM SPEED: **255 mph (426 km/h)**
SERVICE CEILING: **22,700 ft (6,920 m)**
RANGE: **1,885 miles (3,034 km)**
CREW: **4**
POWERPLANT: **2 x Bristol Pegasus**
ARMAMENT: **6 x 0.303in MG**
BOMB LOAD: **4,000 lb (1,814 kg)**
FIRST FLIGHT: **June 21, 1936**
INITIAL CLIMB: **980 ft (300 m) per min**
WEIGHT (EMPTY): **11,780 lb (5,343 kg)**
WEIGHT (LOADED): **22,500 lb (10,206 kg)**
RANGE: **1,630 miles (2,623 km)**

SHORT STIRLING

MANUFACTURER: **Short Bros., Ltd.**
TYPE: **Heavy Bomber**
LENGTH: **87 ft 3 in (26.59 m)**
SPAN: **99 ft 1 in (30.20 m)**
HEIGHT: **22 ft 9 in (6.93 m)**
MAXIMUM SPEED: **270 mph (434 km/h)**
SERVICE CEILING: **not given**
RANGE: **2,010 miles (3,235 km)**
CREW: **7 or 8**
POWERPLANT: **4 x Bristol Hercules XVI**
ARMAMENT: **7 x 0.303in MG**
BOMB LOAD: **14,000 lb (6,350 kg)**
FIRST FLIGHT: **May 14, 1939**
INITIAL CLIMB: **800 ft (244 m) per min**
WEIGHT (EMPTY): **46,900 lb (21,274 kg)**
WEIGHT (LOADED): **70,000 lb (31,752 kg)**
RANGE: **1,125 miles (1,810 km)**

The Vickers Wellesley emerged for its first flight in 1935 as a fabric-covered cantilever monoplane, with its bombs carried in two underwing panniers. The Mk I entered service in 1937. The aircraft was distinguished by the very long-span wing, extreme cruise efficiency, and a reliable engine. The Wellesley saw useful service until late 1942. The Wellington bore the brunt of the British bomber effort early in the war, until large numbers of four-engined heavy bombers became available later.

VICKERS WELLESLEY

MANUFACTURER: Vickers-Armstrong Ltd.
TYPE: General-Purpose Bomber
LENGTH: 39 ft 3 in (11.96 m)
SPAN: 74 ft 7 in (22.73 m)
HEIGHT: 12 ft 4 in (3.75 m)
MAXIMUM SPEED: 228 mph (369 km/h)
SERVICE CEILING: 33,000 ft (10,060 m)
RANGE: 1,110 miles (1,786 km)
CREW: 2
POWERPLANT: 1 x Bristol Pegasus XX
ARMAMENT: 2 x 0.303in MG
BOMB LOAD: 2,000 lb (907 kg)
FIRST FLIGHT: June 9, 1935
INITIAL CLIMB: 1,200 ft (366 m) per min
WEIGHT (EMPTY): 6,369 lb (2,889 kg)
WEIGHT (LOADED): 11,100 lb (5,035 kg)

VICKERS WELLINGTON

MANUFACTURER: Vickers-Armstrong Ltd.
TYPE: Medium Bomber
LENGTH: 64 ft 7 in (19.68 m)
SPAN: 86 ft 2 in (26.26 m)
HEIGHT: 17 ft 5 in (5.31 m)
MAXIMUM SPEED: 255 mph (410 km/h)
SERVICE CEILING: 22,000 ft (6,705 m)
RANGE: 1,885 miles (3,033 km)
CREW: 6
POWERPLANT: 2 x Bristol Hercules
ARMAMENT: 7 x 0.303in MG
BOMB LOAD: 4,500 lb (2,041 kg)
FIRST FLIGHT: June 15, 1936
INITIAL CLIMB: 1,050 ft (320 m) per min
WEIGHT (EMPTY): 22,474 lb (10,194 kg)
WEIGHT (LOADED): 36,500 lb (16,556 kg)

As Mussolini's Italy began to expand by restoring its "lost colonies" overseas, a need arose for aircraft suitable for use in these new territories. The Caproni series served as bomber, troop-carrier, reconnaissance, ground-attack, and supply aircraft. The SM 79 was a robust bomber that operated in difficult conditions and is recognized as one of the finest torpedo bombers of World War II.

CAPRONI CA 133

MANUFACTURER: Societa Italiana Caproni
TYPE: Bomber and Transport
LENGTH: 50 ft 4.75 in (15.36 m)
SPAN: 68 ft 8 in (21.24 m)
HEIGHT: 13 ft 1 in (4 m)
MAXIMUM SPEED: 165 mph (265 km/h)
SERVICE CEILING: 18,045 ft (5,500 m)
RANGE: 838 miles (1,350 km)
CREW: 3
POWERPLANT: 3 x Piaggio Stella PVII
ARMAMENT: 4 x 7.7mm MG
BOMB LOAD: 2,646 lb (1,200 kg)
FIRST FLIGHT: 1935
INITIAL CLIMB: not available
WEIGHT (EMPTY): 9,237 lb (4,190 kg)
WEIGHT (LOADED): 14,771 lb (6,700 kg)

SAVOIA-MARCHETTI SM 79 SPARVIERO

MANUFACTURER: Savoia Marchetti
TYPE: Medium Recon' Bomber
LENGTH: 51 ft 3.1 in (15.62 m)
SPAN: 69 ft 2.7 in (21.20 m)
HEIGHT: 14 ft 5.25 in (4.40 m)
MAXIMUM SPEED: 267 mph (430 km/h)
SERVICE CEILING: 21,325 ft (6,500 m)
RANGE: 1,181 miles (1,900 km)
CREW: 4 or 5
POWERPLANT: 3 x Alfa Romeo RC.34
ARMAMENT: 4 x MG
BOMB LOAD: 2,756 lb (1,250 kg)
FIRST FLIGHT: Late 1934
INITIAL CLIMB: 830 ft (253 m) per min
WEIGHT (EMPTY): 14,991 lb (6,800 kg)
WEIGHT (LOADED): 23,104 lb (10,480 kg)

The G4M "Betty" was the Japanese Air Force's premier heavy bomber during World War II. The initial production run was 1,200 aircraft in several variants.

MITSUBISHI G4M "BETTY"

MANUFACTURER: Mitsubishi
TYPE: Medium Bomber
LENGTH: 65 ft 7.25 in (20 m)
SPAN: 82 ft 0.25 in (25 m)
HEIGHT: 19 ft 8.25 in (6 m)
MAXIMUM SPEED: 266 mph (428 km/h)
SERVICE CEILING: not available
RANGE: 3,749 miles (6,033 km)
CREW: 7
POWERPLANT: 2 x Mitsubishi MK4A
ARMAMENT: 1 x cannon, 2 x MG
BOMB LOAD: 1,764 lb (800 kg)
FIRST FLIGHT: October 1939
INITIAL CLIMB: 1,800 ft (550 m) per min
WEIGHT (EMPTY): 14,991 lb (6,800 kg)
WEIGHT (LOADED): 20,944 lb (9,500 kg)

BOEING B-17 FLYING FORTRESS

MANUFACTURER: Boeing Aircraft Company
TYPE: (B-17G) Heavy Bomber
LENGTH: 74 ft 9 in (22.78 m)
SPAN: 103 ft 9.4 in (31.63 m)
HEIGHT: 19 ft 1 in (5.82 m)
MAXIMUM SPEED: 302 mph (486 km/h)
SERVICE CEILING: 35,600 ft (10,850 m)
RANGE: 1,800 miles (2,897 km)
CREW: 10
POWERPLANT: 4 x Wright R-1820-97
ARMAMENT: 12 x 0.50in MG
BOMB LOAD: 17,600 lb (7,983 kg)
FIRST FLIGHT: July 28, 1935
INITIAL CLIMB: 540 ft (164 m) per min
WEIGHT (EMPTY): 44,560 lb (20,212 kg)
WEIGHT (LOADED): 72,000 lb (32,659 kg)

BOEING B-29 SUPERFORTRESS

MANUFACTURER: Boeing
TYPE: Long-range Heavy Bomber
LENGTH: 99 ft (30.18 m)
SPAN: 141 ft 2.75 in (43.05 m)
HEIGHT: 29 ft 7 in (9.02 m)
MAXIMUM SPEED: 358 mph (576 km/h)
RANGE: 5,830 miles (9,382 km)
CREW: 9
POWERPLANT: 4 x Wright R-3350-23
ARMAMENT: 1 x cannon, 8 x MG
BOMB LOAD: 20,000 lb (9,072 kg)
WEIGHT (EMPTY): 70,140 lb (31,816 kg)
WEIGHT (LOADED): 124,000 lb (56,246 kg)

CONSOLIDATED B-24 LIBERATOR

MANUFACTURER: Consolidated Vultee
TYPE: Long-range Heavy Bomber
LENGTH: 66 ft 4 in (20.22 m)
SPAN: 110 ft (33.53 m)
HEIGHT: 17 ft 11 in (4.46 m)
MAXIMUM SPEED: 303 mph (488 km/h)
SERVICE CEILING: 32,000 ft (9,755 m)
RANGE: 2,850 miles (4,586 km)
CREW: 10
POWERPLANT: 4 x P & W R-1830-43
ARMAMENT: 9 x 0.50in MG
BOMB LOAD: 8,800 lb (3,992 kg)
FIRST FLIGHT: December 29, 1939
INITIAL CLIMB: 900 ft (274 m) per min
WEIGHT (EMPTY): 32,605 lb (14,490 kg)
WEIGHT (LOADED): 60,000 lb (27,216 kg)

CURTISS SB2C HELLDIVER

MANUFACTURER: Curtiss-Wright Corp.
TYPE: Scout and Dive-Bomber
LENGTH: 36 ft 8 in (11.18 m)
SPAN: 49 ft 8.26 in (15.15 m)
HEIGHT: 13 ft 1.5 in (4.00 m)
MAXIMUM SPEED: 281 mph (452 km/h)
SERVICE CEILING: 24,200 ft (7,375 m)
RANGE: 1,375 miles (2,213 km)
CREW: 2
POWERPLANT: 1 x Wright R-2600-8
ARMAMENT: 2 x cannon, 2 x MG
BOMB LOAD: 3,000 lb (1,361 kg)
FIRST FLIGHT: December 18, 1940
INITIAL CLIMB: not available
WEIGHT (EMPTY): 10,114 lb (4,588 kg)
WEIGHT (LOADED): 16,812 lb (7,626 kg)

DOUGLAS A-20

MANUFACTURER: Douglas Aircraft Co.
TYPE: Light Attack Bomber
LENGTH: 47 ft 11.88 in (14.63 m)
SPAN: 61 ft 4 in (18.69 m)
HEIGHT: 17 ft 7 in (5.36 m)
MAXIMUM SPEED: 339 mph (546 km/h)
SERVICE CEILING: 23,700 ft (7,225 m)
RANGE: 2,100 miles (3,380 km)
CREW: 3
POWERPLANT: 2 x Wright R-2600-23
ARMAMENT: 9 x 0.50in MG
BOMB LOAD: 4,000 lb (1,814 kg)
FIRST FLIGHT: October 26, 1938
INITIAL CLIMB: 1,164 ft (355 m) per min
WEIGHT (EMPTY): 16,993 lb (7,708 kg)
WEIGHT (LOADED): 27,200 lb (12,338 kg)

THE HARDWARE

Undeniably the best American dive-bomber of the war, the SBD Dauntless was developed in 1934 for the American carrier fleet then under construction. A batch of 54 were delivered to the U.S. Navy from 1937. The last aircraft was delivered in 1938, in much modified form. From 1940 until it was retired four years later, this was one of the most important U.S. warplanes, playing a decisive role in the battles at Coral Sea, Midway, and in the Solomons.

DOUGLAS SBD DAUNTLESS

MANUFACTURER: Douglas Aircraft Co.
TYPE: Scout and Dive-Bomber
LENGTH: 33 ft 1.25 in (10.09 m)
SPAN: 41 ft 6.38 in (12.66 m)
HEIGHT: 13 ft 7 in (4.14 m)
MAXIMUM SPEED: 255 mph (410 km/h)
SERVICE CEILING: 25,530 ft (7,780 m)
RANGE: 1,565 miles (2,519 km)
CREW: 2
POWERPLANT: 1 x Wright R-1820-60
ARMAMENT: 4 x MG
BOMB LOAD: 2,250 lb (1,021 kg)
FIRST FLIGHT: July 23, 1938
INITIAL CLIMB: 1,500 ft (457 m) per min
WEIGHT (EMPTY): 6,404 lb (2,905 kg)
WEIGHT (LOADED): 10,700 lb (4,853 kg)

GRUMMAN TBF AVENGER

MANUFACTURER: Grumman Aircraft
TYPE: Torpedo Bomber
LENGTH: 40 ft 9 in (12.42 m)
SPAN: 54 ft 2 in (16.51 m)
HEIGHT: 13 ft 9 in (4.19 m)
MAXIMUM SPEED: 257 mph (414 km/h)
SERVICE CEILING: 21,400 ft (6,525 m)
RANGE: 2,685 miles (4,321 km)
CREW: 3
POWERPLANT: 1 x Wright R-2600-8
ARMAMENT: 4 x MG
BOMB LOAD: 2,500 lb (1,134 kg)
FIRST FLIGHT: August 1941
INITIAL CLIMB: 770 ft (235 m) per min
WEIGHT (EMPTY): 10,555 lb (4,788 kg)
WEIGHT (LOADED): 17,364 lb (7,876 kg)

LOCKHEED HUDSON

MANUFACTURER: Lockheed
TYPE: Coastal Recon' Bomber
LENGTH: 44 ft 3.75 in (13.50 m)
SPAN: 65 ft 6in (19.96 m)
HEIGHT: 10 ft 10.5 in (3.32 m)
MAXIMUM SPEED: 222 mph (357 km/h)
SERVICE CEILING: 21,000 ft (6,400 m)
RANGE: 1,960 miles (3,154 km)
CREW: 6
POWERPLANT: 2 x GR-1820-G102A
ARMAMENT: 7 x 0.303in MG
BOMB LOAD: 1,350 lb (612 kg)
FIRST FLIGHT: December 10, 1938
INITIAL CLIMB: 1,000 ft (305 m) per min
WEIGHT (EMPTY): 12,091 lb (5,484 kg)
WEIGHT (LOADED): 19,500 lb (8,845 kg)

LOCKHEED VENTURA

MANUFACTURER: Lockheed
TYPE: Coastal Recon' Bomber
LENGTH: 51 ft 9 in (15.77 m)
SPAN: 65 ft 6 in (19.96 m)
HEIGHT: 11 ft 11 in (3.63 m)
MAXIMUM SPEED: 322 mph (518 km/h)
SERVICE CEILING: 26,300 ft (8,015 m)
RANGE: 1,660 miles (2,671 km)
CREW: 5
POWERPLANT: 2 x P & W R-2800-31
ARMAMENT: 6 x MG
BOMB LOAD: 5,000 lb (2,268 kg)
FIRST FLIGHT: July 31, 1941
INITIAL CLIMB: 2,230 ft (680 m) per min
WEIGHT (EMPTY): 20,197 lb (9,161 kg)
WEIGHT (LOADED): 34,000 lb (15,422 kg)

MARTIN B-10B

MANUFACTURER: Glenn L. Martin Co.
TYPE: Medium Bomber
LENGTH: 44 ft 2 in (13.46 m)
SPAN: 70 ft 10.5 in (21.60 m)
HEIGHT: 11 ft 7 in (3.53 m)
MAXIMUM SPEED: 200 mph (322 km/h)
SERVICE CEILING: 25,200 ft (7,680 m)
RANGE: 590 miles (950 km)
CREW: 4
POWERPLANT: 2 x Wright R-1820
ARMAMENT: 3 x 0.303in MG
BOMB LOAD: 2,260 lb (1,025 kg)
FIRST FLIGHT: January 1932
INITIAL CLIMB: 1,860 ft (567 m) per min
WEIGHT (EMPTY): 10,322 lb (4,682 kg)
WEIGHT (LOADED): 15,894 lb (7,210 kg)

With its established reputation in bomber design and production, Martin made concerted efforts to win the 1939 Medium Bomber competition run by the U.S. Army, and boldly entered a design featuring a wing optimized for high cruise efficiency rather than landing. This Model 179 was ordered off the drawing board in July 1939 and first flew in November 1940. Production B-26A Marauder aircraft were deployed to Australia the day after the attack on Pearl Harbor, and although inexperienced pilots found the aircraft more than a handful as a result of its high wing loading and high landing speed, once mastered the Marauder was an excellent warplane that achieved good results.

MARTIN B-26 MARAUDER

MANUFACTURER: Glenn L. Martin Co.
TYPE: Medium Attack Bomber
LENGTH: 56 ft (17.07 m)
SPAN: 65 ft (18.81 m)
HEIGHT: 19 ft 10 in (6.05 m)
MAXIMUM SPEED: 315 mph (507 km/h)
SERVICE CEILING: 25,000 ft (7,620 m)
RANGE: 1,000 miles (1,609 km)
CREW: 7
POWERPLANT: 2 x P & W R-2800-5
ARMAMENT: 4 x 0.50in MG
BOMB LOAD: 4,800 lb (2,177 kg)
FIRST FLIGHT: November 25, 1940
INITIAL CLIMB: 1,199 ft (366 m) per min
WEIGHT (EMPTY): 21,375 lb (9,696 kg)
WEIGHT (LOADED): 32,000 lb (14,515 kg)

NORTH AMERICAN B-25 MITCHELL

MANUFACTURER: North American Aviation
TYPE: (B-25C) Medium Bomber
LENGTH: 52 ft 11 in (16.12 m)
SPAN: 67 ft 7 in (20.60 m)
HEIGHT: 15 ft 10 in (4.82 m)
MAXIMUM SPEED: 284 mph (457 km/h)
SERVICE CEILING: 21,200 ft (6,460 m)
RANGE: 1,525 miles (2,454 km)
CREW: 5
POWERPLANT: 2 x Wright R-2600-13
ARMAMENT: 6 x 0.50in MG
BOMB LOAD: 3,000 lb (1,361 kg)
FIRST FLIGHT: January 1939
INITIAL CLIMB: 1,100 ft (338 m) per min
WEIGHT (EMPTY): 20,300 lb (9,208 kg)
WEIGHT (LOADED): 41,800 lb (18,960 kg)

The Pe-2 was one of the best Allied combat aircraft to see service in World War II. By dint of continual improvement, it remained in the front line right up to the German surrender in 1945. The prototype flew in 1939, but it was then revised as the PB-100. The Pe-2 multi-role dive- and attack bomber was supplanted from 1942 by the Pe-2FT. Versions of the Pe-2 were also used for long-range reconnaissance and training. The Pe-3 multi-purpose fighter version had cannon, machine guns, and underwing provision for rockets. Some 11,427 were built.

PETLYAKOV PE-2

MANUFACTURER: Petlyakov
TYPE: Multi-Role Attack Bomber
LENGTH: 41 ft 6.5 in (12.66 m)
SPAN: 56 ft 3.7 in (17.16 m)
HEIGHT: 13 ft 1.5 in (4 m)
MAXIMUM SPEED: 335 mph (540 km/h)
SERVICE CEILING: 28,870 ft (8,800 m)
RANGE: 932 miles (1,500 km)
CREW: 3
POWERPLANT: 2 x Klimov VK-105RA
ARMAMENT: 4 x 7.62mm MG
BOMB LOAD: 3,527 lb (1,600 kg)
FIRST FLIGHT: 1939
INITIAL CLIMB: 1,430 ft (436 m) per min
WEIGHT (EMPTY): 12,943 lb (5,870 kg)
WEIGHT (LOADED): 18,728 lb (8,495 kg)

PETLYAKOV PE-8

MANUFACTURER: Tupolev
TYPE: Heavy Bomber
LENGTH: 73 ft 9 in (22.49 m)
SPAN: 131 ft (39.94 m)
HEIGHT: 20 ft (6.1 m)
MAXIMUM SPEED: 272 mph (438 km/h)
SERVICE CEILING: 22,965 ft (7,065 m)
RANGE: 3,383 miles (5,445 km)
CREW: 10
POWERPLANT: 4 x Mikulin AM-35A
ARMAMENT: 2 x cannon, 3 x MG
BOMB LOAD: 8,818 lb (4,000 kg)
FIRST FLIGHT: December 27, 1936
INITIAL CLIMB: not available
WEIGHT (EMPTY): not given
WEIGHT (LOADED): 73,469 lb (33,325 kg)

FIGHTERS

All the combatant nations continually improved their fighter aircraft during the war. The Spitfire, for example, went through over 20 variants. The German Bf 109 evolved through 11 major production variants, plus many sub-types and experimentals.

The Focke Wulf Fw 190 was the only new fighter design to enter service with the Luftwaffe during World War II. The prototype flew in June 1939, and 100 Fw 190A-1 fighters were deployed for combat service in fall 1940. Although the design was known to the Allies prior to the outbreak of the war, the Fw 190 still caused a shock when it was first encountered in combat over France in May 1941, as the plane was light, fast, agile, powerfully armed, and immensely strong. A number of variants were subsequently built.

FOCKE WULF FW 190

MANUFACTURER: **Focke Wulf Flugzeugbau**
TYPE: **Single-Seat Fighter**
LENGTH: **28 ft 10.5 in (8.80 m)**
SPAN: **34 ft 5.5 in (10.5 m)**
HEIGHT: **12 ft 11.5 in (3.95 m)**
MAXIMUM SPEED: **12 ft 11.5 in (3.95 m)**
SERVICE CEILING: **34,775 ft (10,600 m)**
RANGE: **497 miles (800 km)**
CREW: **1**
POWERPLANT: **1 x BMW 801D-2 radial**
ARMAMENT: **4 x cannon, 2 x MG**
FIRST FLIGHT: **June 1, 1939**
INITIAL CLIMB: **2,830 ft (863 m) per min**
WEIGHT (EMPTY): **6,393 lb (2,900 kg)**
WEIGHT (LOADED): **8,770 lb (3,980 kg)**

HEINKEL HE 112

MANUFACTURER: **Ernst Heinkel A.G.**
TYPE: **Fighter, Ground-Attack**
LENGTH: **30 ft 6 in (9.30 m)**
SPAN: **29 ft 10.25 in (9.1 m)**
HEIGHT: **12 ft 7.5 in (3.85 m)**
MAXIMUM SPEED: **317 mph (510 km/h)**
SERVICE CEILING: **27,890 ft (8,500 m)**
RANGE: **683 miles (1,100 km)**
CREW: **1**
POWERPLANT: **1 x Junkers Jumo 210Ea**
ARMAMENT: **2 x cannon, 2 x MG**
BOMB LOAD: **132 lb (60 kg)**
FIRST FLIGHT: **September 1935**
INITIAL CLIMB: **2,300 ft (700 m) per min**
WEIGHT (EMPTY): **3,571 lb (1,620 kg)**
WEIGHT (LOADED): **4,960 lb (2,250 kg)**

MESSERSCHMITT BF 109

MANUFACTURER: **Messerschmitt A.G**
TYPE: **Fighter, Fighter-Bomber**
LENGTH: **29 ft 0.5 in (8.85 m)**
SPAN: **32 ft 6.5 in (9.92 m)**
HEIGHT: **8 ft 2.5 in (2.5 m)**
MAXIMUM SPEED: **386 mph (621 km/h)**
SERVICE CEILING: **37,890 ft (11,550 m)**
RANGE: **621 miles (1,000 km)**
CREW: **1**
POWERPLANT: **1 x DB 605**
ARMAMENT: **1 x cannon, 2 x MG**
BOMB LOAD: **551 lb (250 kg)**
FIRST FLIGHT: **Late 1935**
INITIAL CLIMB: **3,116 ft (950 m) per min**
WEIGHT (EMPTY): **5,893 lb (2,673 kg)**
WEIGHT (LOADED): **7,496 lb (3,400 kg)**

MESSERSCHMITT BF 110

MANUFACTURER: **Messerschmitt A.G**
TYPE: **Heavy Fighter**
LENGTH: **39 ft 8.33 in (12.10 m)**
SPAN: **53 ft 2 in (16.2 m)**
HEIGHT: **13 ft 6.5 in (4.13 m)**
MAXIMUM SPEED: **248 mph (560 km/h)**
SERVICE CEILING: **32,810 ft (10,000 m)**
RANGE: **680 miles (1,095 km)**
CREW: **2 or 3**
POWERPLANT: **2 x DB 601A-1**
ARMAMENT: **1 x cannon, 5 x MG**
BOMB LOAD: **not available**
INITIAL CLIMB: **1,755 ft (585 m) per min**
WEIGHT (EMPTY): **11,354 lb (5,150 kg)**
WEIGHT (LOADED): **14,881 lb (6,750 kg)**

MESSERSCHMITT ME 410

MANUFACTURER: **Messerschmitt A.G**
TYPE: **Heavy Fighter**
LENGTH: **40 ft 11.5 in (12.48 m)**
SPAN: **53 ft 7.75 in (16.35 m)**
HEIGHT: **14 ft (4.28 m)**
MAXIMUM SPEED: **388 mph (624 km/h)**
SERVICE CEILING: **32,810 ft (10,000 m)**
RANGE: **1,050 miles (1,670 km)**
CREW: **2**
POWERPLANT: **2 x DB 603A**
ARMAMENT: **4 x cannon, 4 x MG**
BOMB LOAD: **not available**
FIRST FLIGHT: **1942**
INITIAL CLIMB: **2,060 ft (628 m) per min**
WEIGHT (EMPTY): **16,574 lb (7,518 kg)**
WEIGHT (LOADED): **23,483 lb (10,650 kg)**

In 1937, the Blackburn Company received a contract from the British Air Ministry for the production of the Skua fighter dive-bomber. The first prototype flew in February 1937, by which time orders for 190 aircraft had already been placed. The Skua represented a significant break from the Royal Navy's traditional carrier-borne biplanes; it was Britain's first naval dive-bomber, and the country's first deck-landing aircraft to have flaps, retractable landing gear, and a variable pitch propeller. Deliveries of the first production aircraft were made in October 1938, and at the outbreak of war in September 1939 there were squadrons of them embarked on HMS *Ark Royal* and HMS *Furious*. Much was expected of the Skua when the fighting started, and, in service, the aircraft performed creditably in the dive-bombing role during the battle for Norway in 1940. However, it was hampered by very limited range and served only until 1941, after which it was progressively replaced by Fairey Fulmars. The survivors were used for target-towing and for training purposes.

BLACKBURN SKUA

MANUFACTURER: **Blackburn Aircraft Ltd.**
TYPE: **Carrier-Borne Fighter**
LENGTH: **35 ft 7 in (10.85 m)**
SPAN: **46 ft 2 in (14.07 m)**
HEIGHT: **12 ft 6 in (3.81 m)**
MAXIMUM SPEED: **225 mph (362 km/h)**
SERVICE CEILING: **20,200 ft (6,160 m)**
RANGE: **760 miles (1,223 km)**
CREW: **2**
POWERPLANT: **1 x Bristol Perseus XII**
ARMAMENT: **4 x 0.303in MG**
BOMB LOAD: **500 lb (227 kg)**
FIRST FLIGHT: **February 9, 1937**
INITIAL CLIMB: **1,580 ft (482 m) per min**
WEIGHT (EMPTY): **5,490 lb (2,490 kg)**
WEIGHT (LOADED): **8,228 lb (3,732 kg)**

BOULTON PAUL DEFIANT

MANUFACTURER: **Boulton Paul Aircraft**
TYPE: **(Defiant Mk I) Fighter**
LENGTH: **35 ft 4 in (10.87 m)**
SPAN: **39 ft 4 in (11.99 m)**
HEIGHT: **14 ft 5 in (4.39 m)**
MAXIMUM SPEED: **304 mph (489 km/h)**
SERVICE CEILING: **30,350 ft (9,250 m)**
RANGE: **465 miles (748 km)**
CREW: **2**
POWERPLANT: **1 x RR Merlin III**
ARMAMENT: **4 x 0.303in MG**
BOMB LOAD: **none**
FIRST FLIGHT: **August 11, 1937**
INITIAL CLIMB: **1,852 ft (565 m) per min**
WEIGHT (EMPTY): **6,078 lb (2,757 kg)**
WEIGHT (LOADED): **8,350 lb (3,788 kg)**

BRISTOL BEAUFIGHTER

MANUFACTURER: **Bristol Aeroplane Co.**
TYPE: **Heavy/Night Fighter**
LENGTH: **41 ft 8 in (12.70 m)**
SPAN: **57 ft 10 in (17.63 m)**
HEIGHT: **15 ft 10 in (4.82 m)**
MAXIMUM SPEED: **333 mph (536 km/h)**
SERVICE CEILING: **26,500 ft (8,077 m)**
RANGE: **1,540 miles (2,478 km)**
CREW: **2**
POWERPLANT: **2 x Bristol Hercules VI**
ARMAMENT: **4 x cannon, 6 x MG**
BOMB LOAD: **none**
FIRST FLIGHT: **July 17, 1939**
INITIAL CLIMB: **1,850 ft (564 m) per min**
WEIGHT (EMPTY): **14,600 lb (6,622 kg)**
WEIGHT (LOADED): **21,600 lb (9,798 kg)**

GLOSTER SEA GLADIATOR

MANUFACTURER: **Gloster Aircraft Co.**
TYPE: **Fighter Biplane**
LENGTH: **27 ft 5 in (8.36 m)**
SPAN: **32 ft 3 in (9.83 m)**
HEIGHT: **11 ft 7 in (3.53 m)**
MAXIMUM SPEED: **257 mph (414 km/h)**
SERVICE CEILING: **33,500 ft (10,120 m)**
RANGE: **440 miles (708 km)**
CREW: **1**
POWERPLANT: **1 x Bristol Mercury IX**
ARMAMENT: **2 x 0.303in MG**
BOMB LOAD: **none**
FIRST FLIGHT: **September 1934**
INITIAL CLIMB: **2,300 ft (700 m) per min**
WEIGHT (EMPTY): **3,444 lb (1,562 kg)**
WEIGHT (LOADED): **4,864 lb (2,206 kg)**

GLOSTER METEOR

MANUFACTURER: **Gloster Aircraft Co.**
TYPE: **Single-Seat Fighter**
LENGTH: **44 ft 7 in (13.58 m)**
SPAN: **37 ft 2 in (11.32 m)**
HEIGHT: **13 ft (3.96 m)**
MAXIMUM SPEED: **598 mph (962 km/h)**
SERVICE CEILING: **43,000 ft (13,106 m)**
RANGE: **980 miles (1,580 km)**
CREW: **1**
POWERPLANT: **2 x RR Derwent turbojet**
ARMAMENT: **4 x 20mm cannon**
BOMB LOAD: **none**
FIRST FLIGHT: **March 5, 1943**
INITIAL CLIMB: **7,216 ft (2,200 m) per min**
WEIGHT (EMPTY): **10,626 lb (4,820 kg)**
WEIGHT (LOADED): **19,100 lb (8,664 kg)**

Although the Supermarine Spitfire is often portrayed as the fighter plane that "won" the Battle of Britain, it was in fact Sidney Camm's robust and durable Hurricane that destroyed more German aircraft than the rest of the British planes combined. Well into 1941, the Hurricane was the RAF's most numerous fighter. Designed as a monoplane version of the earlier Fury, the Hurricane was not as technically advanced as the Spitfire and had an unstressed, largely fabric, covering. The prototype first flew in November 1935, and the Hurricane Mk I entered service late in 1937 as the RAF's first monoplane fighter. Early Hurricane aircraft were fitted with a two-blade, fixed-pitch propeller that later gave way to a three-blade, constant-speed unit. Some 19 squadrons operated with Mk I Hurricanes on the outbreak of World War II in September 1939 and some 32 squadrons were equipped by August 1940. The production total was about 3,650 aircraft. Some 7,500 of the improved Mk II fighter-bomber Hurricanes, with an uprated powerplant, heavier armament, and enhancements such as metal-skinned wings, three-blade propeller, and better armor protection, were delivered from September 1940 onward, in various configurations. Many aircraft were tropicalized for North African and Far Eastern service with a special chin air filter. The Mk IV Hurricane was the final British production model and was fitted with uprated engine, additional armor, and provision for underwing stores, including antitank guns. The Sea Hurricane was a naval version of the plane.

HAWKER HURRICANE

CREW: 1
POWERPLANT: 1 x RR Merlin III
MANUFACTURER: **Hawker Aircraft Ltd.**
ARMAMENT: **8 x 0.303in MG**
TYPE: **Single-Seat Fighter**
BOMB LOAD: **none**
LENGTH: **31 ft 4 in (9.55 m)**
FIRST FLIGHT: **November 6, 1935**
SPAN: **40 ft (12.19 m)**
HEIGHT: **13 ft 4.5 in (4.07 m)**
INITIAL CLIMB: **2,520 ft (770 m) per min**
MAXIMUM SPEED: **324 mph (521 km/h)**
WEIGHT (EMPTY): **5,085 lb (2,308 kg)**
SERVICE CEILING: **33,200 ft (10,120 m)**
WEIGHT (LOADED): **6,661 lb (3,024 kg)**
RANGE: **445 miles (716 km)**

SUPERMARINE SEAFIRE

CREW: 1
POWERPLANT: 1 x RR Merlin 55M
MANUFACTURER: **Supermarine Aviation**
ARMAMENT: **2 x cannon, 4 x MG**
TYPE: **Carrier-Borne Fighter**
BOMB LOAD: **500 lb (227 kg)**
LENGTH: **30 ft 2.5 in (9.21 m)**
FIRST FLIGHT: **not given**
SPAN: **36 ft 10 in (11.23 m)**
HEIGHT: **11 ft 2.5 in (3.42 m)**
INITIAL CLIMB: **2,501 ft (762 m) per min**
MAXIMUM SPEED: **348 mph (560 km/h)**
WEIGHT (EMPTY): **6,204 lb (2,814 kg)**
SERVICE CEILING: **24,000 ft (7,315 m)**
WEIGHT (LOADED): **7,640 lb (3,465 kg)**
RANGE: **553 miles (890 km)**

SUPERMARINE SPITFIRE MK I

CREW: 1
POWERPLANT: 1 x RR Merlin 45
MANUFACTURER: **Supermarine Aviation**
ARMAMENT: **8 x 0.303in MG**
TYPE: **Fighter-Bomber**
BOMB LOAD: **500 lb (227 kg)**
LENGTH: **29 ft 11 in (9.12 m)**
FIRST FLIGHT: **March 5, 1936**
SPAN: **36 ft 10 in (11.23 m)**
HEIGHT: **9 ft 11 in (3.02 m)**
INITIAL CLIMB: **3,950 ft (1,204 m) per min**
MAXIMUM SPEED: **394 mph (594 km/h)**
WEIGHT (EMPTY): **4,998 lb (2,267 kg)**
SERVICE CEILING: **36,500 ft (11,125 m)**
WEIGHT (LOADED): **6,417 lb (2,911 kg)**
RANGE: **1,135 miles (1,827 km)**

SUPERMARINE SPITFIRE PR MK XI

RANGE: **980 miles (1,576 km)**
CREW: 1
MANUFACTURER: **Supermarine Aviation**
POWERPLANT: 1 x RR Merlin 61
TYPE: **Fighter, Fighter-Bomber**
ARMAMENT: **2 x cannon, 4 x MG**
LENGTH: **31 ft (9.46 m)**
BOMB LOAD: **1,000 lb (454 kg)**
SPAN: **36 ft 10 in (11.23 m)**
HEIGHT: **12 ft 7.75 in (3.85 m)**
INITIAL CLIMB: **3,950 ft (1,204 m) per min**
MAXIMUM SPEED: **408 mph (655 km/h)**
WEIGHT (EMPTY): **5,610 lb (2,545 kg)**
SERVICE CEILING: **43,000 ft (12,105 m)**
WEIGHT (LOADED): **9,500 lb (4,309 kg)**

The finest Italian fighter planes of World War II all came from a team led by Mario Castoldi at Macchi of Varese. The Macchi 202 Folgore prototype first flew in August 1940. Due to supply problems, only 1,500 were built. A further improved version of the same airframe was the MC.205V Veltro, which first flew in April 1942. Later machines had 20mm cannon rather than machine guns.

MACCHI 202 FOLGORE

MANUFACTURER: **Aeronautica Macchi**
TYPE: **Interceptor Fighter**
LENGTH: **29 ft 0.5in (8.85 m)**
SPAN: **34 ft 8.5 in (10.58 m)**
HEIGHT: **9 ft 11.5 in (3.04 m)**
MAXIMUM SPEED: **370 mph (595 km/h)**
SERVICE CEILING: **37,730 ft (11,500 m)**
RANGE: **475 miles (765 km)**
CREW: **1**
POWERPLANT: **1 x Alfa Romeo RC 41-1**
ARMAMENT: **2 x 12.7mm MG**
BOMB LOAD: **none**
FIRST FLIGHT: **10 August 1940**
INITIAL CLIMB: **not available**
WEIGHT (EMPTY): **5,181 lb (2,350 kg)**
WEIGHT (LOADED): **6,636 lb (3,010 kg)**

KAWASAKI KI 61 "TONY"

MANUFACTURER: **Kawasaki**
TYPE: **(Ki-61-Ib) Fighter**
LENGTH: **28 ft 8.5 in (8.75 m)**
SPAN: **39 ft 4 in (12.1 m)**
HEIGHT: **12 ft 1.75 in (3.70 m)**
MAXIMUM SPEED: **368 mph (592 km/h)**
SERVICE CEILING: **37,730 ft (11,600 m)**
RANGE: **684 miles (1,100 km)**
CREW: **1**
POWERPLANT: **1 x Kawasaki Ha-40**
ARMAMENT: **4 x 12.7mm MG**
BOMB LOAD: **none**
FIRST FLIGHT: **December 1941**
INITIAL CLIMB: **2,200 ft (675 m) per min**
WEIGHT (EMPTY): **4,872 lb (2,210 kg)**
WEIGHT (LOADED): **7,165 lb (3,250 kg)**

MITSUBISHI A6M ZERO-SEN

MANUFACTURER: **Mitsubishi**
TYPE: **Fighter, Fighter-Bomber**
LENGTH: **29 ft 8.75 in (9.06 m)**
SPAN: **39 ft 4.5 in (12 m)**
HEIGHT: **10 ft (3.05 m)**
MAXIMUM SPEED: **332 mph (534 km/h)**
SERVICE CEILING: **32,810 ft (10,000 m)**
RANGE: **1,929 miles (3,104 km)**
CREW: **1**
POWERPLANT: **1 x Nakajima NK1C**
ARMAMENT: **2 x cannon, 2 x MG**
BOMB LOAD: **265 lb (120 kg)**
FIRST FLIGHT: **April 1, 1939**
INITIAL CLIMB: **4,500 ft (1,370 m) per min**
WEIGHT (EMPTY): **3,704 lb (1,680 kg)**
WEIGHT (LOADED): **6,164 lb (2,796 kg)**

BREWSTER F2S BUFFALO

MANUFACTURER: **Brewster Aeronautical**
TYPE: **Fighter, Fighter-Bomber**
LENGTH: **26 ft 4 in (8 m)**
SPAN: **35 ft (10.67 m)**
HEIGHT: **12 ft 1 in (3.68 m)**
MAXIMUM SPEED: **321 mph (517 km/h)**
SERVICE CEILING: **33,200 ft (10,120 m)**
RANGE: **1,680 miles (2,704 km)**
CREW: **1**
POWERPLANT: **1 x Wright R-1820-40**
ARMAMENT: **4 x 0.50in MG**
BOMB LOAD: **232 lb (105 kg)**
INITIAL CLIMB: **2,290 ft (698 m) per min**
WEIGHT (EMPTY): **4,732 lb (2,146 kg)**
WEIGHT (LOADED): **7,159 lb (3,247 kg)**

CURTISS P-40D (KITTYHAWK MK I)

MANUFACTURER: **Curtiss-Wright Corp.**
TYPE: **Fighter-Bomber**
LENGTH: **33 ft 4 in (10.1 m)**
SPAN: **37 ft 3.5 in (11.37 m)**
HEIGHT: **10 ft 7 in (3.23 m)**
MAXIMUM SPEED: **343 mph (552 km/h)**
SERVICE CEILING: **31,000 ft (9,450 m)**
RANGE: **750 miles (1,207 km)**
CREW: **1**
POWERPLANT: **1 x Allison V-1710-81**
ARMAMENT: **6 x 0.50in MG**
BOMB LOAD: **1,500 lb (680 kg)**
INITIAL CLIMB: **2,120 ft (646 m) per min**
WEIGHT (EMPTY): **6,200 lb (2,812 kg)**
WEIGHT (LOADED): **11,400 lb (5,171 kg)**

In 1934, Curtiss began to develop a new "Hawk" fighter with cantilever monoplane wing, retracting landing gear, R-1830 radial engine, and all-metal construction. This was put into production as the P-36. More than 1,300 were built before the decision was made to build the P-40 with a liquid-cooled Allison engine. The R-1830 engine was reliable, but, as it lacked the potential for development into more powerful forms, Curtiss sought new means of exploiting the Model 75 airframe by installing the 775 kW (1040 hp) liquid-cooled Allison V-1710 Vee engine. This was significant in a country where aircraft engines had become almost universally air-cooled, and there were many teething troubles. The first production model was the P-40, which entered service in 1940. This was followed by the P-40B, P-40C, P-40D, and P-40E, as well as Tomahawk Mks I, II, and III for the British RAF, Australian RAAF, and South African SAAF, which were used as low-level army cooperation machines in Britain, and as ground-attack fighters in North Africa.

CURTISS P-40B (TOMAHAWK MK I)

MANUFACTURER: **Curtiss-Wright Corp.**
TYPE: **(P-40B) Fighter**
LENGTH: **31 ft 8.5 in (9.66 m)**
SPAN: **37 ft 3.5 in (11.37 m)**
HEIGHT: **10 ft 7 in (3.22 m)**
MAXIMUM SPEED: **352 mph (567 km/h)**
SERVICE CEILING: **32,400 ft (9,875 m)**
RANGE: **940 miles (1,513 km)**
CREW: **1**
POWERPLANT: **1 x Allison V-1710-33**
ARMAMENT: **4 x MG**
BOMB LOAD: **none**
INITIAL CLIMB: **2,650 ft (807 m) per min**
WEIGHT (EMPTY): **5,590 lb (2,536 kg)**
WEIGHT (LOADED): **7,600 lb (3,447 kg)**

GRUMMAN F4F WILDCAT

MANUFACTURER: **Grumman Aircraft**
TYPE: **Fighter, Fighter-Bomber**
LENGTH: **28 ft 9 in (8.76 m)**
SPAN: **38 ft (11.58 m)**
HEIGHT: **9 ft 2.5 in (2.81 m)**
MAXIMUM SPEED: **318 mph (512 km/h)**
SERVICE CEILING: **34,000 ft (10,365 m)**
RANGE: **1,250 miles (2,012 km)**
CREW: **1**
POWERPLANT: **1 x P & W R-1830-86**
ARMAMENT: **6 x 0.50in**
BOMB LOAD: **200 lb (91 kg)**
FIRST FLIGHT: **September 2, 1937**
INITIAL CLIMB: **1,950 ft (594 m) per min**
WEIGHT (EMPTY): **5,758 lb (2,612 kg)**
WEIGHT (LOADED): **7,952 lb (3,607 kg)**

LOCKHEED P-38 LIGHTNING

MANUFACTURER: **Lockheed**
TYPE: **Long-range Fighter**
LENGTH: **37 ft 10 in (11.53 m)**
SPAN: **52 ft (15.85 m)**
HEIGHT: **12 ft 10 in (3.91 m)**
MAXIMUM SPEED: **414 mph (666 km/h)**
SERVICE CEILING: **44,000 ft (13,410 m)**
RANGE: **2,600 miles (4,184 km)**
CREW: **1**
POWERPLANT: **2 x Allison V-1710-111**
ARMAMENT: **1 x cannon, 4 x MG**
BOMB LOAD: **4,000 lb (1,814 kg)**
FIRST FLIGHT: **not given**
INITIAL CLIMB: **2,850 ft (870 m) per min**
WEIGHT (EMPTY): **12,800 lb (5,806 kg)**
WEIGHT (LOADED): **21,600 lb (9,798 kg)**

NORTH AMERICAN P-51 MUSTANG

MANUFACTURER: **North American Aviation**
TYPE: **Fighter, Fighter-Bomber**
LENGTH: **32 ft 3.25 in (9.84 m)**
SPAN: **37 ft (11.28 m)**
HEIGHT: **13 ft 8 in (4.16 m)**
MAXIMUM SPEED: **437 mph (703 km/h)**
SERVICE CEILING: **41,900 ft (12,770 m)**
RANGE: **2,301 miles (3,703 km)**
CREW: **1**
POWERPLANT: **1 x Packard V-1650-7**
ARMAMENT: **6 x 0.50in MG**
BOMB LOAD: **2,000 lb (907 kg)**
INITIAL CLIMB: **3,475 ft (1,060 m) per min**
WEIGHT (EMPTY): **6,840 lb (3,103 kg)**
WEIGHT (LOADED): **12,100 lb (5,493 kg)**

REPUBLIC P-43 LANCER

MANUFACTURER: **Republic Aviation Corp.**
TYPE: **Fighter**
LENGTH: **28 ft 6 in (8.69 m)**
SPAN: **36 ft (10.97 m)**
HEIGHT: **14 ft (4.27 m)**
MAXIMUM SPEED: **349 mph (562 km/h)**
SERVICE CEILING: **38,000 ft (11,580 m)**
RANGE: **800 miles (1,287 km)**
CREW: **1**
POWERPLANT: **1 x P & W R-1830-47**
ARMAMENT: **4 x MG**
BOMB LOAD: **none**
FIRST FLIGHT: **1939**
INITIAL CLIMB: **not available**
WEIGHT (EMPTY): **5,654 lb (2,565 kg)**
WEIGHT (LOADED): **7,935 lb (3,599 kg)**

REPUBLIC P-47 THUNDERBOLT

MANUFACTURER: **Republic Aviation Corp.**
TYPE: **Fighter-Bomber**
LENGTH: **36 ft 1 in (10.99 m)**
SPAN: **40 ft 9 in (12.42 m)**
HEIGHT: **14 ft 7 in (4.44 m)**
MAXIMUM SPEED: **435 mph (700 km/h)**
SERVICE CEILING: **42,000 ft (12,800 m)**
RANGE: **1,725 miles (2,776 km)**
CREW: **1**
POWERPLANT: **1 x P & W R-2800-59**
ARMAMENT: **8 x 0.50in MG**
BOMB LOAD: **2,500 lb (1,134 kg)**
INITIAL CLIMB: **2,800 ft (855 m) per min**
WEIGHT (EMPTY): **10,700 lb (4,858 kg)**
WEIGHT (LOADED): **16,200 lb (7,355 kg)**

VOUGHT F4U CORSAIR

MANUFACTURER: **Chance Vought Aircraft**
TYPE: **Fighter-Bomber**
LENGTH: **33 ft 8.25 in (10.27 m)**
SPAN: **40 ft 11.75 in (12.49 m)**
HEIGHT: **14 ft 9 in (4.50 m)**
MAXIMUM SPEED: **446 mph (718 km/h)**
SERVICE CEILING: **41,500 ft (12,650 m)**
RANGE: **1,560 miles (2,511 km)**
CREW: **1**
POWERPLANT: **1 x P & W R-2800-18W**
ARMAMENT: **6 x 0.50in MG**
BOMB LOAD: **2,000 lb (907 kg)**
INITIAL CLIMB: **3,870 ft (1,180 m) per min**
WEIGHT (EMPTY): **9,205 lb (4,175 kg)**
WEIGHT (LOADED): **19,500 lb (8,845 kg)**

The aircraft design bureau led by Semyon Lavochkin produced some of the best fighters for the Soviet air force's fleets during the war. The LaG-5 was a successful design and up to late 1944, 9,920 aircraft were built in variants such as the La-5, the La-5F, the definitive La-5FN, and the La-5FN Type 41, with a metal rather than wooden wing.

LAVOCHKIN LA-5

MANUFACTURER: **Lavochkin**
TYPE: **Fighter, Fighter-Bomber**
LENGTH: **28 ft 5.33 in (8.67 m)**
SPAN: **32 ft 1.75 in (9.80 m)**
HEIGHT: **8 ft 4 in (2.54 m)**
MAXIMUM SPEED: **403 mph (648 km/h)**
SERVICE CEILING: **36,090 ft (11,000 m)**
RANGE: **475 miles (765 km)**
CREW: **1**
POWERPLANT: **1 x Shvetsov ASh-82FN**
ARMAMENT: **2 x 20mm cannon**
BOMB LOAD: **1,102 lb (500 kg)**
FIRST FLIGHT: **January 1942**
INITIAL CLIMB: **3,280 ft (1,000 m) per min**
WEIGHT (EMPTY): **5,743 lb (2,605 kg)**
WEIGHT (LOADED): **7,500 lb (3,402 kg)**

MIKOYAN-GUREVICH MIG-3

MANUFACTURER: **Mikoyan-Gurevich**
TYPE: **Fighter, Fighter-Bomber**
LENGTH: **26 ft 9 in (8.15 m)**
SPAN: **33 ft 9.5 in (10.3 m)**
HEIGHT: **8 ft 7 in (2.61 m)**
MAXIMUM SPEED: **398 mph (640 km/h)**
SERVICE CEILING: **37,705 ft (11,500 m)**
RANGE: **742 miles (1,195 km)**
CREW: **1**
POWERPLANT: **1 x Mikulin AM-35A**
ARMAMENT: **3 x MG**
BOMB LOAD: **441 lb (200 kg)**
FIRST FLIGHT: **May 1941**
INITIAL CLIMB: **3,937 ft (1,200 m) per min**
WEIGHT (EMPTY): **5,721 lb (2,595 kg)**
WEIGHT (LOADED): **7,385 lb (3,350 kg)**

POLIKARPOV I-16

MANUFACTURER: **Polikarpov**
TYPE: **Fighter, Fighter-Bomber**
LENGTH: **20 ft 1.3 in (6.13 m)**
SPAN: **29 ft 6.33 in (9.00 m)**
HEIGHT: **8 ft 5 in (2.57 m)**
MAXIMUM SPEED: **304 mph (489 km/h)**
SERVICE CEILING: **29,530 ft (9,000 m)**
RANGE: **435 miles (700 km)**
CREW: **1**
POWERPLANT: **1 x Shvetsov M-63**
ARMAMENT: **4 x 7.62mm MG**
BOMB LOAD: **1,102 lb (500 kg)**
FIRST FLIGHT: **December 31, 1933**
INITIAL CLIMB: **2,790 ft (850 m) per min**
WEIGHT (EMPTY): **3,285 lb (1,490 kg)**
WEIGHT (LOADED): **4,619 lb (2,095 kg)**

RECONNAISSANCE AIRCRAFT

All air forces deployed aircraft designed to gather intelligence, usually by visual observation and aerial photography.

BLOHM UND VOSS BV 141

MANUFACTURER: Blohm und Voss
TYPE: Tactical Reconnaissance
LENGTH: 45 ft 9.25 in (13.95 m)
SPAN: 57 ft 3.5 in (17.46 m)
HEIGHT: 11 ft 9.75 in (3.60 m)
MAXIMUM SPEED: 272 mph (438 km/h)
SERVICE CEILING: 32,810 ft (10,000 m)
RANGE: 1,181 miles (1,900 km)
CREW: 3
POWERPLANT: 1 x BMW 801A radial
ARMAMENT: 4 x 7.92mm MG
BOMB LOAD: 441 lb (200 kg)
WEIGHT (EMPTY): 10,362 lb (4,700 kg)
WEIGHT (LOADED): 13,448 lb (6,100 kg)

DORNIER DO 18

MANUFACTURER: Dornier-Werke GmbH
TYPE: Maritime Reconnaisance
LENGTH: 63 ft 7 in (19.37 m)
SPAN: 77 ft 9.25 in (23.70 m)
HEIGHT: 17 ft 5.5 in (5.32 m)
MAXIMUM SPEED: 166 mph (267 km/h)
SERVICE CEILING: 13,780 ft (4,200 m)
RANGE: 2,175 miles (3,500 km)
CREW: 5 or 6
POWERPLANT: 2 x Jumo 205D diesels
ARMAMENT: 1 x cannon, 1 x MG
BOMB LOAD: 220 lb (100 kg)
INITIAL CLIMB: 374 ft (114 m) per min
WEIGHT (EMPTY): 13,183 lb (5,980 kg)
WEIGHT (LOADED): 23,809 lb (10,800 kg)

FIESELER FI 156 STORCH

MANUFACTURER: Gerhard Fieseler Werke
TYPE: Communications
LENGTH: 32 ft 5.75 in (9.90 m)
SPAN: 46 ft 9 in (14.25 m)
HEIGHT: 10 ft (3.05 m)
MAXIMUM SPEED: 109 mph (175 km/h)
SERVICE CEILING: 17,060 ft (5,200 m)
RANGE: 631 miles (1,015 km)
CREW: 1
POWERPLANT: 1 x Argus inverted-Vee
ARMAMENT: 1 x 7.92mm MG
INITIAL CLIMB: 937 ft (286 m) per min
WEIGHT (EMPTY): 2,072 lb (940 kg)
WEIGHT (LOADED): 2,910 lb (1,320 kg)

FOCKE WULF FW 189 UHU

MANUFACTURER: Focke Wulf Flugzeugbau
TYPE: Reconnaissance
LENGTH: 39 ft 5.5 in (12.03 m)
SPAN: 60 ft 4.5 in (18.40 m)
HEIGHT: 10 ft 2 in (3.10 m)
MAXIMUM SPEED: 217 mph (350 km/h)
SERVICE CEILING: 23,950 ft (7,300 m)
RANGE: 416 miles (670 km)
CREW: 3
POWERPLANT: 2 x Argus As 410A-1
ARMAMENT: 4 x 7.92mm MG
INITIAL CLIMB: 1,590 ft (485 m) per min
WEIGHT (EMPTY): 7,154 lb (3,245 kg)
WEIGHT (LOADED): 9,193 lb (4,170 kg)

HEINKEL HE 60

MANUFACTURER: Ernst Heinkel A.G
TYPE: Reconnaissance Seaplane
LENGTH: 37 ft 8 in (11.48 m)
SPAN: 44 ft 3 in (13.5 m)
HEIGHT: not available
MAXIMUM SPEED: 140 mph (225 km/h)
SERVICE CEILING: 16,400 ft (5,000 m)
RANGE: 447 miles (720 km)
CREW: 2
POWERPLANT: 1 x BMW VI 6.0ZU
ARMAMENT: 2 x MG
FIRST FLIGHT: 1933
BOMB LOAD: none
INITIAL CLIMB: not available
WEIGHT (EMPTY/LOADED): not available

HENSCHEL HS 126

MANUFACTURER: Henschel Flugzeug-Werke
TYPE: Reconnaissance
LENGTH: 35 ft 7 in (10.85 m)
SPAN: 47 ft 6.75 in (14.50 m)
HEIGHT: 12 ft 3.5 in (3.75 m)
MAXIMUM SPEED: 221 mph (355 km/h)
SERVICE CEILING: 27,000 ft (8,230 m)
RANGE: 447 miles (720 km)
CREW: 2
POWERPLANT: 1 x BMW-Bramo 323A-1
ARMAMENT: 2 x 7.92mm MG
BOMB LOAD: 331 lb (150 kg)
FIRST FLIGHT: Fall 1936
INITIAL CLIMB: not given
WEIGHT (EMPTY): 4,480 lb (2,032 kg)
WEIGHT (LOADED): 7,209 lb (3,270 kg)

AVRO ANSON

MANUFACTURER: **A.V. Roe & Co., Ltd.**
TYPE: **Coastal Recon'**
LENGTH: **42 ft 3 in (12.88 m)**
SPAN: **56 ft 6 in (17.22 m)**
HEIGHT: **13 ft 1 in (3.99 m)**
MAXIMUM SPEED: **188 mph (303 km/h)**
SERVICE CEILING: **19,000 ft (5,790 m)**
RANGE: **790 miles (1,271 km)**
CREW: **3 or 4**
POWERPLANT: **2 x Cheetah IX**
ARMAMENT: **4 x 0.303in MG**
BOMB LOAD: **500 lb (227 kg)**
FIRST FLIGHT: **March 1935**
INITIAL CLIMB: **960 ft (293 m) per min**
WEIGHT (EMPTY): **5,375 lb (2,438 kg)**
WEIGHT (LOADED): **9,300 lb (4,218 kg)**

SHORT SUNDERLAND

MANUFACTURER: **Short Bros., Ltd.**
TYPE: **Maritime Recon'**
LENGTH: **85 ft 3.5 in (26 m)**
SPAN: **112 ft 9.5 in (34.38 m)**
HEIGHT: **34 ft 6 in (10.52 m)**
MAXIMUM SPEED: **209 mph (336 km/h)**
SERVICE CEILING: **15,000 ft (4,570 m)**
RANGE: **2,500 miles (4,023 km)**
CREW: **10**
POWERPLANT: **4 x Bristol Pegasus XXII**
ARMAMENT: **8 x 0.303in MG**
BOMB LOAD: **2,000 lb (907 kg)**
INITIAL CLIMB: **720 ft (220 m) per min**
WEIGHT (EMPTY): **30,589 lb (13,875 kg)**
WEIGHT (LOADED): **49,000 lb (22,226 kg)**

SUPERMARINE WALRUS

MANUFACTURER: **Supermarine Aviation**
TYPE: **Spotter Amphibian**
LENGTH: **37 ft 3in (11.35 m)**
SPAN: **45 ft 10 in (13.97 m)**
HEIGHT: **15 ft 3 in (4.65 m)**
MAXIMUM SPEED: **135 mph (217 km/h)**
SERVICE CEILING: **17,100 ft (5,210 m)**
RANGE: **600 miles (966 km)**
CREW: **4**
POWERPLANT: **1 x Bristol Pegasus VI**
ARMAMENT: **3 x 0.303in MG**
BOMB LOAD: **600 lb (272 kg)**
WEIGHT (EMPTY): **4,900 lb (2,223 kg)**
WEIGHT (LOADED): **7,200 lb (3,266 kg)**

WESTLAND LYSANDER

MANUFACTURER: **Westland Aircraft Ltd.**
TYPE: **Tactical Recon'**
LENGTH: **30 ft 6 in (9.30 m)**
SPAN: **50 ft (15.24 m)**
HEIGHT: **11 ft (3.35 m)**
MAXIMUM SPEED: **229 mph (369 km/h)**
SERVICE CEILING: **26,000 ft (7,925 m)**
RANGE: **600 miles (966 km)**
CREW: **1 or 2**
POWERPLANT: **1 x Bristol Mercury XII**
ARMAMENT: **3 x 0.303in MG**
BOMB LOAD: **500 lb (227 kg)**
FIRST FLIGHT: **June 15, 1936**
INITIAL CLIMB: **1,900 ft (580 m) per min**
WEIGHT (EMPTY): **4,065 lb (1,844 kg)**
WEIGHT (LOADED): **7,500 lb (3,402 kg)**

KAWANISHI E7K2 "ALF"

MANUFACTURER: **Kawanishi**
TYPE: **Recon' Floatplane**
LENGTH: **34 ft 5.5 in (10.50 m)**
SPAN: **45 ft 11.25 in (14 m)**
HEIGHT: **15 ft 10.5 in (4.85 m)**
MAXIMUM SPEED: **171 mph (275 km/h)**
SERVICE CEILING: **23,165 ft (7,060 m)**
RANGE: **not available**
CREW: **3**
POWERPLANT: **1 x Mitsubishi Zuisei 11**
ARMAMENT: **3 x MG**
BOMB LOAD: **265 lb (120 kg)**
FIRST FLIGHT: **August 1938**
WEIGHT (EMPTY): **4,630 lb (2,100 kg)**
WEIGHT (LOADED): **7,275 lb (3,300 kg)**

CONSOLIDATED CATALINA

MANUFACTURER: **Consolidated Vultee**
TYPE: **Maritime Recon'**
LENGTH: **63 ft 10 in (19.45 m)**
SPAN: **104 ft (31.70 m)**
HEIGHT: **18 ft 11 in (5.76 m)**
MAXIMUM SPEED: **179 mph (288 km/h)**
SERVICE CEILING: **14,700 ft (4,480 m)**
RANGE: **3,550 miles (5,713 km)**
CREW: **9**
POWERPLANT: **2 x P & W R-1830-92**
ARMAMENT: **5 x MG**
BOMB LOAD: **4,500 lb (2,041 kg)**
WEIGHT (EMPTY): **20,910 lb (9,485 kg)**
WEIGHT (LOADED): **35,420 lb (16,067 kg)**

TRANSPORT AIRCRAFT

GOTHA GO 242 & 244

MANUFACTURER: Gotha Waggonfabrik
TYPE: Troop Transporter
LENGTH: 51 ft 10 in (15.80 m)
SPAN: 80 ft 4.5 in (24.50 m)
HEIGHT: 15 ft 1 in (4.60 m)
MAXIMUM SPEED: 180 mph (290 km/h)
SERVICE CEILING: 25,100 ft (7,650 m)
RANGE: 460 miles (740 km)
CREW: 2
POWERPLANT: 2 x Gnome-Rhône radial
ARMAMENT: 4 x 7.92mm MG
BOMB LOAD: not available
FIRST FLIGHT: not given
INITIAL CLIMB: 885 ft (270 m) per min
WEIGHT (EMPTY): 11,517 lb (5,225 kg)
WEIGHT (LOADED): 17,196 lb (7,800 kg)

JUNKERS JU 52

MANUFACTURER: Junkers Flugzeug
TYPE: Transport
LENGTH: 62 ft (18.90 m)
SPAN: 95 ft 10 in (29.20 m)
HEIGHT: 14 ft 10 in (4.52 m)
MAXIMUM SPEED: 178 mph (286 km/h)
SERVICE CEILING: 19,360 ft (5,900 m)
RANGE: 811 miles (1,305 km)
CREW: 3
POWERPLANT: 3 x BMW 132T-2 radial
ARMAMENT: 4 x 7.92mm MG
BOMB LOAD: not available
FIRST FLIGHT: October 13, 1930
INITIAL CLIMB: 562 ft (171 m) per min
WEIGHT (EMPTY): 14,328 lb (6,500 kg)
WEIGHT (LOADED): 24,317 lb (11,030 kg)

MESSERSCHMITT 323

MANUFACTURER: Messerschmitt A.G
TYPE: Heavy Transport
LENGTH: 93 ft 6 in (8.5 m)
SPAN: 180 ft 5.33 in (55 m)
HEIGHT: 31 ft 6 in (9.6 m)
MAXIMUM SPEED: 157 mph (253 km/h)
SERVICE CEILING: 14,760 ft (4,500 m)
RANGE: 808 miles (1,300 km)
CREW: 10 or 11
POWERPLANT: 6 x Gnome-Rhône radials
ARMAMENT: 1 x 20mm; 5 x MG
BOMB LOAD: none
FIRST FLIGHT: 1942
INITIAL CLIMB: not available
WEIGHT (EMPTY): 65,256 lb (29,600 kg)
WEIGHT (LOADED): 99,206 lb (45,000 kg)

AVRO YORK

MANUFACTURER: A.V. Roe & Co. Ltd.
TYPE: Long-range Transport
LENGTH: 78 ft 6 in (23.93 m)
SPAN: 102 ft 6 in (31.09 m)
HEIGHT: 17ft 10 in (5.44 m)
MAXIMUM SPEED: 298 mph (480 km/h)
SERVICE CEILING: 23,000 ft (7,010 m)
RANGE: 2,700 miles (4,345 km)
CREW: 4
POWERPLANT: 4 x RR Merlin XX
ARMAMENT: none
BOMB LOAD: none
FIRST FLIGHT: July 5, 1942
INITIAL CLIMB: not available
WEIGHT (EMPTY): 42,040 lb (19,069 kg)
WEIGHT (LOADED): 68,597 lb (31,115 kg)

DOUGLAS DC-3

MANUFACTURER: Douglas Aircraft Co.
TYPE: Transport
LENGTH: 64 ft 5.5 in (19.63 m)
SPAN: 95 ft (28.9 m)
HEIGHT: 16 ft 11 in (5.20 m)
MAXIMUM SPEED: 230 mph (370 km/h)
SERVICE CEILING: 24,000 ft (7,315 m)
RANGE: 1,600 miles (2,575 km)
CREW: 2 or 3
POWERPLANT: 2 x P & W R-1830-92
ARMAMENT: none
BOMB LOAD: none
FIRST FLIGHT: December 17, 1935
INITIAL CLIMB: 1,200 ft (366 m) per min
WEIGHT (EMPTY): 17,865 lb (8,103 kg)
WEIGHT (LOADED): 31,000 lb (14,061 kg)

CLOSE SUPPORT AIRCRAFT

Designed by Henschel, this twin-engine ground-attack aircraft could carry at least two 20mm cannon. The Hs 129 first flew in spring 1939. Its poor fields of vision and sluggish handling forced Henschel to make a series of improvements that resulted in the later Hs 129B-1.

HENSCHEL HS 129

MANUFACTURER: Henschel Flugzeug-Werke
TYPE: Close-Support, Antitank
LENGTH: 31 ft 11.75 in (9.75 m)
SPAN: 46 ft 7 in (14.2 m)
HEIGHT: 10 ft 8 in (3.25 m)
MAXIMUM SPEED: 253 mph (407 km/h)
SERVICE CEILING: 29,530 ft (9,000 m)
RANGE: 348 miles (560 km)
CREW: 1
POWERPLANT: 2 x Gnome-Rhône radial
ARMAMENT: 2 x cannon, 2 x MG
BOMB LOAD: 992 lb (450 kg)
FIRST FLIGHT: Spring 1939
INITIAL CLIMB: 1,595 ft (486 m) per min
WEIGHT (EMPTY): 8,862 lb (4,020 kg)
WEIGHT (LOADED): 11,574 lb (5,250 kg)

The Typhoon excelled as a ground-attack fighter. The Mk IB was the definitive version, with fixed forward-firing armament of four 20mm cannon, a sliding bubble canopy, and the powerful Sabre II engine. On D-Day, the Typhoon was a decisive weapon.

HAWKER TYPHOON

MANUFACTURER: Hawker Aircraft Ltd.
TYPE: Ground-Attack Fighter
LENGTH: 31 ft 11 in (9.73 m)
SPAN: 41 ft 7in (12.67 m)
HEIGHT: 15 ft 4 in (4.67 m)
MAXIMUM SPEED: 412 mph (663 km/h)
RANGE: 980 miles (1,577 km)
CREW: 1
POWERPLANT: 1 x Napier Sabre
ARMAMENT: 4 x 20mm cannon
BOMB LOAD: 2,000 lb (907 kg)
FIRST FLIGHT: 1939
INITIAL CLIMB: 3,000 ft (914 m) per min
WEIGHT (EMPTY): 9,800 lb (4,445 kg)
WEIGHT (LOADED): 13,250 lb (6,010 kg)

The Ba 65 was planned to fill the roles of interceptor, light bomber, or reconnaissance/attack plane. However, during the early days of World War II over the North African desert, Ba 65s suffered from reliability problems and by 1941 none remained in service.

BREDA BA 65

MANUFACTURER: Societa Ernesto Breda
TYPE: Ground-Attack
LENGTH: 30 ft 6.25 in (9.30 m)
SPAN: 39 ft 8.5 in (12.10 m)
HEIGHT: 10 ft 6 in (3.20 m)
MAXIMUM SPEED: 267 mph (430 km/h)
SERVICE CEILING: 20,670 ft (6,300 m)
RANGE: 342 miles (550 km)
CREW: 1
POWERPLANT: 1 x Fiat A.80 RC.41
ARMAMENT: 4 x MG
BOMB LOAD: 1,102 lb (500 kg)
FIRST FLIGHT: 1935
INITIAL CLIMB: not available
WEIGHT (EMPTY): 5,291 lb (2,400 kg)
WEIGHT (LOADED): 6,504 lb (2,950 kg)

Comparable in size, shape, weight, and performance with the British Fairey Battle, the Il-2 Shturmovik was by far the more successful aircraft and sustained what is known to have been the biggest production run of any aircraft in history.

ILYUSHIN IL-2 SHTURMOVIK

MANUFACTURER: Ilyushin
TYPE: Close-Support, Antitank
LENGTH: 39 ft 4.5 in (12 m)
SPAN: 47 ft 11 in (14.6 m)
HEIGHT: 11 ft 1.75 in (3.4 m)
MAXIMUM SPEED: 258 mph (415 km/h)
SERVICE CEILING: 19,685 ft (6,000 m)
RANGE: 497 miles (800 km)
CREW: 2
POWERPLANT: 1 x Mikulin AM-38F
ARMAMENT: 2 x cannon, 3 x MG
BOMB LOAD: 2,205 lb (1,000 kg)
FIRST FLIGHT: 1939
INITIAL CLIMB: 490 ft (150 m) per min
WEIGHT (EMPTY): 9,976 lb (4,525 kg)
WEIGHT (LOADED): 14,021 lb (6,360 kg)

LIGHT TANKS

During the early war years, light tanks were used to good effect by the Germans. However, by 1941 they had been superseded by more heavily armed models.

CHAR LÉGER H-38

DESIGNATION: **Char Léger Hotchkiss H-38**
TYPE: **Light Tank**
LENGTH: **13.83 ft (4.21 m)**
WIDTH: **6.39 ft (1.95 m)**
HEIGHT: **7 ft (2.13 m)**
WEIGHT: **26,880 lb (12,218 kg)**
CREW: **2**
MAIN ARMAMENT: **37mm**
SECONDARY ARMAMENT: **1 x 7.5mm**
ENGINE: **Hotchkiss six-cylinder**
RANGE: **93.75 miles (150 km)**
SPEED: **22 mph (36 km/h)**
FORDING: **2.78 ft (.85 m)**
TRENCH CROSSING: **5.9 ft (1.8 m)**
ARMOR (HULL): **1.3 in (34 mm)**
ARMOR (TURRET): **1.77 in (45 mm)**

CHAR LÉGER R-35

DESIGNATION: **Char Léger Renault R-35**
TYPE: **Light Tank**
LENGTH: **13.16 ft (4 m)**
WIDTH: **6.06 ft (1.85 m)**
HEIGHT: **6.83 ft (2.08 m)**
WEIGHT: **22,400 lb (10,181 kg)**
CREW: **2**
MAIN ARMAMENT: **37mm**
SECONDARY ARMAMENT: **1 x 7.5mm**
ENGINE: **Renault four-cylinder**
RANGE: **87.5 miles (140 km)**
SPEED: **12 mph (19.2 km/h)**
FORDING: **2.62 ft (.8 m)**
TRENCH CROSSING: **5.25 ft (1.6 m)**
ARMOR (HULL): **1.25 in (32 mm)**
ARMOR (TURRET): **1.77 in (45 mm)**

RENAULT FT

DESIGNATION: **Renault FT**
TYPE: **Light Tank**
LENGTH: **13.25 ft (4 m)**
WIDTH: **5.61 ft (1.71 m)**
HEIGHT: **7 ft (2.13 m)**
WEIGHT: **14,560 lb (6,618 kg)**
CREW: **2**
MAIN ARMAMENT: **1 x 7.5mm/ 37mm gun**
SECONDARY ARMAMENT: **none**
ENGINE: **Renault four-cylinder**
RANGE: **22 miles (35.4 km)**
SPEED: **4.8 mph (7.68 km/h)**
FORDING: **3 ft (.9 m)**
TRENCH CROSSING: **5.9 ft (1.8 m)**
ARMOR (HULL): **.63 in (16 mm)**
ARMOR (TURRET): **.86 in (22 mm)**

PANZER I

DESIGNATION: **SdKfz 101**
TYPE: **Light Tank**
LENGTH: **13.18 ft (4.02 m)**
WIDTH: **6.75 ft (2.06 m)**
HEIGHT: **5.64 ft (1.72 m)**
WEIGHT: **12,096 lb (5,498 kg)**
CREW: **2**
MAIN ARMAMENT: **2 x 7.92mm**
SECONDARY ARMAMENT: **none**
ENGINE: **Krupp M305**
RANGE: **90.62 miles (145 km)**
SPEED: **23.12 mph (37 km/h)**
FORDING: **2.78 ft (.85 m)**
TRENCH CROSSING: **5.74 ft (1.75 m)**
ARMOR (HULL): **.51 in (13 mm)**
ARMOR (TURRET): **.51 in (13 mm)**

PANZER II

DESIGNATION: **SdKfz 121**
TYPE: **Light Tank**
LENGTH: **15.78 ft (4.81 m)**
WIDTH: **7.5 ft (2.3 m)**
HEIGHT: **6.52 ft (1.99 m)**
WEIGHT: **19,936 lb (9,061 kg)**
CREW: **3**
MAIN ARMAMENT: **20mm**
SECONDARY ARMAMENT: **1 x 7.92mm**
ENGINE: **Maybach HL62TR**
RANGE: **125 miles (200 km)**
SPEED: **25 mph (40 km/h)**
FORDING: **2.78 ft (.85 m)**
TRENCH CROSSING: **5.74 ft (1.75 m)**
ARMOR (HULL): **.57 in (14.5 mm)**
ARMOR (TURRET): **.57 in (14.5 mm)**

PANZER 35(T)

DESIGNATION: **Panzerkampfwagen 35(t)**
TYPE: **Light Tank**
LENGTH: **16.07 ft (4.9 m)**
WIDTH: **6.88 ft (2.1 m)**
HEIGHT: **7.7 ft (2.35 m)**
WEIGHT: **23,520 lb (10,690 kg)**
CREW: **4**
MAIN ARMAMENT: **37mm**
SECONDARY ARMAMENT: **2 x 7.92mm**
ENGINE: **Skoda T11**
RANGE: **119 miles (190 km)**
SPEED: **21.87 mph (35 km/h)**
FORDING: **3.25 ft (1 m)**
TRENCH CROSSING: **6.23 ft (1.9 m)**
ARMOR (HULL): **.98 in (25 mm)**
ARMOR (TURRET): **.98 in (25 mm)**

PANZER 38(T)

x 7.92mm

DESIGNATION: Panzerkampfwagen 38(t)
TYPE: Light Tank
LENGTH: 15.12 ft (4.61 m)
WIDTH: 7 ft (2.13 m)
HEIGHT: 7.87 ft (2.4 m)
WEIGHT: 21,280 lb (9,672 kg)
CREW: 4
MAIN ARMAMENT: 37mm
SECONDARY ARMAMENT: 2

ENGINE: Praga EPA
RANGE: 156 miles (250 km)
SPEED: 26.25 mph (42 km/h)
FORDING: 3 ft (.9 m)
TRENCH CROSSING: 6.13 ft (1.87 m)
ARMOR (HULL): .98 in (25 mm)
ARMOR (TURRET): .98 in (25 mm)

LIGHT TANK MK VI

SECONDARY ARMAMENT: none

DESIGNATION: Light Tank Mk VI
TYPE: Light Tank
LENGTH: 13.2 ft (4.02 m)
WIDTH: 6.83 ft (2.08 m)
HEIGHT: 7.5 ft (2.28 m)
WEIGHT: 11,648 lb (5,294 kg)
CREW: 3
MAIN ARMAMENT: 1 x .303in, 1 x .5in

ENGINE: Meadows ESTB/A
RANGE: 125 miles (200 km)
SPEED: 35 mph (56 km/h)
FORDING: 3 ft (.9 m)
TRENCH CROSSING: 4.98 ft (1.52 m)
ARMOR (HULL): .15 in (4 mm)
ARMOR (TURRET): .59 in (14 mm)

TYPE 94

DESIGNATION: Tankette Type 94 TK
TYPE: Tankette
LENGTH: 10 ft (3 m)
WIDTH: 5.33 ft (1.62 m)
HEIGHT: 5.33 ft (1.62 m)
WEIGHT: 7,840 lb (3,563 kg)
CREW: 2
MAIN ARMAMENT: 7.7mm
SECONDARY ARMAMENT:

ENGINE: Four-cylinder petrol 32 hp
RANGE: 100 miles (160 km)
SPEED: 25 mph (40 km/h)
FORDING: unknown
TRENCH CROSSING: unknown
ARMOR (HULL): .15 in (4 mm)
ARMOR (TURRET): .47 in (12 mm)

TYPE 95

x 7.7mm

DESIGNATION: Light Tank Type 95
TYPE: Light Tank
LENGTH: 13.46 ft (4.1 m)
WIDTH: 6.72 ft (2.05 m)
HEIGHT: 7.5 ft (2.28 m)
WEIGHT: 16,576 lb (7,534 kg)
CREW: 3
MAIN ARMAMENT: 37mm
SECONDARY ARMAMENT: 2

ENGINE: Diesel six-cylinder
RANGE: 156 miles (250 km)
SPEED: 25 mph (40 km/h)
FORDING: 3.25 ft (1 m)
TRENCH CROSSING: 6.56 ft (2 m)
ARMOR (HULL): .23 in (6 mm)
ARMOR (TURRET): .55 in (14 mm)

LIGHT TANK 7TP

x 7.92mm

DESIGNATION: Light Tank 7TP
TYPE: Light Tank
LENGTH: 15 ft (4.57 m)
WIDTH: 8 ft (2.43 m)
HEIGHT: 7 ft (2.13 m)
WEIGHT: 21,056 lb (9,571 kg)
CREW: 3
MAIN ARMAMENT: 37mm
SECONDARY ARMAMENT: 1

ENGINE: Saurer Diesel six-cylinder
RANGE: 100 miles (160 km)
SPEED: 20 mph (32 km/h)
FORDING: unknown
TRENCH CROSSING: 10.23 ft (3.12 m)
ARMOR (HULL): .59 in (15 mm)
ARMOR (TURRET): 1.57 in (40 mm)

COMBAT CAR M1

SECONDARY ARMAMENT: none

DESIGNATION: Combat Car M1
TYPE: Light Tank
LENGTH: 14.6 ft (4.45 m)
WIDTH: 7.75 ft (2.36 m)
HEIGHT: 7.75 ft (2.36 m)
WEIGHT: 19,530 lb (8,877 kg)
CREW: 4
MAIN ARMAMENT: 4 x .5in

ENGINE: Guiberson 250 hp
RANGE: 70 miles (112 km)
SPEED: 45 mph (72 km/h)
FORDING: 3 ft (.9 m)
TRENCH CROSSING: 6 ft (1.83 m)
ARMOR (HULL): .5 in (12.7 mm)
ARMOR (TURRET): .75 in (19 mm)

LIGHT TANK M2A2

DESIGNATION: Light Tank M2A2
TYPE: Light Tank
LENGTH: 13.6 ft (4.14 m)
WIDTH: 7.83 ft (2.38 m)
HEIGHT: 7.75 ft (2.36 m)

WEIGHT: 19,100 lb (8,681 kg)
CREW: 4
MAIN ARMAMENT: .5in
SECONDARY ARMAMENT: 2 x .3in
ENGINE: Continental Radial
250 hp

RANGE: 62.5 miles (100 km)
SPEED: 45 mph (72 km/h)
FORDING: 3.25 ft (1 m)
TRENCH CROSSING: 6 ft (1.83 m)
ARMOR (HULL): .5 in (12.7 mm)
ARMOR (TURRET): .75 in (19 mm)

LIGHT TANK M2A4

DESIGNATION: Light Tank M2A4
TYPE: Light Tank
LENGTH: 13.6 ft (4.14 m)
WIDTH: 8.3 ft (2.52 m)
HEIGHT: 7.75 ft (2.36 m)
WEIGHT: 19,100 lb (8,681 kg)
CREW: 4
MAIN ARMAMENT: 37mm
SECONDARY ARMAMENT: 1 x .5in, 4 x .3in
ENGINE: Continental Radial 250 hp
RANGE: 80 miles (128 km)
SPEED: 37 mph (59.2 km/h)
FORDING: 3.25 ft (1 m)
TRENCH CROSSING: 6 ft (1.83 m)
ARMOR (HULL): .5 in (12.7 mm)
ARMOR (TURRET): .75 in (19 mm)

LIGHT TANK M3

DESIGNATION: Light Tank M3
TYPE: Light Tank
LENGTH: 14.8 ft (3.29 m)
WIDTH: 7.34 ft (2.24 m)
HEIGHT: 8.25 ft (2.51 m)
WEIGHT: 27,552 lb (12,523 kg)
CREW: 4
MAIN ARMAMENT: 37mm
SECONDARY ARMAMENT: 3 x .3in
ENGINE: Continental Radial 250 hp
RANGE: 70 miles (112.6 km)
SPEED: 35 mph (56 km/h)
FORDING: 3 ft (.9 m)
TRENCH CROSSING: 6 ft (1.83 m)
ARMOR (HULL): 1 in (25.4 mm)
ARMOR (TURRET): 1.5 in (38.1 mm)

M22 LOCUST

DESIGNATION: Light Tank T9E1
TYPE: Light Tank
LENGTH: 12.9 ft (3.93 m)
WIDTH: 7.25 ft (2.2 m)
HEIGHT: 5.66 ft (1.72 m)
WEIGHT: 16,400 lb (7,454 kg)
CREW: 3
MAIN ARMAMENT: 37mm
SECONDARY ARMAMENT: 1 x .3in
ENGINE: Lycoming 162 hp
RANGE: 140 miles (224 km)
SPEED: 35 mph (56 km/h)
FORDING: 3 ft (.9 m)
TRENCH CROSSING: 5 ft (1.52 m)
ARMOR (HULL): .75 in (19.05 mm)
ARMOR (TURRET): 1 in (25.4 mm)

M24 CHAFFEE

DESIGNATION: Light Tank M24
TYPE: Light Tank
LENGTH: 18 ft (5.48 m)
WIDTH: 9.67 ft (2.95 m)
HEIGHT: 8.1 ft (2.46 m)
WEIGHT: 40,500 lb (18,409 kg)
CREW: 5
MAIN ARMAMENT: 75mm
SECONDARY ARMAMENT: 2 x .3in, 1 x .5in
ENGINE: 2 x Cadillac 110 hp
RANGE: 100 miles (160 km)
SPEED: 35 mph (56 km/h)
FORDING: 3.34 ft (1.02 m)
TRENCH CROSSING: 8 ft (2.44 m)
ARMOR (HULL): 1.1 in (28 mm)
ARMOR (TURRET): 1.49 in (38 mm)

T-26

DESIGNATION: T-26
TYPE: Light Tank
LENGTH: 15.75 ft (4.8 m)
WIDTH: 8 ft (2.44 m)
HEIGHT: 6.75 ft (2.05 m)
WEIGHT: 19,040 lb (8,654 kg)
CREW: 3
MAIN ARMAMENT: 37mm
SECONDARY ARMAMENT: 2 x 7.62mm
ENGINE: Armstrong Siddeley 75 hp
RANGE: 140.6 miles (225 km)
SPEED: 22 mph (35.2 km/h)
FORDING: Unknown
TRENCH CROSSING: 7.2 ft (2.2 m)
ARMOR (HULL): .23 in (6 mm)
ARMOR (TURRET): .51 in (13 mm)

A Soviet-built version of the British Vickers-Armstrong 6-ton Tank, the original T-26s were manufactured in both twin-turret and single-turret versions. However, from 1933 onward production was concentrated on the single-turret model, in which a larger gun could be mounted. Production continued until 1939. The T-26 was an important factor in the tank strength of the Soviet Union in the 1930s, and was used against the Finns and the Germans in 1941. However, by this time it was obsolete and was soon phased out of service.

MEDIUM TANKS

Medium tanks were an excellent combination of firepower, range, and armor protection. Some of the most decisive tanks of the war were in the medium class, such as the German Panzer IV, the Soviet T-34, and the U.S. M4 Sherman.

VICKERS MEDIUM TANK

DESIGNATION: Vickers Medium Mk IIA
TYPE: Medium Tank
LENGTH: 17.6 ft (5.36 m)
WIDTH: 9.1 ft (2.77 m)
HEIGHT: 8.8 ft (2.68 m)
WEIGHT: 29,568 lb (13,440 kg)
CREW: 3
MAIN ARMAMENT: 3pdr QF
SECONDARY ARMAMENT: 4 x 7.5mm & 2 x .303in
ENGINE: Armstrong-Siddeley V-8
RANGE: 160 miles (257 km)
SPEED: 15 mph (24 km/h)
FORDING: 2.78 ft (.85 m)
TRENCH CROSSING: 5.75 ft (1.75 m)
ARMOR (HULL): .32 in (8.25 mm)
ARMOR (TURRET): .32 in (8.25 mm)

CHAR S-35

DESIGNATION: Char de Cavalerie S-35
TYPE: Medium Tank
LENGTH: 17.33 ft (5.28 m)
WIDTH: 6.06 ft (1.85 m)
HEIGHT: 8.58 ft (2.6 m)
WEIGHT: 44,800 lb (20,363 kg)
CREW: 3
MAIN ARMAMENT: 47mm
SECONDARY ARMAMENT: 1 x 7.5mm
ENGINE: Somua V-8 190 hp
RANGE: 160.6 miles (257 km)
SPEED: 25 mph (40 km/h)
FORDING: 2.62 ft (.8 m)
TRENCH CROSSING: 5.25 ft (1.6 m)
ARMOR (HULL): 1.4 in (36 mm)
ARMOR (TURRET): 2.16 in (55 mm)

PANZER III AUSF F

DESIGNATION: SdKfz 141
TYPE: Medium Tank
LENGTH: 17.65 ft (5.38 m)
WIDTH: 9.67 ft (2.95 m)
HEIGHT: 8 ft (2.44 m)
WEIGHT: 44,352 lb (20,160 kg)
CREW: 5
MAIN ARMAMENT: 37mm
SECONDARY ARMAMENT: 2 x 7.92mm
ENGINE: Maybach HL120TRM
RANGE: 101 miles (165 km)
SPEED: 25 mph (40 km/h)
FORDING: 2.62 ft (.8 m)
TRENCH CROSSING: 8.5 ft (2.59 m)
ARMOR (HULL): 1.18 in (30 mm)
ARMOR (TURRET): 1.18 in (30 mm)

PANZER III AUSF J

DESIGNATION: SdKfz 141
TYPE: Medium Tank
LENGTH: 18.11 ft (5.52 m)
WIDTH: 9.67 ft (2.95 m)
HEIGHT: 8.2 ft (2.5 m)
WEIGHT: 48,160 lb (21,890 kg)
CREW: 5
MAIN ARMAMENT: 50mm
SECONDARY ARMAMENT: 2 x 7.92mm
ENGINE: Maybach HL120TRM
RANGE: 96.8 miles (155 km)
SPEED: 25 mph (40 km/h)
FORDING: 2.62 ft (.8 m)
TRENCH CROSSING: 8.5 ft (2.59 m)
ARMOR (HULL): 1.18 in (30 mm)
ARMOR (TURRET): 1.96 in (50 mm)

PANZER III AUSF N

DESIGNATION: SdKfz 141/2
TYPE: Medium Tank
LENGTH: 18.53 ft (5.65 m)
WIDTH: 9.67 ft (2.95 m)
HEIGHT: 8.2 ft (2.5 m)
WEIGHT: 51,520 lb (23,418 kg)
CREW: 5
MAIN ARMAMENT: 75mm
SECONDARY ARMAMENT: 2 x 7.92mm
ENGINE: Maybach HL120TRM
RANGE: 96.8 miles (155 km)
SPEED: 25 mph (40 km/h)
FORDING: 2.62 ft (.8 m)
TRENCH CROSSING: 8.5 ft (2.59 m)
ARMOR (HULL): 1.96 in (50 mm)
ARMOR (TURRET): 1.96 in (50 mm)

By far the most enduring of the main types of German tank, the Panzer IV was specified as a medium tank in the 20-ton class, to be armed with a 75mm gun. The order to build the vehicle was awarded to the Krupp company, who initially proposed interleaved road wheels for suspension. However, the actual suspension used on the tank was much more simple: eight road wheels on each side suspended in pairs on leaf springs. Like other German tanks of the period, the Panzer IV's engine was located at the rear, with the transmission led forward to the final drive via sprockets at the front of the track. The Ausf C, which was armed with the KwK 37 l/24 gun, incorporated a number of minor changes to the design of the Ausf B, including improved turret face, a new gun mantlet housing, an altered motor mount, and an armored sleeve that protected the coaxial machine gun. Later, to extend combat life, additional armor plates were bolted to the hull and superstructure sides. An initial order for the Ausf C was for 300 vehicles, but only 134 were actually completed. Production took place between September 1938 and August 1939, and the Ausf C saw service in World War II during the German invasion of Poland in September 1939 and also in the invasion of western Europe in the summer of 1940. The vehicle remained in service until 1943, but by that time the numbers that were available had dwindled drastically due to battlefield attrition.

PANZER IV AUSF C

DESIGNATION: SdKfz 161
TYPE: Medium Support Tank
LENGTH: 19.42 ft (5.92 m)
WIDTH: 10.79 ft (3.29 m)
HEIGHT: 8.79 ft (2.68 m)
WEIGHT: 42,560 lb (19,345 kg)
CREW: 5
MAIN ARMAMENT: 75mm
SECONDARY ARMAMENT: 1 x 7.92mm
ENGINE: Maybach HL120TRM
RANGE: 125 miles (200 km)
SPEED: 25 mph (40 km/h)
FORDING: 3.25 ft (1 m)
TRENCH CROSSING: 7.25 ft (2.2 m)
ARMOR (HULL): 1.18 in (30 mm)
ARMOR (TURRET): 1.18 in (30 mm)

PANZER IV AUSF H

DESIGNATION: SdKfz 161/2
TYPE: Medium Tank
LENGTH: 23.03 ft (7.02 m)
WIDTH: 10.79 ft (3.29 m)
HEIGHT: 8.79 ft (2.68 m)
WEIGHT: 56,000 lb (25,454 kg)
CREW: 5
MAIN ARMAMENT: 75mm
SECONDARY ARMAMENT: 1 x 7.92mm
ENGINE: Maybach HL120TRM
RANGE: 131 miles (210 km)
SPEED: 23.75 mph (38 km/h)
FORDING: 3.25 ft (1 m)
TRENCH CROSSING: 7.25 ft (2.2 m)
ARMOR (HULL): 3.14 in (80 mm)
ARMOR (TURRET): 1.96 in (50 mm)

PANZER V AUSF D

DESIGNATION: SdKfz 171
TYPE: Heavy Medium Tank
LENGTH: 29.06 ft (8.86 m)
WIDTH: 11.25 ft (3.43 m)
HEIGHT: 9.67 ft (2.95 m)
WEIGHT: 96,320 lb (43,781 kg)
CREW: 5
MAIN ARMAMENT: 75mm
SECONDARY ARMAMENT: 2 x 7.92mm
ENGINE: Maybach HL 230P30
RANGE: 125 miles (200 km)
SPEED: 28.75 mph (46 km/h)
FORDING: 5.57 ft (1.7 m)
TRENCH CROSSING: 6.26 ft (1.91 m)
ARMOR (HULL): 3.14 in (80 mm)
ARMOR (TURRET): 3.93 in (100 mm)

PANZER V AUSF G

DESIGNATION: SdKfz 171
TYPE: Heavy Medium Tank
LENGTH: 29.06 ft (8.86 m)
WIDTH: 11.25 ft (3.43 m)
HEIGHT: 9.77 ft (2.98 m)
WEIGHT: 101,920 lb (46,327 kg)
CREW: 5
MAIN ARMAMENT: 75mm
SECONDARY ARMAMENT: 2 x 7.92mm
ENGINE: Maybach HL230P30
RANGE: 125 miles (200 km)
SPEED: 28.75 mph (46 km/h)
FORDING: 5.57 ft (1.7 m)
TRENCH CROSSING: 6.26 ft (1.91 m)
ARMOR (HULL): 3.14 in (80 mm)
ARMOR (TURRET): 4.33 in (110 mm)

PZKPFW M15/42

DESIGNATION: M15/42 738(i)
TYPE: Medium Tank
LENGTH: 16.53 ft (5.04 m)
WIDTH: 7.31 ft (2.23 m)
HEIGHT: 7.84 ft (2.39 m)
WEIGHT: 32,928 lb (14,967 kg)
CREW: 4
MAIN ARMAMENT: 47mm
SECONDARY ARMAMENT: 1 x 8mm
ENGINE: 15TB V-8 petrol
RANGE: 112 miles (180 km)
SPEED: 23.75 mph (38 km/h)
FORDING: 3.25 ft (1 m)
TRENCH CROSSING: 6.88 ft (2.1 m)
ARMOR (HULL): 1.18 in (30 mm)
ARMOR (TURRET): 1.92 in (49 mm)

Under the terms of the Lend-Lease scheme, the British purchased a number of Medium Tank M3s from the U.S. government. The vehicle was slightly modified, with changes to the turret. The vehicle's silhouette was reduced by doing away with the cupola, and the turret was reduced by at least 12 in (305 mm), although the end result was still an excellent target for antitank gunners. The M3 in British service was known as the Grant, after the American Civil War general U.S. Grant. The Grant Canal Defense Light version was not a tank, but an armored housing with a powerful searchlight in the place of the original tank turret to light up the battlefield during night actions.

GRANT MEDIUM TANK

DESIGNATION: **Grant Medium Tank**
TYPE: **Medium Tank**
LENGTH: **18.5 ft (5.63 m)**
WIDTH: **8.5 ft (2.51 m)**
HEIGHT: **9.25 ft (2.81 m)**
WEIGHT: **60,000 lb (27,272 kg)**
CREW: **6**
MAIN ARMAMENT: **75mm**
SECONDARY ARMAMENT:
1 x 37mm
ENGINE: **Wright Continental R-975**
RANGE: **160 miles (257 km)**
SPEED: **26 mph (41.6 km/h)**
FORDING: **3.34 ft (1.02 m)**
TRENCH CROSSING: **6.26 ft (1.91 m)**
ARMOR (HULL): **1.5 in (38.1 mm)**
ARMOR (TURRET): **.5 in (12.7 mm)**

MEDIUM TANK MK II

DESIGNATION: **Medium Tank Mk II**
TYPE: **Medium Tank**
LENGTH: **17.5 ft (5.33 m)**
WIDTH: **9.1 ft (2.77 m)**
HEIGHT: **8.8 ft (2.68 m)**
WEIGHT: **29,568 lb (13,440 kg)**
CREW: **5**
MAIN ARMAMENT: **3pdr**
SECONDARY ARMAMENT:
6 x .303in
ENGINE: **Armstrong-Siddeley 90 hp**
RANGE: **160 miles (257 km)**
SPEED: **15 mph (24 km/h)**
FORDING: **2.9 ft (.85 m)**
TRENCH CROSSING: **5.75 ft (1.75 m)**
ARMOR (HULL): **.32 in (8.25 mm)**
ARMOR (TURRET): **.32 in (8.25 mm)**

SHERMAN FIREFLY

DESIGNATION: **Sherman Firefly**
TYPE: **Medium Tank**
LENGTH: **20.57 ft (6.27 m)**
WIDTH: **8.79 ft (2.68 m)**
HEIGHT: **11.25 ft (3.43 m)**
WEIGHT: **71,024 lb (32,284 kg)**
CREW: **5**
MAIN ARMAMENT: **17pdr**
SECONDARY ARMAMENT: **1 x .3in, 1 x .5in**
ENGINE: **Ford V-8 500 hp**
RANGE: **100 miles (160 km)**
SPEED: **29 mph (47 km/h)**
FORDING: **3 ft (.9 m)**
TRENCH CROSSING: **7.41 ft (2.26 m)**
ARMOR (HULL): **.59 in (15 mm)**
ARMOR (TURRET): **3.93 in (100 mm)**

CARRO ARMATO M11/39

DESIGNATION: **Carro Armato M11/39**
TYPE: **Medium Tank**
LENGTH: **15.5 ft (4.72 m)**
WIDTH: **7.08 ft (2.15 m)**
HEIGHT: **7.33 ft (2.23 m)**
WEIGHT: **24,640 lb (11,200 kg)**
CREW: **3**
MAIN ARMAMENT: **37mm**
SECONDARY ARMAMENT: **2 x 8mm**
ENGINE: **Spa 8T 105 hp**
RANGE: **125 miles (200 km)**
SPEED: **20 mph (32 km/h)**
FORDING: **3.25 ft (1 m)**
TRENCH CROSSING: **6.88 ft (2.1 m)**
ARMOR (HULL): **.23 in (6 mm)**
ARMOR (TURRET): **1.18 in (30 mm)**

CARRO ARMATO M13/40

DESIGNATION: **Carro Armato M13/40**
TYPE: **Medium Tank**
LENGTH: **16.18 ft (4.93 m)**
WIDTH: **7.08 ft (2.15 m)**
HEIGHT: **7.8 ft (2.37 m)**
WEIGHT: **31,360 lb (14,254 kg)**
CREW: **3**
MAIN ARMAMENT: **47mm**
SECONDARY ARMAMENT: **2 x 8mm**
ENGINE: **Spa 15T 145hp**
RANGE: **125 miles (200 km)**
SPEED: **22 mph (35.2 km/h)**
FORDING: **3.25 ft (1 m)**
TRENCH CROSSING: **6.88 ft (2.1 m)**
ARMOR (HULL): **1.18 in (30 mm)**
ARMOR (TURRET): **1.57 in (40 mm)**

COMMAND TANK SHI-KI

DESIGNATION: Command Tank
TYPE: Medium Tank
LENGTH: 18 ft (5.48 m)
WIDTH: 18 ft (5.48 m)
HEIGHT: 7.33 ft (2.23 m)
WEIGHT: 33,600 lb (15,272 kg)
CREW: 4
MAIN ARMAMENT: 37mm
SECONDARY ARMAMENT: none
ENGINE: Diesel V-12 170 hp
RANGE: 143.75 miles (230 km)
SPEED: 23.5 mph (37.6 km/h)
FORDING: 2.62 ft (.8 m)
TRENCH CROSSING: 8.53 ft (2.6 m)
ARMOR (HULL): .31 in (8 mm)
ARMOR (TURRET): .98 in (25 mm)

TYPE 97

DESIGNATION: Medium Tank Type 97
TYPE: Medium Tank
LENGTH: 18.04 ft (5.5 m)
WIDTH: 7.64 ft (2.33 m)
HEIGHT: 7.8 ft (2.38 m)
WEIGHT: 35,392 lb (16,087 kg)
CREW: 4
MAIN ARMAMENT: 57mm
SECONDARY ARMAMENT: 1 x 7.7mm
ENGINE: Mitsubishi V-12
RANGE: 131.25 miles (210 km)
SPEED: 23.75 mph (38 km/h)
FORDING: 3.25 ft (1 m)
TRENCH CROSSING: 6.5 ft (2 m)
ARMOR (HULL): .23 in (6 mm)
ARMOR (TURRET): 1.29 in (33 mm)

MEDIUM TANK T3

DESIGNATION: Medium Tank T3
TYPE: Medium Tank
LENGTH: 18 ft (5.49 m)
WIDTH: 7.3 ft (2.2 m)
HEIGHT: 7.5 ft (2.28 m)
WEIGHT: 24,640 lb (11,200 kg)
CREW: 3
MAIN ARMAMENT: 37mm
SECONDARY ARMAMENT: 1 x .3in
ENGINE: Liberty V-12 338 hp
RANGE: unknown
SPEED: 69 mph (110 km/h)
FORDING: 3.25 ft (1 m)
TRENCH CROSSING: 10.7 ft (2.1 m)
ARMOR (HULL): .23 in (6 mm)
ARMOR (TURRET): .51 in (13 mm)

MEDIUM TANK M3

DESIGNATION: Medium Tank M3
TYPE: Medium Tank
LENGTH: 18.5 ft (5.63 m)
WIDTH: 8.92 ft (2.72 m)
HEIGHT: 10.25 ft (3.12 m)
WEIGHT: 30,000 lb (27,272 kg)
CREW: 6
MAIN ARMAMENT: 75mm
SECONDARY ARMAMENT: 1 x 37mm, 3 x .3in
ENGINE: Wright Continental 340 hp
RANGE: 120 miles (193 km)
SPEED: 26 mph (41.6 km/h)
FORDING: 3.3 ft (1.02 m)
TRENCH CROSSING: 6.25 ft (1.9 m)
ARMOR (HULL): 1.5 in (38 mm)
ARMOR (TURRET): 2 in (50.8 mm)

MEDIUM TANK M4A1

DESIGNATION: Medium Tank M4A1
TYPE: Medium Tank
LENGTH: 19.16 ft (5.83 m)
WIDTH: 8.53 ft (2.6 m)
HEIGHT: 9 ft (2.74 m)
WEIGHT: 66,500 lb (30,227 kg)
CREW: 5
MAIN ARMAMENT: 75mm
SECONDARY ARMAMENT: 2 x .3in, 1 x .5in
ENGINE: Continental 400 hp
RANGE: 100 miles (160 km)
SPEED: 24 mph (38.4 km/h)
FORDING: 3 ft (.9 m)
TRENCH CROSSING: 7.41 ft (2.26 m)
ARMOR (HULL): 1 in (25.4 mm)
ARMOR (TURRET): 2 in (50.8 mm)

MEDIUM TANK M4A3

DESIGNATION: Medium Tank M4A3
TYPE: Medium Tank
LENGTH: 19.66 ft (6 m)
WIDTH: 8.53 ft (2.6 m)
HEIGHT: 9 ft (2.74 m)
WEIGHT: 68,500 lb (31,136 kg)
CREW: 5
MAIN ARMAMENT: 75mm
SECONDARY ARMAMENT: 2 x .3in, 1 x .5in
ENGINE: Ford GAA-III 500 hp
RANGE: 100 miles (160 km)
SPEED: 25 mph (40 km/h)
FORDING: 3 ft (.9 m)
TRENCH CROSSING: 7.41 ft (2.26 m)
ARMOR (HULL): 1 in (25.4 mm)
ARMOR (TURRET): 2 in (50.8 mm)

In December 1930, the Soviet Union purchased two U.S. Christie M1928 convertible tanks, which became known in Soviet service as the BT-1. The first Soviet prototypes, known as the BT-2, were completed in October 1931 and took part in the Moscow parade on November 7 of that year. The BT series of medium tanks were designed as fast vehicles that were intended to undertake the traditional cavalry role of exploitation. Production of the BT-2 began in 1932 and was ended the following year, by which time 4,000 vehicles had been built. The tank was fast, but was somewhat unreliable, and its interior was cramped for the three-man crew. The tank did, however, possess some interesting features, such as the capability of running either on its tracks or on its road wheels as required. Armament was satisfactory for its intended role, with a 37mm main gun and a ball-mounted machine gun. Amazingly, this tank was still in service in 1940. The BT-3 was a modified version of the BT-2, with solid disc wheels in place of the spoked type of earlier vehicles. It was also up-gunned with a 45mm gun. The BT-4 was a prototype with hull features similar to the BT-3, but with twin turrets replacing the single turret. The T-34/76 and the T-34/85 Soviet tanks were the mainstay of the Red Army in the later years of World War II and played a vital role in the ultimate defeat of Germany. They were produced in vast numbers.

BT-2

DESIGNATION: **BT-2**
TYPE: **Medium Tank**
LENGTH: **18 ft (5.48 m)**
WIDTH: **7.33 ft (2.23 m)**
HEIGHT: **6.33 ft (1.92 m)**
WEIGHT: **24,640 lb (11,200 kg)**
CREW: **3**
MAIN ARMAMENT: **37mm**
SECONDARY ARMAMENT: **1 x 7.62mm**
ENGINE: **400 hp**
RANGE: **187 miles (300 km)**
SPEED: **45 mph (72 km/h)**
FORDING: **3.25 ft (1 m)**
TRENCH CROSSING: **10.7 ft (2.1 m)**
ARMOR (HULL): **.23 in (6 mm)**
ARMOR (TURRET): **.51 in (13 mm)**

BT-5

DESIGNATION: **BT-5**
TYPE: **Medium Tank**
LENGTH: **18 ft (5.48 m)**
WIDTH: **7.33 ft (2.23 m)**
HEIGHT: **7.25 ft (2.2 m)**
WEIGHT: **25,760 lb (11,709 kg)**
CREW: **3**
MAIN ARMAMENT: **45mm**
SECONDARY ARMAMENT: **1 x 7.62mm**
ENGINE: **Type M5 350 hp**
RANGE: **125 miles (200 km)**
SPEED: **43.75 mph (70 km/h)**
FORDING: **3.25 ft (1 m)**
TRENCH CROSSING: **3.25 ft (1 m)**
ARMOR (HULL): **.23 in (6 mm)**
ARMOR (TURRET): **.51 in (13 mm)**

BT-7

DESIGNATION: **BT-7**
TYPE: **Medium Tank**
LENGTH: **18.65 ft (5.68 m)**
WIDTH: **7.98 ft (2.43 m)**
HEIGHT: **7.5 ft (2.28 m)**
WEIGHT: **30,912 lb (14,050 kg)**
CREW: **3**
MAIN ARMAMENT: **45mm**
SECONDARY ARMAMENT: **2 x 7.62mm**
ENGINE: **450 hp**
RANGE: **156.25 miles (250 km)**
SPEED: **53.75 mph (86 km/h)**
FORDING: **5.1 ft (1.56 m)**
TRENCH CROSSING: **10.7 ft (2.1 m)**
ARMOR (HULL): **.23 in (6 mm)**
ARMOR (TURRET): **.86 in (22 mm)**

T-34/76

DESIGNATION: **T-34/76**
TYPE: **Medium Tank**
LENGTH: **21.6 ft (6.58 m)**
WIDTH: **9.84 ft (3 m)**
HEIGHT: **8 ft (2.43 m)**
WEIGHT: **58,912 lb (26,778 kg)**
CREW: **4**
MAIN ARMAMENT: **76.2mm**
SECONDARY ARMAMENT: **2 x 7.62mm**
ENGINE: **V-2-34 V-12 500 hp**
RANGE: **115 miles (186 km)**
SPEED: **31 mph (50 km/h)**
FORDING: **4.5 ft (1.37 m)**
TRENCH CROSSING: **9.66 ft (2.95 m)**
ARMOR (HULL): **.78 in (20 mm)**
ARMOR (TURRET): **2.04 in (52 mm)**

T-34/85

DESIGNATION: **T-34/85**
TYPE: **Medium Tank**
LENGTH: **24.6 ft (7.49 m)**
WIDTH: **9.61 ft (2.93 m)**
HEIGHT: **7.8 ft (2.37 m)**
WEIGHT: **70,560 lb (32,073 kg)**
CREW: **5**
MAIN ARMAMENT: **85mm**
SECONDARY ARMAMENT: **1 x 7.62mm**
ENGINE: **V-12 diesel, 500 hp**
RANGE: **193.75 miles (310 km)**
SPEED: **34.37 mph (55 km/h)**
FORDING: **4.26 ft (1.3 m)**
TRENCH CROSSING: **9.66 ft (2.95 m)**
ARMOR (HULL): **3.93 in (100 mm)**
ARMOR (TURRET): **3.54 in (90 mm)**

HEAVY TANKS

The desire to produce tanks with more armor protection and greater firepower resulted in some steel monsters being built in World War II. Though they were capable of knocking out most enemy tanks, their slow speed, high fuel consumption, and even higher production costs meant relatively few were built. Only 1,300 of the German Tiger I, for example, were manufactured. The U.S. M6 Heavy Tank, originally planned for 5,500 units, never reached the battlefield—the project was scrapped because of technical difficulties.

CHAR B1

DESIGNATION: **Char de Bataille B1**
TYPE: **Heavy Tank**
LENGTH: **20.92 ft (6.37 m)**
WIDTH: **8.11 ft (2.5 m)**
HEIGHT: **9.2 ft (2.8 m)**
WEIGHT: **67,200 lb (30,545 kg)**
CREW: **4**
MAIN ARMAMENT:
1 x 75mm, 1 x 47mm
SECONDARY ARMAMENT:
2 x 7.5mm
ENGINE: **Renault six-cylinder**
RANGE: **112 miles (180 km)**
SPEED: **17 mph (27.5 km/h)**
FORDING: **unknown**
TRENCH CROSSING: **9 ft (2.74 m)**
ARMOR (HULL): **.6 in (14 mm)**
ARMOR (TURRET): **.6 in (14 mm)**

CHAR B1-BIS

DESIGNATION: **Char de Bataille B1-bis**
TYPE: **Heavy Tank**
LENGTH: **20.94 ft (6.38 m)**
WIDTH: **8.11 ft (2.5 m)**
HEIGHT: **9.17 ft (2.79 m)**
WEIGHT: **71,680 lb (32,581 kg)**
CREW: **4**
MAIN ARMAMENT:
1 x 75mm, 1 x 47mm
SECONDARY ARMAMENT:
2 x 7.5mm
ENGINE: **Renault six-cylinder**
RANGE: **112 miles (180 km)**
SPEED: **17.2 mph (27.52 km/h)**
FORDING: **unknown**
TRENCH CROSSING: **9 ft (2.74 m)**
ARMOR (HULL): **.6 in (14 mm)**
ARMOR (TURRET): **2.6 in (65 mm)**

TIGER I

DESIGNATION: **SdKfz 181**
TYPE: **Heavy Tank**
LENGTH: **27.72 ft (8.45 m)**
WIDTH: **12.13 ft (3.7 m)**
HEIGHT: **9.61 ft (2.93 m)**
WEIGHT: **125,400 lb (57,000 kg)**
CREW: **5**
MAIN ARMAMENT: **88mm**
SECONDARY ARMAMENT:
2 x 7.92mm
ENGINE: **Maybach**
HL210P45
RANGE: **87.5 miles (140 km)**
SPEED: **23.75 mph (38 km/h)**
FORDING: **5.1 ft (1.56 m)**
TRENCH CROSSING: **7.51 ft (2.29 m)**
ARMOR (HULL): **3.93 in (100 mm)**
ARMOR (TURRET): **3.93 in (100 mm)**

TIGER II

DESIGNATION: **SdKfz 182**
TYPE: **Heavy Tank**
LENGTH: **33.79 ft (10.3 m)**
WIDTH: **12.33 ft (3.76 m)**
HEIGHT: **10.1 ft (3.08 m)**
WEIGHT: **154,000 lb (70,000 kg)**
CREW: **5**
MAIN ARMAMENT: **88mm**
SECONDARY ARMAMENT:
2 x 7.92mm
ENGINE: **Maybach**
HL230P30
RANGE: **106 miles (170 km)**
SPEED: **26.25 mph (42 km/h)**
FORDING: **5.24 ft (1.63 m)**
TRENCH CROSSING:
9.84 ft (3 m)
ARMOR (HULL): **3.93 in (100 mm)**
ARMOR (TURRET): **7 in (180 mm)**

HEAVY TANK M6

The U.S. Army originally planned to produce 5,500 M6s, but this was reduced when testing showed it to be too heavy, undergunned, poorly shaped, and having a faulty transmission. As a result, only 40 M6s were built.

DESIGNATION: **Heavy Tank M6**
TYPE: **Heavy Tank**
LENGTH: **24.75 ft (7.54 m)**
WIDTH: **10.16 ft (3.09 m)**
HEIGHT: **9.8 ft (2.98 m)**
WEIGHT: **126,500 lb (57,500 kg)**
CREW: **6**
MAIN ARMAMENT: **1 x 3in, 1 x 37mm**

SECONDARY ARMAMENT: **4 x .5in**
ENGINE: **Wright G-200 800 hp**
RANGE: **unknown**
SPEED: **22 mph (35.2 km/h)**
FORDING: **3.3 ft (1.01 m)**
TRENCH CROSSING: **10 ft (3.04 m)**
ARMOR (HULL): **1 in (25.4 mm)**
ARMOR (TURRET): **3.25 in (82.55 mm)**

The Joseph Stalin series of heavy tanks was a development of the basic KV heavy tank, which the Red Army had wanted to give it superiority over the best German tanks then in service. The same engine was used as in the KV series, but with a synchromesh transmission and regenerative steering to simplify driving and increase maneuverability. The idlers, sprockets, and return rollers of the chassis were lowered to allow the superstructure to overhang the tracks and thus accommodate the larger turret. Hull shape was improved to increase protection, and the tank mounted the 85mm tank gun in a three-man turret. This version was known as the IS-1A, but was soon replaced by the IS-1B, which mounted the 100mm gun. In early 1944, the IS-2 appeared, which was armed with the 122mm gun. The armor-piercing round it fired could penetrate 7.5 in (185 mm) of armor at 3,280 ft (1,000 m). Joseph Stalin tanks were at the head of the advance to Berlin in 1945 and remained in production after the war. The model remained the most powerful tank in service in the world for well over a decade.

IS-2 JOSEPH STALIN

DESIGNATION: **IS-2**
TYPE: **Heavy Tank**
LENGTH: **27.3 ft (8.32 m)**
WIDTH: **10.13 ft (3.09 m)**
HEIGHT: **8.9 ft (2.73 m)**
WEIGHT: **101,200 lb (46,000 kg)**
CREW: **4**
MAIN ARMAMENT: **122mm**
SECONDARY ARMAMENT:
4 x 7.62mm
ENGINE: **V-2-IS V-12 diesel 600 hp**
RANGE: **149 miles (240 km)**
SPEED: **23 mph (37 km/h)**
FORDING: **unknown**
TRENCH CROSSING: **8.16 ft (2.49 m)**
ARMOR (HULL): **4.72 in (120 mm)**
ARMOR (TURRET): **5.19 in (132 mm)**

KV-1

DESIGNATION: **KV-1**
TYPE: **Heavy Tank**
LENGTH: **21.9 ft (6.68 m)**
WIDTH: **10.89 ft (3.32 m)**
HEIGHT: **8.75 ft (2.71 m)**
WEIGHT: **94,600 lb (43,000 kg)**
CREW: **5**
MAIN ARMAMENT: **76.2mm**
SECONDARY ARMAMENT:
3 x 7.62mm
ENGINE: **V-2K V-12 diesel 600 hp**
RANGE: **93.2 miles (150 km)**
SPEED: **21.75 mph (35 km/h)**
FORDING: **unknown**
TRENCH CROSSING: **unknown**
ARMOR (HULL): **1.18 in (30 mm)**
ARMOR (TURRET): **4.72 in (120 mm)**

KV-2

DESIGNATION: **KV-2**
TYPE: **Heavy Assault Tank**
LENGTH: **22.3 ft (6.79 m)**
WIDTH: **10.89 ft (3.32 m)**
HEIGHT: **12 ft (3.65 m)**
WEIGHT: **118,720 lb (53,963 kg)**
CREW: **6**
MAIN ARMAMENT: **152mm**
SECONDARY ARMAMENT:
2 x 7.62mm
ENGINE: **V-2K V-12 diesel 600 hp**
RANGE: **87.5 miles (140 km)**
SPEED: **16 mph (25.6 km/h)**
FORDING: **unknown**
TRENCH CROSSING: **8.5 ft (2.59 m)**
ARMOR (HULL): **1.18 in (30 mm)**
ARMOR (TURRET): **4.33 in (110 mm)**

SELF-PROPELLED GUNS

Artillery mounted on tracked chassis gave armies highly mobile fire support units that could keep up with tanks and wheeled vehicles.

The Grille was first ordered for construction on the new self-propelled gun chassis that BMM was developing, the resultant vehicle being designated Sf 38(t) Ausf K. However, wartime demands resulted in Panzer 38(t)s being used instead, being converted by BMM as they returned from the front for refits. A total of 90 were produced between February and April 1943. Grilles were issued to the heavy infantry assault gun companies of panzergrenadier regiments, serving in Russia, Tunisia, Italy, and France from early 1943. In June 1944, at the time of the D-Day landings, the Grille was still in service in Normandy. The Praga EPA/2 engine had five forward gears and one reverse, and gave a top speed of 21.87 mph (35 km/h). As with most infantry assault guns, the crew were housed in an open superstructure, though the provision of an MG34 machine gun gave them some protection from enemy infantry antitank squads.

GRILLE

DESIGNATION: SdKfz 138/1
TYPE: SP Heavy Infantry Gun
LENGTH: 14 ft (4.61 m)
WIDTH: 7.08 ft (2.16 m)
HEIGHT: 7.87 ft (2.4 m)
WEIGHT: 25,760 lb (11,709 kg)
CREW: 5
MAIN ARMAMENT: 150mm
SECONDARY ARMAMENT:
1 x 7.92mm
ENGINE: Praga EPA/2
RANGE: 115.6 miles (185 km)
SPEED: 21.87 mph (35 km/h)
FORDING: 3 ft (.9 m)
TRENCH CROSSING: 6.13 ft
(1.87 m)
ARMOR (HULL): 1.96 in (50 mm)
ARMOR (TURRET): .98 in (25 mm)

HUMMEL

DESIGNATION: SdKfz 165
TYPE: SP Heavy Howitzer
LENGTH: 23.52 ft (7.17 m)
WIDTH: 9.41 ft (2.87 m)
HEIGHT: 9.23 ft (2.81 m)
WEIGHT: 53,760 lb (24,436 kg)
CREW: 5
MAIN ARMAMENT: 150mm
SECONDARY ARMAMENT:
1 x 7.92mm
ENGINE: HL 120TRM
RANGE: 134.4 miles (215 km)
SPEED: 26.25 mph (42 km/h)
FORDING: 3.25 ft (1 m)
TRENCH CROSSING: 7.25 ft (2.2m)
ARMOR (HULL): 1.18 in (30 mm)
ARMOR (TURRET): .39 in (10 mm)

SIG33

DESIGNATION: sIG33 (SF)
TYPE: SP Heavy Infantry Gun
LENGTH: 15.32 ft (4.67 m)
WIDTH: 7.05 ft (2.15 m)
HEIGHT: 9.18 ft (2.8 m)
WEIGHT: 19,040 lb (8,654 kg)
CREW: 4
MAIN ARMAMENT: 150mm
SECONDARY ARMAMENT: none
ENGINE: Maybach NL38TR
RANGE: 87 miles (140 km)
SPEED: 25 mph (40 km/h)
FORDING: 3 ft (.9 m)
TRENCH CROSSING: 5.74 ft (1.75 m)
ARMOR (HULL): .51 in (13 mm)
ARMOR (SUPERSTRUCTURE): .51 in
(13 mm)

This self-propelled gun mounted the 75mm cannon, and was useful in tank-versus-tank actions. However, it proved inadequate against T-34s and KV-1s on the Eastern Front. The M40 did prove useful in North Africa against light British tanks, and was still being used there in early 1943.

SEMOVENTE M40/41

DESIGNATION:
Semovente M40/41
TYPE: Self-propelled
Gun
LENGTH: 16.1 ft
(4.91 m)
WIDTH: 7.48 ft (2.28 m)
HEIGHT: 6.06 ft (1.85 m)
WEIGHT: 30,016 lb
(13,643 kg)
CREW: 3
MAIN ARMAMENT:
75mm
SECONDARY ARMAMENT:
none
ENGINE: 87.5 miles
(140 km)
RANGE: 93.75 miles
(150 km)
SPEED: 21.25 mph
(34 km/h)
FORDING: 3.25 ft (1 m)
TRENCH CROSSING:
6.88 ft (2.1 m)
ARMOR (HULL): .55 in
(14 mm)
ARMOR (TURRET):
1.18 in (30 mm)

CRUISER TANKS

Prior to World War II, the British Army saw the tank's main role as infantry support, as demonstrated by the heavily armored Matilda I, which only had a machine gun and low speed. However, the Tank Corps insisted that it also be equipped with fast moving, light tanks, which could strike at the enemy's rear. These became known as "Cruiser Tanks," so called because they undertook a similar role to the cruisers in the Royal Navy.

CENTURION

DESIGNATION: Cruiser Tank Centurion
TYPE: Heavy Cruiser Tank
LENGTH: 12.16 ft (7.66 m)
WIDTH: 11.12 ft (3.39 m)
HEIGHT: 9.6 ft (2.92 m)
WEIGHT: 113,792 lb (51,723 kg)
CREW: 4
MAIN ARMAMENT: 17pdr
SECONDARY ARMAMENT: 2 x 7.92mm
ENGINE: Meteor 620 hp
RANGE: 127 miles (205 km)
SPEED: 21.4 mph (32.24 km/h)
FORDING: 4.75 ft (1.45 m)
TRENCH CROSSING: 11 ft (3.35 m)
ARMOR (HULL): .97 in (51 mm)
ARMOR (TURRET): 5.98 in (152 mm)

COMET

DESIGNATION: Cruiser Tank Comet
TYPE: Heavy Cruiser Tank
LENGTH: 25.1 ft (7.65 m)
WIDTH: 10 ft (3.04 m)
HEIGHT: 8.75 ft (2.66 m)
WEIGHT: 72,800 lb (33,090 kg)
CREW: 5
MAIN ARMAMENT: 77mm
SECONDARY ARMAMENT: 2 x 7.92mm
ENGINE: Meteor 600 hp
RANGE: 156.25 miles (250 km)
SPEED: 29 mph (46 km/h)
FORDING: 4 ft (1.12 m)
TRENCH CROSSING: 7.5 ft (2.28 m)
ARMOR (HULL): .98 in (25 mm)
ARMOR (TURRET): 3.97 in (101 mm)

CROMWELL

DESIGNATION: Cruiser Tank Mk VIII
TYPE: Cruiser Tank
LENGTH: 20.8 ft (6.33 m)
WIDTH: 10 ft (3.04 m)
HEIGHT: 8.2 ft (2.5 m)
WEIGHT: 67,720 lb (28,509 kg)
CREW: 5
MAIN ARMAMENT: 75mm
SECONDARY ARMAMENT: 1 x 7.92mm
ENGINE: Meteor 600 hp
RANGE: 173 miles (278 km)
SPEED: 40 mph (64 km/h)
FORDING: 4 ft (1.21 m)
TRENCH CROSSING: 7.5 ft (2.28 m)
ARMOR (HULL): .31 in (8 mm)
ARMOR (TURRET): 2.99 in (76 mm)

CROMWELL MK VI

DESIGNATION: Cruiser Tank Mk VI
TYPE: Cruiser Tank
LENGTH: 20.8 ft (6.33 m)
WIDTH: 10 ft (3.04 m)
HEIGHT: 8.2 ft (2.5 m)
WEIGHT: 67,720 lb (28,509 kg)
CREW: 5
MAIN ARMAMENT: 95mm
SECONDARY ARMAMENT: 1 x 7.92mm
ENGINE: Meteor 600 hp
RANGE: 156.25 miles (250 km)
SPEED: 40 mph (64 km/h)
FORDING: 4 ft (1.21 m)
TRENCH CROSSING: 7.5 ft (2.28 m)
ARMOR (HULL): .31 in (8 mm)
ARMOR (TURRET): 2.99 in (76 mm)

CHALLENGER

DESIGNATION: Cruiser Tank Challenger
TYPE: Cruiser Tank
LENGTH: 26.3 ft (8 m)
WIDTH: 9.5 ft (2.89 m)
HEIGHT: 8.75 ft (2.66 m)
WEIGHT: 71,680 lb (32,581 kg)
CREW: 5
MAIN ARMAMENT: 17pdr
SECONDARY ARMAMENT: 1 x 7.92mm
ENGINE: Meteor 600 hp
RANGE: 162.5 miles (260 km)
SPEED: 32 mph (51 km/h)
FORDING: 4 ft (1.21 m)
TRENCH CROSSING: 7.5 ft (2.28 m)
ARMOR (HULL): .78 in (20 mm)
ARMOR (TURRET): 4 in (102 mm)

By the time of the Allied invasion of France in June 1944, the Cromwell (see page 215) was the most important British tank in service, yet it was still under-armed when compared to the German Panthers and Tigers. Nevertheless, it was fast and reliable and, by equipping their armored reconnaissance units with Cromwells, the British in effect added an extra medium tank battalion to their armored divisions. Fast the Cromwell may have been, but when it came to tank-versus-tank action it suffered alarmingly. An example was Operation Goodwood,

launched in Normandy in July 1944, during which an estimated 1,350 British tanks faced 400 German armored vehicles in a desperate battle. What followed has been described as a "tactical holocaust", and indeed losses were fearful. German tanks, firing from good positions at optimum ranges, destroyed 300 British tanks in 72 hours. The Cromwell had been produced in large numbers, with manufacture beginning in 1943, and, despite its shortcomings, the Cromwell VI and VIII remained in British Army service until the 1950s.

CRUISER TANK MK I

DESIGNATION: Cruiser Tank Mk I (A9)
TYPE: Cruiser Tank
LENGTH: 19.25 ft (5.86 m)
WIDTH: 8.33 ft (2.53 m)
HEIGHT: 8.3 ft (2.52 m)
WEIGHT: 26,880 lb (12,218 kg)
CREW: 6
MAIN ARMAMENT: 2pdr
SECONDARY ARMAMENT: 3 x .330in
ENGINE: AEG 150 hp
RANGE: 131.25 miles (210 km)
SPEED: 25 mph (40 km/h)
FORDING: 3 ft (.9 m)
TRENCH CROSSING: 7.41 ft (2.26 m)
ARMOR (HULL): .23 in (6 mm)
ARMOR (TURRET): .55 in (14 mm)

CRUISER TANK MK IV

DESIGNATION: Cruiser Tank Mk IV
TYPE: Cruiser Tank
LENGTH: 19.75 ft (6 m)
WIDTH: 8.33 ft (2.53 m)
HEIGHT: 8.5 ft (2.59 m)
WEIGHT: 31,360 lb (14,254 kg)
CREW: 4
MAIN ARMAMENT: 2pdr
SECONDARY ARMAMENT: 1 x .303in
ENGINE: Liberty 340 hp
RANGE: 144 miles (232 km)
SPEED: 30 mph (48 km/h)
FORDING: 3 ft (.9 m)
TRENCH CROSSING: 7.41 ft (2.26 m)
ARMOR (HULL): .23 in (6 mm)
ARMOR (TURRET): 1.18 in (30 mm)

CRUISER TANK MK V

DESIGNATION: Cruiser Tank Mk V
TYPE: Cruiser Tank
LENGTH: 19 ft (5.79 m)
WIDTH: 8.6 ft (2.62 m)
HEIGHT: 7.3 ft (2.22 m)
WEIGHT: 40,320 lb (18,327 kg)
CREW: 4
MAIN ARMAMENT: 2pdr
SECONDARY ARMAMENT: 1 x 7.92mm
ENGINE: Meadows Flat-12 300 hp
RANGE: 125 miles (200 km)
SPEED: 31 mph (50 km/h)
FORDING: 3.25 ft (1 m)
TRENCH CROSSING: 4.98 ft (1.52 m)
ARMOR (HULL): .27 in (7 mm)
ARMOR (TURRET): 1.57 in (40 mm)

CRUISER TANK MK VII

DESIGNATION: Cruiser Tank Mk VII
TYPE: Cruiser Tank
LENGTH: 19.8 ft (6.33 m)
WIDTH: 9.5 ft (2.89 m)
HEIGHT: 8 ft (2.4 m)
WEIGHT: 59,360 lb (26,981 kg)
CREW: 5
MAIN ARMAMENT: 6pdr
SECONDARY ARMAMENT: 2 x 7.92mm
ENGINE: Liberty 410 hp
RANGE: 125 miles (200 km)
SPEED: 24 mph (38.4 km/h)
FORDING: 3.25 ft (1 m)
TRENCH CROSSING: 8.49 ft (2.59 m)
ARMOR (HULL): .78 in (20 mm)
ARMOR (TURRET): 3 in (76 mm)

CRUSADER III

DESIGNATION: Cruiser Tank Mk VI
TYPE: Cruiser Tank
LENGTH: 19.68 ft (6 m)
WIDTH: 8.66 ft (2.64 m)
HEIGHT: 7.31 ft (2.23 m)
WEIGHT: 44,147 lb (20,067 kg)
CREW: 3
MAIN ARMAMENT: 6pdr
SECONDARY ARMAMENT: 2 x 7.92mm
ENGINE: Nuffield Liberty 340 hp
RANGE: 127 miles (204 km)
SPEED: 31 mph (50 km/h)
FORDING: 3.25 ft (1 m)
TRENCH CROSSING: 8.49 ft (2.59 m)
ARMOR (HULL): .27 in (7 mm)
ARMOR (TURRET): 1.57 in (40 mm)

TANK DESTROYERS

Antitank vehicles made their first major appearance in World War II. In German designs, the turret was removed from an existing tank design, and a larger gun was mounted with a limited traverse in the hull. The weight and space savings of removing the turret allowed a smaller chassis to carry a larger gun. In U.S. designs, the turret was retained, but left open on top for more working room with the larger gun. The larger guns required a weight to be added to the rear of the turret, which could be seen on designs such as the M10.

The Jagdpanther was one of the finest tank destroyers of the war. The first vehicles were issued to the 559th and 654th Antitank Battalions, though only the 654th received the full complement of 42 vehicles. The largest assembly of Jagdpanthers took place during the Ardennes Offensive in 1944. Thereafter they were issued to the tank detachments of at least seven panzer divisions. In total, 392 were built between January 1944 and March 1945.

JAGDPANTHER

DESIGNATION: SdKfz 173
TYPE: Heavy Tank Destroyer
LENGTH: 32.8 ft (9.9 m)
WIDTH: 10.72 ft (3.27 m)
HEIGHT: 8.92 ft (2.72 m)
WEIGHT: 103,040 lb (46,836 kg)
CREW: 5
MAIN ARMAMENT: 88mm
SECONDARY ARMAMENT: 1 x 7.92mm
ENGINE: Maybach HL230P30
RANGE: 100 miles (160 km)
SPEED: 28.75 mph (46 km/h)
FORDING: 5.57 ft (1.7 m)
TRENCH CROSSING: 6.23 ft (1.9 m)
ARMOR (HULL): 2.36 in (60 mm)
ARMOR (TURRET): 3.14 in (80 mm)

MARDER II

DESIGNATION: SdKfz 131
TYPE: SP Antitank Gun
LENGTH: 20.86 ft (6.36 m)
WIDTH: 7.48 ft (2.28 m)
HEIGHT: 7.21 ft (2.2 m)
WEIGHT: 24,192 lb (10,996 kg)
CREW: 3
MAIN ARMAMENT: 75mm
SECONDARY ARMAMENT: 1 x 7.92mm
ENGINE: Maybach HL62TRM
RANGE: 118.7 miles (190 km)
SPEED: 25 mph (40 km/h)
FORDING: 2.78 ft (.85 m)
TRENCH CROSSING: 5.74 ft (1.75 m)
ARMOR (HULL): 1.37 in (35 mm)
ARMOR (SUPERSTRUCTURE): 1.18 in (30 mm)

MARDER III

DESIGNATION: SdKfz 138
TYPE: SP Antitank Gun
LENGTH: 16.24 ft (4.95 m)
WIDTH: 7.05 ft (2.15 m)
HEIGHT: 8.13 ft (2.48 m)
WEIGHT: 23,520 lb (10,691 kg)
CREW: 4
MAIN ARMAMENT: 75mm
SECONDARY ARMAMENT: 1 x 7.92mm
ENGINE: Praga AC
RANGE: 118.75 miles (190 km)
SPEED: 26.25 mph (42 km/h)
FORDING: 3 ft (.9 m)
TRENCH CROSSING: 6.13 ft (1.87 m)
ARMOR (HULL): .78 in (20 mm)
ARMOR (SUPERSTRUCTURE): .39 in (10 mm)

NASHORN

DESIGNATION: SdKfz 164
TYPE: SP Heavy Antitank Gun
LENGTH: 27.69 ft (8.44 m)
WIDTH: 9.38 ft (2.86 m)
HEIGHT: 8.69 ft (2.65 m)
WEIGHT: 53,760 lb (24,436 kg)
CREW: 4
MAIN ARMAMENT: 88mm
SECONDARY ARMAMENT: 1 x 7.92mm
ENGINE: Maybach HL120TRM
RANGE: 118.7 miles (190 km)
SPEED: 26 mph (42km/h)
FORDING: 2.62 ft (.8 m)
TRENCH CROSSING: 7.54 ft (2.3 m)
ARMOR (HULL): 1.18 in (30 mm)
ARMOR (SUPERSTRUCTURE): .39 in (10 mm)

With the capture of so many vehicles following the fall of France in June 1940, the Germans set about converting them for their own use. This was not an immediate decision, as the army was flushed with victory and few believed that large numbers of non-German fighting vehicles would be needed. It was only with the huge losses experienced on the Eastern Front, plus the appearance of the Soviet T-34 tank, that prompted the necessity for large numbers of antitank platforms. One such vehicle was the PaK40 (SF), a self-propelled antitank gun on a light tank chassis. The conversion was unusual in that the engine was left in the rear. The superstructure and engine cover were removed and a new plate for the driver was fitted as part of the new self-propelled gun conversion. The numbers converted were not great: a total of 24 were modified to carry the 75mm gun, while a further 48 were modified to mount the larger 105mm gun. In both models, the gun had a traverse of 30 degrees to the left and right. These self-propelled armored fighting vehicles were assigned to the 8th Panzerartillerie Abteilung serving in France, and they saw action following the Allied D-Day landings in Normandy in June 1944.

PAK 40 (SF)

DESIGNATION: **Geschützwagen 39H(f)**
TYPE: **SP Antitank Gun**
LENGTH: **17.42 ft (5.31 m)**
WIDTH: **6 ft (1.83 m)**
HEIGHT: **7.31 ft (2.23 m)**
WEIGHT: **19,017 lb (8,644 kg)**
CREW: **4**
MAIN ARMAMENT: **75mm**
SECONDARY ARMAMENT:
1 x 7.92mm
ENGINE: **Hotchkiss six-cylinder**
RANGE: **93.75 miles (150 km)**
SPEED: **22.5 mph (36 km/h)**
FORDING: **2.62 ft (.8 m)**
TRENCH CROSSING: **5.25 ft (1.6 m)**
ARMOR (HULL): **1.18 in (30 mm)**
ARMOR (SUPERSTRUCTURE):
1.18 in (30 mm)

PANZERJÄGER

DESIGNATION: **Panzerjäger**
TYPE: **SP Antitank Gun**
LENGTH: **14.5 ft (4.42 m)**
WIDTH: **6.75 ft (2.06 m)**
HEIGHT: **7.38 ft (2.25 m)**
WEIGHT: **14,336 lb (6,516 kg)**
CREW: **3**
MAIN ARMAMENT: **47mm**
SECONDARY ARMAMENT: **none**
ENGINE: **Maybach NL38TR**
RANGE: **87 miles (140 km)**
SPEED: **25 mph (40 km/h)**
FORDING: **2.78 ft (.85 m)**
TRENCH CROSSING: **5.74 ft (1.75 m)**
ARMOR (HULL): **.51 in (13 mm)**
ARMOR (SUPERSTRUCTURE):
.51 in (13 mm)

PANZERJÄGER 38(T)

DESIGNATION: **Marder III**
TYPE: **SP Antitank Gun**
LENGTH: **19.19 ft (5.85 m)**
WIDTH: **7.08 ft (2.16 m)**
HEIGHT: **8.2 ft (2.5 m)**
WEIGHT: **23,900 lb (10,864 kg)**
CREW: **4**
MAIN ARMAMENT: **76.2mm**
SECONDARY ARMAMENT:
1 x 7.92mm
ENGINE: **Praga EPA**
RANGE: **116 miles (185 km)**
SPEED: **26.25 mph (42 km/h)**
FORDING: **3 ft (.9 m)**
TRENCH CROSSING: **6.13 ft (1.87 m)**
ARMOR (HULL): **1.96 in (50 mm)**
ARMOR (TURRET): **1.96 in (50 mm)**

Production of the M10 began in September 1942 and ended by December of the same year. By then, 7,000 vehicles had been produced. In the field, the concept of separate tank-destroyer battalions proved ineffective, and so most M10s were used for offensive purposes to support attacks. The M10 continued in service until the end of the war, but by then had become obsolete.

TANK DESTROYER M10

DESIGNATION: **Gun Motor Carriage M10**
TYPE: **Tank Destroyer**
LENGTH: **22.5 ft (6.83 m)**
WIDTH: **10 ft (3.05 m)**
HEIGHT: **8.4 ft (2.57 m)**
WEIGHT: **65,861 lb (29,937 kg)**
CREW: **5**
MAIN ARMAMENT: **76mm**
SECONDARY ARMAMENT: **1 x .5in**
ENGINE: **General Motors 375 hp x 2**
RANGE: **200 miles (322 km)**
SPEED: **32 mph (51 km/h)**
FORDING: **3 ft (.9 m)**
TRENCH CROSSING: **7.5 ft (2.26 m)**
ARMOR (HULL): **.47 in (12 mm)**
ARMOR (TURRET): **1.46 in (37 mm)**

INFANTRY TANKS

The Infantry Tank came about as a result of a 1934 requirement by the British General Staff for a tank that would directly support an infantry attack. Armament would consist of a machine gun and the tank would have a speed of 15 mph (24 km/h).

In North Africa, the Afrika Korps captured many British armored vehicles. One such vehicle was the Matilda tank, which in German use was designated Infanterie Panzerkampfwagen Mk II 748(e).

PZKPFW MKII 748 (E)

DESIGNATION: **PzKpfw Mk II 748 (E)**
TYPE: **Infantry Tank**
LENGTH: **18.5 ft (5.63 m)**
WIDTH: **8.5 ft (2.59 m)**
HEIGHT: **8 ft (2.44 m)**
WEIGHT: **59,360 lb (26,981 kg)**
CREW: **4**
MAIN ARMAMENT: **2pdr**
SECONDARY ARMAMENT: **1 x 7.92mm**
ENGINE: **Leyland diesel 190 hp**
RANGE: **160 miles (257 km)**
SPEED: **15 mph (24 km/h)**
FORDING: **3 ft (.9 m)**
TRENCH CROSSING: **7 ft (2.13 m)**
ARMOR (HULL): **.78 in (20 mm)**
ARMOR (TURRET): **3 in (78 mm)**

Originally, the Churchill was intended to fight on the Western Front, which, at the outbreak of World War II, was envisaged as being similar to the conditions experienced in World War I. First production models were delivered in 1941, but they were plagued by mechanical faults. Nevertheless, the Churchill became one of the most successful British tank designs of the war. It served in many roles, including close-support, anti-mine vehicle and flamethrower. The first models were armed with a two-pounder or six-pounder gun, but later Churchills carried a 75mm gun. The Churchill Crocodile was a Mk VII tank armed with a 75mm gun and a flame projector. It towed an armored trailer containing fuel for the flame projector. If set on fire, the trailer could be jettisoned by a quick-release gear.

CHURCHILL

DESIGNATION: **Infantry Tank Mk IV**
TYPE: **Infantry Tank**
LENGTH: **24.5 ft (7.46 m)**
WIDTH: **7.97 ft (2.43 m)**
HEIGHT: **9 ft (2.74 m)**
WEIGHT: **40,727 kg (89,600 lb)**
CREW: **5**
MAIN ARMAMENT: **75mm**
SECONDARY ARMAMENT: **2 x 7.92mm**
ENGINE: **Bedford 350 hp**
RANGE: **90 miles (145 km)**
SPEED: **15.5 mph (24.8 km/h)**
FORDING: **3.31 ft (1.01 m)**
TRENCH CROSSING: **10 ft (3.04 m)**
ARMOR (HULL): **.98 in (25 mm)**
ARMOR (TURRET): **4 in (102 mm)**

INFANTRY TANK MK II

DESIGNATION: **Infantry Tank Mk II**
TYPE: **Infantry Tank**
LENGTH: **18.5 ft (5.63 m)**
WIDTH: **8.5 ft (2.59 m)**
HEIGHT: **8 ft (2.44 m)**
WEIGHT: **59,360 lb (26,981 kg)**
CREW: **4**
MAIN ARMAMENT: **2pdr**
SECONDARY ARMAMENT: **1 x 7.92mm**
ENGINE: **Leyland diesel 190 hp**
RANGE: **160 miles (257 km)**
SPEED: **15 mph (24 km/h)**
FORDING: **3 ft (.9 m)**
TRENCH CROSSING: **7 ft (2.13 m)**
ARMOR (HULL): **.78 in (20 mm)**
ARMOR (TURRET): **3 in (78 mm)**

VALENTINE II

DESIGNATION: **Infantry Tank Mk III**
TYPE: **Infantry Tank**
LENGTH: **17.75 ft (5.41 m)**
WIDTH: **8.59 ft (2.62 m)**
HEIGHT: **7.5 ft (2.28 m)**
WEIGHT: **38,080 lb (17,309 kg)**
CREW: **3**
MAIN ARMAMENT: **2pdr**
SECONDARY ARMAMENT: **1 x 7.92mm**
ENGINE: **GM diesel 138 hp**
RANGE: **90 miles (145 km)**
SPEED: **15 mph (24 km/h)**
FORDING: **3 ft (.9 m)**
TRENCH CROSSING: **7.48 ft (2.28 m)**
ARMOR (HULL): **.31 in (8 mm)**
ARMOR (TURRET): **2.55 in (65 mm)**

ASSAULT GUNS

The German StuG III assault gun was an effective weapon/vehicle combination. Relatively cheap to build, over 7,700 were manufactured. Originally designed for infantry support, the up-gunned versions were used in an antitank role.

The Sturmpanzer IV (Brummbär) carried the 150mm StuH43 gun on a standard Panzer IV chassis. Production began in April 1943, and the first units were issued to Sturmpanzer Abteilung 216 prior to the Kursk Offensive in July. A further three Sturmpanzer Abteilungs were raised, and saw service on the Eastern Front, as well as in the West and in Italy.

BRUMMBÄR

DESIGNATION: **StuG IV 15cm StuH43**
TYPE: **Assault Infantry Gun**
LENGTH: **19.45 ft (5.93 m)**
WIDTH: **9.44 ft (2.88 m)**
HEIGHT: **8.26 ft (2.52 m)**
WEIGHT: **63,168 lb (28,712 kg)**
CREW: **5**
MAIN ARMAMENT: **150mm**
SECONDARY ARMAMENT: **2 x 7.92mm**
ENGINE: **Maybach HL120TRM**
RANGE: **131 miles (210 km)**
SPEED: **28.12 mph (45 km/h))**
FORDING: **3.25 ft (1 m)**
TRENCH CROSSING: **7.25 ft (2.2 m)**
ARMOR (HULL): **3.14 in (80 mm)**
ARMOR (TURRET): **3.93 in (100 mm)**

STUG III AUSF B

DESIGNATION: **SdKfz 142**
TYPE: **Assault Gun**
LENGTH: **17.71 ft (5.4 m)**
WIDTH: **9.67 ft (2.95 m)**
HEIGHT: **6.49 ft (1.98 m)**
WEIGHT: **45,248 lb (20,567 kg)**
CREW: **4**
MAIN ARMAMENT: **75mm**
SECONDARY ARMAMENT: **none**
ENGINE: **Maybach HL120TRM**
RANGE: **100 miles (160 km)**
SPEED: **25 mph (40 km/h)**
FORDING: **2.62 ft (.8 m)**
TRENCH CROSSING: **8.49 ft (2.59 m)**
ARMOR (HULL): **1.96 in (50 mm)**
ARMOR (SUPERSTRUCTURE): **1.96 in (50 mm)**

STUG III AUSF G

DESIGNATION: **SdKfz 142/1**
TYPE: **Assault Gun**
LENGTH: **22.21 ft (6.77 m)**
WIDTH: **9.67 ft (2.95 m)**
HEIGHT: **7.08 ft (2.16 m)**
WEIGHT: **53,536 lb (24,334 kg)**
CREW: **4**
MAIN ARMAMENT: **75mm**
SECONDARY ARMAMENT: **2 x 7.92mm**
ENGINE: **Maybach HL120TRM**
RANGE: **97 miles (155 km)**
SPEED: **25 mph (40 km/h)**
FORDING: **2.62 ft (.8 m)**
TRENCH CROSSING: **8.49 ft (2.59 m)**
ARMOR (HULL): **3.14 in (80 mm)**
ARMOR (SUPERSTRUCTURE): **3.14 in (80 mm)**

MINE EXPLODER

The problem of having to deal with enemy mines resulted in a number of special variants of the Sherman tank. The T3 mine exploder was based on the British Scorpion flail device. It consisted of two booms extending forward from the tank with a rotating shaft fitted with chains to beat the ground as the tank advanced.

MINE EXPLODER T3

DESIGNATION: **Mine Exploder T3**
TYPE: **Anti-mine Tank**
LENGTH: **27 ft (8.23 m)**
WIDTH: **11.48 ft (3.5 m)**
HEIGHT: **9 ft (2.74 m)**
WEIGHT: **70,000 lb (31,818 kg)**
CREW: **5**
MAIN ARMAMENT: **75mm**
SECONDARY ARMAMENT: **2 x .3in. 1 x .5in**
ENGINE: **Ford GAA V-8 500 hp**
RANGE: **100 miles (160 km)**
SPEED: **28.75 mph (46 km/h)**
FORDING: **3 ft (.9 m)**
TRENCH CROSSING: **7.5 ft (2.26 m)**
ARMOR (HULL): **1 in (25.4 mm)**
ARMOR (TURRET): **2.99 in (76 mm)**

In World War II, flamethrower tanks were valuable for their ability to deal with enemy bunkers. The German Army converted a number of StuGs to flamethrowers. Of the 220 StuGs delivered in June 1943, 10 were converted as flamethrowers.

STUG (F1)

DESIGNATION: StuG (FI)
TYPE: **Flamethrower**
LENGTH: **18.11 ft (5.52 m)**
WIDTH: **9.67 ft (2.95 m)**
HEIGHT: **7 ft (2.16 m)**
WEIGHT: **51,520 lb (23,418 kg)**
CREW: **4**

MAIN ARMAMENT:
14mm Flammenwerfer
SECONDARY ARMAMENT:
1 x 7.92mm
ENGINE: **Maybach HL120TRM**
RANGE: **97 miles (155 km)**
SPEED: **25 mph**

(40 km/h)
FORDING: **2.62 ft (.8 m)**
TRENCH CROSSING:
8.49 ft (2.59 m)
ARMOR (HULL): **50 mm (1.96 in)**
ARMOR (SUPERSTRUCTURE):
1.96 in (50 mm)

The L35/Lf was a flamethrower conversion that towed a 1,100 lb (500 kg) armored fuel trailer, while the flame gun was mounted in the hull, replacing the machine guns. On some later vehicles, the fuel tank was mounted on the rear superstructure.

L 35/LF

DESIGNATION: **Carro Armato L35/Lf**
TYPE: **Flamethrower**
LENGTH: **10.4 ft (3.16 m)**
WIDTH: **5.6 ft (1.7 m)**
HEIGHT: **4.25 ft (1.29 m)**
WEIGHT: **7,056 lb**

(3,207 kg)
CREW: **2**
MAIN ARMAMENT:
Flame Gun
SECONDARY ARMAMENT:
none
ENGINE: **20 hp**
RANGE: **93.75 miles (150 km)**

SPEED: **26 mph (41.6 km/h)**
FORDING: **1.64 ft (.5m)**
TRENCH CROSSING:
4.59 ft (1.4 m)
ARMOR (HULL): **.59 in (15 mm)**
ARMOR (TURRET): **.19 in (5 mm)**

Flamethrowers exert a powerful psychological effect on an enemy. It was therefore logical that the Americans should develop a flamethrower version of their main battle tank. The M4-3 was a standard Sherman that could be fitted with a flamethrower kit.

FLAME THROWER

DESIGNATION:
Flamethrower Tank
TYPE: **Medium Tank**
LENGTH: **19.66 ft (6 m)**
WIDTH: **8.53 ft (2.6 m)**
HEIGHT: **9 ft (2.74 m)**
WEIGHT: **68,500 lb**

(31,136 kg)
CREW: **5**
MAIN ARMAMENT: **75mm**
SECONDARY ARMAMENT:
2 x .3in, 1 x .5in
ENGINE: **Ford GAA-III 500 hp**
RANGE: **100 miles (160 km)**

SPEED: **25 mph (40 km/h)**
FORDING: **3 ft (.9 m)**
TRENCH CROSSING:
7.41 ft (2.26 m)
ARMOR (HULL): **1 in (25.4 mm)**
ARMOR (TURRET): **2 in (50.8 mm)**

The T-33 had a single propeller and rudder fitted on the rear hull, with a power takeoff from the engine for the propeller. Encased in sheet metal, balsa-wood floats were fitted in the form of trackguards to provide additional buoyancy to the watertight hull.

T-33

DESIGNATION: **T-33**
TYPE: **Amphibious Tank**
LENGTH: **12.23 ft (3.73 m)**
WIDTH: **6.26 ft (1.94 m)**
HEIGHT: **6.03 ft (1.84 m)**
WEIGHT: **7,150 lb**

(3,250 kg)
CREW: **2**
MAIN ARMAMENT:
1 x 7.62mm
SECONDARY ARMAMENT: **none**
ENGINE: **GAZ-AA 70 hp**
RANGE: **115.6 miles (185 km)**

SPEED: **21.82 mph (35 km/h)**
FORDING: **Amphibious**
TRENCH CROSSING:
unknown
ARMOR (HULL): **.15 in (4 mm)**
ARMOR (TURRET): **.35 in (9 mm)**

FIELD GUNS

Field artillery served a vital role in World War II. Areas could be softened up before an attack or, when the artillery moved and set up in stages to keep the frontline within range, field gun fire could be called in at any time by troops to offer support.

CANON DE 75 1897

TYPE: **Light Towed Field Gun**
CALIBER: **75mm**
VEHICLE LENGTH: n/a
LENGTH OF BARREL: **101.85 in (2.587 m)**
WEIGHT TRAVELLING: **4,344 lb (1,970 kg)**
WEIGHT IN ACTION: **2,514 lb (1,140 kg)**
ELEVATION ARC: **-11° to +18°**
TRAVERSE ARC: **6°**
EFFECTIVE CEILING: n/a
ROAD RANGE: n/a
RANGE: **12,140 yards (11,100 m)**
PROJECTILE WEIGHT: **13.66 lb (6.195 kg)**
ARMOR: n/a
ENGINE: n/a
MUZZLE VELOCITY: **1,886 fps (575 mps)**
SPEED: n/a

CANON DE 155 G.P. PUISSANCE

TYPE: **Heavy Towed Gun**
CALIBER: **155mm**
VEHICLE LENGTH: n/a
LENGTH OF BARREL: **225.4 in (5.725 m)**
WEIGHT TRAVELLING: **25,794 lb (11,700 kg)**
WEIGHT IN ACTION: **23,700 lb (10,750 kg)**
ELEVATION ARC: **0° to +35°**
TRAVERSE ARC: **60°**
EFFECTIVE CEILING: n/a
ROAD RANGE: n/a
RANGE: **21,325 yards (19,500 m)**
PROJECTILE WEIGHT: **94.8 lb (43 kg)**
ARMOR: n/a
ENGINE: n/a
MUZZLE VELOCITY: **2,411 fps (735 mps)**
SPEED: n/a

FELDKANONE 38

TYPE: **Light Towed Gun**
CALIBER: **75mm**
VEHICLE LENGTH: n/a
LENGTH OF BARREL: **91.9 in (2.33 m)**
WEIGHT TRAVELLING: **4,101 lb (1,860 kg)**
WEIGHT IN ACTION: **3,009 lb (1,860 kg)**
ELEVATION ARC: **-5° to +45°**
TRAVERSE ARC: **50°**
EFFECTIVE CEILING: n/a
ROAD RANGE: n/a
RANGE: **12,575 yards (11,500 m)**
PROJECTILE WEIGHT: **12.85 lb (5.83 kg)**
ARMOR: n/a
ENGINE: n/a
MUZZLE VELOCITY: **1,985 fps (605 mps)**
SPEED: n/a

KANONE 44

TYPE: **Heavy Towed Field Gun**
CALIBER: **128mm**
VEHICLE LENGTH: n/a
LENGTH OF BARREL: **260.8 in (6.625 m)**
WEIGHT TRAVELLING: **unknown**
WEIGHT IN ACTION: **22,39 lb (10,160 kg)**
ELEVATION ARC: **-7° to +45° 27'**
TRAVERSE ARC: **360°**
EFFECTIVE CEILING: n/a
ROAD RANGE: n/a
RANGE: **26,685 yards (24,400 m)**
PROJECTILE WEIGHT: **62.4 lb (28.3 kg)**
ARMOR: n/a
ENGINE: n/a
MUZZLE VELOCITY: **3,018 fps (920 mps)**
SPEED: n/a

KANONE 39

TYPE: **Heavy Towed Field Gun**
CALIBER: **149mm**
VEHICLE LENGTH: n/a
LENGTH OF BARREL: **309.7 in (7.868 m)**
WEIGHT TRAVELLING: n/a
WEIGHT IN ACTION: **26,896 lb (12,200 kg)**
ELEVATION ARC: **-3 to +46°**
TRAVERSE ARC: **60–360°**
EFFECTIVE CEILING: n/a
ROAD RANGE: n/a
RANGE: **27,010 yards (24,700 m)**
PROJECTILE WEIGHT: **94.8 lb (43 kg)**
ARMOR: n/a
ENGINE: n/a
MUZZLE VELOCITY: **2,838 fps (865 mps)**
SPEED: n/a

In the 1930s, when it was appreciated that the current program of adapting existing 60-pdr gun carriages to take a new 4.5in gun barrel would not satisfy the full requirement of the Royal Artillery's medium regiments, the British Army decided to create a new weapon that combined a new 4.5in gun on the carriage being planned for the new 5.5in howitzer. The new design was developed and built by 1940, but difficulties with the new carriage meant that it was 1941 before the equipment entered service. The task of the 4.5in gun was long-range interdiction and counter-battery fire, but experience soon revealed that capability in these tasks was hampered by the modest 3.875 lb (1.76 kg) high explosive load of the shell. Production priority was then switched to the 5.5in howitzer, and the last 4.5in guns were pulled out of service after the end of World War II in 1945. The gun was conventional in concept and average in performance, but notable for its strength, while the two carriage variants, which differed only in

modest detail, were of the split-trail type and featured very prominent equilibrators. It served the British Army well in its various campaigns. Also in the mid-1930s, the British Army decided it required a modern long-range gun for the counter-battery and interdiction roles. The result was to exceed all expectations, and would create a gun that had a career of some 40 years. A requirement was accordingly issued for a 5in gun to fire a 100 lb (45.4 kg) shell over a range of 16,000 yards (14,630 m). The requirement was altered in 1939 to cover a gun of 5.5in caliber, and prototype guns were successfully evaluated in 1940. Designed for the originally schemed 5in weapon, the carriage was too light for the larger-caliber weapon, so a new carriage had to be created and the new equipment thus entered service only in 1941. From this time onward, however, the 5.5in guns proved to be a major success, and the type remained in service with some armies into the early 1980s.

4.5IN GUN MK II

TYPE: **Heavy Towed Gun**
CALIBER: **4.5in**
VEHICLE LENGTH: n/a
LENGTH OF BARREL:
187.55 in (4.764 m)
WEIGHT TRAVELLING:
33,600 lb (15,251 kg)
WEIGHT IN ACTION:
12,880 lb (5,842 kg)
ELEVATION ARC: **-5° to 45°**
TRAVERSE ARC: **60°**
EFFECTIVE CEILING: n/a
ROAD RANGE: n/a
RANGE: **20,500 yards
(18,745 m)**
PROJECTILE WEIGHT: **55 lb
(24.97 kg)**
ARMOR: n/a
ENGINE: n/a
MUZZLE VELOCITY:
2,250 fps (686 mps)
SPEED: n/a

5.5IN GUN MK III

TYPE: **Heavy Towed Gun**
CALIBER: **5.5in**
VEHICLE LENGTH: n/a
LENGTH OF BARREL:
164.4 in (4.176 m)
WEIGHT TRAVELLING: n/a
WEIGHT IN ACTION:
12,770 lb (5,792 kg)
ELEVATION ARC: **-5° to
+45°**
TRAVERSE ARC: **60°**
EFFECTIVE CEILING: n/a
ROAD RANGE: n/a
RANGE: **16,200 yards
(14,815 m)**
PROJECTILE WEIGHT: **80 lb
(36.32 kg)**
ARMOR: n/a
ENGINE: n/a
MUZZLE VELOCITY:
2,500 fps (762 mps)
SPEED: n/a

6IN GUN MK VII

TYPE: **Heavy Towed Gun**
CALIBER: **6in**
VEHICLE LENGTH: n/a
LENGTH OF BARREL:
219.7 in (5.58 m)
WEIGHT TRAVELLING:
unknown
WEIGHT IN ACTION:
24,250 lb (10,999 kg)
ELEVATION ARC: **0° to
+38°**
TRAVERSE ARC: **8°**
EFFECTIVE CEILING: n/a
ROAD RANGE: n/a
RANGE: **18,150 yards
(16,595 m)**
PROJECTILE WEIGHT:
100 lb (45.4 kg)
ARMOR: n/a
ENGINE: n/a
MUZZLE VELOCITY:
2,525 fps (770 mps)
SPEED: n/a

6IN GUN MK XIX

TYPE: **Heavy Towed Gun**
CALIBER: **6in**
VEHICLE LENGTH: n/a
LENGTH OF BARREL:
210 in (5.33 m)
WEIGHT TRAVELLING:
22,790 lb (10,338 kg)
WEIGHT IN ACTION:
unknown
ELEVATION ARC: **0° to
+38°**
TRAVERSE ARC: **8°**
EFFECTIVE CEILING: n/a
ROAD RANGE: n/a
RANGE: **18,750 yards
(17,145 m)**
PROJECTILE WEIGHT:
100 lb (45.4 kg)
ARMOR: n/a
ENGINE: n/a
MUZZLE VELOCITY:
2,405 fps (733 mps)
SPEED: n/a

GUN 75/27 MO 11

TYPE: **Light Towed Gun**
CALIBER: **75mm**
VEHICLE LENGTH: n/a
LENGTH OF BARREL:
83.9 in (2.132 m)
WEIGHT TRAVELLING:
4,189 lb (1,900 kg)
WEIGHT IN ACTION:
2,372 lb (1,076 kg)
ELEVATION ARC: **-15° to +65°**
TRAVERSE ARC: **52°9'**
EFFECTIVE CEILING: n/a
ROAD RANGE: n/a
RANGE: **11,200 yards (10,240 m)**
PROJECTILE WEIGHT: **14 lb (6.35 kg)**
ARMOR: n/a
ENGINE: n/a
MUZZLE VELOCITY:
1,647 fps (502 mps)
SPEED: n/a

GUN 149/40 MO 35

TYPE: **Heavy Towed Gun**
CALIBER: **149mm**
VEHICLE LENGTH: n/a
LENGTH OF BARREL:
234.8 in (5.964 m)
WEIGHT TRAVELLING: n/a
WEIGHT IN ACTION:
25,000 lb (11,340 kg)
ELEVATION ARC: **0° to +45°**
TRAVERSE ARC: **60°**
EFFECTIVE CEILING: n/a
ROAD RANGE: n/a
RANGE: **25,920 yards (23,700 m)**
PROJECTILE WEIGHT:
101.4 lb (46 kg)
ARMOR: n/a
ENGINE: n/a
MUZZLE VELOCITY:
2,625 fps (800 mps)
SPEED: n/a

The most advanced item of light field artillery equipment that was available to the Imperial Japanese Army in World War II was the 75mm Field Gun Type 90. This weapon entered service in 1930 under conditions of the greatest secrecy, as the Japanese commanders thought that the weapon would confer upon their armed forces a number of significant tactical advantages against enemies who knew nothing of the type. In design, the 75mm Field Gun Type 90 was akin to the Canon de 85 modèle 1927 supplied to Greece by the French armaments manufacturer Schneider, and it is probable that the basic concept of the gun was copied by the Japanese rather than produced under license. Manufacture of the Type 90 was the responsibility of the Japanese Army's own Osaka Arsenal, and, while the first examples used the Schneider type of breech, the later weapons were revised with a breech of the sliding wedge type. The equipment was also produced with large-diameter wooden spoked wheels that were later succeeded by smaller wheels fitted with pneumatic rubber tires to suit the Type 90 to motor towing. The first knowledge of the Type 90 outside Japan came to light during 1940, when the weapon was used in China. During World War II, although China and Manchuria were the operational theaters that absorbed most of Type 90 production, the weapon was also used in Malaya during 1942.

75MM FIELD GUN TYPE 38

TYPE: **Light Towed Gun**
CALIBER: **75mm**
VEHICLE LENGTH: n/a
LENGTH OF BARREL: **90 in (2.285 m)**
WEIGHT TRAVELLING:
4,211 lb (1,910 kg)
WEIGHT IN ACTION:
2,502 lb (1,135 kg)
ELEVATION ARC: **-8° to +43°**
TRAVERSE ARC: **7°**
EFFECTIVE CEILING: n/a
ROAD RANGE: n/a
RANGE: **13,095 yards (11,975 m)**
PROJECTILE WEIGHT:
13.27 lb (6.025 kg)
ARMOR: n/a
ENGINE: n/a
MUZZLE VELOCITY:
1,985 fps (605 mps)
SPEED: n/a

75MM FIELD GUN TYPE 90

TYPE: **Light Towed Field Gun**
CALIBER: **75mm**
VEHICLE LENGTH: n/a
LENGTH OF BARREL:
112.4 in (2.855 m)
WEIGHT TRAVELLING:
4,405 lb (2,000 kg)
WEIGHT IN ACTION:
3,086 lb (1,400 kg)
ELEVATION ARC: **-8° to +43°**
TRAVERSE ARC: **50°**
EFFECTIVE CEILING: n/a
ROAD RANGE: n/a
RANGE: **16,405 yards (15,000 m)**
PROJECTILE WEIGHT:
13.27 lb (6,025 kg)
ARMOR: n/a
ENGINE: n/a
MUZZLE VELOCITY:
2,297 fps (700 mps)
SPEED: n/a

The lessons of World War I on the Western Front, as they pertained to long-range artillery work, were reflected in the United States by the recommendations of the Caliber Board established in 1919 to consider the U.S. Army's artillery needs. The board felt that a modern long-range gun of 8in caliber was needed, but the USA's poor economic situation meant that work on the new weapon was suspended in 1924 and resumed only in 1939 for the first firing of the T2 prototype weapon in 1941, the year in which the new weapon was standardized for service as the 8in Gun M1. This was planned for use of the same Carriage M1 as the 240mm Howitzer M1, but the need for limited modifications meant that the carriage for the gun became the Carriage M2. The 8in Gun M1 entered service during 1942, but only 139 units had been completed before the end of World War II in 1945, as the weapon was very large, heavy, and costly. Movement was possible only on special wagons (one for the gun and its mounting, and another for the split trail required to handle the recoil forces) generally towed by converted M3 tanks, and the equipment had to be assembled in the firing position with the aid of a truck-mounted crane. The M1 had an initial rate of fire of one round per minute, declining to just one round every two minutes after 10 minutes.

8IN GUN M1

TYPE: **Heavy Mobile Gun**
CALIBER: **8in**
VEHICLE LENGTH: **n/a**
LENGTH OF BARREL: **409.5 in (10.401 m)**
WEIGHT TRAVELLING: **69,300 lb (31,434 kg)**
WEIGHT IN ACTION: **unknown**
ELEVATION ARC: **-10° to +50°**
TRAVERSE ARC: **40°**
EFFECTIVE CEILING: **n/a**
ROAD RANGE: **n/a**
RANGE: **35,000 yards (32,005 m)**
PROJECTILE WEIGHT: **240.37 lb (109.13 kg)**
ARMOR: **n/a**
ENGINE: **n/a**
MUZZLE VELOCITY: **2,950 fps (899 mps)**
SPEED: **n/a**

76.2MM FIELD GUN 1941

TYPE: **Light Towed Gun**
CALIBER: **76.2mm**
VEHICLE LENGTH: **n/a**
LENGTH OF BARREL: **125.76 in (3.194 m)**
WEIGHT TRAVELLING: **2,447 lb (1,110 kg)**
WEIGHT IN ACTION: **unknown**
ELEVATION ARC: **-10° to +18°**
TRAVERSE ARC: **56°**
EFFECTIVE CEILING: **n/a**
ROAD RANGE: **n/a**
RANGE: **14,215 yards (13,000 m)**
PROJECTILE WEIGHT: **13.69 lb (6.21 kg)**
ARMOR: **n/a**
ENGINE: **n/a**
MUZZLE VELOCITY: **2,231 fps (680 mps)**
SPEED: **n/a**

76.2MM FIELD GUN 1942

TYPE: **Light Towed Gun**
CALIBER: **76.2mm**
VEHICLE LENGTH: **n/a**
LENGTH OF BARREL: **117.87 in (2.994 m)**
WEIGHT TRAVELLING: **2,469 lb (1,120 kg)**
WEIGHT IN ACTION: **unknown**
ELEVATION ARC: **-5° to +37°**
TRAVERSE ARC: **54°**
EFFECTIVE CEILING: **n/a**
ROAD RANGE: **n/a**
RANGE: **14,545 yards (13,300 m)**
PROJECTILE WEIGHT: **13.69 lb (6.21 kg)**
ARMOR: **n/a**
ENGINE: **n/a**
MUZZLE VELOCITY: **2,231 fps (680 mps)**
SPEED: **n/a**

122MM FIELD GUN A-19

TYPE: **Heavy Towed Gun**
CALIBER: **122mm**
VEHICLE LENGTH: **n/a**
LENGTH OF BARREL: **215.86 in (5.483 m)**
WEIGHT TRAVELLING: **17,196 lb (7,800 kg)**
WEIGHT IN ACTION: **15,653 lb (7,100 kg)**
ELEVATION ARC: **-4° to +45°**
TRAVERSE ARC: **56°**
EFFECTIVE CEILING: **n/a**
ROAD RANGE: **n/a**
RANGE: **22,825 yards (20,870 m)**
PROJECTILE WEIGHT: **55.1 lb (25 kg)**
ARMOR: **n/a**
ENGINE: **n/a**
MUZZLE VELOCITY: **2,625 fps (800 mps)**
SPEED: **n/a**

HOWITZERS

During World War II, artillery caused nearly 60 percent of all battlefield casualties, and howitzers (indirect fire weapons) were responsible for the majority of those casualties.

CANON DE 105 C

TYPE: **Medium Towed Howitzer**
CALIBER: **105mm**
VEHICLE LENGTH: **n/a**
LENGTH OF BARREL: **76.7 in (1.95 m)**
WEIGHT TRAVELLING: **unknown**
WEIGHT IN ACTION: **3,797 lb (1,722 kg)**
ELEVATION ARC: **-8° to +50°**
TRAVERSE ARC: **58°**
EFFECTIVE CEILING: **n/a**
ROAD RANGE: **n/a**
RANGE: **11,265 yards (10,300 m)**
PROJECTILE WEIGHT: **34.4 lb (15.6 kg)**
ARMOR: **n/a**
ENGINE: **n/a**
MUZZLE VELOCITY: **1,444 fps (440 mps)**
SPEED: **n/a**

CANON DE 155C

TYPE: **Heavy Gun/Howitzer**
CALIBER: **155mm**
VEHICLE LENGTH: **n/a**
LENGTH OF BARREL: **85.6 in (2.176 m)**
WEIGHT TRAVELLING: **8,203 lb (3,720 kg)**
WEIGHT IN ACTION: **7,277 lb (3,300 kg)**
ELEVATION ARC: **0° to +42° 20'**
TRAVERSE ARC: **6°**
EFFECTIVE CEILING: **n/a**
ROAD RANGE: **n/a**
RANGE: **12,360 yards (11,300 m)**
PROJECTILE WEIGHT: **96.16 lb (43.61 kg)**
ARMOR: **n/a**
ENGINE: **n/a**
MUZZLE VELOCITY: **1,476 fps (450 mps)**
SPEED: **n/a**

CANON DE 155 1932

TYPE: **Heavy Howitzer**
CALIBER: **155mm**
VEHICLE LENGTH: **n/a**
LENGTH OF BARREL: **335.6 in (8.525 m)**
WEIGHT TRAVELLING: **n/a**
WEIGHT IN ACTION: **36,155 lb (16,400 kg)**
ELEVATION ARC: **-8° to +45°**
TRAVERSE ARC: **360°**
EFFECTIVE CEILING: **n/a**
ROAD RANGE: **n/a**
RANGE: **30,075 yards (27,500 m)**
PROJECTILE WEIGHT: **110 lb (50 kg)**
ARMOR: **n/a**
ENGINE: **n/a**
MUZZLE VELOCITY: **2,953 fps (900 mps)**
SPEED: **n/a**

LE FH 18/40

TYPE: **Medium Field Howitzer**
CALIBER: **105mm**
VEHICLE LENGTH: **n/a**
LENGTH OF BARREL: **106.7 in (2.71 m)**
WEIGHT TRAVELLING: **4,310 lb (1,955 kg)**
WEIGHT IN ACTION: **n/a**
ELEVATION ARC: **-6° to +40°**
TRAVERSE ARC: **56°**
EFFECTIVE CEILING: **n/a**
ROAD RANGE: **n/a**
RANGE: **13,480 yards (12,325 m)**
PROJECTILE WEIGHT: **32.65 lb (14.81 kg)**
ARMOR: **n/a**
ENGINE: **n/a**
MUZZLE VELOCITY: **1,772 fps (540 mps)**
SPEED: **n/a**

STUG III 10.5CM

TYPE: **SP Assault Howitzer**
CALIBER: **n/a**
VEHICLE LENGTH: **18ft 0.5 in (5.50 m)**
LENGTH OF BARREL: **n/a**
WEIGHT TRAVELLING: **n/a**
WEIGHT IN ACTION: **51,520 lb (23,370 kg)**
ELEVATION ARC: **n/a**
TRAVERSE ARC: **n/a**
EFFECTIVE CEILING: **n/a**
ROAD RANGE: **96 miles (155 km)**
RANGE: **n/a**
PROJECTILE WEIGHT: **n/a**
ARMOR: **3.15 in (80 mm)**
ENGINE: **one Maybach HL 120**
MUZZLE VELOCITY: **n/a**
SPEED: **25 mph (40 km/h) on roads and 15 mph (24 km/h) across country**

QF 25-PDR

TYPE: **Medium Gun/ Howitzer**
CALIBER: **3.45in**
VEHICLE LENGTH: n/a
LENGTH OF BARREL: **92.5 in (2.35 m)**
WEIGHT TRAVELLING: **3,968 lb (1,801 kg)**
WEIGHT IN ACTION: n/a
ELEVATION ARC: **-5° to +40°**
TRAVERSE ARC: **8°– 360°**
EFFECTIVE CEILING: n/a
ROAD RANGE: n/a
RANGE: **13,400 yards (12,255 m)**
PROJECTILE WEIGHT: **25 lb (11.34 kg)**
ARMOR: n/a
ENGINE: n/a
MUZZLE VELOCITY: **1,745 fps (532 mps)**
SPEED: n/a

6IN HOWITZER MK I

TYPE: **Heavy Towed Howitzer**
CALIBER: **6in**
VEHICLE LENGTH: n/a
LENGTH OF BARREL: **79.8 in (2.027m)**
WEIGHT TRAVELLING: **9,850 lb (4,468 kg)**
WEIGHT IN ACTION: unknown
ELEVATION ARC: **0° to +45°**
TRAVERSE ARC: **8°**
EFFECTIVE CEILING: n/a
ROAD RANGE: n/a
RANGE: **11,400 yards (10,425 m)**
PROJECTILE WEIGHT: **100.19 lb (45.48 kg)**
ARMOR: n/a
ENGINE: n/a
MUZZLE VELOCITY: **1,410 fps (430 mps)**
SPEED: n/a

7.2IN HOWITZER MK V

TYPE: **Heavy Towed Howitzer**
CALIBER: **7.2in**
VEHICLE LENGTH: n/a
LENGTH OF BARREL: **161.1 in (4.092 m)**
WEIGHT TRAVELLING: **22,900 lb (10,387 kg)**
WEIGHT IN ACTION: n/a
ELEVATION ARC: **0° to +45°**
TRAVERSE ARC: **8°**
EFFECTIVE CEILING: n/a
ROAD RANGE: n/a
RANGE: **16,900 yards (15,455 m)**
PROJECTILE WEIGHT: **202 lb (91.7 kg)**
ARMOR: n/a
ENGINE: n/a
MUZZLE VELOCITY: **1,700 fps (518 mps)**
SPEED: n/a

7.2IN HOWITZER MK VI

TYPE: **Heavy Towed Howitzer**
CALIBER: **7.2in**
VEHICLE LENGTH: n/a
LENGTH OF BARREL: **248 in (6.30 m)**
WEIGHT TRAVELLING: n/a
WEIGHT IN ACTION: **29,125 lb (13,211 kg)**
ELEVATION ARC: **-2° to +65°**
TRAVERSE ARC: **60°**
EFFECTIVE CEILING: n/a
ROAD RANGE: n/a
RANGE: **19,675 yards (17,990 m)**
PROJECTILE WEIGHT: **200 lb (91.7 kg)**
ARMOR: n/a
ENGINE: n/a
MUZZLE VELOCITY: **1,630 fps (497 mps)**
SPEED: n/a

In the late 1920s, the Italian Army decided it needed a modern heavy howitzer. Although work on a new weapon began in 1930, it was 1938 before the first examples of the Obice da 149/19 modello 37 appeared. The Italian Army ordered 1,392 production examples from Ansaldo and OTO, but only 50 had been delivered by September 1943, the date Italy quit the war on the Axis side. All variants were of orthodox design, mounted on a two-wheeled carriage. The production line was located in northern Italy, so after the partition of Italy in 1943, the Germans kept the weapon in production for their own use with the revised designation 15cm schwere Feldhaubitze 404(i).

GUN 149/19 MO 41

TYPE: **Heavy Towed Howitzer**
CALIBER: **149mm**
VEHICLE LENGTH: n/a
LENGTH OF BARREL: **114 in (2.90 m)**
WEIGHT TRAVELLING: **14,771 lb (6,700 kg)**
WEIGHT IN ACTION: **12,125 lb (5,500 kg)**
ELEVATION ARC: **+5° to +60°**
TRAVERSE ARC: **50°**
EFFECTIVE CEILING: n/a
ROAD RANGE: n/a
RANGE: **15,585 yards (14,250 m)**
PROJECTILE WEIGHT: **15,585 yards (14,250 m)**
ARMOR: n/a
ENGINE: n/a
MUZZLE VELOCITY: **1,969 fps (600 mps)**
SPEED: n/a

GUN 210/22 MO 35

TYPE: **Heavy Towed Howitzer**
CALIBER: **210mm**
VEHICLE LENGTH: n/a
LENGTH OF BARREL: **196.9 in (5 m)**
WEIGHT TRAVELLING: **unknown**
WEIGHT IN ACTION: **35,020 lb (15,885 kg)**
ELEVATION ARC: **0° to +70°**
TRAVERSE ARC: **75–360°**
EFFECTIVE CEILING: n/a
ROAD RANGE: n/a
RANGE: **16,840 yards (15,400 m)**
PROJECTILE WEIGHT: **293 lb (133 kg)**
ARMOR: n/a
ENGINE: n/a
MUZZLE VELOCITY: **1,837 fps (560 mps)**
SPEED: n/a

105MM HOWITZER TYPE 91

TYPE: **Medium Towed Howitzer**
CALIBER: **105mm**
VEHICLE LENGTH: n/a
LENGTH OF BARREL: **100 in (2.54 m)**
WEIGHT TRAVELLING: **4,365 lb (1,980 kg)**
WEIGHT IN ACTION: **3,307 lb (1,500 kg)**
ELEVATION ARC: **-5° to +45°**
TRAVERSE ARC: **45°**
EFFECTIVE CEILING: n/a
ROAD RANGE: n/a
RANGE: **11,785 yards (10,775 m)**
PROJECTILE WEIGHT: **34.7 lb (15.77 kg)**
ARMOR: n/a
ENGINE: n/a
MUZZLE VELOCITY: **1,788 fps (545 mps)**
SPEED: n/a

Work on the 75mm Pack Howitzer M1A1 started in 1920, and the weapon was standardized as the M1 in 1927. Slight changes to the breech ring and block were then effected to create the M1A1. The barrel was installed on the Carriage M1 with tireless and spoked wheels. It was designed for mountain warfare, as the equipment could be broken down into six loads. The weapon was modern in design and strong in construction. A slow initial production rate meant that just under 100 were in service by the middle of 1940, but by the time of the USA's entry into World War II in December 1941, there were 450 in service and total production was 4,939 by the end of the war.

75MM PACK HOWITZER M1

TYPE: **Light Towed Howitzer**
CALIBER: **2.95in**
VEHICLE LENGTH: n/a
LENGTH OF BARREL: **47 in (1.19 m)**
WEIGHT TRAVELLING: **1,296 lb (588 kg)**
WEIGHT IN ACTION: **unknown**
ELEVATION ARC: **-5° to +45°**
TRAVERSE ARC: **6°**
EFFECTIVE CEILING: n/a
ROAD RANGE: n/a
RANGE: **9,750 yards (8,915 m)**
PROJECTILE WEIGHT: **13.76 lb (6.242 kg)**
ARMOR: n/a
ENGINE: n/a
MUZZLE VELOCITY: **1,250 fps (381 mps)**
SPEED: n/a

105MM FIELD HOWITZER M2

TYPE: **Medium Towed Howitzer**
CALIBER: **4.13in**
VEHICLE LENGTH: n/a
LENGTH OF BARREL: **101.35 in (2.574 m)**
WEIGHT TRAVELLING: **4,260 lb (1,932 kg)**
WEIGHT IN ACTION: n/a
ELEVATION ARC: **-5° to +65°**
TRAVERSE ARC: **46°**
EFFECTIVE CEILING: n/a
ROAD RANGE: n/a
RANGE: **12,500 yards (11,430 m)**
PROJECTILE WEIGHT: **33 lb (14.9 kg)**
ARMOR: n/a
ENGINE: n/a
MUZZLE VELOCITY: **1,550 fps (472 mps)**
SPEED: n/a

105MM HOWITZER M7

TYPE: **Medium SP Howitzer**
CALIBER: n/a
VEHICLE LENGTH: **19ft 9 in (6.02 m)**
LENGTH OF BARREL: n/a
WEIGHT TRAVELLING: n/a
WEIGHT IN ACTION: **50,634 lb (22,967 kg)**
ELEVATION ARC: n/a
TRAVERSE ARC: n/a
EFFECTIVE CEILING: n/a
ROAD RANGE: **125 miles (200 km)**
RANGE: n/a
PROJECTILE WEIGHT: **33 lb (14.9 kg)**
ARMOR: **.5–4.5 in (12.7–114 mm)**
ENGINE: **Continental R-975**
MUZZLE VELOCITY: n/a
SPEED: **26 mph (42 km/h) on roads and 15 mph (24 km/h) across country**

155MM HOWITZER M1

TYPE: **Heavy Towed Howitzer**
CALIBER: **155mm**
VEHICLE LENGTH: n/a
LENGTH OF BARREL: **150 in (3.81 m)**
WEIGHT TRAVELLING: **11,966 lb (5,428 kg)**
WEIGHT IN ACTION: unknown
ELEVATION ARC: **-2° to +65°**
TRAVERSE ARC: **53°**
EFFECTIVE CEILING: n/a
ROAD RANGE: n/a
RANGE: **16,000 yards (14,630 m)**
PROJECTILE WEIGHT: **95 lb (43.14 kg)**
ARMOR: n/a
ENGINE: n/a
MUZZLE VELOCITY. **1,850 fps (564 mps)**
SPEED: n/a

8IN HOWITZER M1

TYPE: **Heavy Towed Howitzer**
CALIBER: **8in**
VEHICLE LENGTH: n/a
LENGTH OF BARREL: n/a
WEIGHT TRAVELLING: **32,000 lb (14,515 kg)**
WEIGHT IN ACTION: **29,700 lb (13,4672 kg)**
ELEVATION ARC: **-2° to +64°**
TRAVERSE ARC: **60°**
EFFECTIVE CEILING: n/a
ROAD RANGE: n/a
RANGE: **18,500 yards (16,915 m)**
PROJECTILE WEIGHT: **200 lb (90.8 kg)**
ARMOR: n/a
ENGINE: n/a
MUZZLE VELOCITY: **1,950 fps (594 mps)**
SPEED: n/a

The 152mm Field Gun Model 1935, or BR-2, was installed on a carriage with caterpillar tracks rather than wheels. Stability in the firing position was aided by the use of a split-trail arrangement, and this was reflected in moderately good accuracy to a considerable range. Only a comparatively small number of these powerful gun/howitzer combinations was manufactured, and, although the type was accorded the German designation 15.2cm Kanone 440(r), there is no evidence that any captured guns were ever used by the Germans during World War II.

152MM FIELD GUN BR-2

TYPE: **Heavy Gun/Howitzer**
CALIBER: **152mm**
VEHICLE LENGTH: n/a
LENGTH OF BARREL: **300 in (7.62 m)**
WEIGHT TRAVELLING: n/a
WEIGHT IN ACTION: **40,123 lb (18,200 kg)**
ELEVATION ARC: **0° to +60°**
TRAVERSE ARC: **8°**
EFFECTIVE CEILING: n/a
ROAD RANGE: n/a
RANGE: **29,530 yards (27,000 m)**
PROJECTILE WEIGHT: **106.9 lb (48.5 kg)**
ARMOR: n/a
ENGINE: n/a
MUZZLE VELOCITY: **2,887 fps (880 mps)**
SPEED: n/a

152MM HOWITZER ML-20

TYPE: **Heavy Gun/Howitzer**
CALIBER: **152mm**
VEHICLE LENGTH: n/a
LENGTH OF BARREL: **173.4 in (4.404 m)**
WEIGHT TRAVELLING: **17,482 lb (7,930 kg)**
WEIGHT IN ACTION: **15,719 lb (7,130 kg)**
ELEVATION ARC: **-2° to +65°**
TRAVERSE ARC: **58°**
EFFECTIVE CEILING: n/a
ROAD RANGE: n/a
RANGE: **18,865 yards (17,250 m)**
PROJECTILE WEIGHT: **96.03 lb (43.56 kg)**
ARMOR: n/a
ENGINE: n/a
MUZZLE VELOCITY: **2,149 fps (655 mps)**
SPEED: n/a

203MM HOWITZER B-4

TYPE: **Heavy Towed Howitzer**
CALIBER: **203mm**
VEHICLE LENGTH: n/a
LENGTH OF BARREL: **193.53 in (4.915 m)**
WEIGHT TRAVELLING: n/a
WEIGHT IN ACTION: **39,021 lb (17,700 kg)**
ELEVATION ARC: **0° to +60°**
TRAVERSE ARC: **8°**
EFFECTIVE CEILING: n/a
ROAD RANGE: n/a
RANGE: **17,500 yards (16,000 m)**
PROJECTILE WEIGHT: **220.5 lb (100 kg)**
ARMOR: n/a
ENGINE: n/a
MUZZLE VELOCITY: **2,001 fps (610 mps)**
SPEED: n/a

ANTITANK GUNS

At the beginning of World War II, antitank guns were small-caliber weapons that were often incapable of knocking out an enemy tank. However, by the end of the war they had increased substantially in caliber, range, and penetrative power.

The 47mm SA modèle 1937 APX and the later but virtually identical SA modèle 1939 APX were both sturdy and capable weapons. Low to the ground and comparatively easy to handle, Germany seized many of these guns for use by its occupation forces right up to the time of the Allied invasion of Normandy in 1944.

CANON DE 47
TYPE: **Light Towed AT Gun**
CALIBER: **47mm**
VEHICLE LENGTH: n/a
LENGTH OF BARREL: **98 in (2.49 m)**
WEIGHT TRAVELLING: n/a
WEIGHT IN ACTION: **2,360 lb (1,070 kg)**
ELEVATION ARC: **-13° to +16.5°**
TRAVERSE ARC: **68°**
EFFECTIVE CEILING: n/a
ROAD RANGE: n/a
RANGE: **unknown**
PROJECTILE WEIGHT: **3.8 lb (1.725 kg)**
ARMOR: n/a
ENGINE: n/a
MUZZLE VELOCITY: **2,805 fps (855 mps)**
SPEED: n/a

PAK 35/36
TYPE: **Light Towed AT Gun**
CALIBER: **37mm**
VEHICLE LENGTH: n/a
LENGTH OF BARREL: **65.5 in (1.665 m)**
WEIGHT TRAVELLING: **952 lb (432 kg)**
WEIGHT IN ACTION: **723 lb (328 kg)**
ELEVATION ARC: **-8° to +25°**
TRAVERSE ARC: **60°**
EFFECTIVE CEILING: n/a
ROAD RANGE: n/a
RANGE: **410 yards (375 m)**
PROJECTILE WEIGHT: **12.5 oz (0.354 kg)**
ARMOR: n/a
ENGINE: n/a
MUZZLE VELOCITY: **3,379 fps (1,030 mps)**
SPEED: n/a

PAK 38
TYPE: **Medium Towed AT Gun**
CALIBER: **50mm**
VEHICLE LENGTH: n/a
LENGTH OF BARREL: **124.9 in (3.173 m)**
WEIGHT TRAVELLING: **2,174 lb (986 kg)**
WEIGHT IN ACTION: unknown
ELEVATION ARC: **-8° to +27°**
TRAVERSE ARC: **65°**
EFFECTIVE CEILING: n/a
ROAD RANGE: n/a
RANGE: **490 yards (450 m)**
PROJECTILE WEIGHT: **4lb 15.25 oz (2.25 kg)**
ARMOR: n/a
ENGINE: n/a
MUZZLE VELOCITY: **3,930 fps (1,198 mps)**
SPEED: n/a

PAK 41
TYPE: **Medium Towed AT Gun**
CALIBER: **75mm**
VEHICLE LENGTH: n/a
LENGTH OF BARREL: **170 in (4.32 m)**
WEIGHT TRAVELLING: **2,989 lb (1,356 kg)**
WEIGHT IN ACTION: unknown
ELEVATION ARC: **0° to +16°**
TRAVERSE ARC: **60°**
EFFECTIVE CEILING: n/a
ROAD RANGE: n/a
RANGE: n/a
PROJECTILE WEIGHT: **5 lb 11.25 oz (2.59 kg)**
ARMOR: n/a
ENGINE: n/a
MUZZLE VELOCITY: **3,690 fps (1,124 mps)**
SPEED: n/a

PAK 43
TYPE: **Heavy Towed AT Gun**
CALIBER: **88mm**
VEHICLE LENGTH: n/a
LENGTH OF BARREL: **260.25 in (6.61 m)**
WEIGHT TRAVELLING: **11,023 lb (5,000 kg)**
WEIGHT IN ACTION: n/a
ELEVATION ARC: **-8° to +40°**
TRAVERSE ARC: **360°**
EFFECTIVE CEILING: n/a
ROAD RANGE: n/a
RANGE: **490 yards (450 m)**
PROJECTILE WEIGHT: **16lb 1.5oz (7.3 kg)**
ARMOR: n/a
ENGINE: n/a
MUZZLE VELOCITY: **3,707 fps (1,130 mps)**
SPEED: n/a

QF 2-PDR

TYPE: **Light Towed AT Gun**
CALIBER: **40mm**
VEHICLE LENGTH: n/a
LENGTH OF BARREL: **81.95 in (2.08 m)**
WEIGHT TRAVELLING: **1,848 lb (832 kg)**
WEIGHT IN ACTION: n/a
ELEVATION ARC: **-13° to +15°**
TRAVERSE ARC: **360°**
EFFECTIVE CEILING: n/a
ROAD RANGE: n/a
RANGE: **655 yards (600 m)**
PROJECTILE WEIGHT: **2 lb 6 oz (1 kg)**
ARMOR: n/a
ENGINE: n/a
MUZZLE VELOCITY: **2,616 fps (792 mps)**
SPEED: n/a

QF 6-PDR

TYPE: **Medium Towed AT Gun**
CALIBER: **57mm**
VEHICLE LENGTH: n/a
LENGTH OF BARREL: **101 in (2.44 m)**
WEIGHT TRAVELLING: **2,471 lb (1,112 kg)**
WEIGHT IN ACTION: n/a
ELEVATION ARC: **-5° to +15°**
TRAVERSE ARC: **90°**
EFFECTIVE CEILING: n/a
ROAD RANGE: n/a
RANGE: **unknown**
PROJECTILE WEIGHT: **6.2 lb (2.84 kg)**
ARMOR: n/a
ENGINE: n/a
MUZZLE VELOCITY: **2,700 fps (823 mps)**
SPEED: n/a

ARCHER

TYPE: **Self-Propelled AT Gun**
CALIBER: n/a
VEHICLE LENGTH: **21 ft 11 in (6.68 m)**
LENGTH OF BARREL: n/a
WEIGHT TRAVELLING: n/a
WEIGHT IN ACTION: **35,840 lb (16,257 kg)**
ELEVATION ARC: n/a
TRAVERSE ARC: n/a
EFFECTIVE CEILING: n/a
ROAD RANGE: **90 miles (145 km)**
RANGE: n/a
PROJECTILE WEIGHT: n/a
ARMOR: **.3–2.36 in (8–60 mm)**
ENGINE: **one GMC diesel**
MUZZLE VELOCITY: n/a
SPEED: **15 mph (24 km/h) on roads and 8 mph (13 km/h) across country**

GUN 90/53 SEMOVENTE

TYPE: **SP Antitank Gun**
CALIBER: **90mm**
VEHICLE LENGTH: **17ft 1 in (5.2 m)**
LENGTH OF BARREL: n/a
WEIGHT TRAVELLING: n/a
WEIGHT IN ACTION: **38,084 lb (17,275 kg)**
ELEVATION ARC: **-2° to +85°**
TRAVERSE ARC: **360°**
EFFECTIVE CEILING: n/a
ROAD RANGE: **124 miles (200 km)**
RANGE: n/a
PROJECTILE WEIGHT: n/a
ARMOR: **.39–1.58 in (10–40 mm)**
ENGINE: **SPA 15 TM 41**
MUZZLE VELOCITY: n/a
SPEED: **21.75 mph (35 km/h)**

37MM GUN TYPE 94

TYPE: **Light AT and Support Gun**
CALIBER: **37mm**
VEHICLE LENGTH: n/a
LENGTH OF BARREL: **66.4 in (1.6865 m)**
WEIGHT TRAVELLING: n/a
WEIGHT IN ACTION: **705.5 lb (320 kg)**
ELEVATION ARC: **-10° to +27°**
TRAVERSE ARC: **60°**
EFFECTIVE CEILING: n/a
ROAD RANGE: n/a
RANGE: **4,975 yards (4,550 m)**
PROJECTILE WEIGHT: n/a
ARMOR: n/a
ENGINE: n/a
MUZZLE VELOCITY: **2,297 fps (700 mps)**
SPEED: n/a

47MM ANTITANK GUN TYPE 1

TYPE: **Light Towed AT Gun**
CALIBER: **47mm**
VEHICLE LENGTH: n/a
LENGTH OF BARREL: **99.5 in (2.527 m)**
WEIGHT TRAVELLING: n/a
WEIGHT IN ACTION: **1,653 lb (750 kg)**
ELEVATION ARC: **-11° to +19°**
TRAVERSE ARC: **60°**
EFFECTIVE CEILING: n/a
ROAD RANGE: n/a
RANGE: **500 yards (460 m)**
PROJECTILE WEIGHT: **3.08 lb (1.4 kg)**
ARMOR: n/a
ENGINE: n/a
MUZZLE VELOCITY: **2,707 fps (825 mps)**
SPEED: n/a

37MM AT GUN M3

TYPE: **Light Towed AT gun**
CALIBER: **37mm**
VEHICLE LENGTH: n/a
LENGTH OF BARREL:
78 in (1.9 m)
WEIGHT TRAVELLING:
912 lb (414 kg)
WEIGHT IN ACTION:
unknown
ELEVATION ARC: **-10° to +15°**
TRAVERSE ARC: **60°**
EFFECTIVE CEILING: n/a
ROAD RANGE: n/a
RANGE: **1,000 yards (915 m)**
PROJECTILE WEIGHT: **1 lb 14.75 oz (0.87 kg)**
ARMOR: n/a
ENGINE: n/a
MUZZLE VELOCITY:
2,900 fps (884 mps)
SPEED: n/a

57MM ANTITANK GUN M1

TYPE: **Medium Towed AT Gun**
CALIBER: **57mm**
VEHICLE LENGTH: n/a
LENGTH OF BARREL:
117 in (2.97 m)
WEIGHT TRAVELLING:
2,700 lb (1,227 kg)
WEIGHT IN ACTION:
unknown
ELEVATION ARC: **-5° to +15°**
TRAVERSE ARC: **90°**
EFFECTIVE CEILING: n/a
ROAD RANGE: n/a
RANGE: **1,000 yards (915 m)**
PROJECTILE WEIGHT:
6.28 lb (2.8 kg)
ARMOR: n/a
ENGINE: n/a
MUZZLE VELOCITY:
2,700 fps (823 mps)
SPEED: n/a

3IN ANTITANK GUN M5

TYPE: **Medium Towed AT Gun**
CALIBER: **3in**
VEHICLE LENGTH: n/a
LENGTH OF BARREL:
158.4 in (4.023 m)
WEIGHT TRAVELLING:
5,850 lb (2,654 kg)
WEIGHT IN ACTION: n/a
ELEVATION ARC: **-5° to +30°**
TRAVERSE ARC: **46°**
EFFECTIVE CEILING: n/a
ROAD RANGE: n/a
RANGE: **1,000 yards (915 m)**
PROJECTILE WEIGHT:
15.43 lb (6.94 kg)
ARMOR: n/a
ENGINE: n/a
MUZZLE VELOCITY:
2,600 fps (792 mps)
SPEED: n/a

HELLCAT

TYPE: **76mm SP AT Gun**
CALIBER: **76mm**
VEHICLE LENGTH: **17ft 4 in (5.38 m)**
LENGTH OF BARREL: n/a
WEIGHT TRAVELLING: n/a
WEIGHT IN ACTION:
39,680 lb (17,999 kg)
ELEVATION ARC: n/a
TRAVERSE ARC: n/a
EFFECTIVE CEILING: n/a
ROAD RANGE: **150 miles (241 km)**
RANGE: n/a
PROJECTILE WEIGHT: n/a
ARMOR: **.28–.47 in (7–12 mm)**
ENGINE: **Continental R-975-C4**
MUZZLE VELOCITY: n/a
SPEED: **50 mph (80 km/h) on roads and 20 mph (32 km/h) across country**

The 45mm Antitank Gun Model 1932 was in essence a scaled-up version of the 3.7cm PaK 35/36. Despite its lightness, the Model 1932 was a robust and capable weapon. The improved Model 1937 was almost identical and in German use was designated as the 4.5cm PaK 184/1(r). A development of the Model 1937 was the Model 1938 tank gun, which, in an effort to quickly create more antitank guns in the desperate times of 1941–43 on the Eastern Front, was installed on an interim carriage to create the 4.5cm PaK 184/6(r). To defeat the increasing thickness of German tank armor in the early 1940s, the Soviets increased the length of the 45mm caliber barrel in order to boost muzzle velocity and armor penetration. The breech block was also strengthened and disc wheels were introduced in the 45mm Antitank Gun Model 42 (specifications at right), which remained in Soviet service until well after World War II.

45MM ANTITANK GUN 1942

TYPE: **Light Towed AT Gun**
CALIBER: **45mm**
VEHICLE LENGTH: n/a
LENGTH OF BARREL:
116.8 in (2.967 m)
WEIGHT TRAVELLING:
unknown
WEIGHT IN ACTION:
1,257 lb (570 kg)
ELEVATION ARC: **-8° to +25°**
TRAVERSE ARC: **60°**
EFFECTIVE CEILING: n/a
ROAD RANGE: n/a
RANGE: **unknown**
PROJECTILE WEIGHT:
3.15 lb (1.43 kg)
ARMOR: n/a
ENGINE: n/a
MUZZLE VELOCITY:
2,690 fps (820 mps)
SPEED: n/a

SU-76

TYPE: **Medium SP AT Gun**
CALIBER: **76mm**
VEHICLE LENGTH: **16 ft 6 in (5.03 m)**
LENGTH OF BARREL: n/a
WEIGHT IN ACTION: **24,228 lb (10,990 kg)**
ELEVATION ARC: n/a
TRAVERSE ARC: n/a
EFFECTIVE CEILING: n/a
ROAD RANGE: **221 miles (355 km)**
PROJECTILE WEIGHT: n/a
ARMOR: **.59–1 in (15–25 mm)**
ENGINE: **two GAZ 202**
MUZZLE VELOCITY: n/a
SPEED: **28 mph (45 km/h) on roads and 19 mph (29 km/h) across country**

Appreciating the urgent need for a robust field weapon to defeat German armored vehicles such as the PzKpfw III and PzKpfw IV tanks, the Soviet Union's military planners rightly decided that in the short term their best bet lay with the installation of a powerful gun on a light chassis to create a nimble yet hard-hitting tank destroyer that could be developed quickly and that could also be placed in production early enough to help to stem the German invasion of the USSR, which had begun in June 1941, under the codename Operation Barbarossa. Such a weapon entered Soviet service in 1942 as the four-man 76mm Self-Propelled Gun (SU-76). This was essentially the 76.2mm Model 1942/SiS-3 gun mounted in a fixed armored

superstructure on a lengthened T-70 light tank chassis. However, the increasing armor thickness of German tanks soon combined with the vulnerability deriving from its own thin armor to make the SU-76 better suited to the infantry support role. The gun could fire HE, APHE, HVAP and HEAT rounds at muzzle velocities of between 1,065 and 3,167 ft (325 and 965 m) per second, and carried 60 mixed rounds for the gun that could be elevated in an arc between -3° and +25°, and traversed 32°. An improved model, the SU-76M, with two uprated GAZ-203 engines, and armor protection over the fighting compartment, appeared late in World War II. The vehicle performed well under combat conditions.

SU-85

TYPE: **Heavy SP AT Gun**
CALIBER: **85mm**
VEHICLE LENGTH: **26 ft 9 in (8.15 m)**
LENGTH OF BARREL: n/a
WEIGHT IN ACTION: **65,256 lb (29,600 kg)**
ELEVATION ARC: n/a
TRAVERSE ARC: n/a
EFFECTIVE CEILING: n/a
ROAD RANGE: **249 miles (400 km)**
RANGE: n/a
ARMOR: **.79–1.77 in (20–45 mm)**
ENGINE: **one Model V-2-34**
MUZZLE VELOCITY: n/a
SPEED: **31 mph (50 km/h) on roads and 15 mph (24 km/h) across country**

SU-100

TYPE: **Heavy SP AT Gun**
CALIBER: **100mm**
VEHICLE LENGTH: **31 ft (9.45 m)**
LENGTH OF BARREL: n/a
WEIGHT TRAVELLING: **69,665 lb (31,600 kg)**
ELEVATION ARC: n/a
TRAVERSE ARC: n/a
EFFECTIVE CEILING: n/a
ROAD RANGE: **200 miles (320 km)**
RANGE: n/a
ARMOR: **.79–2.13 in (20–54 mm)**
ENGINE: **Model V-2-34**
MUZZLE VELOCITY: n/a
SPEED: **30 mph (48 km/h) roads and 20 mph (32 km/h) across country**

SU-122

TYPE: **Heavy SP AT Gun**
CALIBER: **122mm**
VEHICLE LENGTH: **32 ft 2 in (9.8 m)**
LENGTH OF BARREL: n/a
WEIGHT TRAVELLING: **97,773 lb (44,350 kg)**
ELEVATION ARC: n/a
TRAVERSE ARC: n/a
EFFECTIVE CEILING: n/a
ROAD RANGE: **211 miles (340 km)**
PROJECTILE WEIGHT: n/a
ARMOR: **.87–2.95 in (22–75 mm)**
ENGINE: **one Model V-2-K**
MUZZLE VELOCITY: n/a
SPEED: **28 mph (45 km/h) on roads and 15 mph (24 km/h) across country**

100MM ANTI-TANK GUN 1944

TYPE: **Heavy Towed AT Gun**
CALIBER: **100mm**
VEHICLE LENGTH: n/a
LENGTH OF BARREL: **235 in (5.97 m)**
WEIGHT IN ACTION: **7,628 lb (3,460 kg)**
ELEVATION ARC: **-5° to +45°**
TRAVERSE ARC: **58**
EFFECTIVE CEILING: n/a
RANGE: **22,965 yards (21,000 m)**
PROJECTILE WEIGHT: **34.4 lb (15.6 kg)**
ARMOR: n/a
ENGINE: n/a
MUZZLE VELOCITY: **2,952 fps (900 mps)**
SPEED: n/a

ANTIAIRCRAFT GUNS

Large- and small-caliber guns designed to give protection from enemy aircraft.

The Canon de 75 1933 represented an effort to modernize the 75mm family of AA guns by installing the modified Schneider barrel on a more modern mounting: a folding cruciform with a conventional pedestal and folding platform for the detachment of one commander and 10 men. Only limited numbers were produced, the Germans taking these for service as the 7.5cm FlaK M.33(f) weapons.

CANON DE 75 1933

TYPE: Medium AA Gun	TRAVELLING: n/a
CALIBER: 75mm	WEIGHT IN ACTION: 9,259 lb (4,200 kg)
VEHICLE LENGTH: n/a	ELEVATION ARC: 0° to +70°
LENGTH OF BARREL: 157 in (4 m)	TRAVERSE ARC: 360°
WEIGHT	EFFECTIVE CEILING: 23,620 ft (7,200 m)
ROAD RANGE: n/a	RANGE: n/a
PROJECTILE WEIGHT: 19.85 lb (9 kg)	ARMOR: n/a
ENGINE: n/a	MUZZLE VELOCITY: 2,346 fps (715 mps)
SPEED: n/a	

FLAK 38

TYPE: Light Towed AA Gun	TRAVERSE ARC: 360°
CALIBER: 20mm	EFFECTIVE CEILING: 6,630 ft (2,200 m)
VEHICLE LENGTH: n/a	ROAD RANGE: n/a
LENGTH OF BARREL: 88.68 in (2.252 m)	RANGE: n/a
WEIGHT TRAVELLING: 1,654 lb (750 kg)	PROJECTILE WEIGHT: 0.2625 lb (0.119 kg)
WEIGHT IN ACTION: 926 lb (420 kg)	ARMOR: n/a
ELEVATION ARC: -20° to +90°	ENGINE: n/a
	MUZZLE VELOCITY: 2,953 fps (900 mps)
	SPEED: n/a

FLAKVIERLING 38

TYPE: Light Towed AA Gun	TRAVERSE ARC: 360°
CALIBER: 20mm	EFFECTIVE CEILING: 7,220 ft (2,200 m)
VEHICLE LENGTH: n/a	ROAD RANGE: n/a
LENGTH OF BARREL: 88.7 in (2.252 m)	RANGE: n/a
WEIGHT TRAVELLING: 4,877 lb (2,212 kg)	PROJECTILE WEIGHT: 0.2625 lb (0.119 kg)
WEIGHT IN ACTION: 3,338 lb (1,514 kg)	ARMOR: n/a
ELEVATION ARC: -10° to +100°	ENGINE: n/a
	MUZZLE VELOCITY: 2,953 fps (900 mps)
	SPEED: n/a

FLAKPANZER IV

TYPE: Self-Propelled AA Gun	ROAD RANGE: 130 miles (210 km)
CALIBER: n/a	RANGE: n/a
VEHICLE LENGTH: 19 ft 4 in (5.89 m)	PROJECTILE WEIGHT: n/a
LENGTH OF BARREL: n/a	ARMOR: .6–3.35 in (16–85 mm)
WEIGHT TRAVELLING: n/a	ENGINE: Maybach HL 120 TR 112
WEIGHT IN ACTION: 48,887 lb (22,175 kg)	MUZZLE VELOCITY: n/a
ELEVATION ARC: n/a	SPEED: 25 mph (40 km/h) on roads or 14.9 mph (24 km/h) across country
TRAVERSE ARC: n/a	
EFFECTIVE CEILING: n/a	

FLAKPANZER WIRBELWIND

TYPE: Self-Propelled AA Gun	EFFECTIVE CEILING: n/a
CALIBER: n/a	ROAD RANGE: 130 miles (210 km)
VEHICLE LENGTH: 19 ft 4 in (5.89 m)	RANGE: n/a
LENGTH OF BARREL: n/a	PROJECTILE WEIGHT: n/a
WEIGHT TRAVELLING: n/a	ARMOR: .63–3.35 in (16–85 mm)
WEIGHT IN ACTION: 48,887 lb (22,175 kg)	ENGINE: Maybach HL 120 TR 112
ELEVATION ARC: n/a	MUZZLE VELOCITY: n/a
TRAVERSE ARC: n/a	SPEED: n/a

234

FLAK 36/37

TYPE: **Light Towed AA Gun**
CALIBER: **37mm**
VEHICLE LENGTH: n/a
LENGTH OF BARREL: **142.7 in (3.626 m)**
WEIGHT TRAVELLING: **5,291 lb (2,400 kg)**
WEIGHT IN ACTION: **unknown**
ELEVATION ARC: **-8° to +85°**
TRAVERSE ARC: **360°**
EFFECTIVE CEILING: **15,750 ft (4,800 m)**
ROAD RANGE: n/a
RANGE: n/a
PROJECTILE WEIGHT: **1.4 lb (0.64 kg)**
ARMOR: n/a
ENGINE: n/a
MUZZLE VELOCITY: **2,690 fps (820 mps)**
SPEED: n/a

FLAK 36/37

TYPE: **Towed AA Gun**
CALIBER: **88mm**
VEHICLE LENGTH: n/a
LENGTH OF BARREL: **199.4 in (4.93 m)**
WEIGHT TRAVELLING: **15,126 lb (6,861 kg)**
WEIGHT IN ACTION: **11,534 lb (5,150 kg)**
ELEVATION ARC: **-3° to +85°**
TRAVERSE ARC: **360°**
EFFECTIVE CEILING: **26,245 ft (8,000 m)**
ROAD RANGE: n/a
RANGE: n/a
PROJECTILE WEIGHT: **20.34 lb (9.24 kg)**
ARMOR: n/a
ENGINE: n/a
MUZZLE VELOCITY: **2,690 fps (820 mps)**
SPEED: n/a

FLAK 38/39

TYPE: **Heavy Towed AA Gun**
CALIBER: **105mm**
VEHICLE LENGTH: n/a
LENGTH OF BARREL: **261.7 in (6.648 m)**
WEIGHT TRAVELLING: **32,187 lb (14,600 kg)**
WEIGHT IN ACTION: **22,575 lb (10,240 kg)**
ELEVATION ARC: **-3° to 85°**
TRAVERSE ARC: **360°**
EFFECTIVE CEILING: **41,995 ft (12,800 m)**
ROAD RANGE: n/a
RANGE: n/a
PROJECTILE WEIGHT: **33.3 lb (15.1 kg)**
ARMOR: n/a
ENGINE: n/a
MUZZLE VELOCITY: **2,887 fps (880 mps)**
SPEED: n/a

QF 3IN AA

TYPE: **Medium Towed AA Gun**
CALIBER: **3in**
VEHICLE LENGTH: n/a
LENGTH OF BARREL: **134.8 in (3.42 m)**
WEIGHT TRAVELLING: **17,585 lb (7,973 kg)**
WEIGHT IN ACTION: **unknown**
ELEVATION ARC: **-10° to +90°**
TRAVERSE ARC: **360°**
EFFECTIVE CEILING: **23,500 ft (7,165 m)**
ROAD RANGE: n/a
RANGE: n/a
PROJECTILE WEIGHT: **16 lb (7.26 kg)**
ARMOR: n/a
ENGINE: n/a
MUZZLE VELOCITY: **2,000 fps (610 mps)**
SPEED: n/a

QF 3.7IN AA

TYPE: **Heavy Towed AA Gun**
CALIBER: **3.7in**
VEHICLE LENGTH: n/a
LENGTH OF BARREL: **185 in (4.7 m)**
WEIGHT TRAVELLING: **20,540 lb (9,317 kg)**
WEIGHT IN ACTION: **unknown**
ELEVATION ARC: **-5° to +80°**
TRAVERSE ARC: **360°**
EFFECTIVE CEILING: **32,000 ft (9,755 m)**
ROAD RANGE: n/a
RANGE: n/a
PROJECTILE WEIGHT: **28.56 lb (12.96 kg)**
ARMOR: n/a
ENGINE: n/a
MUZZLE VELOCITY: **2,600 fps (793 mps)**
SPEED: n/a

75MM AA GUN TYPE 88

TYPE: **Medium Towed AA Gun**
CALIBER: **75mm**
VEHICLE LENGTH: n/a
LENGTH OF BARREL: **130.5 in (3.315 m)**
WEIGHT TRAVELLING: **6,063 lb (2,750 kg)**
WEIGHT IN ACTION: **5,390 lb (2,445 kg)**
ELEVATION ARC: **0° to +85°**
TRAVERSE ARC: **360°**
EFFECTIVE CEILING: **23,620 ft (7,200 m)**
ROAD RANGE: n/a
RANGE: n/a
PROJECTILE WEIGHT: **14.5 lb (6.58 kg)**
ARMOR: n/a
ENGINE: n/a
MUZZLE VELOCITY: **2,362 fps (720 mps)**
SPEED: n/a

Without doubt, the 40mm Bofors gun, designed in a country that remained neutral, was the most widely employed antiaircraft gun of World War II. The first weapon appeared in 1930, and by 1939 the Bofors gun was in service with some 18 countries. The specification (right) is for the British Gun Mk 1.

40MM BOFORS GUN

TYPE: **Medium Towed AA Gun**
CALIBER: **40mm**
VEHICLE LENGTH: n/a
LENGTH OF BARREL: **88.58 in (2.249 m)**
WEIGHT TRAVELLING: **5,423 lb (2,460 kg)**
WEIGHT IN ACTION: **unknown**
ELEVATION ARC: **-5° to +90°**
TRAVERSE ARC: **360°**
EFFECTIVE CEILING: **23,600 ft (7,200 m)**
ROAD RANGE: n/a
RANGE: n/a
PROJECTILE WEIGHT: **1.96 lb (0.89 kg)**
ARMOR: n/a
ENGINE: n/a
MUZZLE VELOCITY: **2,800 fps (854 mps)**
SPEED: n/a

37MM AA GUN M1

TYPE: **Light Towed AA Gun**
CALIBER: **37mm**
VEHICLE LENGTH: n/a
LENGTH OF BARREL: **78 in (1.9 m)**
WEIGHT TRAVELLING: **6,125 lb (2,778 kg)**
WEIGHT IN ACTION: **unknown**
ELEVATION ARC: **-5° to +90°**
TRAVERSE ARC: **360°**
EFFECTIVE CEILING: **18,600 ft (5,670 m)**
ROAD RANGE: n/a
RANGE: n/a
PROJECTILE WEIGHT: **1 lb 5.5 oz (0.61 kg)**
ARMOR: n/a
ENGINE: n/a
MUZZLE VELOCITY: **2,800 fps (853 mps)**
SPEED: n/a

90MM AA GUN M1

TYPE: **Heavy Towed AA Gun**
CALIBER: **90mm**
VEHICLE LENGTH: n/a
LENGTH OF BARREL: **186.5 in (4.737 m)**
WEIGHT TRAVELLING: **19,000 lb (8,618 kg)**
WEIGHT IN ACTION: **unknown**
ELEVATION ARC: **0° to +80°**
TRAVERSE ARC: **360°**
EFFECTIVE CEILING: **39,500 ft (12,040 m)**
ROAD RANGE: n/a
RANGE: n/a
PROJECTILE WEIGHT: **23.415 lb (10.62 kg)**
ARMOR: n/a
ENGINE: n/a
MUZZLE VELOCITY: **2,700 fps (823 mps)**
SPEED: n/a

76.2MM AA GUN 1931

TYPE: **Medium Towed AA Gun**
CALIBER: **76.2mm**
VEHICLE LENGTH: n/a
LENGTH OF BARREL: **165 in (4.19 m)**
WEIGHT TRAVELLING: **9,281 lb (4,210 kg)**
WEIGHT IN ACTION: **6,724 lb (3,050 kg)**
ELEVATION ARC: **-3° to +82°**
TRAVERSE ARC: **360°**
EFFECTIVE CEILING: **30,510 ft (9,300 m)**
ROAD RANGE: n/a
RANGE: n/a
PROJECTILE WEIGHT: **14.575 lb (6.61 kg)**
ARMOR: n/a
ENGINE: n/a
MUZZLE VELOCITY: **2,674 fps (815 mps)**
SPEED: n/a

85MM AA GUN 1944

TYPE: **Medium Towed AA Gun**
CALIBER: **85mm**
VEHICLE LENGTH: n/a
LENGTH OF BARREL: **184.76 in (4.693 m)**
WEIGHT TRAVELLING: **9,303 lb (4,220 kg)**
WEIGHT IN ACTION: **6,746 lb (3,060 kg)**
ELEVATION ARC: **-2° to +82°**
TRAVERSE ARC: **360°**
EFFECTIVE CEILING: **34,450 ft (10,500 m)**
ROAD RANGE: n/a
RANGE: n/a
PROJECTILE WEIGHT: **20.29 lb (9.2 kg)**
ARMOR: n/a
ENGINE: n/a
MUZZLE VELOCITY: **2,625 fps (800 mps)**
SPEED: n/a

INFANTRY SUPPORT GUNS

LE IG 18

TYPE: **Infantry Support Gun**
CALIBER: **75mm**
VEHICLE LENGTH: **n/a**
LENGTH OF BARREL: **34.8 in (0.884 m)**
WEIGHT TRAVELLING: **unknown**
WEIGHT IN ACTION: **882 lb (400 kg)**
ELEVATION ARC: **-10° to +73°**
TRAVERSE ARC: **12°**
EFFECTIVE CEILING: **n/a**
ROAD RANGE: **n/a**
RANGE: **3,885 yards (3,550 m)**
PROJECTILE WEIGHT: **12–13.2 lb (5.45–6 kg)**
ARMOR: **n/a**
ENGINE: **n/a**
MUZZLE VELOCITY: **689 fps (210 mps)**
SPEED: **n/a**

SIG33

TYPE: **Infantry Support Gun**
CALIBER: **150mm**
VEHICLE LENGTH: **n/a**
LENGTH OF BARREL: **64.9 in (1.650 m)**
WEIGHT TRAVELLING: **unknown**
WEIGHT IN ACTION: **3,858 lb (1,750 kg)**
ELEVATION ARC: **0° to +73°**
TRAVERSE ARC: **11° 30'**
EFFECTIVE CEILING: **n/a**
ROAD RANGE: **n/a**
RANGE: **5,140 yards (4,700 m)**
PROJECTILE WEIGHT: **83.8 lb (38 kg)**
ARMOR: **n/a**
ENGINE: **n/a**
MUZZLE VELOCITY: **787 fps (240 mps)**
SPEED: **n/a**

76.2MM INFANTRY GUN

TYPE: **Medium Support Gun**
CALIBER: **76.2mm**
VEHICLE LENGTH: **n/a**
LENGTH OF BARREL: **49.5 in (1.257 m)**
WEIGHT TRAVELLING: **n/a**
WEIGHT IN ACTION: **1,323 lb (600 kg)**
ELEVATION ARC: **-8° to +25°**
TRAVERSE ARC: **60°**
EFFECTIVE CEILING: **n/a**
ROAD RANGE: **n/a**
RANGE: **9,350 yards (8,550 m)**
PROJECTILE WEIGHT: **13.69 lb (6.21 kg)**
ARMOR: **n/a**
ENGINE: **n/a**
MUZZLE VELOCITY: **1,270 fps (387 mps)**
SPEED: **n/a**

MOUNTAIN GUNS

GEBIRGSGESCHÜTZ 36

TYPE: **Light Mountain Gun**
CALIBER: **75mm**
VEHICLE LENGTH: **n/a**
LENGTH OF BARREL: **57 in (1.4475 m)**
WEIGHT TRAVELLING: **unknown**
WEIGHT IN ACTION: **1,653 lb (750 kg)**
ELEVATION ARC: **-10° to +70°**
TRAVERSE ARC: **40°**
EFFECTIVE CEILING: **n/a**
ROAD RANGE: **n/a**
RANGE: **10,390 yards (9,150 m)**
PROJECTILE WEIGHT: **12.85 lb (5.83 kg)**
ARMOR: **n/a**
ENGINE: **n/a**
MUZZLE VELOCITY: **1,558 fps (475 mps)**
SPEED: **n/a**

75MM PACK GUN TYPE 94

TYPE: **Light Pack Gun**
CALIBER: **75mm**
VEHICLE LENGTH: **n/a**
LENGTH OF BARREL: **61.5 in (1.56 m)**
WEIGHT TRAVELLING: **n/a**
WEIGHT IN ACTION: **1,179 lb (535 kg)**
ELEVATION ARC: **-10° to +45°**
TRAVERSE ARC: **40°**
EFFECTIVE CEILING: **n/a**
ROAD RANGE: **n/a**
RANGE: **8,940 yards (8,175 m)**
PROJECTILE WEIGHT: **13.62 lb (6.18 kg)**
ARMOR: **n/a**
ENGINE: **n/a**
MUZZLE VELOCITY: **1,165 fps (355 mps)**
SPEED: **n/a**

TANK HUNTERS

Tank hunters were self-propelled antitank guns that had no turret, but possessed thick frontal armor. The larger vehicles, such as the Jagdtiger, were not produced in sufficient numbers to make a significant impact on the battlefield.

Manufactured from 1943 to provide the German forces with a dedicated Panzerjäger (tank hunter) capable of defeating the Allied powers' latest armored fighting vehicles, the Jagdpanzer 38(t) "Hetzer" (baiter) was based on the redesigned hull of the PzKpfw 38(t) light tank of Czechoslovak origins. Production totalled 1,577 vehicles.

JAGDPANZER 38(T)

TYPE: **Four-Man Tank Hunter**
CALIBER: **n/a**
VEHICLE LENGTH: **20 ft 7 in (6.27 m)**
LENGTH OF BARREL: **n/a**
WEIGHT TRAVELLING: **unknown**
WEIGHT IN ACTION: **35,108 lb (15,925 kg)**
ELEVATION ARC: **n/a**
TRAVERSE ARC: **n/a**
EFFECTIVE CEILING: **n/a**
ROAD RANGE: **99 miles (160 km)**
RANGE: **n/a**
ARMOR: **.3–2.36 in (8–60 mm)**
ENGINE: **one EPA TZJ**
MUZZLE VELOCITY: **n/a**
SPEED: **16 mph (25.75 km/h) on roads and 9 mph (14.5 km/h) across country**

JAGDPANZER IV

TYPE: **Four-Man Tank Hunter**
CALIBER: **n/a**
VEHICLE LENGTH: **23 ft 11 in (7.29 m)**
LENGTH OF BARREL: **n/a**
WEIGHT TRAVELLING: **n/a**
WEIGHT IN ACTION: **52,443 lb (23,788 kg)**
ELEVATION ARC: **n/a**
TRAVERSE ARC: **n/a**
EFFECTIVE CEILING: **n/a**
ROAD RANGE: **130 miles (208 km)**
RANGE: **n/a**
ARMOR: **.3–2.36 in (10–60 mm)**
ENGINE: **Maybach HL 120 TRM**
MUZZLE VELOCITY: **n/a**
SPEED: **28 mph (45 km/h)**

JAGDTIGER

TYPE: **Heavy Tank Destroyer**
CALIBER: **n/a**
VEHICLE LENGTH: **34 ft 11.5 in (10.6 m)**
LENGTH OF BARREL: **n/a**
WEIGHT TRAVELLING: **155,556 lb (70,560 kg)**
WEIGHT IN ACTION: **n/a**
ELEVATION ARC: **n/a**
TRAVERSE ARC: **n/a**
EFFECTIVE CEILING: **n/a**
ROAD RANGE: **99 miles (160 km)**
RANGE: **n/a**
ARMOR: **1.1–9.95 in (30–250 mm)**
ENGINE: **Maybach HL 230 P30**
MUZZLE VELOCITY: **n/a**
SPEED: **23.5 mph (38 km/h) on roads and 14.5 mph (19 km/h) across country**

ASSAULT GUNS

Also known as the 7.5cm Sturmgeschütz III, the 7.5cm Sturmgeschütz 40 was an assault gun series based on the chassis of the PzKpfw III medium tank. The first variants were armed with the 7.5cm KwK L/24 short-barrel gun, and were the StuG III Ausf A (1940), the StuG III Ausf B/D with chassis variations, and the StuG III Ausf E (1942). The data (right) is for the StuG 40 Ausf F.

STUG III 7.5CM

TYPE: **Four-Man Assault Gun**
CALIBER: **7.5cm**
VEHICLE LENGTH: **18 ft (5.49 m)**
LENGTH OF BARREL: **n/a**
WEIGHT TRAVELLING: **n/a**
WEIGHT IN ACTION: **24,391 lb (21,950 kg)**
ELEVATION ARC: **n/a**
TRAVERSE ARC: **n/a**
EFFECTIVE CEILING: **n/a**
ROAD RANGE: **96 miles (155 km)**
RANGE: **n/a**
ARMOR: **1.2–3.15 in (30–80 mm)**
ENGINE: **Maybach HL 120 TRM**
MUZZLE VELOCITY: **n/a**
SPEED: **25 mph (40 km/h)**

BEHIND
THE LINES

Countries involved in World War II

What started out as a conflict in Europe quickly spread to engulf the whole globe. World War II was a truly global conflict, and touched the lives of hundreds of millions of people. The European mainland was ravaged by the war, as armies raged to and fro across its terrain. The conflict never touched countries on the periphery of the war theaters directly, such as South Africa and New Zealand.

- Albania
- Algeria
- Australia
- Austria
- Belgium
- Borneo
- Bulgaria
- Burma
- Canada
- Ceylon
- Chile
- China
- Congo
- Cuba
- Czechoslovakia
- Denmark
- Egypt

- Eritrea
- Ethiopia
- Finland
- France
- Germany
- Gibraltar
- Greece
- Grenada
- Gilbert Islands
- Hong Kong
- Hungary
- India
- Iran
- Iraq
- Italy
- Japan
- Korea

- Malaya
- Malta
- Marshall Islands
- Morocco
- Netherlands
- New Guinea
- New Zealand
- Nicaragua
- Norway
- Pakistan
- Palestine
- Philippines
- Poland
- Portugal
- Romania
- Sicily
- Singapore

- Solomon Islands
- Somalia
- South Africa
- Soviet Union (USSR)
- Spain (neutral, but sent troops to fight for the Axis on Eastern Front)
- Sweden
- Switzerland
- Syria
- Thailand
- Tunisia
- Turkey
- United Kingdom
- United States
- Vietnam
- Yugoslavia

Axis casualties in World War II

Country	Pop.	Killed/Missing	Wounded	Total (Military)	Civilian (deaths)
Germany	78 m	3.5 million	4.6 million	8.1 million	2 million
Italy	44 m	330,000	66,000	396,000	145,000
Japan	72 m	2.12 million	4 million	6.12 million	145,100
Romania	20 m	500,000	300,000	800,000	400,000
Bulgaria	6 m	22,000	28,000	50,000	3,000
Hungary	10 m	120,000	250,000	370,000	200,000
Finland	4 m	100,000	45,000	145,000	4,000

Allied casualties in World War II

COUNTRY	POP.	KILLED/MISSING	WOUNDED	TOTAL (MILITARY)	CIVILIAN (DEATHS)
China	450 m	1.3 million	1.8 million	3.1 million	9 million
Poland	35 m	130,000	200,000	330,000	2.5 million
UK	48 m	400,000	300,000	700,000	60,000
France	42 m	250,000	350,000	600,000	270,000
Australia	7 m	30,000	40,000	70,000	Unknown
India	360 m	36,000	64,000	100,000	Unknown
New Zealand	2 m	10,000	20,000	30,000	Unknown
South Africa	10 m	9,000	14,000	23,000	Unknown
Canada	11 m	42,000	50,000	92,000	Unknown
Denmark	4 m	2,000	Unknown	Unknown	1,000
Norway	3 m	10,000	Unknown	Unknown	6,000
Belgium	8 m	12,000	16,000	28,000	100,000
Netherlands	9 m	14,000	7,000	21,000	250,000
Greece	7 m	90,000	Unknown	Unknown	400,000
Yugoslavia	15 m	320,000	Unknown	Unknown	1.3 million
USSR	194 m	9 million	18 million	27 million	19 million
USA	129 m	300,000	300,000	600,000	Unknown

The Holocaust – Jewish deaths by country

COUNTRY	DEATHS
Poland	3,000,000
Ukraine	900,000
Hungary	450,000
USSR	352,000
Romania	300,000
Baltic Countries	228,000
Germany/Austria	210,000
Netherlands	105,000
France	90,000
Slovakia	75,000
Greece	54,000
Belgium	40,000
Yugoslavia	26,000
Bulgaria	14,000
Italy	8,000
Luxembourg	1,000
Norway	900

TOTAL: 5,853,900

Materials produced during World War II

Coal
In millions of metric tonnes
1. Germany = 2,420.3
2. United States = 2,149.7
3. United Kingdom = 1,441.2
4. Soviet Union = 590.8
5. Japan = 184.5
6. Canada = 101.9
7. Italy = 16.9
8. Hungary = 6.6
9. Romania = 1.6

Iron Ore
In millions of metric tonnes
1. United States = 396.9
2. Germany = 240.7
3. United Kingdom = 119.3
4. Soviet Union = 71.3
5. Japan = 21.0
6. Hungary = 14.1
7. Romania = 10.8
8. Italy = 4.4
9. Canada = 3.6

Crude Oil
In millions of metric tonnes
1. United States = 833.2
2. Soviet Union = 110.6
3. United Kingdom = 90.8
4. Germany = 33.4 (including 23.4 synthetic)
5. Romania = 25.0
6. Canada = 8.4
7. Japan = 5.2
8. Hungary = 3.2

Major Nazi Concentration and Death Camps

CAMP	FUNCTION	LOCATION	ESTABLISHED	EVACUATED	LIBERATED	NUMBER MURDERED IN
Auschwitz	Concentration	Oswiecim, Poland	May 20, 1940		January 27, 1945, by Soviets	1,100,000
Belzec	Extermination	Belzec, Poland	March 17, 1942	Liquidated by Nazis December 1942		600,000
Bergen-Belsen	Concentration	near Hanover, Germany	April 1943		April 15, 1945, by British	35,000
Buchenwald	Concentration	Buchenwald, Germany	July 16, 1937	April 6, 1945	April 11, 1945 by Americans	33,462
Chelmno	Extermination	Chelmno, Poland	Dec. 7, 1941	Liquidated by Nazis July 1944		320,000
Dachau	Concentration	Dachau, Germany	March 22, 1933	April 26, 1945	April 29, 1945, by Americans	32,000
Dora/Mittelbau	Concentration	Nordhausen, Germany	Aug. 27, 1943	April 1, 1945	April 9, 1945, by Americans	unknown
Drancy	Detention	Drancy, France	August 1941		August 17, 1944, by Allies	unknown
Flossenbürg	Concentration	Flossenbürg, Germany	May 3, 1938	April 20, 1945	April 23, 1945 by Americans	73,000
Gross-Rosen	Concentration	near Wroclaw, Poland	August 1940	February 13, 1945	May 8, 1945, by Soviets	40,000
Janowska	Extermination	Lvov, Ukraine	Sept. 1941	November 1943		40,000
Majdanek	Extermination	Lublin, Poland	Feb. 16, 1943	July 1944	July 22, 1944, by Soviets	360,000
Mauthausen	Concentration	Mauthausen, Austria	Aug. 8, 1938		May 5, 1945, by Americans	120,000
Natzweiler	Concentration	near Strasbourg, France	May 1, 1941	September 1944		12,000
Neuengamme	Concentration	Hamburg, Germany	Dec. 13, 1938	April 29, 1945	May 1945 by British	56,000
Plaszow	Concentration	Krakow, Poland	October 1942	Summer 1944	January 15, 1945, by Soviets	8,000
Ravensbrück	Concentration	near Berlin, Germany	May 15, 1939	April 23, 1945	April 30, 1945, by Soviets	92,000
Sachsenhausen	Concentration	Berlin, Germany	July 1936	March 1945	April 27, 1945, by Soviets	105,000
Sered	Concentration	Sered, Slovakia	1941/42		April 1, 1945, by Soviets	13,500
Sobibor	Extermination	Sobibor, Poland	March 1942	Liquidated by Nazis October 1943		250,000
Stutthof	Concentration	near Danzig, Poland	Sept. 2, 1939	January 25, 1945	May 9, 1945, by Soviets	65,000
Theresienstadt	Concentration	Terezin, Czech Republic	Nov. 24, 1941		May 8, 1945, by Soviets	33,000
Treblinka	Extermination	Treblinka, Poland	July 23, 1942	Liquidated April 1943		900,000
Vaivara	Concentration	Estonia	Sept. 1943	Closed June 28, 1944		1,000

Weapons produced during World War II

Tanks and self-propelled guns (bottom, right)
1. Soviet Union = 105,251 (*92,595*)
2. United States = 88,410 (*71,067*)
3. Germany = 46,857 (*37,794*)
4. United Kingdom = 27,896
5. Canada = 5,678
6. Japan = 2,515
7. Italy = 2,473
8. Hungary = 500

Note: Number in parentheses equals the number of tanks and self-propelled guns equipped with main weapons of 75mm caliber or larger. Smaller producing countries do not have this differentiation.

Artillery
Artillery includes antiaircraft and antitank weapons with calibers above 37mm.
1. Soviet Union = 516,648
2. United States = 257,390
3. Germany = 159,147
4. United Kingdom = 124,877
5. Japan = 13,350
6. Canada = 10,552
7. Italy = 7,200
8. Other Commonwealth = 5,215
9. Hungary = 447

Mortars (over 60mm)
1. Soviet Union = 200,300
2. United States = 105,055
3. United Kingdom = 102,950
4. Germany = 73,484
5. Commonwealth = 46,014

Machine guns
Machine guns do not include submachine guns, or machine guns used for arming aircraft.
1. United States = 2,679,840
2. Soviet Union = 1,477,400
3. Germany = 674,280
4. Japan = 380,000
5. United Kingdom = 297,336
6. Canada = 251,925
7. Other Commonwealth = 37,983
8. Hungary = 4,583

Military trucks
1. United States = 2,382,311
2. Canada = 815,729
3. United Kingdom = 480,943
4. Germany = 345,914
5. Soviet Union = 197,100
6. Japan = 165,945
7. Italy = 83,000

Aircraft produced during World War II

Military aircraft of all types
1. United States = 324,750
2. Germany = 189,307
3. Soviet Union = 157,261
4. United Kingdom = 131,549
5. Japan = 76,320
6. Canada = 16,431
7. Italy = 11,122
8. France *(09/39–06/40)* = 4,016
9. Other Commonwealth = 3,081
10. Hungary = 1,046
11. Romania = 1,000

Fighter aircraft
1. United States = 99,950
2. Soviet Union = 63,087
3. Germany = 55,727
4. United Kingdom = 49,422
5. Japan = 30,447
6. Italy = 4,510
7. France *(09/39–06/40)* = 1,597

Attack aircraft
1. Soviet Union = 37,549
2. Germany = 12,539
3. France *(09/39–06/40)* = 280

Bomber aircraft
1. United States = 97,810
2. United Kingdom = 34,689
3. Soviet Union = 21,116
4. Germany = 18,495
5. Japan = 15,117
6. Italy = 2,063
7. France *(09/39–06/40)* = 712

Transport aircraft (below left)
1. United States = 23,929
2. Soviet Union = 17,332
3. Germany = 3,079
4. Japan = 2,110
5. United Kingdom = 1,784
6. Italy = 468

Training aircraft
1. United States = 57,623
2. United Kingdom = 31,864
3. Japan = 15,201
4. Germany = 11,546
5. Soviet Union = 4,061
6. Italy = 1,769

MORE PRODUCTION

Ships and submarines produced in World War II

Aircraft carriers
1. United States = 22 (*141*)
2. Japan = 16
3. United Kingdom = 14
4. Germany = 0
5. Italy = 0
Figure in parentheses indicates merchant vessels converted to escort carriers.

Battleships
1. United States = 8
2. United Kingdom = 5
3. Italy = 3
4. Japan = 2
5. Germany = 2

Cruisers
1. United States = 48
2. United Kingdom = 32
3. Japan = 9
4. Italy = 6
5. Soviet Union = 2

Destroyers
1. United States = 349
2. United Kingdom = 240
3. Japan = 63
4. Soviet Union = 25
5. Germany = 17
6. Italy = 6

Convoy escorts
1. United States = 420
2. United Kingdom = 413
3. Canada = 191
4. Germany = 23

Submarines
1. Germany = 1,337
2. United States = 422
3. Japan = 167
4. United Kingdom = 167
5. Soviet Union = 52
6. Italy = 28

One person's weekly food allowance (United Kingdom)

Owing to shortages during the war, many items were rationed to allow everyone to get their fair share. Before the war many everyday items were imported. The outbreak of war and the dangers to ships from German U-boats meant that many goods were in short supply. Even goods that were made in Britain were no longer available, as factories were converted to make items to help the war effort, such as weapons and munitions.

- 4 oz (113 g) lard or butter
- 12 oz (340 g) sugar
- 4 oz (113 g) bacon
- 2 eggs
- 6 oz (170 g) meat
- 2 oz (57 g) tea

Clothes Rationing

Everyone was given a book of 66 coupons to use to buy new clothes for one year. This was cut to 48 in 1942 and 36 in 1943. Each item of clothing cost a certain number of coupons.

ITEM	MEN	WOMEN	CHILDREN
Raincoat	16	15	11
Overcoat	7	7	4
Jacket	13	12	8
Shirt/Blouse	5	4	3
Sweater/Cardigan	5	5	3
Trousers	8	8	6
Shorts	3	3	2
Skirt	8	6	5
Boots/Shoes	7	5	3
Nightdress/Pyjamas	8	6	6
Underwear/Vest	3	3	2
Socks/Stockings	2	2	1

British Medals

Order of Precedence for the British Commonwealth. The lists only contains the most common decorations from World War II or with any relation to World War II:

- Victoria Cross VC
- George Cross GC
- Knight/Lady of The Garter KG/LG
- Knight/Lady of The Thistle KT/LT
- Knight/Dame Grand Cross of the Order of the Bath GCB
- Order of Merit OM
- Knight/Dame Grand Cross of the Order of St Michael and St George GCMG
- Knight/Dame Grand Cross of The Royal Victorian Order GCVO
- Knight/Dame Grand Cross of the Order of the British Empire GBE
- Companion of Honour CH
- Knight/Dame Commander of the Order of the Bath KCB/DCB
- Knight/Dame Commander of the Order of St Michael and St George KCMG/DCMG
- Knight/Dame Commander of The Royal Victorian Order KCVO/DCVO
- Knight/Dame Commander of the Order of The British Empire KBE/DBE
- Knight Bachelor (NB: Confers title of "Sir." No post-nominals)
- Companion of the Order of the Bath CB
- Companion of the Order of St Michael and St George CMG
- Commander of The Royal Victorian Order CVO
- Commander of the Order of the British Empire CBE
- Companion of the Distinguished Service Order DSO
- Distinguished Service Cross DSC
- Lieutenant of The Royal Victorian Order LVO
- Officer of the Order of the British Empire OBE
- Companion of the Imperial Service Order ISO
- Member of The Royal Victorian Order MVO
- Member of the Order of the British Empire MBE
- Royal Red Cross (1st class) RRC
- Distinguished Service Cross DSC
- Military Cross MC
- Distinguished Flying Cross DFC

U.S. Medals

Order of Precedence of U.S. World War II medals and ribbons:

1. Medal of Honor
2. Distinguished Service Cross
3. Navy Cross
4. Air Force Cross
5. Army Distinguished Service Medal
6. Navy Distinguished Service Medal
7. Silver Star
8. Legion of Merit
9. Distinguished Flying Cross
10. Soldier's Medal
11. Navy and Marine Corps Medal
12. Gold Lifesaving Medal
13. Bronze Star Medal
14. Purple Heart
15. Air Medal
16. Silver Lifesaving Medal
17. Army Commendation Medal
18. Navy & Marine Corps Commendation Medal
19. Combat Action Ribbon
20. Distinguished Unit Badge
21. Navy Presidential Unit Citation
22. Navy Unit Commendation
23. Army Meritorious Unit Commendation
24. Prisoner of War Medal
25. Army Good Conduct Medal
26. Reserve Special Commendation Ribbon
27. Navy Good Conduct Medal
28. Marine Corps Good Conduct Medal
29. Coast Guard Good Conduct Medal
30. Selected Marine Corps Reserve Medal

USSR Medals

Highest Decorations
- Medal "Zolotaya Zvezda" *(Geroi Sovetskogo Soyuza) (Medal of the Gold Star (Hero of the Soviet Union))*
- Medal "Serp i Molot" *(Geroi Sotsialisticheskogo Truda) (Medal of the Sickle and Hammer (Hero of Socialist Labor))*

Orders
- Orden Pobeda *(Order of Victory)*
- Orden Lenina *(Order of Lenin)*
- Orden Krasnogo Znameni *(Order of the Red Banner)*
- Orden Suvorova *(Order of Suvorov)*
- Orden Ushakova *(Order of Ushakov)*
- Orden Kutuzova *(Order of Kutuzov)*
- Orden Nakhimova *(Order of Nakhimov)*
- Orden Bogdana Khmelnitskogo *(Order of Bogdan Khmelnitsky)*
- Orden Aleksandra Nevskogo *(Order of Aleksandr Nevsky)*
- Orden Otechestvennoi voiny *(Order of the Patriotic War)*
- Orden Trudovogo Krasnogo Znameni *(Order of the Red Banner of Labor)*
- Orden Krasnoi Zvezdy *(Order of the Red Star)*
- Orden Znak Pocheta *(Order of the Badge of Honor)*
- Orden Slavy *(Order of Glory)*
- Orden "Mat Geroinya" *(Order of Mother Heroine)*
- Orden Materinskaya Slava *(Order of Maternal Glory)*

Medals for Merit and Bravery
- Medal Ushakova *(Medal of Ushakov)*
- Medal Nakhimova *(Medal of Nakhimov)*
- Medal "Za otvagu" *(Medal for Bravery)*
- Medal "Za boyeviye zaslugi" *(Medal for Military Merit)*

Campaign and Service Awards
- Medal "Partizanu Otechestvennoi voiny" *(Medal to the Partisan of the Patriotic War)*
- Medal "Za oboronu Odessy" *(Medal for the Defense of Odessa)*
- Medal "Za oboronu Sevastopolya" *(Medal for the Defense of Sevastopol)*
- Medal "Za oboronu Sovetskogo Zapolyarya" *(Medal for the Defense of the Soviet Polar Region)*
- Medal "Za oboronu Kavkaza" *(Medal for the Defense of the Caucasus)*
- Medal "Za oboronu Kieva" *(Medal for the Defense of Kiev)*
- Medal "Za oboronu Leningrada" *(Medal for the Defense of Leningrad)*
- Medal "Za oboronu Moskvy" *(Medal for the Defense of Moscow)*
- Medal "Za oboronu Stalingrada" *(Medal for the Defense of Stalingrad)*
- Medal "Za vzyatiye Veny" *(Medal for the Capture of Vienna)*
- Medal "Za vzyatiye Budapeshta" *(Medal for the Capture of Budapest)*
- Medal "Za vzyatiye Kyonigsberga" *(Medal for the Capture of Koenigsberg)*
- Medal "Za vzyatiye Berlina" *(Medal for the Capture of Berlin)*
- Medal "Za osvobozhdeniye Belgrada" *(Medal for the Liberation of Belgrade)*
- Medal "Za osvobozhdeniye Pragi" *(Medal for the Liberation of Prague)*
- Medal "Za osvobozhdeniye Varshavy" *(Medal for the Liberation of Warsaw)*
- Medal "Za pobedu nad Germaniei v Velikoi Otechestevennoi voine 1941–1945" *(Medal for the Victory over Germany in the Great Patriotic War of 1941–1945)*
- Medal "Za pobedu nad Yaponiei" *(Medal for the Victory over Japan)*

Commemorative Medals
- Yubileinaya medal "20 let pobedy v Velikoi Otechestvennoi voine 1941–1945" *(Jubilee Medal for 20 years of Victory in the Great Patriotic War of 1941–1945)*
- Yubileinaya medal "30 let pobedy v Velikoi Otechestvennoi voine 1941–1945" *(Jubilee Medal for 30 years of Victory in the Great Patriotic War of 1941–1945)*
- Yubileinaya medal "40 let pobedy v Velikoi Otechestvennoi voine 1941–1945" *(Jubilee Medal for 40 years of Victory in the Great Patriotic War of 1941–1945)*

German Medals

German Orders
- Eisernes Kreuz *(Iron Cross)*
- Kriegsverdienstkreuz *(War Merit Cross)*
- Kriegsorden des Deutschen Kreuzes *(German Cross)*
- Verdienstorden vom Deutschen Adler *(Order of the German Eagle)*
- Deutscher Orden des Großdeutschen Reiches *(German Order of the Great German Empire)*

Medals for Merit and Bravery
- Nahkampfspange *(Close Combat Bar)*
- Nahkampfspange der Luftwaffe *(Close Combar Bar of the Luftwaffe)*
- Ehrenblattspange *(Honor Roll Clasp)*
- Spanienkreuz *(Spanish Cross)*
- Wehrmachtbericht *(Army Record)*

Campaign Awards
- Ehrenkreuz des Weltkrieges *(Cross of Honor 1914–1918)*
- Medaille zur Erinnerung an den 13. März 1938 *(Commemorative Medal 13 March 1938)*
- Medaille zur Erinnerung an den 1. Oktober 1938 *(Commemorative Medal 1 October 1938)*
- Spange zur Medaille zur Erinnerung an den 1. Oktober 1938 *(Clasp to the Commemorative Medal 1 October 1938)*
- Medaille zur Erinnerung an die Heimkehr des Memellandes *(Medal to Commemorate the homecoming of the Memelland)*
- Deutsches Schutzwall-Ehrenzeichen *(Westwall Medal)*
- Medaille "Winterschlacht im Osten 1941/42" *(Ostmedaille)* *(Russian Front Medal)*
- Narvikschild *(Narvik Shield)*
- Krimschild *(Krim Shield)*
- Cholmschild *(Cholm Shield)*
- Demjanskschild *(Demjansk Shield)*
- Kubanschild *(Kuban Shield)*
- Lapplandschild *(Lapland Shield)*
- Warsawschild *(Warsaw Shield)*
- Lorientschild *(Lorient Shield)*
- Ärmelband Spanien *(Spanish Civil War Cuff Title)*
- Ärmelband Kreta *(Kreta Cuff Title)*
- Ärmelband Afrika *(Afrika Cuff Title)*
- Ärmelband Metz 1944 *(Metz Cuff Title)*
- Ärmelband Kurland *(Kurland Cuff Title)*

Japanese Medals

Highest Decoration
- Bukosho *(Medal of Honor)*

Orders
- Daikun'i kikkash *(Supreme Order of the Chrysanthemum)*
- Kinshi Kunsho *(Order of the Golden Kite)*
- Kyuokujitsu_sho *(Order of the Rising Sun)*
- Zuiho_sho *(Order of the Sacred Treasure)*

Campaign and Service Awards
- 1931 China Incident Medal
- 1937 China Incident Medal
- Border War Medal
- 1942 China Incident Medal
- Great East Asia War Medal

Wounded Awards
- Shoigunjinsho *(Wounded Badge)*

War Decorations: Japanese Army
- Enlisted Man's Proficiency Tank Badge
- Sharpshooter's Badge
- Army Air Force Badge
- Badge for Military Horsemanship
- Army NCO's Proficiency Badge
- Machine Gun Marksmen Badge
- Marshal's Badge
- Badge for Graduates of Army Staff College
- Commander's Badge
- Army Worker's Badge

Index

Index